Supervising

Supervising

Christina Christenson
Ohio University

Thomas W. Johnson
California State University at Fullerton

John E. Stinson
Ohio University

▲▼ Addison-Wesley Publishing Company

Reading, Massachusetts   Menlo Park, California
London   Amsterdam   Don Mills, Ontario   Sydney

Cover photograph: Four by Five, Inc.

Library of Congress Cataloging in Publication Data

Christenson, Christina.
  Supervising.

  Bibliography: p.
  Includes index.
  1. Supervision of employees. I. Johnson, Thomas
William, 1946–   II. Stinson, John E.   III. Title.
HF5549.C458   658.3′02   81-8003
ISBN 0-201-03431-X   AACR2

ISBN 0-201-03431-X
CDEFGHIJ-DO-898765

Preface

Supervision is an "in" topic today. There are discussions of what supervisors do and how they do it (or should do it) in books and at conventions, seminars, and meetings of managers. Supervisors and the impact they have on workers and productivity are increasingly recognized as critical elements in organizational success.

This book is the result of our growing concern over the need for effective supervisors in organizations of all types. Through our activities as teachers, consultants, and supervisors, we have seen the impact of effective—and ineffective—supervisors. We have also come to understand the problems faced by supervisors and the demands placed on them by higher level management and by their workers.

Historically, the most capable and responsible workers were made supervisors—but they were provided little or no education or development regarding supervision. The assumption seemed to be that workers should know the technology and job, and if they needed any other knowledge or skills, they could be developed through experience.

Today, it is becoming more evident that it isn't sufficient for supervisors to have knowledge of the technology and jobs of the workers they supervise. Supervisors face a variety of challenges and have to respond to different pressures. The challenge of making workers more productive is an increasingly complex one. To meet such challenges, supervisors need managerial skills. They need to know how to plan, organize, and control the work and the work force. They need to be able to understand human behavior and to work effectively with people.

We address these areas in a practical way in this book. *Supervising* is designed to provide you with a basic understanding of what activities and skills are required to supervise workers effectively. However, we are fully aware that learning concepts and actually applying them are two entirely different processes. Therefore we have included a variety of exercises and cases that you can use to "try out" the supervisory skills and activities discussed in the book.

Our overall objective in *Supervising* is to give you the opportunity to better prepare yourself for your first supervisory job as well as to develop yourself further as a supervisor. We describe the supervisor's job as it really is in organizations. The major problems faced by countless supervisors on a daily basis are discussed and suggestions for resolving them are given. We have incorporated the common situations faced by supervisors throughout the book. In addition, we have included situations some supervisors face today and most others will certainly face in the near future.

We have enjoyed writing *Supervising*. The book itself is the product of the ideas and efforts of many people. Numerous people offered many fine suggestions that we have incorporated. In particular, the following individuals reviewed the entire manuscript and made many valuable suggestions: Larry Bailey, San Antonio College; Jack Brill, San Diego City College; C. Mallory Graves, Central Virginia Community College; Kathryn Hegar, Mountain View College; and Jeffery Olson, North Central Technical Institute. Ginger Adams did a tremendous job typing the manuscript under very tight deadlines. We thank her very much. We would also like to thank the people at Addison-Wesley for their help.

Finally, we should express our appreciation to our families and our co-workers. They have tolerated our single-minded concentration on the book for long periods of time and have provided the necessary support and encouragement.

Athens, Ohio   C. C.
Fullerton, California   T. W. J.
December 1981   J. E. S.

Contents

IV Supervisory staffing   299

12 Selecting and orienting workers   300

13 Training and developing workers   331

16 Working safely   418

Supervising

The supervisor

1

The supervisor's job

Objectives

After reading this chapter you should be able to

- [ ] Identify the common features of supervisory jobs.
- [ ] Distinguish between supervisors and higher-level managers and supervisors and hourly workers.
- [ ] Describe the role of supervisors as a "linking pin" and as the "person in the middle."
- [ ] Discuss the importance of supervision in organizations.

Introduction to supervision

So you want to be a supervisor—or do you? Supervising is a challenging and sometimes taxing activity. Supervisors are responsible for the work of others as well as their own work. They must solve problems, make decisions, and take action. They experience pressures from higher-level managers and pressures from workers. Supervisors never seem to have enough time to get their work done.

But supervising is also a very rewarding activity. You can experience a real sense of accomplishment when your work group is cooperating and performing effectively. Knowing that you have helped your workers develop their skills and abilities can be satisfying. Helping to create an environment that workers find rewarding also provides satisfaction.

Supervising is an increasingly important activity in today's society, as the role of the supervisor relates to two major areas of concern in business and most other organizations. One concern is the problem of productivity. As we will discuss in Chapter 2, the rate of productivity in business organizations in the United States has started to decline. This deterioration has a significant impact on our economy and society. The second concern is the quality of life of the American worker, also discussed in Chapter 2. Many workers are experiencing high levels of job dissatisfaction, and this stress carries over and affects all areas of their life.

Effective supervision is a key to resolving both of these issues. Supervisors work directly with the workers who produce products and provide services. If they perform their supervisory job effectively, they can have a positive impact on the effort and productivity of the workers. And, they also can help create a work environment which provides a higher level of job satisfaction and contributes to a better quality work life.

How can you become an effective supervisor? Experience is one answer. You can be placed in a supervisory position and learn from your successes and failures. But, experience is not the only answer. A systematic study of supervision can also help your performance. By studying concepts and ideas that supervisors have found helpful, you can prepare yourself to meet the challenges of a supervisor's job. While study alone cannot make you an effective supervisor, it can help you learn from your experience more rapidly and more effectively.

You are about to begin a systematic study of supervision. Let's start by looking at Bill Smith's situation. A little over eight years ago, Bill Smith was hired as a maintenance person at the Demco Plant. At that time Demco had a work force of sixty-five hourly workers and seven salaried employees. Bill was responsible for maintaining lights, air conditioning, generator, and miscellaneous equipment in proper operating condition.

The plant grew in succeeding years, and in seven years, floor space had more than tripled and the work force expanded to almost 400. Bill Smith's duties and responsibilities also increased. He discovered that he was often required to work overtime and was frequently called back to the plant during the night to make necessary repairs. He performed his work without complaint and was a devoted and loyal employee. Additional people were occasionally added to the maintenance department. Last year Bill Smith was appointed Plant Maintenance Supervisor, placed on salary, and given the responsibility of supervising seven maintenance workers.

The plant manager soon noted that Bill Smith still preferred to make repairs on equipment personally rather than direct the efforts of his workers. As a result, the plant manager sat down with Bill to talk to him about his new job. He was told that with plant expansion, the work of the maintenance department had grown in complexity and responsibility. The plant manager indicated that one person could no longer perform the work required of the entire department. As a supervisor, he should have been selecting capable workers, training those workers to maintain machinery, and directing them in such a way that work was performed in an efficient manner. As a result of this conversation, Bill Smith agreed to appear each day in the dress required of the supervisor, white shirt and tie, and to perform the functions of the supervisor.

The plant manager was disappointed to learn in the following months that Bill Smith was still supervisor in title only. Other department heads were complaining that machinery was in need of repair, and quite often work scheduling was delayed as a result. It was reported that when maintenance department workers were summoned, more likely than not, they were unable to complete the work without calling Bill Smith. Bill Smith had returned to his blue denims after finding that his white shirt was ruined by the end of the day after repairing oily machinery. One department head informed the plant manager that Bill Smith was inclined to be possessive in regard to machinery, resenting anyone else who made repairs. He preferred, instead, working long hours of overtime and returning to the plant in the early morning. He also had hesitated to select and train competent subordinates. The plant manager, realizing some action should be taken, was reminded by at least one department head that Bill Smith was a valuable employee and had devoted many years to the plant and exhibited unique loyalty. To discharge or to demote such a man would be a poor way indeed to compensate him for such devotedness.

The supervisor's job

When you talk to many different supervisors, as we have, you get a variety of descriptions of the supervisor's job. You find that they perform many different activities and face different problems. These supervisors even seem to be describing quite different jobs.

These differences are to be expected. Supervisors work in a variety of organizations. Some, like Bill Smith, work in manufacturing organizations which historically have been the focus of the study of supervision. There are also, however, supervisors in retail stores, fast food restaurants, banks, hospitals, and government offices. These organizations have different goals and the workers being supervised perform quite different functions. The problems faced by supervisors, and the activities they perform, therefore, vary greatly.

While differences do exist, all supervisors' jobs share some common features. All **supervisors** have people working for them; they get work accomplished through other people rather than performing the work themselves. All supervisors are responsible for accomplishing goals. They are expected to supervise their workers to meet performance goals set by higher-level managers.

This common feature indicates the major supervisory function: working with and through hourly-level workers to accomplish established work-unit goals. This function separates workers from supervisors. Consider Bill Smith. As a worker, his responsibility was to maintain equipment in the plant in proper operating condition. When he became plant maintenance supervisor, however, his function was *supposed* to change. He was still responsible for maintaining the equipment. He was not expected to do the maintenance himself, however. He was expected to train other workers, provide them with direction, coordinate their efforts, and give them the necessary assistance so that they could maintain the equipment. In short, as a supervisor, he was supposed to maintain the equipment through the efforts of other workers.

Supervisory activities

How do supervisors accomplish their goals? What do supervisors do? What types of activities do they perform?

First, we should keep in mind that supervisors are managers. They are first-line managers working directly with individual hourly workers. As managers, they are involved in each of these management activities:

Planning. Determining goals, deciding how goals can be accomplished, setting courses of action, establishing policies and procedures. Setting work schedules for the department is an example.

Organizing. Assigning jobs to individuals, grouping jobs together to coordinate effort, assigning authority and responsibility.

Staffing. Selecting people to fill jobs, placing people on jobs and orienting them, training workers, and evaluating their performance.

Directing. Guiding and influencing people to perform work, communicating with them, creating positive motivation, and handling any people problems.

Controlling. Collecting information on accomplishments, comparing this to planned accomplishments, and taking corrective action when necessary.

Supervisors and managers

Supervisors are managers and all managers are involved in performing each of these activities. However, supervisors are unique among managers, since they are the only ones who directly manage hourly-level workers. Thus the amount of time they spend on each activity and the emphasis of the activity differ from that of other managers.

To understand these differences, let's look at each of the management activities and compare the involvement of supervisors and higher-level managers.

■ **Planning.** Higher-level managers generally spend more time on planning activities than do supervisors. In addition, planning at higher levels generally focuses on a longer time period. While top management may be making plans for the next year or even five years into the future, most supervisors plan for the next day, or week, or month.

■ **Organizing.** Higher-level managers spend more time on organizing, and their organizational efforts cover a much wider scope. Supervisors' attention to organizing is usually restricted to mapping out the work and making work assignments just for their section.

■ **Staffing.** Supervisors tend to be directly responsible for more people than higher-level managers. In addition, they work directly with people to get their work done, whereas higher-level managers work more with information than people. Consequently, supervisors generally spend more time on staffing activities than higher-level managers.

■ **Directing.** Supervisors also tend to spend more time on directing activities. As indicated, the very essence of supervision is getting things done through other people. Supervisors work with people, not with things as do workers, or with information as do higher-level managers. Thus directing occupies a great deal of time for most supervisors and generally somewhat less for higher-level managers.

■ **Controlling.** All levels of management, from supervisors to top-level managers, spend a similar amount of time on controlling activities. The nature of involvement, however, tends to vary. Higher-level managers devote most of their controlling activities to analyzing information about the total organization. They review quality control and production reports, budget and expense summaries, and a variety of progress reports to see if the organization is meeting its objectives. In contrast, supervisors spend most of their time monitoring activities in their own area, providing the control reports which will be analyzed by higher levels of management, and taking corrective action either on their own or at the request of higher management.

The importance of supervision

Historically, most books on the subject of **supervision** viewed the supervisor as a key person in management.[1] Supervisors make decisions and interpret company policy. They schedule work and direct the work force. They motivate workers and help them derive satisfaction from their work.

A natural extension of this concept is to view the supervisor as a linking pin between workers and higher-level management. They represent management's policies and points of view to workers. And, equally important, they represent the workers' points of view to higher-level management. They link together management's goals and efforts and workers' goals and efforts.

In practice, however, the supervisor often becomes the person in the middle. Management expects the supervisor to control performance and carry out organizational plans. Workers expect the supervisor to react to their wants and provide support. Sometimes management's expectations and workers' expectations are in conflict. Then supervisors feel pressured by both management and workers and wonder how to satisfy the needs of both groups.

The introduction of technical specialists to "help" supervisors has made this situation worse. Production planners schedule the work. Personnel specialists select and hire workers. Training specialists train workers. Labor relations specialists handle grievances. These specialists have absorbed many supervisory responsibilities.

The supervisor has become less central in supervising the work force and in representing workers to management. The pressures, however, have not decreased. Even though supervisors have less control, the expectations of workers and management have not decreased.

Does it make a difference whether the supervisor is the key person in management or the person in the middle? Does the supervisor make a difference in the performance of the organization? Consider the following situation.[2]

In 1974 Tri/Valley Growers faced significant problems in their Plant 7 in Modesto, California. Plant 7, only five years old, was among the largest and most modern canneries in the world. Productivity and quality, however, were less than expected. Operating costs were higher. Significant safety problems and indications of worker dissatisfaction were evident also, including high turnover, high absenteeism, and excessive grievances.

A thorough investigation of the problems at Plant 7 was conducted by an outside consultant. One of the major problems found was the quality of supervision. In particular, different groups viewed the supervisor's job differently.

- Supervisors considered themselves responsible only for product flow. They assumed that technical specialists were responsible for other activities such as quality, staffing, safety, and discipline. Further, they felt that higher-level managers had a single-minded focus on productivity. They reacted to this pressure from management by pressuring their workers.

- Managers saw the technical specialists as advisors only. They assumed the supervisors were responsible for all normal supervisory activities. They just concluded that the supervisors were poor performers.

- The technical specialists felt it was their responsibility to fill the decision-making gaps left by the supervisors.
- Workers considered most supervisors to be weak and ineffective. They were frustrated by having to get information and decisions from a variety of technical specialists.

Tri/Valley recognized they had to take action to clarify the supervisors' job and improve conditions. They decided to "reconstitute" the supervisory job to its original level of responsibility.

- Each supervisory job was analyzed and described in writing.
- Each job was described in terms of both content and specific skills required.
- Relationships between supervisors and technical specialists were defined. Technical specialists were to be advisors only. The authority of the supervisor was clearly established.
- A selection procedure was established to hire qualified candidates for available supervisory positions.
- The "reconstituted" supervisory job was thoroughly explained to the supervisors.
- The supervisors were thoroughly trained for their specific responsibilities.

These actions reoriented the supervisory job to that of a key person in management and provided a basis for selecting and training supervisors. What were the results?

- Turnover in 1975 was 50% for nonseniority workers and 17% for seniority workers. By 1979 it was 26.7% for nonseniority workers and 4.1% for seniority workers. Estimated cost savings were $133,000.
- Absenteeism decreased from 12.2% in 1975 to 7.1% in 1979. Estimated cost savings were $355,000.
- Accident frequency rate decreased by 38%. Savings were $288,000.
- More than 1800 grievances were filed in 1975. In 1979 there were 787 grievances.
- Direct labor productivity improved 21% between 1975 and 1979. The dollar benefit was $1,728,000.

These are, of course, very impressive improvements. While this is a study of only one plant, it does demonstrate the importance of good supervisors functioning as key people in management.

We thoroughly believe that the supervisor is the key person in management. Supervisors work directly with the employees who are producing products or providing services. If they are given appropriate authority and if they are competent, they can have a major impact on results. They can work with their workers to obtain an effective level of performance and provide a satisfying work environment.

Becoming supervisors

For those who are promoted to supervisor, the shift from worker to supervisor—from doing work yourself to getting work done through others—is sometimes problematic. Remember Bill Smith? The shift requires a reorientation in thinking.

Many newly appointed supervisors report feeling both a sense of added responsibility and a lack of control. They are responsible for the results of other people's work, not just their own. But, they cannot control others' efforts the way they did their own. They cannot be as sure of the results of others' efforts as they were of their own.

Sometimes making the transition from worker to supervisor is difficult. With experience, however, most newly appointed supervisors begin to develop a managerial point of view. They learn to get their sense of achievement through the accomplishments of their workers. They learn that while their workers may not perform a specific task exactly as they might, jobs still get done and get done well. Most importantly, new supervisors learn that they have a set of new activities that, although quite different from their old activities, are even more important.

Moving from worker to supervisor thus requires a change in orientation and the development of a managerial point of view. It also requires the development of supervisory skills. Both achievements are necessary to become a good supervisor. Bill Smith, for example, may have failed as a supervisor either because he could not change his orientation or because he didn't have the supervisory skills.

Supervisory skills

What are the supervisory skills? A recent study of training needs of supervisors identified twenty-three skills.[3] These are shown in Fig. 1.1. In this study, supervisors were also asked to indicate which skill areas were most important to them, so the skills are listed in that order.

One area of supervisory skills is not included in the list. These are the **technical skills, the supervisors' knowledge of the technical aspects of the jobs their workers perform.** Technical skills are extremely important to supervisors. You cannot train and develop employees unless you know the job you are training them for. Likewise

1. Motivating	**13.** Counseling
2. Developing employees	**14.** Functioning in the organization
3. Communication	
4. Leadership	**15.** Time management
5. Planning/organizing	**16.** Delegation
6. Human relations	**17.** Affirmative action/equal employment opportunity
7. Performance appraisal	
8. Disciplining	**18.** Safety (for example, OSHA, first aid)
9. Decision making	
10. Handling complaints and grievances	**19.** Conducting meetings
	20. Termination procedures
11. Management methods (for example, MBO)	**21.** Interviewing
	22. Hiring procedures
12. Reporting systems (written information)	**23.** Budgeting

Figure 1.1 Supervisory skills listed according to importance to role of a supervisor

Source: Adapted from Katherine Culbertson and Mark Thompson, "An Analysis of Supervisory Training Needs," *Training and Development Journal,* February 1980, pp. 58–62.

you cannot appraise their performance or provide leadership if you do not know how to perform the job.

Technical skills, however, are unique to each type of job. As such, they cannot be taught in a course on supervision. Rather, in general courses in supervision, and in this book, we must concentrate on the skills that are common to all supervisors.

Plan of this book

This book is based on the identified supervisory skills. In Chapter 2, we focus on the environment that affects supervisors. We describe changes that are occurring and discuss how these might affect the supervisor's job.

Supervisors function within organizations. In Chapter 3 we discuss the nature of organizations and note how different organizational characteristics affect supervisors. We also discuss the informal relationships that develop in organizations and how supervisors can deal with them.

Supervisors often feel pressured and frustrated because of lack of time to do their job. Chapter 4 covers time management techniques and provides approaches to using time better.

Chapter 5 concentrates on the development of communication skills. The nature of communication within organizations is discussed. Special skills including writing, interviewing, and conducting meetings are also emphasized.

The question of motivation is the topic of Chapter 6. Theories and concepts of motivation are briefly discussed and techniques for motivating workers are emphasized.

In Chapter 7, we concentrate on the leadership role of the supervisor. We emphasize developing skills for analyzing situations and choosing an effective leadership style.

Chapter 8 concentrates on problem workers. Techniques for disciplining effectively, handling complaints, and counseling workers are discussed.

Decision making and problem solving are covered in Chapter 9. The development of more effective problem-solving skills is emphasized. In addition, the use of group versus individual decision making is discussed.

Chapters 10 and 11 concentrate on planning and controlling. In Chapter 10, the planning and control process is described. While supervisors are not involved in all planning activities, they are affected by the developed plans. This impact is discussed. In Chapter 11, specific planning and control techniques such as MBO and budgeting are discussed.

The process of selecting workers is discussed in Chapter 12. Supervisory techniques for bringing in new employees and orienting them to their jobs are emphasized. In addition, the topics of equal employment opportunity and affirmative action are discussed.

Chapter 13 emphasizes the area of training and developing workers. On-the-job training and informal coaching are discussed.

Performance review is discussed in Chapter 14. The chapter covers both informal and formal performance review. In addition, discussing performance reviews with workers is emphasized.

The influence of unions is discussed in Chapter 15. Handling complaints and grievances is emphasized. In addition, there is a discussion of union organizing efforts.

Chapter 16 covers safety. The Occupational Safety and Health Act is discussed. Techniques for developing work safety are emphasized.

Building supervisory skills

Supervising is a complex activity that doesn't conform to hard and fast rules. We can't tell you "how to do it" in a book. We can, however, make certain that your study of supervision involves more than simply reading descriptions of concepts. Throughout this book, we emphasize application of concepts. In addition to describing ideas, we provide some guidelines for applying them in your own work situation, now or in the future.

To give you some experience in applying concepts, cases and practical exercises conclude each chapter. The cases are descriptions of supervisory situations. You will be asked to use the concepts discussed in the chapter to either (1) analyze what happened and explain why, or (2) analyze the situation and make a decision. In addition, longer cases appear at the end of each section. These cases cover a variety of issues and will give you an opportunity to try out your ideas in more complex situations.

A word of caution: this book will not make you a supervisor. Supervising is a skill and, like any skill, it requires experience as well as study. A good understanding of the concepts in the book, however, can make analyzing your experiences easier so you can profit from your mistakes as well as your successes.

Being a supervisor isn't an easy job. Sometimes it is extremely frustrating, a seemingly continual flow of problems and challenges. Likewise, learning to supervise isn't easy. It requires study; it requires experience. Both activities, however, can be exceptionally rewarding. Ultimately we hope each of you will experience the satisfaction of seeing people work together effectively and knowing you have played a part in achieving this goal.

Summary

☐ Supervising is a challenging and rewarding activity. It is an increasingly important activity. Effective supervision is fundamental to increased productivity and quality of life.

☐ Supervisors are found in all types of organizations. While their activities differ, all supervisory jobs involve working with and through hourly-level workers to accomplish established work-unit goals. As first-line managers, supervisors plan, organize, staff, direct, and control.

☐ Higher-level managers spend more time planning and organizing. Supervisors spend more time staffing and directing. All levels of management control activities.

☐ Supervisors are often viewed as a linking pin between workers and higher-level management. Often, however, they become caught in the middle when management's and workers' expectations conflict. One thing we do know is that effective supervisors are key people in management.

☐ The shift from worker to supervisor can be difficult. New supervisors often experience both a sense of added responsibility and lack of control. They must reorient their thinking from doing work themselves to getting work done through others. They must develop a managerial viewpoint.

☐ Supervising is a skill. It requires experience as well as study. As a result, we emphasize application as well as concepts throughout this book.

Questions for review and discussion

1. What makes supervisors different from workers?
2. Why can the shift from worker to supervisor be difficult?
3. What is a managerial viewpoint?
4. What are the management activities? How does the supervisor's involvement in these activities differ from that of higher-level managers?

Key terms

Controlling	Staffing
Directing	Supervision
Organizing	Supervisors
Planning	Technical skills

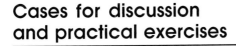

Cases for discussion and practical exercises

1. Bill Jones, general manager of a small manufacturing plant, had to select a new supervisor for Department 1 to replace a supervisor who was retiring. He wanted to select the worker from the plant who had the best potential to be a good supervisor. Unfortunately, no established criteria existed for making this decision. Bill had talked to a number of people and had received suggestions regarding criteria he should use in selecting the new supervisor. Now he had to decide just what qualifications he would use. The following criteria have been suggested:

   a) Select the worker with the greater seniority in the plant.

   b) Select the worker who has the best productivity record.

   c) Select the worker with the greatest technical knowledge of the work process.

   d) Select the worker who has the best communication skills.

   e) Select the worker who has the best common sense.

   f) Select the worker who has been a natural leader in informal activities.

   g) Select the worker who is outgoing and has a likeable personality.

   Discuss each of the possible criteria. Which would you recommend for Bill Jones' use? Why? If you recommend more than one, discuss their relative importance.

2. Interview someone who is presently a supervisor. Preferably this should be someone you do not work closely with at the present time. Structure your interview around the following questions:

   a) What do you do? What are your major activities and responsibilities?

   b) What are some of the major problems you face?

   Try to get as much information as possible. Compare the information you receive from your interview with the material discussed in this chapter. How do the activities relate to those discussed in the chapter?

Notes

1. Keith Davis, *Human Behavior at Work* (New York: McGraw Hill Book Company, 1977), p. 126.

2. Ernest A. Doud, Jr. and Edward J. Miller, "First-Line Supervisors: The Key to Improved Performance." *Management Review*, December 1980, 18–24.

3. Katherine Culbertson and Mark Thompson, "An Analysis of Supervisory Training Needs." *Training and Development Journal*, February 1980, pp. 58–62.

2

The challenge of supervision

Objectives

After reading this chapter you should be able to

- ☐ Explain the problems presented by technological change and how they affect the supervisor's job.
- ☐ Identify major changes in the work force and explain how they affect the supervisor's job.
- ☐ Explain how the economy affects the supervisor's job.
- ☐ Explain how government regulation influences the supervisor's job.
- ☐ Explain why declining productivity is a major problem which must be resolved.
- ☐ Explain how quality circles and Quality of Work Life programs operate and how they affect the supervisor's job.

The environment of supervision

The supervisor's job is challenging and is becoming increasingly complex. Supervisors must react to a number of new and different pressures. We are in a period of significant change in our society and in our economy. In many cases, supervisors will have to adapt to these changes. Traditional ways of doing the job must be updated.

In this chapter we will examine the changing conditions in four areas of the supervisor's environment: technology, people, the economy, and government. Then we will examine what is probably the major problem confronting supervisors today—declining productivity.

The changing technology

Today's world is one of rapidly changing technology, with "breakthroughs" in the industrial sector occurring daily. Assessing the challenges posed by new technology is, at best, a risky task. This risk results in part from not knowing what technology and innovations may appear in the next ten years. Predicting how people using the new technologies will react is also difficult. While some see a futuristic society similar to that portrayed in "Star Wars," others see merely a continuance of the lifestyle to which we have grown accustomed over the past several decades. Actually, the future will probably be somewhere between these two extremes. The world of work will proceed in its usual pattern but with key dramatic changes directly attributable to new technology. While we have no crystal ball to help us, a brief look at some recent technological developments gives some insight into what you as supervisors can expect in the future.

A major development of the sixties was the evolution of micro-electronics. The semi-conductor and electronic chip paved the way for electronic controls in all areas of the economy. In the office this has resulted in computer-controlled accounting processes. In the plant it has led to computer-aided design and computer-aided manufacturing (CAD-CAM) techniques, and even to a major new form of mechanization—robotics. These developments in turn have created an entirely new environment to which supervisors and workers alike must adapt or face obsolescence.

This cycle of change and adaptation is not new. Similar circumstances arose with the introduction of the wheelright in the nineteenth century and automobile mechanization in the twentieth century. Then as now, change is not ominous, necessarily, but can be seen as both a challenge and an opportunity.

Neither the worker nor the supervisor will go untouched in the next decade. In fact, the success of organizations in the future will largely depend on how effectively they utilize the new technology. New technology will be incorporated and people will have to adjust and learn to use the technology. Directing workers in the new era is perhaps one of the most challenging tasks supervisors will face.

Robotics Computer-aided manufacturing or robot assembly is no longer a rarity. There are currently more than 2000 robots working in the United States and as many as 13,000 worldwide.[1] Unfortunately, the reasons for their use are still not understood either by workers or most supervisors.

Robots are not substitutes for human effort. They are an extension of human effort in an attempt to increase productivity, enhance the quality of working life, and increase product quality. They represent the use of preprogrammed activities through mechanized operations. Robots are tools to be used and directed by people, *not* substitutes for human involvement in the work process. Robots on the welding line in Detroit or the packaging line in Omaha perform a wide variety of preprogrammed tasks but *never* without the involvement of people. Admittedly, fewer people are used on any specific operation, but their presence is critical, and their tasks and responsibilities are necessary.

Directing workers in the new work environment   Whole lines of welded parts have been rejected solely because someone failed to replace electrodes. Hours of meat production have been wasted because of clogged polyethelene wrapping tubes. The list is endless. These failures point to the critical need for human "supervision" of robot production. How accepting workers are of this new tool and their role in the production process become an important aspect of the supervisor's job.

While conditions vary from location to location, the general impact of this increasing technical complexity at work includes: (1) a decrease in numbers of blue collar workers and the use of manual or physical skills; (2) an increase in white collar workers and mental, unobservable skills; (3) a shift in emphasis from direct production to maintenance of the production process; and (4) a reduction in the number of low-skilled jobs available. To these, a fifth aspect may be added. While the labor–management environment in the past has been all too often adversarial in nature, mechanized production requires a more cooperative relationship.

Instead of being one more cog in the wheel of the production process, workers in the future may be responsible for the functioning of multimillion dollar robot systems. Instead of merely totaling lines of accounting figures, "clerks" may be responsible for computer entries on which a whole organization depends. Simply put, for every mechanized operation there will be responsibilities borne by workers. Machine skills, manual dexterity, and brute strength will give way to attentiveness, quick thinking, and a degree of responsibility never before experienced by most workers. Workers will be forced to make the transition from the role of a producer to that of a monitor of a very sophisticated and very expensive mechanized production process, from being a human adding machine to being a computer programmer. Their relationship to their work will radically change.

Obviously, new technology has its costs. Organizations must be able to make substantial investments in equipment. Workers must face the necessity for upgraded and new and different skills. While company training efforts may aid some workers, the fact remains that some jobs will disappear and some workers will not have appropriate skills. The future will be difficult. However, the responsibility for determining whether or not the future will be met as a challenging opportunity or a devastating calamity lies to a large extent with line supervisors.

Increased technological complexity has a direct impact on the supervisor's job. With more automated operations, supervisors find they no longer perform some of the traditional supervisory functions. For example, they may have little or no say in determining work methods, procedures, or design of jobs performed by workers. Planning and scheduling of work is done by higher-level managers or staff specialists. Supervisors monitor the implementation of the work plan.

While the traditional supervisory functions are decreased, the supervisor's role as a "linking pin" increases. Supervisors will feel greater pressure to keep employees fully informed of goals, objectives, and plans established by higher-level managers. Representing employees and their interests to higher-level managers will be increasingly important. In short, as a linking pin, the supervisor will become less a manager of things and more a manager of information.

The importance of the supervisor's role as a manager of people will also increase. At the same time, managing people will become more of a challenge. As technology becomes more complex, the level of skills required by the employees increases. Not only do skill levels become more sophisticated and technical, they require more mental effort and become less directly observable. Thus it will be difficult, if not impossible, for the supervisor to possess all the technical capabilities needed to perform all the activities of his or her workers.

Supervisors will be managing workers who have greater technical capabilities than they do. As a result they will be spending less time telling workers what to do and how to perform their activities. Rather, the focus will be on creating an environment that encourages positive motivation and the acceptance of responsibility, as well as providing the necessary support, tools, equipment, and supplies that promote a high level of performance.

The nature of people

As we have discussed, managing people is becoming increasingly complicated. The new technology contributes to this complexity, but is not the only factor. The changing mix of employees and changing social and work values are also factors. A generation ago the average worker typically was a white male needing work to support his family. This is no longer the case.

Women now make up more than 40% of the work force. More than 25% of managers and supervisors are women. More than 10% of the work force is black and over 5% is Spanish-speaking. The average age of the work force is increasing. It is currently 32 years, and by 1990, the average age will be 40 years. The work force is becoming better educated, as the average worker today has a high school diploma. It is reasonable to expect that individuals entering the work force during the 1980s will have graduated from high school and most will have had some college or technical school education.[2]

Women workers   The entry of more women into paid working jobs has affected supervisors. Women may have been educated and socialized to accept the work role, but have others in the organization adjusted to these changes? Problems of discrimination still exist. The problem of the sexes learning to relate to each other on a professional basis still remains to be resolved. Supervisors may encounter many difficulties as they attempt to insure the acceptance of female workers by the work group, foster their development, and cope with their own anxieties.

Dual-career marriages   More women and men are participating in **dual-career marriages.** In dual-career marriages both husband and wife work. Both view their work as a central and important part of their life. Both adjust and accommodate their work life to balance the responsibilities of home and family. These adjustments are not without strains which may affect their work. Some employees, for example, are unwilling to accept a move to another location because it would interfere with or interrupt their spouse's career.

Black workers   Despite legal efforts to eliminate racial discrimination, the problem still exists. Whereas less than twenty years ago, blacks were forced to take relatively lower-level jobs, today they can be found in all levels and types of jobs. Supervisors find themselves responsible for assuring that blacks have the equal opportunity guaranteed them by law.

Cultural minorities In recent years the influence of cultural minorities on this country has increased. While Spanish-speaking persons represent the largest cultural minority, Vietnamese, Indians, and others have entered the work force as well.

There appears to be a trend toward viewing America as a culturally diverse society, rather than as a "melting pot." Organizations will still expect minorities to conform to accepted patterns of job behavior. Supervisors, however, will have to adapt to a broader range of cultural values.

Older workers In contrast to what was expected a decade ago, the trend is to later rather than earlier retirement. More people are enjoying good health and physical and mental vitality to a later age. They want and often need to remain active and productive. Organizations can no longer require people to retire at age 65, and an increasing number of people are continuing to work who are age 65 or older. For supervisors this means an increased need to train older workers to function effectively with the new technology.

Education Better educated people tend to have higher expectations regarding their work and life-styles. People invest much time and money in education in the hope of obtaining greater rewards. They expect to be able to use their capabilities, and receive rewards, both financial and nonfinancial, that are meaningful to them. These workers tend to want work that is challenging and rewarding to perform. But, even though workers are becoming more educated, there are still numerous relatively unchallenging, low-level jobs that must be done. The problem becomes one of getting people to perform these jobs and perform them well.

Values Along with greater education, today's workers seem to bring somewhat different work values with them. Many of today's younger workers no longer agree with the Protestant work ethic that work is good in and of itself. They no longer feel obligated to accept without question the orders or directions of their bosses. Many do not believe that money is the only reward they should get from their work. Rather, they want to contribute to the organization. They expect their ideas, opinions, and feelings to be considered. They want personal satisfaction as well as a paycheck from their job. As a result, many organizations are redesigning jobs to incorporate opportunities for greater personal satisfaction.

In summary, the work force is becoming more varied, since the people doing the work have different needs and wants. They experience personal pressures that affect their work. They bring different expectations to their jobs. Further, differences in values and lifestyles introduce more strains and conflict to the work place.

In the face of this increasing variety and complexity, supervisors are expected to mold their workers into a more productive work group. To meet this challenge, tomorrow's supervisor must have an accurate understanding of human behavior. The skills of leadership and the ability to resolve differences and create positive motivation will be critical. When coupled with the needs of new technology, effectively managing people may well be the most important function supervisors will perform.

Economic forces

All organizations—private or public, profit or nonprofit—are affected by the state of the national and international economy. A stable, predictable economy is an ideal environment for effective organizational functioning. Unfortunately, that is not the nature of today's economy. At present, our economy is unstable and unpredictable, and this instability will probably continue well into the future. It is characterized by a high level of inflation, soaring energy costs, pockets of very high unemployment in certain industries and certain regions, and volatile but generally high interest rates.

High interest rates can significantly decrease business activities in industries that are heavily dependent on consumer credit. The housing industry is an example. When mortgage rates are high, people are less likely to borrow money to buy or build a new house. Thus fewer new houses are constructed. While this credit problem directly affects contractors and their employees, it also spills over to companies that provide goods and services to the housing industry. The auto industry is another example. High interest rates discourage people from borrowing money to purchase new cars, reducing business activity and employment in the auto industry as well as in the network of companies dependent on the industry.

Organizations also borrow money to finance internal operations. Retail organizations, for example, often borrow money to buy goods to stock their stores. When interest rates are high, these organizations pay more to carry their inventory. Pressure builds to stock fewer goods and/or raise prices to cover the high inventory costs. Many companies borrow money to invest in plant and equipment. When interest rates are high, companies frequently delay building new plants and modernizing equipment.

A high level of inflation has an even broader impact on the functioning of organizations. Organizations are pressured to raise wages so that their employees can keep up with the increasing cost of living. At the same time companies are trying to hold down costs so that they do not have to raise their prices accordingly. The result is frequently greater pressure to increase productivity and hold down costs.

Increased inflation in the United States also has an impact on international trade. As the cost of goods produced in the United States goes up, exporting these goods to other countries becomes more difficult. Likewise, goods produced in other countries become cheaper in the United States. This imbalance causes a decrease in the demand for U.S. goods, and employment in U.S. industries goes down.

What impact do these economic forces have on you as a supervisor? They may affect the setting in which you work. Some industries are declining or even dying in the United States. In such a situation you may find yourself supervising a scaled-down operation or even an operation that is being phased out completely. In the worst case you will be faced with the challenge of maintaining a positive motivational climate and keeping people productive, while they are concerned about being out of a job in six months or a year. At best you will be faced with making your work group more productive—producing more with similar or less resources—in order to avoid the negative picture just presented. This situation is similar to that which supervisors in the auto industry find themselves in today.

As organizations are faced with increasing inflationary pressures, supervisors will be more involved with efforts to closely control costs and increase productivity. This may be particularly problematic for supervisors in nonprofit or public organizations. In the public sector, prices simply cannot be raised to cover the increased costs of providing services. Thus, as costs increase, with no increase in funding, the challenge is one of providing the same level of service with less money.

Government regulation

Government has become increasingly interested in the way organizations are conducting their affairs. This concern has resulted in government agencies that enforce laws and regulations that cover business activity. Regulation was initiated with the Interstate Commerce Commission in 1887 and has ballooned to about fifty agencies today. Twenty of these were added in the 1970s alone. The Code of Federal Regulations was 77,498 pages long in 1978, filling more than 15 feet of bookshelves. It is estimated that private industry spent $100 billion in 1979 trying to understand, comply with, dispute, and cope with the paperwork the agencies create.[3] Whether or not we like the idea of government regulating business, it is a reality.

Government regulation of business directly affects you as a supervisor. Government regulations provide directives which limit business activity or specify action. Because of their impact on many supervisory activities, government regulations will be discussed throughout this book. However, a quick look at some of the regulations will give you an idea of the magnitude of the problem.

Environmental protection   Legislation and regulations concerned with protecting the quality of the environment have received considerable publicity. Laws such as the Air Quality Act and the Water Quality Act restrict an organization's impact on the environment. They have caused organizations to change the way they handle gas, liquid, and solid wastes.

For example, an electric company can no longer simply burn coal to generate electricity. It must control the composition of the smoke leaving its smokestack. Government regulations specify the maximum amount of sulfur dioxide and suspended solid particles allowed in the smoke. Electric companies must find ways to conform to these regulations.

Supervisors seldom make decisions regarding how the organization will conform to **environmental protection** legislation. They are involved, however, in implementing any changes in processes that are required to meet the regulations.

Consumer protection   Consumer protection, like environmental protection, has received much attention in the press. The activities of Ralph Nader and his Nader's Raiders—as well as other consumer advocates—have drawn a great deal of public attention to consumer rights.

Government involvement in consumer protection goes back to 1906 when the Food and Drug Administration was established. The government has become more active, however, since 1962 when President Kennedy proclaimed four basic consumer rights. These rights are (1) the right to safety, (2) the right to be heard, (3) the right to choose, and (4) the right to be informed. To implement these rights the federal government passed twenty-five major pieces of consumer legislation from 1966–1969. These laws prohibit companies from violating consumer rights and provide specific remedies when rights are violated.

Automobile recalls illustrate the impact of consumer protection legislation. Automotive companies have been forced to recall and repair cars in which faulty design or construction threatens the safety of the occupants. Even though consumers have chosen to buy the cars, the company is responsible for guaranteeing the car is not inherently unsafe.

Supervisors are affected indirectly by consumer legislation. In particular, they must insure an acceptable level of quality in the product produced or service provided to consumers. The need for this is reflected in a popular warning in Detroit: never buy a car assembled on a Monday or Friday.

Employment Numerous laws have been established that affect the employment process. The Civil Rights Act prohibits discrimination in employment because of race, color, sex, religion, or national origin. The Equal Pay Act requires that women performing work comparable to that performed by men receive equal pay. The Age Discrimination in Employment Act prohibits discrimination in employment for people between 40 and 70 years of age.

These and similar laws are designed to insure that all people receive equal consideration and treatment. They have dramatically affected the employment process in most companies, limiting what can be done and specifying what must be done in the selection, promotion, and compensation of employees. Since these laws have an important, direct effect on supervisors, they will be discussed in more detail in Chapter 12.

Management-union activities American workers were given the right to form unions and bargain collectively with employers under the National Labor Relations Act (the Wagner Act) in 1935. Since that time laws have been established to govern the relationship among management, unions, and workers.

The Wagner Act identified and forbid unfair labor practices by employers. The Act also established the National Labor Relations Board to administer the law. The Taft-Hartley Act prohibited unfair labor practices by unions. Many of the rights given workers in the private sector were extended to those in the public sector through Executive Orders 10988 and 11491.

These and numerous other similar laws and regulations affect most supervisors today. If you are a supervisor in a company with a union, the way you work with your employees is governed by labor laws as well as the union contract and company policies. Government regulation of the union–management relationship affects the way you function daily on the job. Because it has such an affect on supervisors, this aspect of government regulation will be discussed in more detail in Chapter 15.

Safety and health The Occupational Safety and Health Act of 1970 (OSHA) regulates organizations in areas affecting the health and safety of employees. Under this law, the Secretary of Labor establishes standards for both safety and health. It also provides for on-site inspection and establishes penalities for violations.

This area of government regulation also directly affects supervisors. Supervisors are responsible for insuring safe conditions at the work place. They are expected to watch continually for threats to worker health or safety and take action to correct any unsafe conditions. The supervisor's responsibility for insuring a safe work environment is discussed in depth in Chapter 16.

The productivity problem

Declining **productivity** is one of the major problems facing the United States today. It is a both a cause and result of each of the forces we have discussed thus far in this chapter: technological development, the state of the economy, the changing work force, and government regulation.

In the years following World War II, the steady growth of productivity was a major factor in creating the highest standard of living in the world. From 1948 to 1965 productivity increased at an average yearly rate of 3%. Starting in the late 1960s the rate of in-

crease started to decline. In 1979 productivity actually decreased by
.9% and this decline continued with a 1.7% decrease in productivity in the first half of 1980.[4]

A decreasing rate of productivity creates major problems for
business and for the people of the United States. Decreasing productivity, when combined with increasing wage rates, increases the cost
of products produced. When increases in material and energy costs
are also considered, the end result is still higher prices and spiraling
inflation rates. In addition, as productivity in the United States decreases relative to that of other countries, American businesses find
they no longer can compete effectively in the world market. A result
is increased unemployment of American workers. These problems—inflation and unemployment—directly lower the standard of
living of the American people

Of all the topics considered here, the most important to the
average American is that of productivity. While our modern society
can define production costs or production/service output in many
ways to suit the needs of the moment, success or failure of our system
eventually comes down to the question of productivity. Put more
simply, productivity affects the cost of each item produced or service
provided. Many factors affect productivity—quality, production
efficiency, worker involvement, company investment, government
regulation, consumer protection, quality of work life, and social mo-
bility. Without improvement in productivity, few of the "good"
things are possible and in fact deterioration in our way of life is assured.

We can expect therefore a greater emphasis on increasing productivity. Business and government will be searching for ways to
produce more with the same amount of resources. There will certainly be an emphasis on developing and using new technology. Tax
laws may be changed to encourage companies to invest in more efficient equipment. There may be alterations in government regulations which result in lower costs and, consequently, higher productivity rates.

Many companies are introducing programs designed to help
workers become more productive. These include changes in job
design, changes in company policies, and changes in the way workers are managed. These programs directly affect the supervisor's job
and the way they must interact with their workers. Examples of such
programs which are gaining popularity include quality circles and
Quality of Work Life programs.

Quality circles

Recently, U.S. organizations have begun to look at management practices employed by companies in other countries. In particular, because of their dramatic increases in productivity, there has been much attention paid to the Japanese approach. Quality circles are one Japanese innovation that has interested American companies. Roughly one in every eight Japanese workers is involved in a quality circle. Many people feel that quality circles have contributed greatly to the increase in Japanese productivity.[5]

Quality circles are autonomous units which are established within work groups. They generally consist of approximately ten workers led by a supervisor or senior worker. In principle they are voluntary study groups that are taught problem-solving techniques and statistical methods and focus on solving job-related problems. Quality circles concentrate on improving production methods, reducing scrap, defects, reworks, and downtime. These efforts are expected to lead to increases in productivity and lower costs.

Quality circles are also intended to improve the morale and motivation of the work force. Frequently problems are solved by improving working conditions. Participants are also involved in skill development. In total, the existence of quality circles indicates the company's belief that hourly workers have an important contribution to make to the organization.

Quality circles have certain characteristics:

- There is a continuous study of the work place, searching for opportunities for improvements. The quality circles are not formed to respond to a specific problem nor are they disbanded when a specific problem is solved.
- They are based on the assumption that the causes of poor quality performance are not easily identified by either managers, supervisors, or workers. They assume study is needed to discover and solve quality problems. The company therefore provides the participants with the training necessary to analyze problems and provide solutions.
- They are based on the assumption that workers are more motivated to carry out solutions to problems if they have been involved in determining that solution.

Quality circles are not without problems, however. Ideally, there should be equal emphasis on productivity and worker development. In practice, companies frequently place more emphasis on productivity, causing workers to question the benefits provided to them. In addition, a minority of workers views quality circles as a burden imposed on them by management rather than as their own program to improve their work place.

Because of the publicity quality circles have received, many American companies have begun to experiment with them. Among those firms are American Airlines, Honeywell, Ford Motor Co., General Motors, and Rockwell International. While we do not know what impact they will have on American industry, we can expect that many more firms will experiment with quality circles in the coming years.

Quality of work life programs

Quality of Work Life (QWL) programs grew out of a concern over increasing worker dissatisfaction. Many jobs had become highly structured, routine, and repetitive, providing little involvement, challenge, or reward for many workers. As a result, these workers were dissatisfied with their work and this dissatisfaction led to increased absenteeism, turnover, and decreased productivity.

QWL programs in organizations often are sponsored jointly by union and management. A joint union–management committee initiates and oversees the QWL program. The basic element of QWL programs is the QWL Committee. There may be one or more QWL committees in specific segments of the organization composed of hourly workers, union representatives, and management representatives. Frequently an outside consultant helps them function.

The QWL committees are cooperative problem-solving groups. They determine their own goals and objectives, analyze problems, and develop action plans to improve the work place. Their mission is to improve the quality of work life and the effectiveness of the organization. Indicators of the quality of work life in an organization include worker satisfaction, absenteeism, turnover, accidents, and mental well-being. Indicators of organizational effectiveness include labor costs, productivity, and the quality of product or service provided.

Although no standard pattern exists, most QWL committees analyze and propose changes in working conditions, employee training, communication with workers, reward systems, and job structure. In particular, most QWL programs focus on providing employees with more responsibility and decision-making authority. Such changes are expected to create a more positive motivational climate for workers, allowing them to more fully use their skills and abilities and leading to both greater worker satisfaction and higher productivity.

Like quality circles, QWL programs are still in the experimental stages in American industry. A number of organizations are experimenting with QWL programs and we can expect more experimentation during the next several years.[6] The success of these programs, however, is yet to be proven.

Company experiments in employee participation programs such as quality circles and QWL programs will have a significant effect on the supervisor's job. Supervisors who previously have functioned primarily as directors of the work force will find that they must develop new relationships and establish new patterns of functioning with employees. They will face the challenge of redefining much of the role of the supervisor as a manager of people.

Summary

- ☐ Supervisors face an increasingly challenging job. Their environment is undergoing significant change in four areas: (1) technology, (2) people, (3) the economy, and (4) government regulation.
- ☐ Technological change has been rapid. Directing workers in the new era of mechanization will be a challenging task.
- ☐ The supervisor's job will change. Supervisors will be required to spend less time planning and organizing work and more time monitoring work. They will need to create an environment that motivates workers to accept higher levels of responsibility.
- ☐ Changes in the work force will also make supervising workers more challenging. Women and minority workers, better educated workers, older workers, and dual-career families all result in new problems supervisors must address. At the same time work values are changing. Supervisors must cope with a diverse group of workers having a variety of needs and expectations.

☐ The instability of our economy poses new challenges for supervisors. High rates of inflation, energy costs, interest rates, and unemployment affect all organizations. Supervisors will be called on to improve productivity in all areas.

☐ Government regulation of business has increased in recent years. Some laws have a greater impact on the supervisor's job than others. In all cases supervisors must do their part to insure these laws are not violated.

☐ The productivity problem is a major problem supervisors must face in the future. Declining productivity hurts business as well as society.

☐ Because of their success in Japan, quality circles have been introduced in some organizations to help increase productivity. Quality of Work Life programs represent another attempt to improve productivity. Both change the way supervisors perform their jobs.

Questions for review and discussion

1. What is the impact of robot assembly on human effort at work?

2. Discuss the changes in the supervisor's job resulting from the new technology.

3. How has the work force changed? How do these changes affect the supervisor's job?

4. What is the impact of an unstable economy on the supervisor's job?

5. What areas of business activity are regulated by the government? How does this influence the supervisor's job? *UNION LAWS*

6. Why is declining productivity a major problem facing U.S. industry today?

7. What are quality circles? What problems are associated with quality circles?

8. What are Quality of Work Life (QWL) programs? How do quality circles and Quality of Work Life programs affect the supervisor's job?

9. If robots are meant to improve work, why do some workers resist their use?

10. Debate the advantages and disadvantages of government regulation of business.

Key terms

Consumer protection

Dual-career marriages

Environmental protection

Government regulation

Productivity

Quality circles

Quality of Work Life (QWL) programs

Robot assembly

Cases for discussion and practical exercises

1. Three supervisors, Jane, Roger, and Joe, sat talking one day in the lunchroom. For years their company had maintained slow but steady growth. Workers tended to join the company after graduating from high school and remained there until retirement. Most of them had family members already employed at the company when they hired in. Turnover was low and the workers seemed like one happy family.

"Things were a lot simpler then," Roger remarked. "I'm kind of glad to see the golden years of retirement lying right before me."

"For you that's fine," Jane replied. "But I've got another fifteen years to go. It's a shame to see this place go downhill like it is."

Joe cut in and said, "But Jane, it didn't have to. Look at what's happened over the past ten years. It's these darn kids we're bringing in here. They haven't learned yet that there's no free lunch."

Nearly ten years ago, the company developed a new manufacturing process and a few new products. From that time on, demand for these new products sharply increased. Workers often had to work overtime and for the first time the company actively had to seek job applicants from outside sources. The result was a large influx of younger, newer workers.

"These kids think they know more about their jobs and mine than I do just because they've been to school," Joe continued. "They think they've got rights to everything under the sun!"

Jane broke into the conversation, "Isn't that the clincher. Never before have I had so many problems. These young folks say they're bored with their jobs and take days off to ease their frustration! Can you believe that? Why one young fellow told me the other day he wanted more responsibility. So yesterday I asked him to work overtime and he refused! Get this—he had to pick up his kids at school!"

Roger spoke up, "The problem is that kids today don't know what it is not to have a job. They grow up feeling work is some God-given right. No, I take that back, they think that to work when they want and doing what they want is a God-given right."

Joe got up from the table saying, "You know, it's really a shame. They are really good kids. Sure, we don't see eye-to-eye on a lot of things. That's okay with me in most respects. I draw the line at work though. In my department, what I say goes. If they don't look good, I don't look good. And I don't like the idea of putting my thirty-five years of good hard work on the line just because some kid feels like taking the day off. I tell you, something has to be done."

a) Are the "kids" referred to in the preceding case really the poor-quality performers that the supervisors make them out to be?

b) What is the real problem at issue in this case?

2. If you are presently employed, consider the government regulations affecting your work place. Identify what you think are the most important regulations that govern a supervisor's actions in the work place. How does each affect the supervisor. If you are not presently employed, pick the type of organization you would like to work in and complete the same assignment.

Notes

1. "Robots Join the Labor Force," *Business Week*, June 9, 1980, pp. 62–76.

2. Barry Tarshis, *The Average American Book* (New York: Signet, 1979).

3. Thomas P. Murphy, "Regulation: Have We Gone Overboard On It?" *Think*, September–October, 1980, pp. 16–25.

4. "An Economic Dream in Peril," *Newsweek*, September 8, 1980, pp. 50–62; and Irwin Ross, "Productivity and Your Pocketbook," *Readers Digest*, December, 1980, pp. 150–154.

5. Robert E. Cole, "Learning from the Japanese: Prospects and Pitfalls," *Management Review*, September 1980, pp. 22–28 and 38–42.

6. Edgar Huse, *Organization Development and Change* (2nd ed.), (Minneapolis: West Publishing Company, 1980).

3

Working in the organization

Objectives

After reading this chapter you should be able to

- ☐ Explain how the organization's structure affects supervisors.
- ☐ Discuss why supervisors need to understand informal groups.
- ☐ Indicate how supervisors can use informal groups to increase performance.
- ☐ Identify ways supervisors can use the political process to their advantage.

Supervisors must work with and through people to accomplish goals. The way they work with people, however, is influenced by the specific type of organization where they work. They may be employed by a hospital, a steel company, or a school system. Each of these organizations is structured in order to achieve its specific purpose. An organization's structure has considerable impact on how supervisors perform their jobs.

An effective organizational structure can make the supervisor's job easier by facilitating communication and helping supervisors coordinate and focus workers' efforts on goal accomplishment. An unsound structure can have the opposite effect. It can create confusion, conflict, duplication of effort, and a host of other difficulties.

Informal organizations also exist within all organizations. The patterns of relationships involved in informal organizations are not formally established, but do influence the opinions, feelings, and actions of workers. As a result they can have a significant impact on the functioning of formal organizations.

Even though supervisors are not in a position to design the structure of an organization, they must function within it. Learning more about organizations and how they are structured and understanding informal organizations can help supervisors anticipate both problems and opportunities. Then they can cope better with the organizational world in which they live and work.

In this chapter we will examine the nature and structure of organizations as they affect the supervisor's job. We will first consider some general characteristics of all organizations. Then we will look at different types of organizational structures and the advantages and disadvantages of each. Next the impact of the informal organization on the supervisor's job will be discussed. The chapter will conclude with a look at an aspect of organizations that is often overlooked—organizational politics.

The characteristics of organizations

All of us are in continuous contact with organizations throughout our lives. We are born in a hospital. We are educated in school systems. We go to work in some type of organization: a business, a hospital, a school system, or a government agency. As diverse as they may seem, all of these organizations have certain characteristics in common. We will call these the defining characteristics of an **organization.**

■ Organizations have goals. They have a reason—or reasons—for existing. Business organizations often have goals of producing a product or providing a service and making a profit. Hospitals exist to provide care for the sick. Schools are established to educate people.

■ Organizations are made up of people working together to accomplish something they could not do as well individually. People use other resources—money, materials, and equipment—to perform work in the organization. Through their efforts, organizational goals are achieved.

■ There is a division of labor in organizations. Not all people do the same job. Some people may be salespersons, for example; others may be accountants. Doctors do one type of work; nurses have a different job. Work is specialized so that the various jobs in an organization can be performed more effectively.

- Organizations also have a formally established structure. This structure establishes the role of every manager, supervisor, and worker and describes the formal relationships between these roles. The structure is designed to coordinate the efforts of members of the organization and is the main vehicle for planning their cooperative effort.

- There is a hierarchy of authority in organizations. Authority is the right to decide and act. It is assumed to flow from the top down. Top managers delegate some of their authority to middle-level managers, supervisors, and workers, giving them the right to make decisions and take action within certain limits.

Organizational charts

Organizational structures often are represented on an **organizational chart.** An example of a partial organizational chart is shown in Fig. 3.1. The organizational chart identifies departments and jobs and shows the flow of authority or chain of command in the organization. Organizational charts are frequently supplemented by job descriptions and organizational manuals. These define in greater detail the tasks involved in the various jobs and the relationships between jobs.

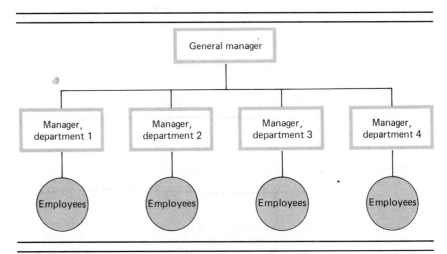

Figure 3.1   A partial organizational chart.

What the chart shows

- It shows division of work into components. These components may be divisions or departments or they may be individuals. (Boxes on the conventional chart represent these units of work.)
- It indicates who is (supposed to be) whose boss. The solid lines on the chart show this superior–subordinate relationship with its implied flow of delegated responsibility, authority, and attendant accountability.
- It states the nature of work performed by the components.
- It shows the grouping of components on a functional, regional, product, or other basis.
- It depicts levels of management in terms of successive layers of superiors and subordinates.

What the chart doesn't show

- It does not show the degree of responsibility and authority exercised by positions on the same managerial level. It does not show power.
- It does not clearly distinguish between line and staff. Making this determination is sometimes difficult and often inconsistent between companies.
- Size and position of boxes do not necessarily reflect importance.
- It does not show all the channels of contact or communication.
- It shows only a few of the key links or relationships in the total organizational network.
- It does not show the informal organization that is a logical and necessary extension of the formal structure.

Figure 3.2 What is and is not on the organizational chart*

Adapted from Howard Carlisle, *Management: Concepts and Situations* (Chicago: Science Research Associates, 1976).

An organizational chart is a simplified model of the organization's structure, but, as shown in Fig. 3.2, the chart has its limitations. It does not show certain important aspects of the organization's structure. Nevertheless, it is a useful guide and provides a good overview of how the various departments within an organization are related.

Establishing departments

Departments are groups of related jobs. Top management determines how the jobs will be grouped in order to establish departments. Supervisors are responsible for the work performed in a department. As a result they need to understand how the departments are created. Several bases exist for grouping jobs into departments. Among the more common are function, product, and location departments.

Functional departments

In **functional departments** jobs requiring similar skills are grouped together. Figure 3.3 shows a chart for an organization based on functions, or related activities. The common functions found in a manufacturing organization—production, marketing, and finance —are the basis for grouping the jobs.

Functional departmentation offers several advantages. Since each department is responsible for only a limited number of specialized activities, experts in these areas can be hired and/or trained. Once on the job, workers can learn more quickly how to perform their jobs. They learn from their experiences in their daily activities. Thus, the skill and knowledge of employees increases rapidly. In addition, functional departmentation simplifies communication within the organization. With departments and jobs identified by function, people in the organization know where to send and get information.

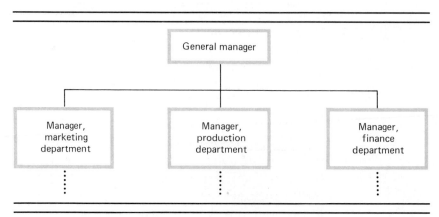

Figure 3.3   Functional departmentation.

There are problems with functional departmentation, however. It tends to create a narrow viewpoint. Workers tend to identify more strongly with their jobs and departments than with the organization as a whole. Thus, greater coordination may be required to make certain all departments work together in achieving organizational goals.

Product departments

Figure 3.4 depicts an organization using **product departments. Here workers and jobs are grouped together on the basis of the product produced or service provided.** For example, General Motors has the Chevrolet Division, the Pontiac Division, and the Cadillac Division. Department stores generally have a men's clothing department, a women's clothing department, a toy department, and a housewares department.

Product departmentation improves the coordination of activities within each product or service area. When employees are working with one product or a group of related products, they can identify with the product. It is easier for them to see the end result of their activities.

Duplication of activities occurs, however. For example, both the Chevrolet Division and the Pontiac Division have marketing departments. Duplication of activities among the different product departments may lead to increased costs for the organization.

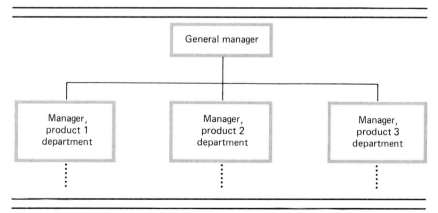

Figure 3.4   Product departmentation.

Location departments

An organization structured according to place or location, using a location department system, is illustrated in Fig. 3.5. Location departmentation groups jobs on the basis of where the work is performed or where the market areas to be served are located. Large city police departments are often organized on a location basis. The police work is divided into several different precincts or districts.

Differences in market or work conditions make this type of departmentation useful. Department store chains, for example, are often organized on the basis of location. Local managers are more knowledgeable about local conditions, buyer preferences, and regional demand. Thus, they are able to take into account any unique local conditions while managing their store.

Most organizations actually use a combination of different types of departments. Figure 3.6 shows an example of an organization using three types of departmentation. At the top, the organization is departmentalized on the basis of function; at the second level, by product; and at the third, by place (location). Using a combination of departmental types enables an organization to obtain the advantages of each, while minimizing their various disadvantages.

Matrix organization is a structure that differs from the ones previously discussed. It exists along with one or a combination of the other types of departmentation. Matrix organization brings together people with special expertise to work on a project for a definite period.

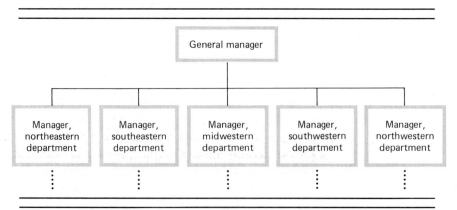

Figure 3.5   Location departmentation.

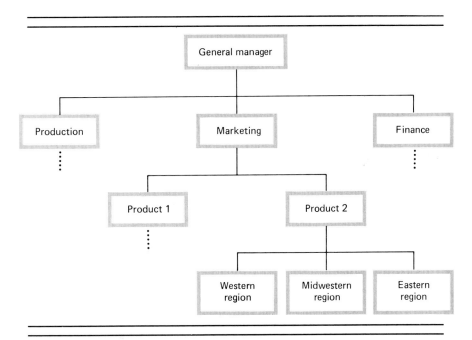

Figure 3.6 Mixed departmentation.

Workers are brought from different departments to work under the direction of the project manager who also is regularly assigned to a permanent department. Each performs a job necessary to complete the special project. As a result, the worker has two superiors, the department supervisor and the project manager, and two sets of job responsibilities, those of the normal job and those required by the project.

Authority relationships

Establishing formal lines of **authority** among the people holding jobs in an organization helps coordinate individual efforts. Authority is the right to decide and take action while using organizational resources: people, money, equipment, and material. A fundamental relationship exists between the responsibilities involved in a job and the authority that is associated with the job. Job responsibilities can be met only if the job holder has the authority to obtain the resources and assistance necessary to carry out these responsibilities.

There are two types of authority in most organizations: line and staff. Managers and supervisors who have **line authority** have the right to direct the work of subordinates and are in the chain of command running from top management down to hourly workers. Production supervisors in a manufacturing organization have line authority, as do marketing managers in their part of the organization. The principal in a school system and the director of nursing in a hospital are additional examples of persons holding line authority.

Managers and supervisors with **staff authority** advise or provide a service to the line. Assume for a moment that you are a sales supervisor and need to hire a salesperson. The personnel department would place ads and attempt to locate candidates for the position (a service). They might also give tests to determine the capabilities of applicants (a service). They might even rank the top four or five candidates on the basis of their evaluation (advice). The final decision, however, would be up to you as the sales supervisor.

Personnel is only one of many examples of staff positions. Maintenance of buildings is a staff function. The accounting department in a plant is another example. The important difference is that staff personnel perform a supplementary role: they give advice and/or provide a service to the line.

Span of control

The number of workers a supervisor must work with is referred to as **span of control**. This number influences how effective supervisors are in their jobs. For many years people have attempted to determine just how many workers one supervisor can effectively supervise. They have concluded that there is no set number. Supervisors have effectively supervised anywhere from seven to fifty workers.

As a rule, if workers perform jobs that are similar in nature and which involve tasks that do not differ widely, more workers can be supervised (larger span of control). The key factor is the amount of one-to-one communication necessary to effectively supervise workers. The more complex the job, as well as the more diverse the tasks, the more individualized attention workers require from supervisors. At the same time, less competent workers require more attention than competent workers. The supervisor's time is limited. You can easily see how meaningful interaction with many workers performing different jobs is difficult, particularly if they have performance problems.

Unfortunately, supervisors have little control over how many workers they supervise. That decision is made by upper management. However, they can cope more effectively with what appears to be an impossible situation. If supervisors find they really don't know each of their workers well enough or they don't have enough time to work with each worker having problems on the job, the span of control is probably too large.

For example, the new insurance claims clerk may have asked you three days ago to explain how to handle claims from members of the United Auto Workers' plan. You want to clarify the procedure because it is different from that typically followed. The policy is a major one and your boss has recently informed you of several complaints about the handling of past claims. But somehow, you just haven't found the time.

When supervisors find they cannot meet workers' demands for their time, what can they do? They cannot overlook the importance of personal direction and attention to worker problems, yet they only have so many hours in a day.

Delegation is one way supervisors can handle this situation. Identify competent, well-trained workers and give them the authority to train new workers or help out in problem situations. Of course, certain activities cannot be delegated. However, if you delegate routine activities, you are free to deal with the real problem situations.

Centralization and decentralization

Centralization and decentralization refer to where the authority to make decisions is located in an organization. In a **centralized organization**, the important decisions are made, or must be approved, by top managers. In a **decentralized organization**, more authority to make decisions is delegated to supervisors. *at the lowest possible level.*

The foundation of a centralized organization is a system of rules and procedures established to govern decisions and actions. Procedures and rules are intended to make the behavior of organization members more predictable and consistent. To the extent that people accept the rules and procedures covering their jobs, they behave in a fairly standard, predictable manner. Also, rules and procedures provide consistency in decisions and actions, even though different people are involved at different times.

Rules and procedures can increase organizational efficiency, since procedures are guidelines for action. As a result, people do not need to spend as much time trying to decide how to deal with each problem they face. Instead of trying to "reinvent the wheel" every time a problem arises, they can refer to procedures that will generally tell what action to take. Procedures do, however, limit the flexibility supervisors have in doing their jobs.

Despite the advantages of centralization, many organizations have found it advantageous to decentralize. Let's consider some of the possible benefits of decentralization. As an organization grows larger, it becomes more difficult for top managers to be knowledgeable about all activities in the organization. It takes longer for top managers to get the information necessary to make decisions. Delegating more authority to supervisors can unclog the decision-making machinery and improve the organization's efficiency.

- Decentralization gives more authority to supervisors who are most knowledgeable about the specific details and circumstances of problems that arise in their departments. Supervisors often make better decisions than top managers who are not in touch with the specifics of the situation.

- Decentralization can create smaller and more autonomous organizational units. Often, supervisors and workers can better understand and identify with such units. People are less likely to feel they are lost in the crowd and under the control of "faceless bureaucrats."

- Workers have a greater opportunity to participate in decision making in a more decentralized organization. Workers who are permitted to have some say in what happens are likely to feel more motivated and satisfied on the job.

We should keep in mind that decentralization is not an either-or proposition; it is a matter of degree. Organizations can range from very centralized to very decentralized. How much decentralization is good for an organization? It all depends. Several factors should be considered:

- How competent are supervisors? The people who will make decisions must have the necessary knowledge and skill.

- Who has the facts necessary to make decisions? Who can get the necessary information? Unless supervisors have sufficient information, they will not be able to make good decisions.

- How important is speed in making decisions? If conditions are rapidly changing and flexibility is important, some decentralization may be very useful.

- How independent are the activities of each organizational unit? How much will the decisions made in one unit "lock in" other units? If the activities of the organization's units must mesh closely, decentralizing decisions may be difficult.

Informal organization

The **informal organization** is the network of personal and social relationships that develops as people associate with one another in the organization. It is not established by the formal organizational structure. The emphasis in the informal organization is on people and their relationships. In a formal organization, the emphasis is on position, authority, and function.

Informal organizations frequently cut across the boundaries of the formal organization. Relationships develop between workers from different departments and at different levels in the organization. These workers associate with each other. They talk about the organization, their work place, and people with whom they work. These informal relationships influence the opinions, ideas, and feelings of workers. The formal organization cannot control the informal organization. Sometimes the informal organization works at cross purposes with the formal organization.

Understanding informal organizations is important to supervisors. Informal group relationships develop within their formal work group. Informal leaders emerge and informal relationships among workers affect their opinions, feelings, and actions. In short, the functioning of the formal work group is influenced by the existence of informal groups. Let's look at some of the characteristics of informal groups and see how they influence the formal work group. Then we will discuss some ways supervisors can work with informal groups.

Group norms

A norm is an informal rule—stated or unstated—regarding how members of a group should or should not behave. **Group norms** serve the same function for informal groups as policies and procedures do for the formal organization. Group members expect each other to conform to group norms. In manufacturing organizations, for example, groups often develop norms concerning how hard group members should work and how much they should produce.

Norms are rarely consciously established; they simply evolve over a period of time. Group members begin developing habits of behavior with one another and others with whom they come into contact. Eventually these habits become "the way we do things around here."

Further, norms are not recorded. In fact, group members often are not even consciously aware of their norms. Only when a group member violates a norm, or goes against an unwritten rule, do other members consciously think of their norms.

While most of us like to think we are fairly independent, we tend to conform closely to what others expect of us. Likewise, we generally conform to norms without question. We want to be accepted by the group and, therefore, we follow its informal rules of behavior.

At times, however, a worker does something that violates a group norm. It may be because the worker is new to the group and/or unaware of the norm. Or, the worker may disagree with the norm for some reason. In either case, the group will take action to attempt to bring the nonconforming worker in line.

The type of action groups take to enforce norms usually follows a predictable pattern. First, one or more members of the group will talk with the worker who has violated the norm. They will explain that the behavior is not acceptable to other group members and encourage a change in behavior.

If the nonconforming worker still does not conform, group members often will take a more "hard-line" approach. They may make fun of the worker or do other things to make him or her feel uncomfortable. In a few cases, threats or physical actions may even be used to force the worker to conform.

Finally, if all else fails, the worker will be ostracized. That is, he or she will be ignored, given the cold shoulder, and generally made to feel excluded from the group.

Informal leadership

A second important characteristic of informal work groups is informal group leadership. It is important to distinguish between formal and informal group leaders. A formal leader (manager or supervisor) is designated by the formal organization and has authority to direct the work activities of the group. In contrast, the informal leader emerges from within the membership of the group. Informal leaders are not appointed or elected. As group members work together, they tend to look more and more to one or more persons in the group for guidance. As group members look more and more to an individual for guidance, that individual comes to be accepted as an informal leader of the group.

Several factors influence who is likely to emerge as an informal group leader.

Expertise. When workers have problems or questions about their work, they tend to seek help from a group member who has more experience or ability. Thus, workers who "know the ropes" are more likely to emerge as informal leaders.

Personality. Workers who have pleasing personalities and good social skills also tend to become informal leaders. Group members tend to look up to and accept guidance from a worker they like as a person. From your own experience you can probably think of several people who became leaders because of their personalities.

Values. Workers who most closely represent the values of the group members are more likely to be accepted as group leaders. Group members tend to trust and respect those workers who personify their values, motives, and goals.

Informal leaders perform a variety of functions for the group. A quick look at these functions will demonstrate how informal leaders can have an impact on the supervisor's job.

Provide direction. Informal leaders give advice and guidance to group members. They may provide counseling on handling on-the-job problems or even personal problems.

Maintain the group. Informal group leaders also help to maintain harmony and resolve conflicts within the group. For example, when members deviate from a group norm, the informal leader is generally expected to make the first attempt to bring them back into line.

Represent the group. Informal leaders represent the group in contacts with those outside the group. For example, they are expected to bring the group's complaints or suggestions to the attention of their supervisor.

One final point should be made about informal leaders. We have been talking as if informal groups have only one informal leader. This is not necessarily true. A group may have only a single leader, but many groups have more. Quite often larger groups have as many as three informal leaders: one who helps with job problems (a task leader), one who resolves conflicts (a social leader), and one who represents the group (a representation leader).

Group cohesiveness

Group cohesiveness is defined as the extent to which members desire to remain members of the group. This factor reflects how important the group is to its members. We find it easier, however, to think of cohesiveness as how "close-knit" the group is or how tightly group members "stick together."

The cohesiveness of a group directly influences the degree to which members conform to norms. This makes sense for two reasons. If being a member of the group is important, members will tend to conform to group norms more readily in order to continue to be accepted by the group. Also, if a member does deviate from accepted group norms, other members generally will react more rapidly to get the worker to change this behavior and conform to accepted practices.

What makes some groups more cohesive than others? Some groups are more cohesive than others for a variety of reasons. Among the most important are: (1) the opportunity for communication among group members, (2) commonality of members' backgrounds, (3) size of the group, (4) accomplishment of goals, and (5) the degree to which the group feels threatened.

■ Communication within the group is probably the most important factor. In general, the more group members communicate, the greater the cohesiveness of the group. As group members communicate more and more with one another, they tend to develop closer personal relationships and the group becomes more cohesive.

[HOMOGENOUS]

■ If group members have fairly similar backgrounds, the group will generally be more cohesive. If members have similar experiences and/or similar interests, they will tend to stick together more than individuals who have different backgrounds and different interests. For example, a group made up entirely of people who were once city-ghetto dwellers will probably be more cohesive than one made up of members from rural, city, and suburban backgrounds.

■ The size of the group influences the level of cohesiveness. In general, smaller groups are more cohesive than larger groups. If we think in terms of the opportunity for communication, this observation makes sense. In small groups, members have more opportunity to communicate. As a result, a higher level of cohesiveness can be expected. In larger groups, members do not have as many opportunities to interact regularly. Thus a lower level of cohesiveness can be expected.

■ Group accomplishment of goals influences cohesiveness. If members feel that the group is accomplishing goals that are important to them, the group will tend to be more cohesive. If they feel the group is failing, cohesiveness will be lower. Consider for a moment the group that makes up a basketball team. If the team is winning, team spirit is high and group members tend to stick together more. If the team is losing, the attitudes of team members tend to become negative and conflict among teammates is more likely to develop.

■ If group members feel their group is threatened in some way, cohesiveness generally will increase. Again, think of the basketball team. If the school decides that due to budget cuts basketball will be dropped, team members will probably band together (become more cohesive) to protest the action, even if the team is having a bad season. They might organize a drive to contact alumni and other interested persons to put pressure on the school to keep the basketball program. In general, a group that feels threatened will become more cohesive and will work together to protect itself against the threat.

Cohesiveness and group performance

Is a high level of group cohesiveness good or bad? If you talked to supervisors you would probably get different answers.

One supervisor we talked to made the following comment: "The more those people get together and talk, the worse things get. All they do is encourage each other to hold down production." This supervisor obviously felt that informal groups, particularly cohesive groups, were bad.

The comments of another supervisor, however, reflect a different opinion: "My people really work well together. They help each other out, and if one of them starts goofing off, the others put pressure on him to get back in line and do a good job. They really make it easy to be a good supervisor." This supervisor would answer that cohesive work groups are good. Why do the supervisors disagree?

No correct answer exists to the question of whether cohesive groups help or hinder job performance. That is, we cannot state that a high level of group cohesiveness always encourages either a high level or a low level of performance. To better understand the relationship between cohesiveness and performance, we must consider the nature of the group's norms.

Norms can be described as positive or negative. Positive norms include those that are consistent or compatible with attaining departmental and organizational goals. The behaviors encouraged by the group are behaviors that contribute positively to goal attainment. Negative norms on the other hand, encourage behavior that thwarts departmental or organizational norms. They result in behaviors that contribute negatively to goal attainment. Examples of positive and negative norms typically found in informal work groups are given in Table 3.1.

Table 3.1

Examples of positive and
negative norms

NEGATIVE NORMS	
Work group	**Behavior**
Factory workers	Keep your mouth shut when the boss is around.
Factory workers	We stop working 15 minutes before quitting time to wash up.
Utility workers	We always take a nice long coffee break in the morning before climbing those poles.
Typists	Don't rush the work. They'll just give you more to do.
Salesclerks	Don't hurry to wait on a customer. They can wait.

POSITIVE NORMS	
Work group	**Behavior**
Factory workers	Do it right the first time.
Typists	Make certain it looks nice. We want to be proud of our work.
Car salespeople	We want to sell more cars than anyone else in the city.
Grocery clerks	Go out of your way to satisfy customers. We want them to come back.
Factory workers	Don't waste materials; they cost money.

If norms are positive, performance is better in more cohesive groups. Positive norms say, "We want to do a good job." If the group is cohesive, workers all try to achieve a high level of performance.

If norms are negative, performance is poor in more cohesive groups. Negative norms say, "We want to do the minimum we possibly can." If the group is cohesive, members conform to the norms; they do as little as possible, and performance is poor.

If cohesiveness is low, performance will vary more within the group. Group members will not conform as closely to norms and average group performance will be neither very high nor very low.

Thus as shown in Fig. 3.7, we can expect the best performance from a cohesive group with positive norms. Poorest performance will come from a cohesive group with negative norms. A low-cohesive group's performance will fall between the two extremes.

Working with the informal organization

Figure 3.7 suggests that supervisors need to encourage positive norms and cohesiveness to build a more effective work group. Groups with these characteristics tend to be more productive and stable, as well as more satisfying for group members. While supervisors cannot directly control the forces at work in an informal group, taking actions that influence them is possible. Let's examine several ideas that may help you work with groups more effectively.

- Groups often develop negative norms because of a lack of information. Group members may not understand what is happening in the organization, or why they are expected to work in a certain way. In some cases, they may not even know what they are expected to do. Thus, it is important to inform group members about the organization and their jobs as quickly and thoroughly as possible. If this is not done, they probably will get their information from the "grapevine," information that may or may not be accurate.

- Giving information is not enough. Listening is also important. You need to work actively to elicit the group's ideas and opinions. If something is bothering the group, you need to listen and try to understand the problem. Keeping the group fully informed and listening to problems helps encourage the development of positive norms.

- Rewarding good work by the group is also useful, especially since this develops pride. As the group works together to accomplish something they feel is significant, the cohesiveness of the group tends to increase. In addition, as pride increases, more positive norms develop.

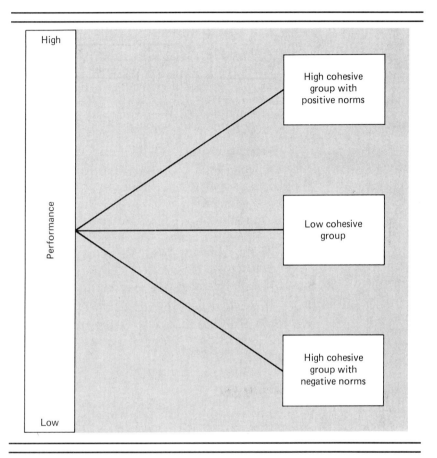

Figure 3.7   Performance levels of cohesive groups.

■ Allowing the group to participate in decisions regarding group work is sometimes useful. Negative norms are often the result of differences between the way workers view their job and the way supervisors view the job. If group members have a voice in decisions that affect them, their ideas are more likely to coincide with their supervisor's. However, increased participation in decision making is not always possible. The conditions under which participative decision making are likely to work are discussed in Chapter 9.

■ As noted earlier, an informal leader holds a special position within the group. The informal leader can often have considerable impact on the group's norms. As a result, supervisors can gain a great deal by working with and through informal leaders.

Often the informal leader can and will represent the group's view. Supervisors can "bounce" their ideas off the informal leader to get an idea regarding how the group will react. This does not mean that they should not talk to and get ideas from all workers, nor does it mean that the informal leader should be shown favoritism. But the informal leader can be used as a barometer of group opinions. Informal leaders can also help communicate with the group and influence their opinions and ideas.

A word of caution: an informal leader who is not able to maintain respect in the eyes of group members is often replaced by someone else. For this reason, supervisors must be careful not to take some action that could accidentally compromise or undermine the informal leader's position in the work group.

Organizational politics

Up to this point, we have described organizations and the people who work in them in fairly sterile terms. But one critical factor isn't found on the organizational chart or discussed in job descriptions, nor is it openly acknowledged by the people who hold jobs in organizations. That factor is the political process found operating in organizations everywhere.

To understand **organizational politics** we need first to look at why it exists. All organizations are concerned with distributing power. Quite simply, power is the ability to get something done by influencing the behavior of others. How much formal power an individual has is determined in part by the authority associated with the particular job. This authority is defined by organizational charts and job descriptions. However, authority is merely the recognized right to exert power. Anyone who has spent any time in an organization knows that the authority that comes with the job is only part of getting things done.

In order to get things done and make yourself look good (a point we will discuss shortly), political maneuvering is usually required.

This involves getting all the information you need to do your job and jockeying for the power to do what the job requires, while insuring that everyone is happy.[1]

Organizational politics is inevitable. Whenever two or more people find themselves working together, they will sooner or later become involved in a struggle for power, as each tries to make the work relationship more desirable for himself or herself. The reasons for this struggle may vary.[2] Some people seek more power. Others hold jobs which have results that are difficult to measure. As a result, they desire to publicize the fact that they are doing an effective job. Others feel insecure and become involved in organizational politics to make their position in the organization more stable. Still others are concerned with advancing their interests and see politics as a means of paving the way upward within the organization. Furthermore, organizational politics provides a vehicle for becoming one of the "in-group." As many people want to be accepted at work, politics may provide a way of satisfying this need.

In a nutshell, successful supervisors are those who are effective in their jobs from other people's point of view. Nearly all people in organizations must, to varying degrees, rely on others to help them do their jobs, as well as advance their interests in the organization. Success depends on a variety of complex relationships with your superiors, peers, and subordinates. The political process is a mechanism to be used to sell yourself—to increase your visibility to your boss, peers, and subordinates. You use the process to publicize what you are doing and to be certain that what you are doing conforms with their expectations.

Building good relations with your boss

Hard work and competence are critical to becoming a success in your boss's eyes. But the way in which you carry out your duties also influences your boss's opinion. Andrew DuBrin offers several suggestions for helping you make a good impression on your boss. His suggestions include:[3]

- **Help your boss succeed.** Never forget why you were hired. You were hired because your boss believed you could help him or her be more successful. The minute you lose sight of this fact, you become less effective.

- Be loyal to your boss. Never publicly attack him or her. Remember, you are part of a team.
- Learn what your boss's objectives are and seek to attain them. Becoming a critical subordinate can do much for your future in the organization.
- Make your boss's life less complicated. Take away some of the problems he or she faces. Don't add to them.
- Maintain regular contact with your boss and actively listen to what he or she has to say. Ask your boss's advice and be concerned about him or her as a person.
- Be a watchdog; keep your boss informed of potential problems.
- Share your accomplishments with your boss. Recognize the team effort involved.

The critical point to remember is that your boss has control over your future. Whether you like it or not, successful performance is defined by the observer—your boss. It requires hard work in the manner your boss sees as effective and successful. The rules of the game are set from above. Finding out what these rules are and conforming to them can greatly enhance your status in the organization.

Building good relations with your workers

Regardless of how well you can perform your job, you will only be as good as your workers let you be. In other words, you can exert only as much power over your workers as they let you exert. Several guides for developing a loyal following have been offered by DuBrin:[4]

- Follow through on commitments.
- Recognize your workers. Show them how important you think they are.
- Be sensitive to your workers' needs. Look at every action you consider taking through their eyes.
- Be courteous. Answer all memos and letters, return phone calls, avoid keeping people waiting to see you, and so forth. Make your workers feel they are important.
- Maintain old ties within the organization. Never become "too good" for your old friends.

Summary

☐ All organizations share certain characteristics. They have goals. They are comprised of people working together to reach these goals. There is division of labor. They have a formally established structure designed to coordinate individual effort. There is a hierarchy of authority.

☐ Supervisors do not design the structure of their organization but their jobs are affected by it. An organizational chart describes the organizational structure. It identifies jobs, departments, and the flow of authority in the organization.

☐ Departments are groups of jobs. Jobs may grouped on the basis of function, product, location, or a combination of these factors. Matrix organization exists along with any one of these types of departmentation and involves bringing workers from different departments together to work on a special project.

☐ Authority is the right to decide and take action while using organizational resources. Each job must have enough authority to insure its responsibilities can be carried out. There are two types of authority: line and staff. Line authority involves the right to direct workers and is part of the chain of command. Staff authority involves advising or providing services to the line.

☐ Span of control refers to the number of workers a supervisor must work with. There is no best span of control. Supervisors can effectively supervise more workers when workers perform similar jobs, the jobs are not complex, and workers are competent.

☐ Supervisors have little control over span of control. Delegating some of your activities to competent workers can help you deal with problems of a span of control that is too large.

☐ Centralization or decentralization refers to the location of authority to make decisions. Authority is located at the top in centralized organizations. Rules and procedures are established which limit the flexibility supervisors have in their jobs.

☑ Decentralization enables supervisors to make decisions about situations with which they are familiar. It creates smaller, more autonomous units workers can more readily identify with and encourages worker participation in decision making. Decentralized organizations provide supervisors with more authority.

☑ How decentralized an organization should be depends upon the competence of supervisors, the person who has the information needed to make decisions, the need to make decisions quickly, and the degree to which organizational units are independent.

☐ The informal organization is the network of personal and social relationships that develops as people associate with each other. It is not a part of the formal organizational structure.

☐ Supervisors need to understand how informal organizations operate because they influence the functioning of the formal work group. Workers form informal groups which influence their opinions, feelings, and actions at work.

☐ Informal groups expect members to conform to norms. Corrective action is taken by the group when norms are violated. Informal leaders emerge from the group, and group members turn to these leaders for guidance and advice.

☐ Informal groups can be described in terms of how cohesive they are. Group cohesiveness influences the degree to which members conform to norms. Several factors affect the cohesiveness of a group. Whether or not cohesive groups help or hinder performance depends on the group's norms. If norms are positive, a cohesive group will result in better job performance. If they are negative, cohesive groups will result in poor performance.

☐ Supervisors should encourage cohesive groups with positive norms by providing information to the group as well as listening to information the group has to offer. Good work by the group should be rewarded. The group's members should be allowed to participate in decisions that affect them. Informal leaders should be recognized and used as a barometer of group opinions.

☐ The political process operates in all organizations for a variety of reasons. It is not shown on an organizational chart but it can have a significant impact on your future. The political process is a mechanism used to increase your visibility and publicize what you are doing right to your boss, peers, and workers.

Questions for review and discussion

1. Distinguish between the formal and informal organization.
2. What is an organizational chart? What does it show? What does it not tell you?
3. Distinguish between the two types of authority found in organizations.
4. To what does span of control refer? What factors influence the appropriate span of control? What can supervisors do when their span of control is too large?
5. What are the advantages and disadvantages of centralization and decentralization? What factors influence how decentralized an organization should be?
6. What types of workers tend to become informal leaders? How can supervisors use informal leaders effectively?
7. What is the relationship between group cohesiveness and performance? How can supervisors encourage cohesive groups with positive norms?
8. What is organizational politics and why does it exist in all organizations? How can you use it to your advantage?

Key terms

Authority
Centralized organization
Decentralized organization
Departments
Functional department
Group cohesiveness
Group norm
Informal leader
Informal organization

Line authority
Location department
Organization
Organizational charts
Organizational politics
Product department
Span of control
Staff authority

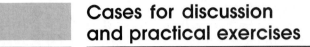

Cases for discussion and practical exercises

1. Abe Fox, one of several construction supervisors for the Monumental Building Company, had just employed another college student for summer work. This new crew member professed a sincere interest in learning something about the construction business; he was majoring in architectural design and needed practical experience. Additionally, the young man was on a football scholarship at the nearby university and seemed to have the perfect physique to do the heavy work required of most summer employees.

   After the first few days of work orientation, all new employees were assigned to work teams under the guidance of an experienced group leader. Abe Fox saw little of the new employees after that except at a distance.

   Two weeks later the student approached Abe and said he thought he would have to quit or face getting fired or hurt. To Abe's chagrin, the young man explained that the harder he worked on the job, the less popular he was with the other workers. No one would talk to him or eat lunch with him. Finally, he said, he had gone to the group leader and asked if there was some problem or if his work was unsatisfactory. He was told that his work was all right, but the way he was working was going to put someone out of a job. He was told either to slow down and pace himself along with the others or to watch out for a beam or something falling on his head! The group leader had continued, "These people won't put up with your kind of hustle for very long. They need employment, you are a newcomer setting too high a standard. Either be one of us or you'll be gone—one way or the other!"*

   a) In what ways do group members exert pressure on newcomers to conform to group norms?

   b) What should Abe Fox do?

*Source: Francis J. Bridges and James E. Chapman, *Critical Incidents in Organizational Behavior and Administration: With Selected Readings.* © 1977, p. 37. Reprinted by permission of Prentice-Hall, Inc., Englewood Cliffs, N.J.

2. Practically everyone on the night shift liked Ralph Bumpers. Bumpers was a veteran mechanic and part of the maintenance crew that worked late hours keeping a fleet of trucks in top condition for the daytime hauling service. Usually at the 9:00 P.M. break all the mechanics got together for coffee and a smoke. Bumpers had top seniority and top pay among the group, but he had never been promoted to management. Still, the other mechanics and helpers looked to Bumpers for guidance and interpretation of company rules and policies. Often they bypassed their own supervisors and searched out Bumpers for suggestions about particular problems.

    Bumpers enjoyed the attention and respect given to him by fellow employees, but he knew that several first-level managers were openly hostile to him. He suspected that they resented the influence he had over their employees.

    At the next employee appraisal meeting with his immediate superior, Bumpers was told that he was a good worker, but that his influence on his fellow workers was disconcerting to management. It was suggested that he direct all problems presented to him by fellow workers to their supervisors and leave the managing to the supervisors.

    During coffee break the following evening, Bumpers told his friends what his supervisor had said to him. The entire group was upset and mad. The general consensus was that if management wanted problems, they would get plenty of them.*
    a) What caused Ralph to become an informal leader?
    b) How should Ralph's immediate supervisor handle the situation?

3. Draw a chart of the organization in which you work. If it is a very large organization, consider only your plant or that part of the organization which is relevant to you. Identify the types of departments used in the organization. Does this organizational structure present any problems for the supervisors in the organization? If so, what are they?

4. Think of a group you have worked with or work with presently. Identify the norms of the group. Classify each of the norms as

---

*Source: Ibid., p. 169. Reprinted by permission of Prentice-Hall, Inc., Englewood Cliffs, N.J.

either a positive or a negative norm from the point of view of the organization. How cohesive was the group? What factors made it cohesive or kept it from being cohesive? Was there an informal leader? Why did that person become the informal leader?

Notes

1. Interview with Marilyn Moats Kennedy, "Playing 'Office Politics'—How Necessary." *U.S. News and World Report,* January 12, 1981, p. 35.

2. Andrew J. DuBrin, *Fundamentals of Organizational Behavior* (2nd ed). (Elmsford, N.Y.: Pergamon Press, 1978).

3. Andrew J. DuBrin. *Winning at Office Politics.* (New York: Van Nostrand Reinhold, 1978).

4. Ibid.

4

Time management
for supervisors

After reading this chapter you should be able to

- ☐ Discuss myths about time management.
- ☐ Explain how to develop and use a master list.
- ☐ Demonstrate how to build and use a daily work plan.
- ☐ Discuss how you can cope with paperwork and meetings more effectively.

Bill started the day shift on Monday and returned to his office. As he sat down to review some inventory reports he had been asked to check, the phone rang. The personnel department was looking for the forms on his workers which were due last week. Setting the inventory reports aside, he began to search his desk drawer for the forms. He muttered about paperwork as he began to complete the forms. Shortly, however, the interoffice mail arrived on his desk. Bill thumbed through it looking for anything important and discovered a memo with a complaint about the tool room.

He read the memo and headed for the tool room to look for the problem. On the way he passed the vending area. The coffee smelled so good he decided to take time out to have a cup. Bill's accomplishments thus far amount to exactly nothing. He has failed even to get started.

Bill feels that he never has enough time. He is bothered by a sensation of being on a treadmill which seems to be moving faster and faster. Where, he asks, is the time to think and plan? He can't seem to keep up with the never-ending stream of here-and-now problems, let alone think about tomorrow.

Maybe you're not in bad shape compared to Bill. But chances are you feel you do not have enough time to complete your work either. At least that's what R. Alec Mackenzie found when he surveyed thousands of supervisors, managers, and executives.[1] Only one in a hundred felt they had enough time. The others were asked how much more time they would need to do the job. More than half said they would need 50% more time.

This statistic is particularly striking when we realize one fundamental fact about time: there isn't any more available. We already have all the time there is. Whether we use our time wisely or fritter it away, we all have twenty-four hours a day, seven days a week, and fifty-two weeks a year. Time cannot be accumulated or stockpiled; it must be spent. We can determine, however, how we spend our time, whether it is managed effectively or mismanaged.

This chapter focuses on some tools and techniques for managing your time. They are not particularly complex or revolutionary but they can help you manage your time, your most precious resource.

Myths of managing time

Before we examine several specific tools and techniques for managing time, let's look at some of the myths about time and time management. Most of us believe some of these myths. Whether we realize it or not, they influence and guide our behavior.

The harder you work the more you get done Some have called this the "buckets of sweat" syndrome. It is based on the assumption that a direct relationship exists between hard work and positive accomplishment. According to some, however, results are seldom proportional to the buckets of sweat generated. If time spent in planning saves time in execution and improves results, supervisors would be better off beginning work when it has been carefully thought out. The old adage, "Work smarter, not harder," is still good advice.

The best way to get a job done is to do it yourself The reasoning here is you save time when you don't have to get someone else to do the job. If you do something yourself, you don't have to check to see that the job was satisfactorily completed. You don't put your fate in someone else's hands and you don't need to spend precious time explaning what to do and how to do it to someone else.

Although doing it yourself is sometimes the answer, most often this is not the case. People have limits to what they can do. Despite our feelings of self-reliance, we often find that a do-it-yourself attitude dilutes our effectiveness. As Michael Le Boeuf has observed:[2]

> *Devoting a little of yourself to everything means committing a great deal of yourself to nothing. This leaves you unable to concentrate on those very few projects that have the highest payoff per investment of your time and energy.*

An open-door policy is necessary This myth generates a great deal of wasted time for many supervisors. The open-door policy gained popularity with the movement toward people-oriented management. Closed doors were believed to inhibit communication and promote a sense of exclusion. However, according to R. Alec Mackenzie, open door policies can waste a supervisor's time:[3]

> *Being always available is no guarantee of success as a manager. On the contrary, it may encourage dependence and serve as an invitation to interruptions that will fragment the supervisor's day. It may also result in the upward delegation of decisions, forcing him to work below his level and involving him in details that take time away from more important matters.*

It's their fault This myth is rooted in human nature. When looking for the causes of our problems we tend to look to others or to external factors. Thus, when asked to identify their time wasters, most supervisors tend to focus on external factors like meetings, phone calls, visitors, and paperwork demanded by others. However, when prodded into a careful analysis of where their time goes and why it is wasted, most discover that they are their own worst enemy. The blame shifts from external factors to procrastination, lack of delegation, a "fire fighting" mentality, and other internal factors.

Once we recognize that we are the major cause of our wasted time, one important conclusion becomes apparent. At the heart of time management is the management of self. By taking control of your time, you take control of your life. This process begins not with others, but with ourselves.

Developing a work plan

Supervisors who have enough time to do their job well organize their days around the important things they need to do. A key to organizing your days is to develop, and *use,* a personal work plan. This plan can be helpful in many different areas of your life: your activities as a student, your home and family responsibilities, as well as your work activities. We will concentrate in this discussion, however, on work activities. A number of steps are involved in developing a personal work plan, including developing a master list, prioritizing tasks, building your daily work plan, and using your work plan.

The master list

The **master list** is a list of duties and tasks facing you in the foreseeable future. Depending on your particular job situation, the period covered might range from the next few weeks to the next few months.

To develop your master list you need to do a personal job analysis. First identify the routine duties you perform daily or on a regular basis, such as work scheduling, reviewing progress reports, filling out payroll sheets, completing production reports, or walking around your department and talking with your people. Keep notes on your activities for a few days to make certain you include all regular, routine duties. The list should also include how much time you spend, on the average, performing each duty.

Once you have identified your routine duties, analyze them to see if you are wasting time. To do this, you should ask yourself three questions about each duty:

- Is this duty necessary?
- Can it be delegated to someone else?
- Is there another way to perform it in less time while still doing it effectively?

The objective is to correctly identify your *necessary* routine duties and *accurately* estimate the amount of time required for each duty. Once this is done, enter them into the routine duties section of your master list.

Next, turn your attention to the nonroutine tasks. These are one-time-only projects or tasks you perform infrequently. Make a list of all tasks you *might* complete in the time considered. Include those things you *should* get done as well as those you *must get done*. These might include tasks such as developing a cross-training program for your workers, completing a budget report, developing a proposal for a change in the inventory control system, or completing a personal development program.

Some of the tasks on your master list may seem so time consuming to complete that you can't see how they can fit in your plan. Typically you're tempted to argue that you'll have to delay working on such big tasks until you can block out a lot of time, maybe days or even weeks. Being practical, though, you realize that the large amount of time you seek is never going to be available.

One solution to this problem is to break down big tasks into a series of smaller tasks. When you break down big tasks in this fashion, you will have a step-by-step understanding of what has to be done. The result is a series of tasks requiring manageable units of time. Instead of looking at a gigantic block of time necessary to complete the overall project, you can get it out of the way in bits and pieces. In due course the whole project will begin to take shape.

One payoff of this approach to big tasks is reduced anxiety. Using this approach you are less likely to feel overwhelmed by the weight of postponed assignments. Time pressures are not as intense because you know which parts of your big tasks can be done right away, and which parts must be done later, and you have a target date set for each part.

After you have broken down your big tasks, enter all identified tasks in the nonroutine section of your master list. When a task has a specific completion date, it should be entered. You should also enter an estimate of the time required to complete each task. These time factors will be important in the development of your daily work plan.

Establishing priorities

Once you have a list of the duties and tasks facing you, your next step is to establish priorities. You establish priorities only for the nonroutine tasks, since you have already determined that the routine duties are necessary. Some time management experts suggest categorizing tasks on your list as high, medium, or low depending on their relative contribution to your goals. They further suggest that you concentrate on those tasks in the "high-goals contribution" category, do as many "medium" tasks as possible, and avoid doing all "low" tasks.

This advice may be useful if you have the freedom to do only those things that you see contributing most to your overall goals. Most of us, however, work for someone else. We are not completely free to choose our tasks. For example, some of the things we personally consider very unimportant, or even foolish, may be very important to the boss's boss.

A more realistic approach to ranking your task list is to designate as high priority those things that are demanded by your boss and/or your organization. Also ranked as high priorities are tasks that are imposed on you by customers or even an emergency of some sort. You should label these tasks as "1"; they are "must tasks." Your job or career may be threatened if you don't get them done on time.

The second category, labeled "2," are "should tasks." Included here are those tasks nobody is forcing on you but that should get done because they will provide real benefits. "Should" tasks might include a productivity-improvement project, improving relations with a particularly important customer, or some other project likely to pay dividends in the future. The important thing about tasks in this second category is that they are not demanded. They can, however, make the difference between the effective supervisor and one who is merely average. They are the discretionary tasks that provide a payoff for your unit, and they are the key to improvement.

The third category is reserved for those tasks remaining. You label these "3." These are truly the leftovers. If you've already attended to all of your "must" and "should" tasks, it's perfectly acceptable to work on them. But, if you must carefully balance demands on your time, these tasks are good candidates to be dropped. They are "back burner" items. If, due to the limits of time, they never move up, so be it.

After you have established your priorities, the master list is complete. It is, of course a "living document" and must be updated periodically. As projects are completed, tasks are dropped from the list. As new tasks arise, they are added to the list. Your master list on any given day, however, forms the basis for your work plan.

Developing your master list may seem to take a lot of time. This is often true, but time spent planning now will pay big dividends in time saved in the future. Further, it's a one-shot investment in time. You need only develop the master list once. After that, updating your master list as changes occur on your job is easy.

+Developing your daily work plan

The first step in developing your **daily work plan** or "to do" list is reviewing your master list. Scan the list to identify routine duties for the day. Enter them on your list and note how much time they will require. You might also schedule the time during the day when you plan to perform each of these duties.

In addition to these routine duties, unanticipated demands on your time that are almost impossible to plan for will arise. People drop in and want to talk. There may be a surge of phone calls. Restrict these demands as much as possible, but be realistic. They will happen. Based on your own experience, block out a reasonable amount of time on your work plan for these unanticipated demands.

Now you are ready to complete your daily work plan. Consider the amount of time required for routine duties and unanticipated demands. Then estimate the time remaining for nonroutine tasks. Select nonroutine tasks from you master list to complete your work plan.

Which nonroutine tasks do you select? You have already categorized each task on your list as "1," "2," or "3" depending on its relation to your job demands. Since the "1" and "2" tasks are the most important ones, no "3" tasks should be scheduled on your "to do" list. Spending your time on "3" tasks, even though you might really enjoy doing them, accomplishes little beyond boosting your ego or lulling you into a false sense of accomplishment. Focus on completing the "1" and "2" tasks. If you get time for some "3" tasks, fine, but if not, it is no great loss to you or your organization.

When selecting the specific "1" or "2" tasks to include on a given day's work plan you need to consider their due dates as well as their priorities. Clearly, those tasks with the earliest due dates should be entered. Included here are all those tasks that you should begin now if you are going to complete them when your boss expects them to be finished.

Regular completion of "1" tasks goes a long way to making you an effective supervisor. To be really outstanding, however, you need to complete "2" tasks consistently. This is difficult. Your boss may not be pushing for their completion, and, in all likelihood, you have plenty to do in any given work day. You may not be able to devote time to "2" tasks during every working day, but sometime during the course of your week you should try to fit in time for them. As time passes, you will make progress on these "2" tasks.

Another issue of some importance is the time to develop your daily work plan. According to some, you should do it at the beginning of each work day. The basis for the suggestion is that by making planning the first step in each day you will ensure that it does not get lost in the shuffle of the day's events. Others disagree. They suggest that you plan each day's activities at the end of the preceding day. According to this view people tend to be most productive during the first part of the day. Thus, it is a waste of time and energy to devote the early part of each day to planning.

Who is right? It's difficult to say. Whichever suggestion you follow it is important to make development of a daily work plan a regular part of your work routine.

Avoiding wasting time with others

In addition to developing and using your daily work plan, you also should attempt to reduce the demands on your time. Meetings and drop-in visitors are a great potential drain on your time and energy, but walling yourself off is no solution. Some of the meetings that consume your time are called by your boss or by others in positions of authority. There may be little you can do about these. What about the others? Even here, as Michael LeBoeuf has noted:[4]

> *Meetings, visitors and telephone calls are not necessarily unproductive any more than gunpowder is a necessarily destructive substance. It's all a matter of application. Unfortunately, the seeming legitimacy of these common time wasters allows them to proliferate unchecked. If we take steps to make judicious use of meetings, visitors, and the telephone, these time wasters can become tools to aid effectiveness.*

The key therefore is not avoiding meetings and contacts with others, but learning to use these interactions efficiently.

First, let's focus on dealing with visitors. For many of us, drop-in visitors represent one of the biggest potential time wasters. Following a few simple suggestions, however, can make a big difference. If you have a separate office, consider the following ideas:

1. Arrange your desk and chair so that you are not facing the door. If your door is open but your back is to it, visitors are less likely to drop in.

2. Remove excess chairs and other invitations to socializing. A coffee pot or a group of chairs might make you a great social director, but it can be a source of much wasted time.

3. Consider closing your door at least for certain periods of time during the day. While an open door might make you more approachable it also invites anyone roaming the halls to drop in.

If someone wants to talk with you, volunteer to go to that person's office. This gives you control over the length of the visit. Once you are done with your business, you can leave. If you talk to the visitor in your office, you may have to waste a lot of time before the conversation is finished.

Once a visitor is in your office, you can control the efficiency of your visit in several ways:

1. Try to get a statement of purpose early in the conversation. You do not have to be rude to accomplish this. If somebody comes to you and says, "Hi, have you got a minute?," find out the purpose of their visit. You need not, however, place time constraints on everybody who comes in contact with you.

2. A more extreme suggestion is to stand up to confer with visitors who walk into your office unexpectedly. Most people understand "body language" pretty well, and this indicates to the visitor that you are busy. Once visitors are allowed to sit down they are much more likely to extend their stay longer than necessary.

3. Another strategy is to become tight-lipped once you feel visitors have overstayed their usefulness. By not contributing to needless conversations, you may be able to minimize them.

Despite the time wasted with visitors, many people waste even more time in meetings. The depth of the problem is illustrated by R. Alec Mackenzie:[5]

> *Ask any group of managers in any country in the world to list their three most time-consuming activities. Give them a few moments to reflect and discuss the question. Invariably "meetings" will appear among the three. I have asked this question of more than 200 groups, and in every case but 3, more than three-fourths of each group indicated that half their time spent in meetings is wasted. The problem, lamented a friend of mine, is in not being sure which half.*

Certainly the best way to avoid wasting time in meetings is to eliminate them unless they are really necessary. The question to consider then is what about those that are really needed? Most time management experts agree that the following suggestions should make meetings more efficient:

1. Determine what you want to accomplish at the meeting. Every meeting should have a specific goal or purpose—it should be what some have called an action/decision meeting. Avoid meetings for the sake of meetings.

2. Each meeting should have a set starting and ending time. Some experts recommend scheduling meetings before lunch or toward the end of the day to prevent long, drawn-out meetings.

3. Prepare an agenda for the meeting and distribute it well in advance. List the topics to be covered and the time frame associated with each item. Position agenda items carefully. Put your most important items first and don't make the mistake of trying to cram too many items into one meeting. Once you are in the meeting, discipline yourself to stay with the agenda and follow the time limits if at all possible.

4. Make a written record of the meeting. You don't need to record everything that was said and keep complete minutes. What you do need is a record of what was decided and who is going to do what. That way you can avoid the problems created when differences of opinion arise regarding what decision was actually made.

Taming the paper avalanche

Another big time eater is paperwork, and unfortunately the avalanche of paper is likely to continue, or perhaps even increase. Government regulation, the knowledge and technology explosion, computers, and copy machines have all contributed to a rising tide of paper that threatens to engulf even the best of us. You can, however, take a number of positive steps that can help you deal effectively with the paper avalanche.

If you analyze your paperwork, you'll find it fits into one of three categories. In the first category are requests for action. They may come from your boss, another department, one of your workers, or a variety of other sources. Their important common denominator is that they require you to do something. Generally, action requests take the form of interoffice memos, letters, or work orders. In the second category is operating information—information that you need to keep abreast of your own operation. Examples of operating information are production and cost reports, inventory records, and requisitions. The third category encompasses all other information. This is a very broad category including a wide range of material—trade and technical publications, general informational bulletins, catalogues, and that seemingly never-ending stream of junk mail.

Organizing your paperwork

Organizing is the first step in taming the paper avalanche. The key to organizing is getting control of your desk rather than allowing it to control you. The messy desk problem is widespread and difficult to control. How do things get into such a mess? R. Alec Mackenzie has recounted the theory of one manager:[6]

> *Because of all the things we don't want to forget, the things we want to remember we put on top of our desk, where we will see them. The problem is, he continued, that it really works. Every time our gaze wanders and we look at them, we remember them and our train of thought is broken. Then as the stacks grow higher, we are unable to remember what's beneath the top. . . .*

The top of your desk should be reserved for action requests only. Any paper that requires a response should be where you can get to it right away. All others should be out of the way. Some time management experts have gone one step further. They suggest that you clear your desk of everything not directly related to the project at hand.

You should set up a reference file for operating information. Organize these papers carefully and make sure the file contains current operating information only. If you don't regularly purge this file, removing the outdated information, you will slowly create a monster that becomes less and less functional. Your operating reference file should be placed in a handy location. Since it contains those items you will need to refer to fairly often, you don't want to waste a lot of time running back and forth to retrieve items from it. The deep drawer found in most desks is set up to hold a file and is probably the best location.

A table top or shelf should be set aside for all other useful reading materials and information. Note that we use the word "useful" here. Those pieces of paper, particularly those in the miscellaneous information category, that do not seem particularly useful should be thrown away. Do not allow them to pile up and clutter up your office and your time.

Handling your paperwork

So far we have discussed how to organize your paperwork to tame the avalanche of paper. How you handle your papers, however, is just as important as how well you organize them. A number of time management experts advise that you handle each piece of paper only once, if at all possible. As you go through your stack of paperwork, do something with each piece of paper that will help move it along. If a memo can be answered with a short note scribbled at the end, do it. If it's something that should be routed to one of your workers for their information or action, scribble your note on it now and send it on its way. If it's something you will need to refer to later on, file it so you know where it will be. And if it's something you really don't need, by all means throw it out right now. If at all possible, avoid setting papers aside as you will only have to shift your train of thought when dealing with them later. You also run the risk of misplacing or losing them, and at the very least you waste precious time by handling each piece of paper twice.

Delegating

Don't do it, delegate it. That's the ultimate approach to managing your time. Authorities on time management agree that all possible tasks should be delegated. Books on supervision and training programs for supervisors emphasize the importance of **delegation**. Teachers in classrooms review lists of reasons for delegation. Everyone seems to be in favor of delegation.

Yet many supervisors indicate that they delegate very little to their subordinates. "Delegation is great in theory, but just doesn't work in practice." In fact, some supervisors seem to subscribe to the principles of nondelegation given in Fig. 4.1. Why?

The person to whom a supervisor delegates a task may not perform the task in exactly the same way the supervisor would. But, is that necessarily bad? Also, the supervisor may need to spend some time on training when a new task is delegated to a subordinate. But, what about the second, third, or fourth time the task is performed? Think of the time the supervisor can save. Sure, not all tasks can be delegated. Perhaps the supervisor is the only one who has the necessary information or resources to accomplish certain tasks. Or maybe the task has been specifically delegated to the supervisor.

There are numerous reasons (or excuses) why supervisors do not delegate. But, in many cases, it remains a question of attitude.

If you don't want to delegate, you can concentrate on all the reasons why you should not. If you do want to delegate, you can concentrate on finding ways you can. As a supervisor thinking about the demands on your time, the choice is up to you.

Delegating successfully

The ability to delegate is not innate, but rather is a skill that must be developed. As with any developmental task, delegation skills improve when past experience has been successful. Delegation is a two-way process. Looking at the supervisor's role in the process is only part of the story. The workers must accept the delegated tasks.

Workers often shy away from added authority because they feel they already have too much to do. They may be afraid to act on their own. Sometimes, workers are delegated tasks they do not have the resources or authority to accomplish. Often they view delegation as requiring additional work without increased rewards.

Do not delegate

If you want to avoid seeing your family or if you want to make certain that you cannot play golf, tennis, or engage in any other leisure-time activity. Refusal to delegate will ensure that you will work twenty hours a day just to get the job done. Therefore, you will not have time for any other activities. This principle can be extended even further. We are all concerned about the well-being of our family. You can make certain your family enjoys the golden years, spending the insurance money they receive when you work yourself to death at an early age.

Do not delegate

If your subordinates are stupid, lazy, and uncommitted, it is obvious that such people will do a poor job, so it is imperative that you do their work for them. This has the added advantage of giving your people ample free time to do crossword puzzles on the job and develop other creative ways of looking busy.

Do not delegate

If you want to make certain that your people never have the opportunity to develop into more effective employees. We all know that people learn from experience. So, a perfect way to keep them from learning is to refuse to delegate tasks to them. This has the added advantage of making certain that none of your people are able to do your job, a very secure feeling indeed.

Do not delegate

If you want to make certain you will not be promoted. Refusal to delegate makes you indispensible on the job. Further, since no one else can do your job, no one can replace you and you cannot be promoted.

Sound silly? A lot of reasons for not delegating sound just as absurd.

Figure 4.1 Common reasons given for not delegating.

Successful delegation requires that supervisors encourage workers to accept and meet added tasks. The tasks must be clearly defined and the goals to be accomplished must be accepted and understood by the worker and supervisor. Workers will be more likely to accept added tasks when they are associated with meaningful rewards, such as recognition, merit increases, and promotional opportunities.

Supervisors must insure workers have the authority and resources necessary to complete the delegated tasks. For example, workers who have been delegated the responsibility of training newcomers must have the time available to do so. Too often, this responsibility is given to good workers who are also expected to maintain their regular job performance. In this instance, effective training of new workers can only be done at the expense of job performance. If the supervisor does not recognize this, delegation will probably be unsuccessful.

Effective delegation also requires that supervisors be able to sit back and let workers do the work. This ability perhaps is the most difficult thing to learn. Even though supervisors can delegate the authority to perform certain tasks, they cannot delegate the responsibility for these tasks. Because they are responsible, supervisors often hesitate to let workers assume greater authority out of a fear they will make mistakes. However, the more opportunities workers have for performing these added tasks, the more competent they will become.

Delegating authority does not mean the supervisor disappears from the scene. You are still there to provide advice and assistance as needed. As workers successfully perform more delegated tasks, their self-confidence increases. Your confidence in them will grow as well.

Summary

☐ All people seem to need more time. The amount of time available is limited, so the time you have must be managed effectively.

☐ There are several myths about time and time management. Looking closely at these myths points out that we are the major cause of wasted time.

☐ Developing and using a work plan can help you organize your days and reduce wasted time. This requires you to: (1) analyze your job and develop a master list, (2) develop task priorities, and (3) build and use a daily work plan.

☐ Your master list contains the regular, routine duties that are necessary to your job. Nonroutine tasks which should be done or must be done are also included. How much time is spent on each task is also indicated.

☐ Priorities are established for nonroutine tasks. "Must" tasks are tasks that must be completed on time. "Should" tasks are those that no one forces you to do but will benefit your department. All other tasks are the back-burner items.

☐ Building and using a daily work plan separates outstanding supervisors from other supervisors. Your "to do" list includes time for routine duties from your master list and time set aside for unanticipated demands. Remaining time is allocated to non-routine items from your master list.

☐ Nonroutine tasks included on your "to do" list should be selected on the basis of due dates as well as their priority. Accomplishing "1" items will make you an effective supervisor. Completing "2" items will help make you an outstanding supervisor.

☐ Reducing routine demands on your time is important. Paperwork should be organized into one of four categories: action requests, operating information, general information, and miscellaneous information. Each piece of paper should be handled once.

☐ Meetings you call do not need to be a drain on your time. One-to-one meetings should come quickly to the point. You do not have to be available at all times. Make decisions as soon as possible and record what you have decided.

☐ You should only call action group meetings. Each meeting should have an agenda with carefully planned items. Record only who will do what.

☐ Delegation is the ultimate way to manage your time effectively. Rather than finding reasons why you can't delegate, find ways that you can.

Questions for review and discussion

1. Discuss four commonly held myths about time management. Why are these myths and not accurate perceptions?

2. What steps are involved in developing a personal work plan?

3. What is a master list? How is it developed?

4. How can you develop priorities for the duties and tasks on your job?

5. What steps are involved in building a work plan or "to-do" list?

6. How can you reduce the amount of time spent on paperwork? In meetings?

7. Some supervisors argue that time management techniques take too much time to use. Discuss both sides of this issue.

Key terms

Action requests	"Must" tasks
Daily work plan	Operating information
Delegation	"Should" tasks
Master list	

Cases for discussion
and practical exercises

1. Lou Spataro and Harv Tschirgi were riding home after attending an evening meeting of their supervisors' club. Lou and Harv were both supervisors in the same company. They frequently attended supervisors' club meetings together and generally they gained some good ideas that helped them on the job. The speaker this evening had talked about time management and they disagreed somewhat on the usefulness of his comments.

   LOU: I can't see this business of making up a master list and a daily work plan. How can I plan what I'm going to be working on in two weeks? It seems like there's a new emergency every day that I have to handle. I can't turn my back on today's problems to follow some list I developed two weeks ago. It might work for some people, but in my job I have to stay more flexible.

   HARV: Sometimes I think we make our own emergencies. I know I get hung up working on one problem and let other things I should be working on slip. Maybe, if I just once sat down and thought through what I should be doing, I might be able to control some of the pressures on my time. It's worth a try. As the speaker said, it's better than fighting fires all the time.
   a) Do you agree with Lou or Harv? Why?

2. As a student, time is an important resource for you. This is particularly true if you are also working or have other obligations. Apply the concepts of time management discussed in this chapter to your activities as a student. Draw up a master list of activities for the next month. From this, make up your daily student work plan for each day during the next two weeks. Try to follow your student work plan. Also remember to update your master list as activities are completed and new activities added. At the end of the two weeks, evaluate the use of the time management techniques. Did they help you? Did you have problems using them? Do you think they would be helpful for a supervisor?

Notes

1. R. Alec Mackenzie, *The Time Trap* (New York: AMACOM, 1972), p. 1.

2. Michael LeBoeuf, *Working Smart: How to Accomplish More in Half the Time* (New York: Warner Books, 1979), p. 27.

3. Mackenzie, *op. cit.*, p. 90.

4. LeBoeuf, *op. cit.*, p. 152.

5. Mackenzie, *op. cit.*, p. 98.

6. *Ibid.*, p. 67.

Cases for section I

The "ninety-day wonder"

In a certain mining company that has been in existence for many years, the miners often "test" new supervisors, especially when they are younger and not very familiar with mining operations. The miners are rough and hardy, and their average age is between 45 and 50. The company has high pay rates for these semiskilled workers and an excellent fringe-benefit package. Also, few other opportunities for employment exist in the area. Because of these factors, the average miner has worked fifteen or more years for the company.

In most instances the mining supervisors are promoted through the ranks, but occasionally younger people with more education and technical training are hired. As indicated, the miners will frequently engage in a game of trying the supervisor's patience. They will ask a new supervisor to solve technical problems when they think he or she lacks the appropriate knowledge, push company rules as far as they can, appear to not understand when they actually do, deliberately engage in slowdowns, ignore or only partially respond to direction, challenge authority (based on the union contract), and send the young supervisor on "wild-goose chases" of trumped-up situations or problems.

Those new supervisors who cannot take the pressure are known as "ninety-day wonders" because they generally remain on the job for ninety days or less. Other young supervisors who effectively respond to the challenge win the esteem of the work group and continue on as respected supervisors.

Questions

1. How do the terms *authority*, *power*, and *influence* relate to this case?
2. Why do the miners test the young supervisors?

3. What action can a new supervisor take that will win favor of the miners?

4. How should a young supervisor use his or her authority during this probation period?

Source: Adapted from *Management Essentials: Concepts and Applications* by Howard M. Carlisle. © 1979, Science Research Associates, Inc. Reprinted by permission of the publisher.

The day the machine department had a new supervisor

Particular Electronics Corporation is a relatively small electronics firm located in a major midwestern city. The company manufactures a variety of small electrical appliances such as outlet plugs and specially wound cords. A privately owned corporation, Particular Electronics has shown a profit each year of its existence since it was purchased by Ed Montgomery and Bill Watkins in 1970. However, profit margins on many items were slim, as Particular had as its major competition small household operators in the Far East, especially Hong Kong. In order to compete with this low-wage competition, Particular had to be cautious about its wages as well. To accomplish this goal, the company adopted a policy of using only part-time help in its factory operation; employees included students, retirees, and foreign nationals. This strategy, coupled with sophisticated time and labor-saving devices (innovations of Montgomery and Watkins), and the fact that Particular was nonunion, enabled them to ease some of the competitive pressures which they faced. In addition, Particular's competitive edge also stemmed from its extremely creative approach to meeting customer needs, solid engineering, and a willingness to take customer orders that larger competitors ignored.

Organization

Most of the products made by Particular pass through each of the three major manufacturing departments: cutting and winding, machining, and assembly. Because of this production flow, a great deal of cooperation and close coordination is needed between the departments.

The incident

On a Friday in January of this year, an unusual combination of events occurred at Particular. To begin, Dick Ruthman, plant manager of Particular, was absent as he was every Friday to attend classes at a local university where he was pursuing an M.B.A. degree. Then, at about 10:00 that morning, Sandra Bandor, machine department supervisor, received a phone call informing her that a fire had occurred in her apartment and her sister had been slightly burned in the blaze. Bandor went back to her department visibly upset but did not say anything to her work crew. She was in tears when she left for home a few moments later. To further complicate matters, Sandra's assistant supervisor was not at work that day because of a death in her family.

Roberta Torino, Particular's controller and office manager, was aware of the dilemma Sandra's departure would cause, especially with the concurrent absences of the plant manager and the assistant machine department supervisor. Frequently involved in factory matters, and also mindful of the organization's small size and informality, Roberta decided to act to fill the supervisory void in the machine department. She told Joan Petit (production scheduler), "You will have to watch the jobs they are working on, and make sure they are working on the right ones according to the daily schedule." Joan was selected by Roberta for this task, even though she had had only two months of experience, because she was familiar with the jobs the machine department was working on that day.

On reaching the machine department, Joan told the women she was taking over for the day because Sandra had gone home. The women seemed to be upset by this news. Some even stopped work and started talking to one another. Joan decided to seek out Liz Candelli, supervisor of the assembly department and senior supervisor on the floor. The two women discussed the situation in Liz's office, which because of the large glass window was clearly visible to the women in the machine department. Joan wondered out loud whether she should separate the two informal leaders of the department who seemed to be talking the most and generally causing disruption among the other department personnel.

When Joan returned to the machine department after her discussion, she found some of the workers were still standing around in small groups and talking. Two of them, the informal leaders, were again the most vocal and demonstrative. Joan then decided to separate the two ringleaders by assigning them to operations which were physically distant from each other. One of the ringleaders told Joan, "Nothing personal, honey, but we don't like to be told what to do by that witch in the assembly department." Joan assured her that the assignments were strictly her idea.

Another woman (the other ringleader) told Joan that she was going home at noon. Joan later found out that she had been the assistant supervisor in the machine department at one time but had been demoted to the ranks about a year before this incident. Joan said nothing but could not help noticing that none of the women looked very happy and that they were working at a very low level of output.

Confused and concerned with what appeared to be a work stoppage, Joan decided to seek executive advice this time. After a brief recitation of her story to Ed Montgomery, Bill Watkins, Roberta Torino, and Rod Tyree (the engineering director), the two owners of the company decided that they would not get involved in the situation. They explained to Joan that the chain of command dictated that Dick Ruthman should handle the problem when he came in on Monday. Moreover, they did not want to "go over Ruthman's head." Rod Tyree, however, asked for and received permission to talk to the machine department women. Rod said he thought he might able to "calm them down."

The women told Rod that they were not really angry at Joan Petit but that they very much resented the job reassignments which they believed Liz Candelli had suggested to Joan. Moreover they felt Candelli was trying to punish them through Joan's intervention. A few women, however, did ask Tyree who had authorized Joan Petit to be the machine department supervisor that day. Tyree's efforts to calm the women proved somewhat fruitful since none of the women left early, and all stayed on the job.

Post-incident events

When Dick Ruthman heard the story of Friday's events, he decided to call a meeting of the entire machine department, including Sandra Bandor and Joan Petit. Joan felt the two ringleaders should be punished. Dick, however, only told the women that Joan had his support whenever she was given a supervisory assignment and that everyone should "just forget the whole thing."

Questions

1. What problems at Particular are illustrated by this incident?

2. How might this situation have been handled more effectively?

3. Describe the situation with reference to the organization and its employees, the behavior of those involved, and the attempts to resolve the problems.

4. What might be done to salvage this situation?

Source: From *Management*, 2nd edition, by William F. Glueck. Copyright © 1980 by the Dryden Press, a division of Holt, Rinehart and Winston Publishers. Reprinted by permission of the publisher.

Matt Hinshaw's problem

Matt Hinshaw didn't like it when his boss told him he needed to pay more attention to the work in his department, and that he needed to concentrate on the important things and leave the rest to other people. "I don't know what he expects," Matt thought. "I never loaf, and I always work overtime. I have more work than one person can do. He must want a dynamo to run this department." With that, he turned his attention to the work of the day.

As the whistle blew, he checked his work stations and saw two empty spots. "Wonder what happened to Slim and Mavis," he mused. Then he noticed that four stations weren't operating. "Wonder why? Before I wade into this, I'd better take an ulcer pill." After a walk to the fountain for water, Matt remembered the weekly report that he always completed. Of course his secretary could do it, but he felt that these production figures should be kept secret. Besides, if everyone knew what was going on, he might lose control.

After finishing the weekly report, Matt turned his attention to what he thought of as his "fun job," computing each employee's efficiency on the basis of the number of rejected products. He knew his secretary could do this as well as he could, but he enjoyed the task, and it didn't take too much time. In the middle of his computations, he remembered Slim and Mavis, and went to check on them. Mavis had come in late, but Slim wasn't at work. Matt decided he would need to double up on Slim's work by putting one of the stock clerks there.

Forty-five minutes later, he was back at his desk waiting for his secretary to finish typing his weekly special report to top management. He always took this to the front office personally and delivered it to the "top brass." In this way he could have a cup of coffee and butter up the bosses.

During his lunch break, he talked to other supervisors about their work, asking for tips on how to get things done. One suggested that he stop going to the routine supervisors' meeting each week. It just took time. Matt knew that Joe Dawson would like to have the assignment, and it would be good training for him since he had been picked to be acting supervisor during Matt's absences. But Matt had always kept this job for himself because he was afraid something would happen that he should know about.

When he got back to his desk, he reviewed the weekly stock report prepared by his storekeeper, which he telephoned into central records at the home office in Chicago. It usually took about 15 or 20 minutes. Joe Dawson could do it, but Matt always believed the report should be accurate and he didn't want the big boss to blame him for mistakes.

Later, his secretary put a stack of routine forms in front of him and as he systematically signed them, he wondered what his boss would say if he saw all the things that he (Matt) had to do. Maybe the boss would not say he needed to pay more attention to the work in his department.

Questions

1. What is Matt's major problem?
2. If you were Matt's boss, how would you handle him?
3. What do you think Matt should do?

Source: Adapted from Claude S. George, *Supervision in Action: The Art of Managing Others*, 1979, p. 237. Reprinted by permission of Reston Publishing Co., Inc., a Prentice-Hall Company, 11480 Sunset Hills Road, Reston, Va. 22090.

Supervising workers

5

Developing communication skills

Objectives

After reading this chapter you should be able to

- ☐ Describe the communication process and different kinds of communication found in organizations.
- ☐ Identify ways supervisors can improve communication with their workers.
- ☐ Identify ways supervisors can improve their written communication.
- ☐ Explain how supervisors can make interviews more effective.
- ☐ Identify the steps to be followed in conducting effective meetings.

"What we have here is a failure to communicate." "Our problem is a breakdown in communication." These comments are heard all too often in organizations. We all spend much of our time communicating, so we get plenty of practice. Yet it is surprising how often our interactions are not completely effective.

Communication breakdowns can cause real trouble for you as a supervisor. You accomplish most of your activities through communication. You coordinate the efforts of your workers through communication. In fact, one study has shown that supervisors spend 90% of their work day communicating: reading, writing, listening, and speaking.[1]

In this chapter, we will discuss ideas that can help you improve your effectiveness as a communicator. First we will discuss the communication process. Next, we will examine communication in work organizations. Finally, we will discuss skills that are particularly important to you as a supervisor.

The communication process

The **communication process** is complex. It is the process of passing information and meaning from one person to another and involves at least two people: a sender and a receiver. The sender develops and transmits a message to the receiver. The main purpose is to achieve common understanding between the sender and the receiver.

Figure 5.1 illustrates the basic communication process. As you can see it includes six stages:

1. The sender has a thought,
2. which is developed into a message.
3. The message is transmitted to the receiver,
4. who receives the message,
5. attaches meaning to the message,
6. and gives feedback to the sender regarding the communication effort.

Communication begins in the mind of the sender. The sender has a thought, either an idea or a feeling, that he or she wants to communicate to the receiver. The sender then develops a message to convey the thought. Most of our messages are conveyed by words. Some, however, are nonverbal. A smile, a nod, a shrug of the shoulder are all examples of "body language" used to send messages.

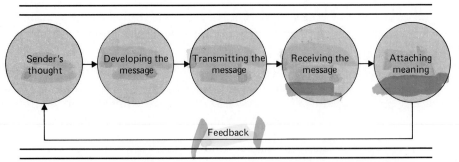

Figure 5.1   The communication process.

The first two steps of the communication process often occur at about the same time; we get an idea and start developing the message. At this stage problems may occur. Some thoughts are simple, others are quite complex. Obviously, it is easier to put a simple thought into a message, but even then caution is necessary. Making certain that the message accurately conveys the intended idea or feeling is important. This same idea is expressed by the old saying, "Be sure the brain is engaged before putting the mouth in gear."

Language skills are also important at this point. Some people seem to know how to express themselves so their ideas are transmitted exactly while others have great difficulty expressing themselves. The following examples, taken from letters to a welfare office, show how a lack of language skills can distort meaning:[2]

- I am very much annoyed to find you have branded my son illiterate. This is a dirty lie as I was married a week before he was born.

- I cannot get sick pay. I have six children. Can you tell me why?

- Mrs. Jones has not had any clothes for a year and has been visited regularly by the clergy.

Once developed, a message must be transmitted. It may be spoken or written, or it may be communicated nonverbally. Communication may take place face-to-face, on the telephone, through letters, or in group meetings. Many potential problems arise at this stage, for people may talk too fast, their handwriting may be unreadable, or there may be noise or other physical distractions. All of these factors may distort a message.

Once transmitted, the message is received and the receiver attaches meaning to it. Again, potential problems may arise. A blockage may keep the message from being received. The receiver may be thinking of something else and not really hear what is being said. A message that is posted on a bulletin board may not be read. A letter sent through the mail may end up in the dead-letter office.

Attaching meaning to a message is also difficult. Words often mean different things to different people, and the same word may have many different meanings. For example, the dictionary lists seventy-nine different meanings for the word "round."

We interpret messages on the basis of past experience and make assumptions about their meaning. Consider the following example.[3] Several hundred women held temporary, rather than permanent, civil-service appointments. Because of variations in the work load, occasional layoffs occurred among these temporary workers. Before the last layoff, the personnel director used the loudspeaker system for the following announcement: "The following women are requested to report to Room 10 at 4:00 P.M." Then, the names of the women were announced. When the women arrived in Room 10, they were told that this was their last day of temporary work.

A few days later the personnel director had a training assignment for some of the women who had "permanent" jobs. He decided to call them to Room 10 at the end of the day to tell them about the program. He went to the loudspeaker in the afternoon and announced: "The following women are requested to report to Room 10 at 4:00 P.M." The names were then read.

As the names of these women were read, many of them were visibly distressed, assuming they would be laid off. Soon, in sympathy with their co-workers, the entire office became upset. They made an assumption about the message on the basis of their past experience.

The final step in the communication process is obtaining **feedback.** Did the receiver understand the message or not? Did he or she comprehend the meaning of the sender's original idea? Feedback can involve action. Did the receiver do what the sender asked? Or the feedback can be a return communication.

Lack of feedback is another source of communication problems. Without feedback, being certain the message was received and the proper meaning attached is difficult. With feedback, any distortion in meaning can be corrected by another communication.

Communication in organizations

Much of the communication in an organization can be described as downward, upward, or lateral communication. These are types of **formal communication,** devoted to work-related matters. A great deal of **informal communication** occurs in an organization as well.

This communication flows through informal channels and may or may not be work related. A supervisor must use both formal and informal communication effectively.

Downward communication

Downward communication flows from higher-level managers to supervisors and workers. Examples of downward communication are job instructions, policy statements, procedures, memos, and company publications. Some types of information are communicated from top management to the entire organization. Policy statements are an example. This form of downward communication is generally written. The majority of downward communication, however, takes place between supervisors and workers, for example, with job instructions. This type of communication is usually oral.

The importance of downward communication cannot be overstated. People want and need information relevant to their jobs. If they do not get this information through formal channels, they either make assumptions or turn to informal communication channels.

Yet supervisors often do a poor job of downward communication. This point was made in a study of common "communication sins."[4] Workers from several different organizations were asked to rank ten communication sins on the basis of how often these sins were committed against them. Figure 5.2 lists the findings. The three most common sins in the ranking were (1) they didn't tell me, (2) they didn't tell me everything, and (3) they told me too late. This result demonstrates the basic principle of downward communication: COMMUNICATE!

Upward communication

Upward communication flows from workers to supervisors and to higher-level managers and is just as vital as downward communication. You need feedback to make certain downward communication is understood. You also receive worker ideas, opinions, and feelings through upward communication.

It is often difficult to achieve effective upward communication, since employees are often unwilling or afraid to express their ideas.

1. Failing to notify me of something I should have known.
2. Giving me incomplete information.
3. Telling me about something too late.
4. Using the wrong method (oral when it should have been written, etc.).
5. Bypassing me in the chain of command.
6. Giving me wrong information.
7. Communicating in a sarcastic, hostile, or emotionally-loaded manner.
8. Talking over my head (language, terms, overly technical words, etc.).
9. Criticizing me in front of others.
10. Acting inconsistently with communications received.

Figure 5.2 Rank order of communication sins.

Source: James A. Lee, "A Study of Communication Sins," Unpublished paper, Ohio University, 1973. Reprinted with permission.

In some case they even feel that the expression of their ideas is not encouraged. Some organizations have tried to improve upward communication by using techniques such as suggestion boxes, group meetings, and employee newsletters. These can be helpful in some situations, but they cannot provide all the upward communication needed in an organization.

Most effective upward communication occurs directly between workers and their supervisor. The effectiveness of upward communication depends on the relationship between supervisor and worker. A supervisor who is receptive and encouraging is more likely to obtain ideas and opinions from employees.

Lateral communication

Communication also flows laterally in an organization. Lateral communication helps coordinate the activities of different departments. For example, a production supervisor and the maintenance supervisor communicate directly without using their managers as intermediaries. Likewise, a nursing supervisor often communicates directly with the supervisor of a laboratory in a hospital. Lateral communications may be face-to-face or through some type of formal information system.

The grapevine

Informal communication, the **grapevine,** flourishes because communication is a natural human tendency. People who know each other in the organization talk together informally. One thing they have in common is the organization where they work, so they talk about what is happening there.

Grapevines carry two types of information: work-related and people-related. As we said earlier, employees want to know what is happening in the organization. When they are not kept informed through formal channels, they seek information from the grapevine. People are also naturally curious about co-workers. Here too grapevines serve a purpose. They carry the type of personal information not generally communicated through formal channels.

Facts about the grapevine   Some workers consider the grapevine their main source of information. They get information quickly, and more information is available than is normally included in formal downward communication. The communication is face-to-face and with people they know. Thus, the grapevine often has a stronger impact on many workers than formal downward communications, which are often written and may originate from someone they do not know.

How accurate is the grapevine? There is some debate. Some have claimed that 78 to 90% of the information is accurate.[5] Messages that do not involve highly emotional or controversial issues tend to be more accurate. However, the danger of misunderstanding increases as the message is passed from person to person. A slight error at each step can greatly change the message. Further, one bit of incorrect information might be sufficient to change the entire meaning of the message.

Keith Davis has provided a good example of how incorrect information can make organizational life miserable.[6] In this instance the message in the grapevine was that a welder married the general manager's daughter. The message was true with regard to his marriage having taken place, the date, the location, and other details, but one detail was wrong. The woman was not the general manager's daughter. She just happened to have the same last name. This one wrong fact caused the whole story to be misleading, even though it was 90% accurate in detail.

Constructively dealing with the grapevine   Supervisors often become frustrated with grapevines, particularly when they carry incorrect rumors. But grapevines exist and you cannot stop them. You can, however, increase the accuracy of the grapevine by feeding it correct information. And you can try to reduce reliance on the grapevine by initiating formal communication that is complete and timely.

Furthermore, the existence of grapevines is not always unfortunate, provided the information is accurate. The grapevine can serve several constructive purposes.[7]

1. It provides an outlet for passing certain information that should not go through formal channels, such as personal information, which helps build a sense of comradeship.
2. It enables people to express emotions which, if kept inside, can lead to problems in the future.
3. It can help translate messages from management into more easily understood language.
4. It can prevent misinformation or unfounded rumors by clarifying details.
5. It provides feedback about workers' feelings.

Improving your communication skills

As a supervisor, you spend much of your time and effort communicating, both sending and receiving, in order to get your job done. Certain communication skills are particularly important for supervisors. These skills include encouraging feedback, listening, understanding nonverbal communication, writing, interviewing, and participating in meetings.

Encouraging feedback

Feedback is critical for communicating effectively with workers. In reality, however, supervisors have difficulty ascertaining their impact on their workers or that of other job-related issues. A worker cannot easily approach his or her supervisor and give the feedback that is requested, let alone freely volunteer feedback. Thus you need to actively encourage a response.

To encourage feedback you must first convince your workers you are receptive. They must feel that you really want to receive their reactions. Then, you must be responsive. Workers will continue to provide feedback only if they believe you are willing and able to do something with the information you receive.

William Dyer has offered several strategies for encouraging feedback.[8]

- **Individual Direct Request.** Ask workers to meet you to discuss whatever you are seeking information about on a one-to-one basis. Be sure they know in advance the purpose of the meeting so they can prepare.
- **Written Feedback.** Directly request workers to share their feelings in writing.
- **Anonymous Strategies.** Often workers will be more likely to provide direct feedback when they don't feel put on the spot. One way to avoid this situation is to give workers some relevant information first, and after opening up the discussion solicit their comments. As an alternative, you can have workers meet on their own, discuss the situation, and provide you with a summary report. In addition, asking for written feedback without identifying the source can be useful.

Obviously, when you encourage feedback you must be able to distinguish between useful and phony feedback. Phony feedback results from:

- **Forced feedback.** Workers don't want to be rude and ignore your question. They may not want to confront you directly with the truth either. The result is either altering the truth or avoiding the issue and ultimately saying nothing.
- **Filtered feedback.** As information moves up the hierarchy it tends to sound better and better.[9]

Phony feedback can easily mislead you if taken seriously. You can reduce the amount of false information by cultivating feedback, not forcing it. In some situations going and observing personally what is happening may be more advantageous than relying on others to tell you.

When you receive feedback from workers, you need to be responsive. Your workers will feel you are more responsive if you:

■ Listen to the feedback given rather than attempting to explain or justify the situation.
■ Encourage continuously flowing information.
■ React honestly to the worker's feedback.
■ Express your appreciation to the worker.
■ Act on the feedback you receive. Do something with the information received from workers.[10]

Listening

Most of us would laugh if we were told we were poor listeners. We spend nearly every minute of the day listening. In reality, however, we maybe good "hearers," but not good listeners. We hear what other people say, but listening means giving those sounds meaning. **Listening** does not occur until we hear, understand, and remember what someone is communicating.

We are capable of understanding speech at a rate of about 600 words per minute. Most people, however, speak at 100 or 140 words per minute.[11] Thus, our brains have a lot of spare time while someone is talking. Rather than using the time to understand the speaker's ideas better, we tend to let our minds wander. We daydream. We think about how we are going to respond. We notice what the speaker is wearing. We think about our plans for the evening. Our wandering minds keep us from really concentrating on the communication and understanding the message.

Listening is also hindered by the volume of communication we face each day. One study indicates that most people spend at least five hours a day listening.[12] We listen to the radio and we watch TV. We are literally bombarded with communication. We cannot keep our attention focused all the time on listening carefully to all communications.

Although problems are involved, effective listening is a skill that can be learned. The following guidelines should help you become as good at listening as you are at hearing.[13]

- Stop talking! You cannot listen if you are talking. Are you listening or thinking about what you want to say next?
- Give the talker your undivided attention.
- Put the talker at ease. Help the person feel free to talk. This is often called "being open."
- Listen to everything that is communicated: facts, feelings, emotions, and impressions.
- Remove distractions. Don't doodle, tap, or shuffle papers. Will it be quieter if you shut your door?
- Look at the other person's point of view. Try to put yourself in the other person's place, so that you can see things from his or her standpoint.
- Don't let your physical actions discourage the talker. Staring out the window, turning away, or giving the talker a disapproving look will surely cause him or her to modify the conversation or abruptly end it.
- Be patient. Allow plenty of time. Do not interrupt. Don't move towards the door or walk away.
- Hold your temper. An angry person interprets words the wrong way.
- Be gentle with argument and criticism. Don't put people on the defensive. They may "clam up" or get angry. Don't argue, since even if you win, you lose.
- Ask questions. This stance is encouraging and shows that you are listening. The speaker will be able to further develop his or her position.
- If there is disagreement force yourself to walk in the other person's shoes. Listen objectively. Restate and defend the position with which you disagree. While this does not mean you will change your mind, you will clarify the disagreement. Also, you will consider information you may have avoided in defending your own position.

Nonverbal communication

People rarely communicate their feelings and emotions only by words. All of us constantly send clues about our feelings, not only by what we say, but by what we do. This is called **nonverbal communication.** Understanding nonverbal communication can help us become more effective communicators.

Nonverbal communications are often expressed through your body: the expression on your face, your posture, your gestures, and a number of other clues. Let's examine some the most important types of "body language."

One way you can tell how people feel about each other is by noting the distance maintained between them. Edward T. Hall has observed that we choose a distance based on our feelings toward the person with whom we are communicating.[14] He has defined four distances:

- **Intimate distance**. Ranging from skin contact to about eighteen inches, we generally reserve this distance for people who are very close to us and restrict it to private situations, such as comforting and protecting. When we let someone into our intimate distance, it is a sign of trust. If someone invades our intimate territory without our consent we generally feel threatened.

- **Personal distance**. Ranging from eighteen inches to four feet, the inner part of this zone is the distance at which most couples stand in public. Friends carrying on a conversation while standing would often be at the outer part of the zone.

- **Social distance.** Ranging overall from four to twelve feet, the inner range, from four to seven feet, is the distance at which conversations between co-workers or customers and salespeople occur. The outer range is reserved for more impersonal and formal situations.

- **Public distance.** Ranging outward from twelve feet, the inner range of this zone is generally used by most teachers in the classroom. As you move out of this zone, say to twenty-five feet and beyond, two-way communication becomes almost impossible.

The distance selected for communication is an indication of the relationship between people. Those we trust or care for are allowed into our personal space. Thus, if someone stands or sits close to us when communicating, they may be saying, "I trust you." A hesitancy to approach you, on the other hand, may indicate dislike or a lack of trust.

We also communicate through our posture, although these messages are easy to miss. For example, a person who is bored seldom leans back and slumps enough to embarrass the other person. A person's posture is relaxed in nonthreatening situations, but may tighten up and become rigid when threatened or fearful.

Gestures are another good source of nonverbal communication. Most of us know that facial expressions are the most obvious way to express emotions. But when people want to hide their feelings, they try to control their facial expressions. Most people are even less aware of the ways they move their eyes, hands, legs, and feet. As a result these movements are often more revealing of how a person feels than are facial expressions.

People often express different and even contradictory messages in their verbal and nonverbal communications. Consider the person with red face and bulging veins who yells, "Angry? No, I'm not angry!" Usually, of course, contradictions are not this obvious. Contradictory verbal and nonverbal messages are an indication of deliberate or unconscious deception. By comparing verbal and nonverbal communication, you can determine if you are actually receiving and understanding the message the sender intends.

Effective writing

Much of the formal communication in an organization is in written form. As a supervisor you will write letters, interoffice memos, and reports. Yet, in our discussions with executives, they say that many of their supervisors, managers, and technical employees do not write effectively.

Although good writing is a natural skill for some people, it is not an inherent ability. It is a skill you can develop. And, as a supervisor, writing is a skill that is important to your success. Your letters, memos, and reports are often read by people who do not know you, and they will form an opinion of your ability based on the effectiveness of your writing. In many cases, higher-level managers have decided that a supervisor lacks ability based solely on a poorly written report. Similarly, in some cases particularly well-written reports create such a positive impression that higher-level managers recommend the supervisor for promotion.

Thus, effective writing is important because much of the information needed for organizational functioning is in written form. Because others form an opinion of your capabilities based on your writing skills, your career will be affected. Even more crucial, effective writing is necessary to ensure that the right message is understood. What can you do to improve the effectiveness of your writing?

- Remember that effective writing is basically effective oral communication that has been put in written form and polished. Don't try to write in an archaic, formal style.
- Take the time to do it right. Don't just "dash off" a memo. Review it, polish it, and make certain of its quality.
- Practice. Work at developing your writing skills. Effective writing is a skill that can be developed through practice.

When communicating in writing, make sure you observe the principles of good writing: completeness, conciseness, clarity, and correctness.

Completeness   Include all the information the reader needs. Incomplete messages are costly. The reader may need to contact you to obtain information that wasn't included in your message, requiring additional time and money for both you and the reader. Even worse, the reader may make assumptions regarding information you omitted, and will misinterpret your message. To ensure completeness, take the time before you write to jot down the information you want to include in your message. Ask yourself what the reader needs to know. Like news reporters, check to see that your written message answers the "five W" questions—who, what, where, when, and why—and any other essentials, such as "how." Finally, always read over the written message, trying to view it from the reader's standpoint before you send it.

Conciseness   Conciseness is important in business writing. A wordy message takes more time and money to prepare and read. Further, busy people are more likely to read and understand a short, concise message than a long, involved one. Be cautious, however.

Conciseness and brevity are not necessarily the same thing. Being concise means saying what is necessary in the fewest possible words without sacrificing completeness. To make your message concise, organize it effectively, including only the relevant facts. Avoid unnecessary repetition and wordy statements. Cut out unnecessary words and phrases. For example, consider the wordy and concise phrases in Table 5.1.

Clarity Clear writing is understandable writing. Unclear writing obscures the meaning of the message, so that the reader must work to understand what you are saying or else get the wrong message. Conciseness contributes to clarity, but conciseness alone does not ensure clarity. To increase clarity you need to be sure information is presented in a logical sequence. You also need to keep your reader in mind by writing at an appropriate level of readability. For the average reader, for example, sentences should average fifteen words each, paragraphs should average about 100 words, and there should be about 150 syllables for every 100 words. Finally, use common words. Avoid jargon unless you are absolutely certain that you reader will understand the terms.

Table 5.1

Examples of wordy and concise phrases

WORDY	CONCISE
The only thing that it is necessary for you to do is . . .	Just
Due to the fact that . . .	Because
Would you please arrange to forward . . .	Please send
In the event that . . .	If
At this time . . .	Now
In spite of the fact . . .	Although

Correctness   Correctness is the final test of business writing. It refers to both form and content. The information you are transmitting should be accurate and should be in correct form. Make certain that there are no errors in spelling, punctuation, capitalization, and grammar. Be sure that the typed copy is clean and attractive. Physical appearance is the first thing the reader notices and can influence his or her reaction to your message. A messy communication, or one that includes errors, indicates to the reader either that you are not capable of writing effectively or you aren't concerned enough to provide a carefully written document. Obviously, either impression may create a negative reaction.

Interviewing

Interviews are really conversations planned to meet specific purposes. Typically they involve two people and are more formal than normal day-to-day conversations with workers. As is true of all communication acts, interviews involve giving and receiving information.

You may conduct a number of different types of interviews as a supervisor. The more important types of interviews, and their stated purposes, are given as follows:

- **Hiring Interviews.** These are designed to gather information about job applicants so that you can decide which applicant best matches job requirements. In the hiring interview you also give applicants information about the organization and the job so they can decide whether or not the job meets their expectations.

- **Performance Review Interviews.** The purpose here is to provide feedback to workers, determine their training needs, and motivate them to a higher level of performance.

- **Counseling Interviews.** These interviews address workers' personal problems so the problems can be resolved before job performance is seriously affected.

- **Disciplinary Interviews.** In these interviews, information regarding unacceptable job performance or behavior is exchanged and action is taken to correct the problem.

■ **Grievance Interviews.** Information regarding a worker's complaint is exchanged and action is taken to resolve the complaint.

Potential problems with interviews

When people leave the interview with incorrect or inaccurate information, the interview has failed. Why might this occur? Often impressions are received or prior opinions are held that influence the way information is interpreted, leading to inaccurate conclusions. Let's look at some of the more common reasons why incorrect opinions might be formed.

Stereotyping Stereotyping involves forming opinions on the basis of readily identifiable characteristics such as race, sex, or age. Individuals are assumed to be "just like" everyone in the particular group even if the individual does not fit the pattern. For example, Table 5.2 indicates typical characteristics sometimes assumed to be possessed by males and females. Even though these stereotyped images are inaccurate, they sometimes have great influence over opinions. Similarly, stereotypes exist for blacks, older workers, overweight workers, and numerous other classes of workers.

When stereotypes influence how supervisors interpret information received during interviews, what the worker says (actual information) becomes less important than who the worker is. As a result, specific individual characteristics are often ignored even though the individual does not fit the mold. The result may be a poor hiring decision or an ineffective plan for performance improvement or problem resolution.

Initial impressions The first impression of a person may affect the interpretation of information received during the interview. Impressions regarding an applicant's suitability for a job are often formed during the first few minutes of the employment interview. These impressions hardly can be based on accurate information about the individual in such a short period of time. If the first impression is negative, even if the applicant is qualified, the supervisor's opinion probably will not change regardless of additional information obtained. Similarly, impressions formed during a worker's first few weeks of employment are lasting.

Table 5.2

Male and female stereotypes

MALE CHARACTERISTICS	FEMALE CHARACTERISTICS
Adventurous	Appearance oriented
Aggressive	Artistic
Blunt	Compassionate
Competitive	Dependent
Confident	Emotional, excitable
Crude	Gentle
Decisive	Humanitarian
Dominant	Neat
Independent	Needing security
Initiative	Passive
Intelligent	Submissive
Logical	Sensitive
Objective	Sympathetic
Rough	Talkative
Worldly	Tender

Source: Adapted from Richard D. Arvey, *Fairness in Selecting Employees* (Reading, Massachusetts: Addison-Wesley, 1979).

Halo effect   The **halo effect** is produced when one particular action or aspect of work performance influences a supervisor's overall opinion of the worker. An extremely favorable or unfavorable comment or characteristic colors reactions to all other information communicated during interviews.

Recent behavior bias   People tend to remember best what they have observed most recently. Since supervisors are in daily contact with their workers, it is easy to see how a worker's recent behavior may unduly influence their reaction to the worker during interviews. This is known as a **recent behavior bias.** Unless recent behavior is consistent with earlier behavior, this influence can distort the information received by supervisors during an interview.

Friendship Supervisors get to know and like some workers better than others. It is difficult at times to separate your role as a supervisor directing workers from that of the worker's friend. Clearly, if performance review, discipline, and other interviews are to be accurate, questions of friendship should not influence your evaluation of information received during the interviewing process.

Similar-to-me effect[15] People tend to relate more easily to people like themselves. While this response is acceptable outside the work relationship, it can lead to trouble if carried over to the interview situation. We tend to interpret information received from workers who are similar to us in attitudes or background more favorably than information received from those who are not. This is called the **similar-to-me effect.**

Conducting better interviews

The problems discussed in the preceding paragraphs can make interviews ineffective. There are, however, steps you can take to help you become a better interviewer.

Prepare in advance Plan what you want to accomplish during the interview. Have your purpose clearly in mind. Write down specific topics you want to discuss or questions you want to ask. If it is not a hiring interview, make certain your workers know in advance the purpose of the interview and the topics to be discussed, so the worker can be prepared too. Plan to hold the interview at a specific time and in an appropriate place.

Create the proper setting The environment in which the interview is conducted can influence its effectiveness. Interviews should be conducted with as much privacy as possible so you can talk without restraint and interruption. In general, people are nervous at first. You can help them feel more at ease by talking about non-job-related areas in the beginning of the interview. After this warm-up period, people will be more likely to feel comfortable talking about job-related areas. Too often supervisors are formal and impersonal during the interview. This may inhibit the conversation, resulting in less sharing of information.

Ask questions The way you get applicants or workers to respond during the interview also influences the quality of the interview. Six main questioning techniques are useful in different situations.[16]

- **Directive, Close-Ended Approach.** This technique involves asking a question which requires a very specific answer. This highly structured approach gives you control over the discussion and saves time. However, it also limits the amount of information received since the person being interviewed is given no opportunity to become involved in the discussion.

- **Nondirective, Open-Ended Approach.** This technique is the opposite of the close-ended approach. Here you ask the question without limiting how the worker may respond. This approach is more likely to provide you with more information as workers are free to respond as they see fit. This flexibility requires more time and may also require you to probe for additional, clarifying information.

- **Probing Approach.** This type of questioning is used to clarify statements made previously or obtain additional information. You probe to achieve greater understanding about the topic you are discussing. As a result, probing questions are often used along with the open-ended approach.

- **Hypothetical Questions.** Another way to obtain information during interviews is to pose "what if" situations to the worker. This approach requires workers to describe what they would do in certain situations.

- **Mirror Response.** This approach helps you comprehend what a worker really means when his or her response is not clear. It involves restating what the worker has said, but in question form. As this method is nonevaluative, and hence not threatening, workers often respond by telling you how they really feel.

Involve the worker in the interview The way you ask questions largely determines how involved workers become in the interview. Obviously close-ended or leading questions leave little room for involvement. The worker merely answers your question. However, the more workers participate in the interview and feel you have given them a chance to express themselves, the more accepting they will be of the information they receive and the resulting decisions or actions taken.

Effective meetings

As we indicated in Chapter 4, meetings are a fact of life for supervisors in any organization. The more you advance in management, the more meetings you will attend. People often complain about meetings and consider them a waste of time, but this does not have to be the case. Meetings are often necessary to share ideas, get opinions, discuss ideas, or make decisions. The following ideas can help you conduct meetings effectively.

State your purpose   Determine and clearly state the purpose(s) for the meeting. If you are scheduling a meeting, there should be a reason. Meetings held for the sake of meeting make little sense. The people who are invited should understand why the meeting is being held and what you want to accomplish.

Use an agenda   Prepare and distribute an agenda. The agenda should indicate the topics to be discussed in the meeting and the actions to be taken relative to each topic. This agenda should be distributed to participants several days before the meeting, giving them time to collect information and prepare to participate in a meaningful manner.

Prepare   Prepare for the meeting. Review the agenda noting all actions to be taken relative to each agenda item. Collect all information necessary for your participation and identify any information you want to share. Make certain that the meeting place is set up properly and any needed equipment is available. Prepare visual aids—charts or diagrams—if they will be useful in conducting the meeting.

Involve the workers   Encourage participation. Meetings are set up so that people can share information, ideas, and opinions. Encourage all participants in the meeting to be involved actively. Attempt to draw out those who tend to be quiet and do not participate fully. It is just as important to discourage those who tend to talk too much and dominate the meeting. Keep in mind the helping and hindering roles we will discuss in Chapter 9. Try to discourage hindering roles and encourage helping roles.

Summarize As the discussion on each agenda item is completed, summarize the discussion to ensure that all participants leave with the same understanding. Finally, at the conclusion of the meeting, summarize the complete discussion. In particular, note any decisions that have been made and any actions assigned to particular individuals. Frequently it is useful to prepare written minutes summarizing the meeting to distribute to participants.

Keep it short Meetings are expensive. They cost time. Further, if meetings drag on some participants lose interest. So keep the meeting as brief as possible while still discussing all necessary items. To ensure that meetings don't drag on it is useful to establish a stopping time as well as a starting time in advance.

Although you will be conducting some meetings, you will also be participating in many meetings conducted by others. You should manage your own participation in other meetings. Prepare just as thoroughly to participate in meetings conducted by others. Collect all information you need for discussing the various agenda items. Note before the meeting any positions you want to take or points you want to express. During the meeting, share your information, ideas, and opinions. Do so in a balanced way, however. Listen carefully to others' contributions and react to them appropriately. Do not dominate the discussion.

Meetings can be a waste of time. However, if they are properly conducted and if participants manage their involvement, they can be a useful means for sharing information.

Summary

- ☐ Supervisors spend 90 % of their day communicating. Communication is the process of passing information and meaning from the sender to the receiver. The purpose of communication is to achieve common understanding.
- ☐ The communication process includes six stages: (1) the sender has a thought, (2) which is developed into a message, (3) the

message is transmitted to the receiver, (4) who receives the message, (5) attaches meaning to it, and (6) gives feedback to the sender. Problems resulting in communication breakdowns can arise at any point in the process.

☐ Formal communication in organizations includes downward, upward, and lateral communication. These formal channels communicate work-related information. Downward communication flows from higher-level managers to supervisors to workers. Upward communication flows from workers to supervisors and managers. Lateral communication flows across different departments.

☐ Informal communication occurs outside formally established channels, through the grapevine. It includes work-related and people-related information. Information travels rapidly through the grapevine and can be quite accurate when messages are not emotional or controversial. However inaccurate messages can be damaging.

☐ Grapevines are inevitable but they do not cause problems necessarily. Supervisors can make them more accurate. Grapevines also serve several constructive purposes if they are dealt with effectively.

☐ Supervisors can become better communicators if they develop good skills in encouraging feedback, listening, communicating nonverbally, writing, interviewing, and participating in meetings.

☐ Supervisors must work to encourage feedback. Workers will give supervisors feedback only if they believe supervisors want feedback and are willing and able to act on the information received. Several strategies for encouraging useful feedback are available.

☐ Most people are poor listeners. Listening does not occur until people hear, understand, and remember what has been communicated. If you follow the guides to better listening you can become as good at listening as you are at hearing.

☐ Nonverbal communication accompanies all verbal communication. Body language communicates much information not communicated through words. The distance selected for communication conveys information about the relationship between the people talking. Posture, gestures, and other nonverbal cues communicate feelings as well. Supervisors can compare verbal and nonverbal communication to determine if they are receiving and understanding the intended message.

☐ Good writing skills are important to a supervisor's success. Important people may form an opinion of you on the basis of your writing. Effective writing is also necessary to ensure your message is understood. Good writing requires completeness, conciseness, clarity, and correctness.

☐ Supervisors conduct several types of interviews as part of their jobs. Interviews are conversations planned to meet a specific purpose. The purpose may be to hire new workers, review job performance with workers, counsel workers, discipline workers, and handle grievances.

☐ Interviews are often ineffective because incorrect or inaccurate information is obtained. Problems which cause interviews to be ineffective include stereotyping, initial impressions, halo effect, recent behavior bias, friendship, and the similar-to-me effect.

☐ Supervisors can make interviews more effective by preparing in advance and conducting the interview in the proper setting. The way questions are asked and the involvement of the worker also influence how effective the interview will be.

☐ Supervisors attend meetings regularly. You can make the meetings you call more effective. Clearly state the purpose of the meeting. Prepare and distribute an agenda. Be prepared for the meeting. Encourage constructive involvement from participants. Summarize what was said about each agenda item, then summarize the complete discussion at the conclusion of the meeting. Keep your meetings brief.

Questions for review and discussion

1. What is the purpose of the communication process? What steps are involved?

2. Distinguish between formal and informal communication in organizations. Define the types of formal communication found in organizations.

3. Why is feedback essential to supervisors? How can supervisors encourage useful feedback and discourage phony feedback?

4. How can supervisors become better listeners?

5. What is nonverbal communication? Why is it important to effective communication?

6. Why is effective writing important for supervisors? What are the characteristics of good written communication?

7. Discuss the problems associated with interviews which cause incorrect or inaccurate information to be exchanged. How can supervisors make their interviews more effective?

8. How can supervisors make meetings they call more effective?

9. Are grapevines good or bad? Discuss both sides of the issue.

10. Identify one activity that a supervisor performs that does not involve communication.

Key terms

Communication process	Informal communication
Counseling interviews	Interviews
Disciplinary interviews	Lateral communication
Downward communication	Listening
Feedback	Nonverbal communication
Formal communication	Performance review interviews
Grapevine	Recent behavior bias
Grievance interviews	Similar-to-me-effect
Halo effect	Stereotyping
Hiring interviews	Upward communication

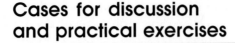

Cases for discussion and practical exercises

1. Rex Swenson is a fry cook for a local drive-in restaurant. He has been employed in this position for three years while working his way through school. He is a dependable employee and well liked by the owner, Tim Wicks. However, something happened in late August that changed their relationship.

   Rex was supposed to work the Sunday evening shift, but his mother was sick in the hospital in Dallas, some twenty miles away, and he had gone to visit her during the afternoon. On the way back, he got caught in a traffic jam after a Dallas Cowboys football game and arrived at work an hour late. Tim was not at the drive-in at the time, but other employees told him that the fry cook on duty had to wait over an hour until Rex got there. On Monday, Rex also had the evening shift, but his car broke down on the way to work, and again he was delayed one hour.

   When he walked into the kitchen, Tim glared at him and said, "Late again, eh? Two times in a row. You know I can't put up with this. When you hired on here, you knew how important it was to be on time. We can't expect everyone else to adjust their schedule to yours. I've had to pay overtime for the past two days because you failed to get here. This is serious, Rex. What've you got to say for yourself."

   Rex was taken aback by Tim's abrupt approach, and he replied rather flippantly, "I had a few problems."

   Before he could say another word, Tim shot back, "You had some problems! What do you think you gave me by not showing up? I'm trying to run this operation with employees who ignore work schedules and you tell me you've got problems. Things better shape up, Rex. What's wrong, anyway?"

   By now Rex was obviously irritated and a little embarrassed. He answered suddenly, "I just had some problems."

   "Is that all you're going to say? I'm going to have to start looking for another fry cook if you can't do better than that."

   "Then why don't you?" Rex countered and turned to leave. *

Source: From *Management: Concepts and Situations* by Howard Carlisle. © 1976, Science Research Associates, Inc. Reprinted by permission of the publisher.

Consider the following questions:
a) What communication breakdowns occurred in this situation?
b) How could the situation have been avoided?

2. Think back over your own working experience. Think of a time when a communication breakdown occurred. What caused the communication breakdown? What happened as a result of the communication breakdown? What could have been done to keep that particular breakdown from occurring?

3. Interview a number of workers regarding communication "sins" that have been committed against them. You may want to use the list given earlier in this chapter. Which of the sins were committed against them most often? How does this compare to the results of the study given in the chapter?

Notes

1. Paul R. Timm, *Managerial Communication: A Finger on the Pulse* (Englewood Cliffs, New Jersey: Prentice Hall, Inc., 1980), p. v.

2. Robert Fulmer, *The New Management* (New York: Macmillan, 1974), p. 34.

3. Keith Davis, *Human Behavior at Work*, 5th Edition (New York: McGraw-Hill, 1977), p. 381.

4. James A. Lee. "A Study of Communication Sins," Unpublished paper, Ohio University, 1973.

5. Timm, *Managerial Communication*, p. 74.

6. Davis, *Human Behavior*, p. 75.

7. Timm, *Managerial Communication*, p. 75.

8. William G. Dyer, "Encouraging Feedback," *The Personnel Administrator*, June 1974.

9. Betsy D. Gelb and Gabriel M. Gelb, "Strategies to Overcome Phoney Feedback," *MSU Business Topics*, Autumn 1974, pp. 5–7.

10. William G. Dyer, "Encouraging Feedback."

11. Ron Adler and Neil Towne, *Looking Out Looking* (San Francisco: Holt, Rinehart and Winston, 1975).

12. *Ibid.*

13. Timm, *Managerial Communication*, pp. 264–268; and Robert Fulmer, *The New Management*, p. 314.

14. Edward T. Hall, *The Hidden Dimension* (Garden City, N.Y.: Anchor Books/Doubleday, 1969).

15. T. M. Rand and K. N. Wexley, "A Demonstration of the Byrne Similarity Hypothesis in Simulated Employment Interviews," *Psychological Reports*, 1975, pp. 535–544.

16. Timm, *Managerial Communication*, pp. 148–151.

6

Motivating workers

Objectives

After reading this chapter you should be able to

- [ ] Explain how assumptions about people can affect your dealings with workers and hinder motivation.
- [ ] Explain how human needs influence behavior.
- [ ] Identify signs of frustration and explain how frustration can be handled.
- [ ] Explain Herzberg's two-factor theory of work motivation.
- [ ] Explain how supervisors can use job enrichment to increase workers' motivation.
- [ ] Explain how supervisors can use behavior modification to increase workers' motivation.

Job enlargement = adding more task to work.

What motivates people?

"Why do people work?" Or, more specifically, "Why don't people work harder?" "What can I do to get my people to do a better job?" "My people don't even care if they do a good job." "How can I work with them so they will be more careful and concerned about their work?" These questions are typical of those asked by many supervisors. Why?

As we indicated earlier, supervisors get work accomplished through the efforts of other people. They are responsible for attaining acceptable performance from people in their departments. Performance is the key, main concern.

Worker performance is influenced by two factors. One is ability. The worker must have the skills and the capabilities necessary to perform the job. Ability is not the only factor influencing performance, however. A second major factor is the worker's level of motivation. Given two people with the same level of ability, the worker who is more motivated—who is more willing to put forth effort to do the work—will perform at a higher level. The more motivated worker will do more work and/or do better work than one who is less motivated. Even very capable workers, if they are not motivated to work, will perform poorly.

In view of these two factors you need to be certain that your workers are adequately trained and have the necessary tools, equipment, and supplies. You must also be sure that workers are motivated to do their jobs. You need to develop a positive motivational climate for your workers. In this chapter, we will concentrate on what you can do to develop a more positive motivational climate.

Assumptions about workers

In order to develop a positive motivational climate, you must have a clear understanding of what motivates your workers. This might seem like an easy task. We would assume that a supervisor working daily with the same people knows them and has a clear understanding of the factors important to them. But this is not always the case. One study makes this point.[1]

This study asked a group of supervisors to rank the importance of a number of possible motivational factors *for their subordinates.* (See Table 6.1.) Note the supervisors were not asked what they felt was important, but what was important to their workers. They ranked the factors they thought were valued by their workers, and then the workers were asked to rank the same ten items for themselves.

As you can see from the results in Table 6.1, this group of supervisors did not predict the importance of the different factors for their workers very accurately. For example, the three items ranked most important by the workers were full appreciation for work done, feeling "in" on things, and sympathetic understanding of personal problems. The supervisors had predicted that these three items would be lowest in importance for their workers. Instead, they had predicted that wages and job security would be the most important factors.

How could these supervisors have been so wrong about their workers? Douglas McGregor offers one possible explanation. He suggests that many supervisors do not try to develop a clear and accurate understanding of their workers. Rather, they tend to make

Table 6.1

What workers want from their jobs

	SUPERVISORS' ESTIMATE	WORKERS' RESPONSE
Good working conditions	4	9
Feeling "in" on things	10	2
Tactful disciplining	7	10
Full appreciation for work done	8	1
Management loyalty to workers	6	8
Good wages	1	5
Promotion and growth with company	3	7
Sympathetic understanding of personal problems	9	3
Job security	2	4
Interesting work	5	6

Source: Adapted from Paul Hersey and Kenneth H. Blanchard, *Management of Organizational Behavior*, 3rd ed., (Englewood Cliffs, N.J.: Prentice-Hall, 1977), p. 47.

general assumptions about the nature of workers and treat them on the basis of those assumptions. To demonstrate the potential problems of behaving on the basis of assumptions, McGregor developed what he called Theory X and Theory Y.[2]

On the basis of his observations, McGregor noted that many supervisors behaved as if they held a very negative view of their workers. He called this view of people **Theory X.** McGregor said that supervisors who hold Theory X assumptions treat their workers as if:

■ They are basically lazy and will avoid work if they can.

■ They are not ambitious, do not want responsibility, and prefer to be directed.

■ They must be closely controlled and often forced to work toward organizational objectives.

They are unwilling and unable to help solve organizational problems.

These supervisors, according to McGregor, tend to behave in an autocratic manner. They make all decisions, structure the work, and closely supervise and control their workers.

McGregor noted that an alternative set of assumptions could be developed. He called these **Theory Y. Supervisors who hold Theory Y assumptions treat their workers as if:**

- Work is an activity as natural as rest or play.
- They will not only accept responsibility, but under the proper conditions they will actively seek it.
- They will exercise self-control or self-direction when working toward objectives to which they are committed.
- They are generally willing and able to help solve organizational problems.

Supervisors who hold Theory Y assumptions treat their workers more democratically. They delegate authority and allow workers to participate in decision making. They allow workers more autonomy.

McGregor did not argue that either set of assumptions is correct. Rather, he was pointing out that supervisors should not make assumptions. If a supervisor holds Theory X assumptions but supervises workers who have Theory Y characteristics, the resulting problem is evident. Closely controlling individuals who are seeking responsibility would quickly dampen their motivation. Likewise, delegating authority to individuals with Theory X characteristics would lead to disastrous performance.

The key is to be careful not to make assumptions about employees' values. Rather, you need to remember that each person is unique. To create a positive motivational climate, you need to analyze your workers, determine what factors motivate them as individuals, and work with them on that basis.

What approaches can you use to analyze people? How can you determine what motivates them? To provide a framework for answering these questions, we will look first at some approaches to the study of motivation. Then we will turn our attention to specific strategies to motivate on-the-job performance.

The process of motivation

Workers have many needs. At any given time, some of these needs are satisfied and others are unsatisfied. An unsatisfied need is the starting point in the **motivation process.** It begins the chain of events leading to behavior.

When workers have an unsatisfied need, they attempt to identify something that will satisfy the need. This is called a **goal.** Once a goal has been identified, they take action to reach that goal and thereby satisfy the need. This process is illustrated in Fig. 6.1. For example, when people are hungry (unsatisfied need), they take action to obtain food (goal). Similarly, when they are lonely (unsatisfied need), they attempt to find and associate with other people (goal).

Human needs

Abraham Maslow, a psychologist, has classified human needs into five categories.[3] The five categories are:

- **Physiological needs** for food, water, air, and shelter. These needs must be satisfied at least partially for continued survival.
- **Security** for protection from physical harm and economic disaster and avoidance of the unexpected. These are the needs to feel free from threat and harm.
- **Social needs** to associate with other people and be accepted by them, to love and be loved. These are sometimes called the love needs or the needs for affiliation.

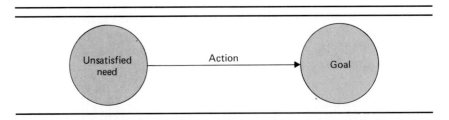

Figure 6.1   The motivation process.

- **Esteem** related to respect and prestige. There are two types: self-esteem and esteem from others. These include the need to be prominent in some way, to be respected by others. They also include the need for self-respect.
- **Self-fulfillment** for realizing one's potential. These include the need for realizing one's capabilities to the fullest: for accomplishing what one is capable of accomplishing and for becoming what one is capable of becoming. These needs are also called needs for self-realization or self-actualization.

Maslow proposes that these categories should be arranged in a hierarchy. As shown in Fig. 6.2, physiological needs are the most basic, followed by safety, social, esteem, and self-fulfillment needs. According to Maslow, people attempt to satisfy lowest-level needs first. As long as these needs are unsatisfied, they dominate behavior. As needs are satisfied, however, they lose their motivational power and the next level of needs, security needs, becomes the dominant motivating force. This process continues up the need hierarchy.

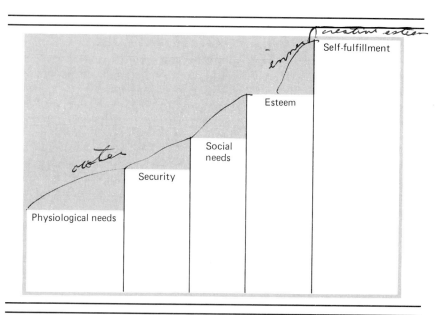

Figure 6.2 Maslow's hierarchy of needs.

As each level of needs becomes satisfied, the next highest level becomes dominant. Figure 6.3 illustrates the need hierarchies of two individuals with different dominant needs.

In Maslow's view, people are motivated to take action to satisfy dominant needs. But once a need is satisfied, it no longer acts as a motivator. Assume you are sitting down after stuffing yourself at Thanksgiving dinner. It is very unlikely that you will immediately get up, go the refrigerator, and get another turkey leg. Your hunger (need for food) is satisfied. You are not motivated to take action to obtain more food.

How accurate is **Maslow's need hierarchy?** Can it be used to make specific predictions about a person's behavior? Probably not, since Maslow himself acknowledged that the order in which needs become dominant is not rigidly fixed. Different people may order their needs differently. Some people—the starving artist is an example—are more preoccupied with self-fulfillment and expression, and less with satisfaction of their lower needs. For other people, esteem needs may become dominant before social needs. Many of us

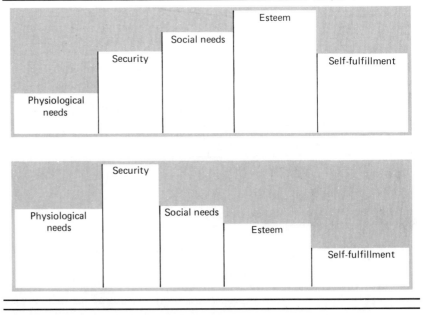

Figure 6.3   Two individuals with different dominant needs.

have known people who were more concerned about their self-image than about acceptance by others. Many "loners" fall into this category.

Most evidence indicates that a two-level hierarchy is more accurate than Maslow's stair-step progression. As shown in Fig. 6.4, this hierarchy contains **primary needs** and **secondary needs**. Primary needs include physical needs and security. Secondary needs include social needs, esteem, and self-realization. As primary needs are satisfied, secondary needs become dominant. The order in which secondary needs become important, however, varies from person to person. It is also likely that many people are motivated simultaneously by several secondary needs.

While studying human needs does not provide a complete understanding of motivation, it does provide an excellent starting point. In particular, the study of needs highlights two important facts:

1. People have many needs. For most people, physical and security needs are fundamental. Once these needs are mainly satisfied, secondary needs become the dominant motivating force.

2. A satisfied need is not a motivator. People take action to satisfy dominant needs, not needs that are already satisfied.

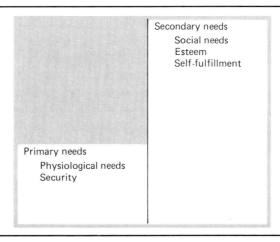

Figure 6.4 Primary and secondary needs.

Frustration behavior

Our discussion thus far has focused on goal-directed behavior. We have examined needs and their influence on people's actions. We have assumed that when people take action, they can reach their goals. This is not always the case, however. Consider, for example, the worker in the automobile assembly plant who intentionally slashes the interior of a car as it moves past on the line, or the child who kicks the dog after being prevented from taking cookies from the cookie jar. Behaviors such as these are often the result of frustration.

Frustration occurs when need satisfaction is blocked (see Fig. 6.5). A person acts to satisfy a need and is not able to reach the goal. The obstacle may be a physical barrier. For example, road construction may detour a saleswoman far out of her way, make her late for an appointment, and cause her to lose a sale. Usually, however, blockages are more complex. The boss, higher levels of management, co-workers, and the nature of the job are just a few possible sources of frustration.

Most people must cope with frustration frequently. Sometimes they cope by changing goals. Or they may simply learn to live with the situation and proceed with other activities. If frustration becomes too intense, however, two reactions are common: aggressive behavior and withdrawal.

Aggression   Aggression is behavior characterized by fighting or some kind of attack. It may be either direct or displaced. Direct aggression is action taken against the actual source of frustration. A

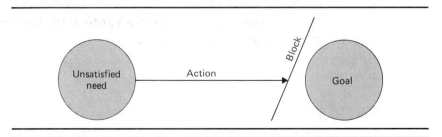

Figure 6.5   Frustration.

worker frustrated by a supervisor, for example, might yell and swear at the supervisor. Or the worker might start a damaging rumor about the supervisor's personal life. Fighting, both physical and psychological, is an example of direct aggression. Displaced aggression is directed at some person or object other than the source of frustration. A common example is the person who takes home on-the-job frustration and yells at the children.

Withdrawal Frustration may also result in **withdrawal.** When people withdraw, they remove themselves from the source of their frustration. They may physically withdraw by being absent from work or quitting their jobs, or they may withdraw psychologically. In psychological withdrawal, a person is present physically but not mentally. Daydreaming and a "turned off" attitude are examples of this form of withdrawal.

Frustration in work organizations

Frustration can create costly problems for any organization. Displaced aggression, in the form of sabotage, is a major cost for some companies. Physical withdrawal—quitting and absences—also can be quite expensive. Even psychological withdrawal can be costly. Turned-off workers usually produce less and do poorer quality work. They also may not work safely.

Frustration may be costly, but what can you do about it? The first step is identification. While this is not easy, some of the symptoms discussed, such as excessive absenteeism, irritability, or slipshod work, are clues. Sometimes a good heart-to-heart talk can bring the problem into the open. These conversations are often difficult to conduct, however, because frustrated workers may be less than rational or so alienated that they are unreceptive.

Once frustration has been identified, the best approach is to remove the source of frustration, although this is not always possible. For example, people tend to carry their off-the-job frustrations into the work place. A marital spat in the morning or a traffic jam on the way to work can wreck what otherwise might have been a pleasant day. Or a person with a problem child at home may be perpetually moody or depressed at work and thus become an irritant to co-workers. In situations such as these, the supervisor cannot remove the source of frustration.

Even when frustration is job-related, it may be difficult to remove. A supervisor cannot usually eliminate all job-related frustrations. Certain troublesome organizational rules, for example, may be beyond the supervisor's power to change.

Unfortunately, the problems created by frustration are not easily solved. If the source of frustration cannot be removed, the supervisor can try to provide opportunities for releasing the tensions created by frustration. Often, just talking out the problem or venting anger can be helpful to a frustrated person.

Motivation at work

Our study of needs and frustration provides some insights about workers and their behavior. Using this understanding as a base, we can now look more specifically at work motivation.

Perhaps the most popular theory of work motivation is based on research by Frederick Herzberg.[4] In his original study, Herzberg and his associates interviewed 200 engineers and accountants. They were asked to think of times when they felt particularly good about their jobs and times when they felt particularly bad. The engineers and accountants then were asked to describe the factors that caused these feelings.

When talking about bad times, the engineers and accountants brought up issues like unfair company policies, poor relationships with their bosses and co-workers, and low pay. In contrast, when asked about good job experiences, they generally did not mention these factors. Instead, they talked about recognition they had received for a well-done job or the opportunities for personal growth and development.

Herzberg and others repeated these interviews with a variety of workers in different organizations. Their results were generally the same. Based on these findings, Herzberg developed the **two-factor theory of work motivation.** According to Herzberg, the absence of certain job factors tends to make workers dissatisfied. The presence of these same factors does not, however, produce higher levels of motivation. They merely help avoid dissatisfaction and the problems it creates, such as absenteeism, turnover, and grievances. Herzberg called these factors **maintenance factors.** Maintenance factors include:

- Fairly administered company policies;
- A supervisor who knows the work;
- A good relationship with one's supervisor;
- A good relationship with one's co-workers;
- A fair salary;
- Job security;
- Good working conditions.

in pay to motivate:

1. must want more pay

2. must see pay related to performance

3. must be able to influence performance

To build higher levels of motivation and job satisfaction a different set of factors is necessary. If these factors are not present, howevr, no strong dissatisfaction results. Herzberg called these **motivator factors.** Motivator factors include:

- The opportunity to accomplish something significant;
- Recognition for significant accomplishments;
- Chance for advancement;
- Opportunity to grow and develop on the job;
- Chance for increased responsibility.

As the lists indicate, the motivator factors are job-centered. They relate directly to the content of the job itself. In contrast, maintenance factors relate more to the conditions and environment in which the work is done.

Herzberg noted that although maintenance factors had long been considered the key to motivation, they are actually more related to job dissatisfaction. When maintenance factors are not present, there may be more absences, more quits, and in union organizations, more grievances. Maintenance factors however, will not in and of themselves motivate people to higher performance. High-level performance can only be obtained through building motivator factors into workers' jobs.

One explanation for the difference between maintenance and motivator factors may be workers' expectations. Workers expect their supervisors to be fair and their working conditions to be good. When they are not, they become dissatisfied or frustrated. Opportunities for accomplishment, advancement, and responsibility are less available in many jobs. Thus, making them available can lead to higher motivation and better performance.

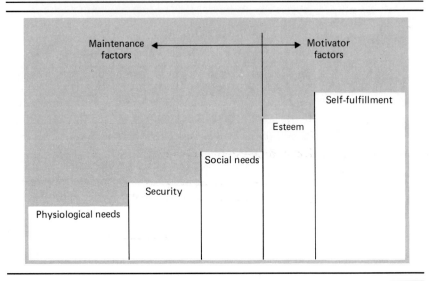

Figure 6.6   Maslow and Herzberg compared.

To a certain extent, Herzberg's theory fits in with the earlier discussion of needs. As shown in Fig. 6.6, the maintenance factors include mainly physiological, security, and some social needs. The motivator factors are directed at social, esteem, and self-fulfillment needs.

Herzberg's theory has received a great deal of attention. Although the theory has been criticized, few would debate that Herzberg has contributed to our thinking on work motivation. His work complements and extends the need-hierarchy concepts. Its focus is directly work-related. Most significantly, he has drawn attention to the importance of the nature of the job in work motivation.

Motivation strategies

What can be done to increase the motivation to work? How can we create a motivational climate that encourages good performance? Organizations are experimenting with a number of different strategies. Among the more popular are job enrichment and behavior modification.

Job enrichment

Job enrichment is a motivation strategy that directly affects the nature of the jobs that workers perform. This strategy is based on Herzberg's conclusion that work motivation can be increased by building more motivator factors into jobs. Job enrichment involves adding more responsibility to the job. The worker is given the opportunity to make decisions regarding what is done and how the work is done. In addition, jobs are restructured to add more opportunities for achievement, recognition, growth, and development.

Volvo's Kalmar plant in Sweden is an example of an extensive job enrichment effort. In the Kalmar plant, the traditional automotive assembly line was eliminated. A special auto carrier was designed and the car is moved from assembly group to assembly group. The car is stationary while the work is being performed. The plant employees are grouped into twenty-five teams of approximately twenty people each. Each team is responsible for an entire assembly process such as door assembly, electrical systems, or interiors. Each team has its own space on the floor and even its own break area. Each team determines how they will do their work. Team members can specialize on one task, they can rotate jobs, or they can perform a number of different operations.

The key is that team members make the decisions. How they do their work is not dictated by others. Team members set their own work pace (within limits) and take breaks when they want. Team members inspect their own work. Finally, a computer flashes hourly productivity figures onto display screens providing rapid feedback to workers.

Note how this set-up differs from the conventional assembly line, where a worker performs a repetitive short-cycle task, designed by others, on a moving line.

The Volvo plant example illustrates some of the suggestions Herzberg and others have made for enriching jobs:

- Decrease the number of external controls on workers' jobs.
- Give them greater authority to decide what to do and how to do it.
- Balance this increased freedom with more individual accountability for work performed.
- Allow people to become "experts" by assigning them specific tasks.

- Create a natural unit of work by giving people tasks with which they can identify.

- Establish a spirit of teamwork.

- Decrease the obvious distinctions between managers and workers, such as special parking and dining facilities and different styles of dress.

- Provide growth and development by emphasizing career training and advancement.

Does job enrichment work? Is it an effective motivational strategy? Numerous organizations have experimented with job enrichment. IBM, Travelers Insurance, Polaroid, Texas Instruments, United Airlines, and the Bell Telephone Systems are examples. The results of these experiments, however, have been mixed.

Once again Volvo is a good example. The Kalmar Plant had higher levels of satisfaction and a lower turnover rate after job enrichment was instituted. Further, there was some evidence of higher product quality. But problems were encountered. The Kalmar plant cost 10 to 30% more to build than a conventional plant. In addition, productivity was below normal and labor costs were higher than normal.

These mixed results are common. Frequently, worker satisfaction will increase as a result of job enrichment. Productivity may not increase.

Experiments with job enrichment must be reviewed carefully. In many experiments changes were made, in addition to the changes in the job, which could have had an impact on workers. For example, a job enrichment program for janitorial employees at Texas Instruments is credited with improving cleanliness, reducing turnover, and substantial cost savings. What was not reported, however, was that wages were increased by 46% and benefits worth about one-third of the workers' wages were added. What caused the improved performance? Was it job enrichment or the increase in pay? Determining the cause is impossible.

Technological factors may also limit the usefulness of job enrichment. Making the technological changes necessary to enrich jobs may be too costly in some situations. The costs of enriching the job would far exceed the value of any benefits obtained.

Workers' wants are also a question. Research indicates that not all workers expect or want more challenge and responsibility on the job. Some workers view their jobs only as a means to an end. They are quite willing to trade time for money if minimal demands are placed on them. A job enrichment program might have a negative impact on these workers.

Is job enrichment a useful motivational technique? In many cases job enrichment has encouraged better quality work and contributed to worker satisfaction. Less evidence exists that it has had an impact on productivity. In addition, job enrichment probably will not work in all situations. Not all people want or expect the same things from their work. Not all jobs can be enriched. Companies should carefully analyze their workers and the work situation before investing heavily in a job enrichment program.

Behavior modification

Behavior modification is a motivational strategy that supervisors may find useful. The basis of behavior modification is that behavior is a function of its consequences. This theory is summarized in the "Law of Effect." This law states that behavior followed by a positive (or rewarding) consequence tends to be repeated and behavior followed by a negative consequence tends not to be repeated.

For example, assume that a student, not particularly gifted in mathematics, studies very hard and does fairly well (B+) on a mathematics examination. If the student's parents offer praise for the effort and accomplishment (positive consequence), the student will tend to study hard for the next examination. On the other hand, if the parents criticize the student for not getting an A (negative consequence), the student will tend not to study as hard for the next examination.

As a supervisor, you are concerned with encouraging positive behaviors, or behaviors that contribute to performance. You also want to discourage negative behaviors, or behaviors that detract from performance. Using behavior modification, you attempt to influence workers' behavior. You use reinforcement to strengthen or modify the behaviors of your workers.

You can use different types of reinforcements such as positive reinforcement, negative reinforcement, punishment, and extinction.

Positive reinforcement   **Positive reinforcement** is a consequence of behavior that increases the likelihood that the behavior will be repeated. It is a "reward" that an individual receives as a result of behaving in a certain way. Many rewards such as praise, money, a sense of accomplishment, and promotion are positive reinforcements.

Negative reinforcement   **Negative reinforcement,** or the removal of unpleasant consequences, increases the likelihood that the behavior will be repeated. In negative reinforcement the "reward" is the removal of something negative. An example would be an employee who learns that if she completes assigned projects on time, her supervisor will stop yelling at her.

Punishment   **Punishment** is an unpleasant consequence of behavior that makes it more likely the behavior will not be repeated. It is used to reduce undesirable behavior rather than to encourage desired behavior. The parent who slaps the hands of a child who has raided the cookie jar is attempting to get the child to stop eating cookies by using punishment. Criticizing an employee's work is using punishment to get the person to stop doing poor work. Many disciplinary programs are based on punishment. An employee who has excessive absences may be suspended; the pro baseball player who hits an umpire is fined.

Extinction   **Extinction** is the withholding rewards when undesirable behavior occurs so that the behavior will eventually disappear. As with punishment, extinction is used to decrease undesirable behavior. The parent who consciously ignores an unruly child is attempting to discourage the undesirable behavior by providing no reinforcement (extinction).

Most proponents of behavior modification encourage the use of positive reinforcement. They argue that the use of punishment simply discourages a behavior. It provides no indication of desirable behavior, and further, has unpredictable results. Positive reinforcement identifies desirable behaviors and encourages the increased use of those behaviors.

How can you use behavior modification to encourage productive behavior on the job? A systematic approach usually involves the following steps.

Step 1. Identify the performance-related target behaviors or behavior you want to encourage or discourage.

Step 2. Measure the frequency of these target behaviors. How often is the employee engaging in the behavior? This is important for establishing a "base-line" so that the success of the behavior modification program can be accurately evaluated.

Step 3. Intervene with reinforcements. Positive reinforcement or negative reinforcement can be used to increase the frequency of desirable target behaviors. Punishment or extinction can be used to decrease the frequency of undesirable target behaviors.

Step 4. Evaluation. Again the frequency of the target behaviors is measured and compared with the base-line measurement from step 2. If undesirable behaviors have decreased or desirable behaviors have increased, the strategy is working and the reinforcements can be maintained. If not, alternative reinforcements should be tried.

As an example of how this systematic approach to behavior modification works, consider June Hargraves' situation. June is the newly appointed supervisor of a group of sales clerks in a department store. During her first few weeks on the job, June noticed that the clerks were lax in providing immediate service to waiting customers. Frequently the clerks chatted among themselves, letting customers wait several minutes after entering the department. Since June had recently attended a seminar on behavior modification, she decided to attempt to use it to decrease customer waiting time.

First, she identified the target behavior, immediate service to customers upon entering the department. Over the next two weeks she observed the clerks and noted the frequency with which they waited on customers immediately. She found that customers were waited on with no avoidable delay only 65% of the time. She then decided on her reinforcement strategy. While she could have defined the target behavior as making customers wait and used punishment to decrease it, she chose instead to use positive reinforcement. She decided she would provide daily feedback on the number of "immediate helps" and praise the clerks whenever they improved the proportion of immediate helps over the preceding day.

June continued her program for a six-week period. At the end of six weeks immediate helps were occuring 90% of the time. While not perfect, this was a substantial improvement over the 65% base-line figure. The new figure indicated to June that the behavior modification was working, and she decided to continue the positive reinforcement of daily feedback and praise for improvement.

Numerous organizations use systematic approaches to behavior modification. These include Emery Air Freight, Michigan Bell, General Electric, Standard Oil of Ohio, and Weyerhauser. While most have reported performance improvements as a result of their programs, we need to remain cautious. Behavior modification was developed in the psychological laboratory. Many studies have been performed in the laboratory to develop the technique. However, relatively few good experiments with behavior modification have been conducted in companies, looking at people in actual work situations. As a result much is still to be learned about the use of behavior modification.

If you decide to use behavior modification to attempt to create a more positive motivational climate, the following guidelines will be useful:

- Reward workers when, but only when, they perform effectively.
- Tell workers what they can do to get rewards.
- If you withhold rewards, explain to workers what they are doing wrong.
- Remember that failure to reward good performance is a form of extinction and may decrease performance.

Increasing motivation

Motivating people at work is not a simple proposition. People have a variety of needs and supervisors have a limited influence on the rewards their organization can offer each employee.

Given these circumstances, what can you do to try to motivate people? Our discusion points up several considerations. Knowing the needs and wants of each person who works in your department is important. Instead of working on the basis of blanket assumptions, such as Theory X or Theory Y, you should analyze each employee. You do not need to play amateur psychologist. Rather, a lot can be learned simply by keeping the lines of communication open and by observation.

Understanding workers' needs should give you a good idea of the kind of rewards you need to offer. Although you may have limited control over what rewards are available, making full use of those that can be offered is important. For example, as new employees learn about and take interest in their jobs, they can be given increased responsibility. Recognition for a job well done, even in the form of a few words of praise, is another example.

Making the right rewards available, however, is not enough. People must believe that by working they will receive rewards that are important to them. This concept is explained by a recent theory, the **expectancy theory of motivation.** People's actions are based on their expectations as well as their needs. Unless there is a positive expectation of receiving a reward that will satisfy a need, an individual will not take action. To illustrate, consider a person who is thirsty. The person may need water, but the action of going to the faucet and getting a drink occurs only if he or she expects that effort to result in obtaining water.

The experience of one manufacturing company dramatically demonstrates the importance of expectations. The company planned to expand its operations, and management knew that a number of new supervisors would be needed. To prepare for the expansion, the company decided to run a training program for hourly employees to prepare them to become supervisors. The program was open to all at no cost. They were required, however, to attend the program on their own time. When the program started, management was shocked —only three people participated.

Interviews with employees who did not participate explained the poor response. Many indicated that they would like to be promoted, but didn't feel that attending the program would help. "Promotion is based on who you know, not what you know" was a commonly expressed opinion. In other words, although promotion was an important reward to many of the employees, they did not participate in the training program because they did not believe it would help them get promoted. They had negative expectations.

Similarly, how hard employees work is affected by their needs and by whether or not they expect good performance to result in rewards that will satisfy these needs. To be motivated, people must believe that by working hard they will fulfill needs that are important to them.

Finally, you should not overlook the importance of trying to minimize damage from dissatisfaction and frustration. Some of the issues that tend to dissatisfy employees can be dealt with directly. Unfair and arbitrary supervision is an example. Also, you can help lessen or ease employees' frustration even when you cannot directly change the source of the frustration.

There are no pat answers to motivational problems and no sure-fire formulas for motivating people. However, a good understanding of work motivation and a genuine concern for channeling the efforts of your people toward improved performance can help.

Summary

☐ Supervisors are responsible for obtaining acceptable levels of performance from their workers. Worker performance is influenced by two factors: (1) ability and (2) motivation. Supervisors must ensure workers are motivated to do their jobs. Workers must be willing to exert themselves.

☐ Supervisors tend to hold general assumptions about the nature of their workers. These assumptions influence how supervisors supervise their workers. If they are inaccurate, motivation problems result.

☐ McGregor identified two sets of assumptions. The Theory X view of people is negative and results in autocratic supervision. Theory Y is a more positive view and results in more democratic supervision.

☐ The motivational process begins with an unsatisfied need (goal). People behave in order to reach a goal that will satisfy a need.

☐ Maslow identified five categories of needs which are arranged in a hierarchy: (1) physiological, (2) safety, (3) social, (4) esteem, and (5) self-fulfillment. He suggested that people satisfy the lowest level, unsatisfied needs first. Once a need is satisfied, it no longer motivates behavior.

☐ A two-level need hierarchy is probably more accurate. As primary needs become satisfied, secondary needs become dominant. Secondary needs are not satisfied in any particular order.

☐ Frustration occurs when people are prevented from satisfying a need. Two common reactions to frustration are aggressive behavior and withdrawal. Supervisors should attempt to remove sources of frustration or provide opportunities for workers to release tension.

☐ Herzberg's two-factor theory of work motivation identifies two sets of factors: (1) maintenance factors and (2) motivator factors. Maintenance factors do not result in increased motivation but do reduce job dissatisfaction. Motivator factors increase motivation and job satisfaction

☐ Job enrichment is a strategy based on Herzberg's work for increasing motivation. It involves designing jobs to include more motivator factors. It has been effective in increasing worker satisfaction but the impact on worker productivity is not clear.

☐ Behavior modification uses reinforcements to encourage desirable behavior and discourage undesirable behavior. There are four types of reinforcement: (1) positive reinforcement, (2) negative reinforcement, (3) punishment, and (4) extinction. Supervisors using behavior modification to increase motivation should follow a systematic approach.

☐ Creating a positive motivational climate is not a simple task. Supervisors must know their workers and understand their needs. They must ensure workers expect that good performance will be rewarded with meaningful rewards.

Questions for review and discussion

1. What are Theory X and Theory Y? Discuss each and indicate what they are telling us about motivating workers.

2. Describe the motivation process.

3. Discuss Maslow's need hierarchy. How does he suggest motivation occurs?

4. What causes frustration? Why should supervisors be concerned with the existence of frustrated workers? How should supervisors deal with frustration?

5. Discuss Herzberg's two-factor theory of motivation. Compare it to Maslow's need-hierarchy theory.

6. What is job enrichment? How effective is job enrichment as a motivation strategy?

7. What is behavior modification? How is it implemented?

8. How do worker expectations influence motivation?

9. Some people argue that motivation comes from within. They say that you cannot motivate another person. Do you agree or disagree? Why?

Key terms

Aggression

Behavior modification

Esteem

Expectancy theory of motivation

Extinction

Frustration

Goal

Herzberg's two-factor theory of motivation

Job enrichment

Maintenance factors

Maslow's need hierarchy

Motivation process

Motivator factors

Negative reinforcement

Physiological needs

Positive reinforcement

Primary needs

Punishment

Secondary needs

Security

Self-fulfillment

Social needs

Theory X

Theory Y

Withdrawal

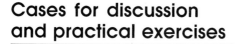

Cases for discussion
and practical exercises

1. Jean Wills supervises a group of data-processing clerks. She has been a supervisor for about five years and previously had worked as a clerk before she was promoted. Jean had always taken care to assign jobs to her clerks, giving them very clear instructions and watching closely to make certain they did the job right. Her people had done adequate work, but she had never been completely happy with their performance levels. She was also a bit disturbed that her employees didn't seem to accept her as one of the group. She felt they resented her and the way she worked.

   As a result of attending a supervisory training program conducted by her company, Jean decided she would change her approach to her clerks. One section of the program was on employee motivation. The program leader presented Herzberg's motivation theory and explained how job enrichment increases motivation. Jean realized the approach she had been using had been rather autocratic and hadn't emphasized any of the motivator factors. She decided to use some job enrichment in her group. She would let her clerks take more responsibility for deciding what should be done rather than spelling everything out for them. She also vowed not to check their work all the time. Instead she would let them control their work pace. She even would let them decide when they would take their morning and afternoon coffee breaks.

   After two months, Jean had to admit her "new motivation program" was a failure. With the exception of a few go-getters, the clerks seemed to resent her new approach. They complained that they didn't know what they were supposed to do and said Jean was never around when they needed her. The only thing they seemed to like about the program was taking breaks, and the breaks seemed to stretch out from 10 minutes to a half hour. One clerk even told her that if she wanted to improve their performance, she should "put things back like they were before and pay us more money."

   Looking at the results, Jean decided that the theory she had been taught in the training program just wouldn't work in practice. As she told her husband, "People don't want responsibility. If I want to keep my job, I'd better go back to the way I was supervising and put on the pressure."

a) Do you agree with Jean's conclusion?

b) What mistakes did Jean make?

2. Interview at least one supervisor and at least four hourly-level workers to find out what they want from their work, the factors that might motivate them to work harder. You may want to ask them to rank the ten items given in Table 6.1, or you may want to develop a list of items you think are more relevant. How much agreement is there among the supervisors and workers? How might you account for any differences? How does what they want relate to the motivation theories discussed in the chapter?

Notes

1. Paul Hersey and Kenneth H. Blanchard, *Management of Organizational Behavior*, 3rd edition, (Englewood Cliffs, New Jersey: Prentice-Hall, 1977), p. 47.

2. Douglas McGregor, *The Human Side of Enterprise* (New York: McGraw-Hill, 1960).

3. Abraham H. Maslow, "A Theory of Human Motivation," *Psychological Review* 50 (1943), pp. 370–396.

4. Frederick Herzberg, *Work and the Nature of Man* (New York: World, 1966).

7

Supervisory leadership

Objectives

After reading this chapter you should be able to

☐ Explain what early studies revealed about effective leaders' characteristics.

☐ Discuss the argument that leadership style depends on the particular situation.

☐ Identify the steps supervisors should follow when choosing a leadership style.

☐ Explain how your leadership style is affected by your workers, time constraints, the job, and your boss.

☐ Identify different types of power that you can use to become a better leader.

The supervisor as leader

"Am I glad it's Friday" Betty Dawson exclaimed. "In a few minutes I can take off and forget about this place for the weekend."

Betty is the supervisor of a group of records clerks at a small university. She had been a supervisor for a little over two years, and, until recently, had enjoyed the work. Now, however, Betty has a problem that she just can't seem to handle. Betty's problem is Barbara Shesky.

When Betty hired Barbara a little over two months ago, she thought she had the qualities of a perfect worker. She seemed bright, she had good high school grades, and she projected enthusiasm. Shortly after she began working however, her imperfections became evident.

In Betty's words, "She's lazy! She just won't work when I give her an assignment. Or if she does, I find out later that it's been done so poorly it has to be redone. I've always had good workers. I try to be friendly with them and am considerate of their ideas and feelings.

I want them to feel involved in the operation of the department. I guess I'm what you would call a participative leader. The problem is Barbara doesn't want to participate. I don't know what I'm going to do. I just can't figure out how to get her to work."

Leadership is an important aspect of the supervisor's job. Supervisors are responsible for the quality of their workers' performance. Effective leadership is necessary to meet this responsibility. Like Betty, supervisors are often concerned about how to approach their workers. Sometimes the approach they use doesn't get the desired results. Sometimes what works in one situation isn't effective in others.

In this chapter we will discuss supervisory leadership. First, we will review briefly the psychological study of leadership. Then we will discuss different supervisory leadership styles and the situations in which those styles can be used. Finally we will examine sources of power available to supervisors and discuss what you can do to become more effective.

Before proceeding any further in our discussion, we should define leadership. **Leadership** is the process of influencing the activities of individuals or groups toward goal accomplishment. As a supervisor, whenever you try to influence your workers so they perform their jobs more effectively, you are engaging in leadership activity.

Leadership effectiveness

Throughout this chapter, we will be discussing effective leadership. A leader's effectiveness is determined by two factors: output factors and human factors.

Output factors are the end results in an organization. They indicate how well the organization is accomplishing its objectives. In a business organization, for example, output factors would include such things as (1) productivity, (2) quality, (3) profitability, and (4) cost effectiveness. In a hospital, output would include quality of patient care and financial solvency.

Human factors reflect the state of the human resources in an organization. They indicate how well people are working together and how satisfied they are with their work. Human factors include such things as (1) morale, (2) amount and type of communication, (3) level of motivation, (4) commitment to objectives, and (5) level of interpersonal and intergroup conflict. The same kinds of human factors tend to be important in all types of organizations.

Both output and human factors are important. If a leader is unable to work with and through people to achieve output factors, the organization (or at least part of the organization) will not accomplish its goals. Similarly, if a leader fails to attend to human factors, communication breakdowns and disagreements are likely to result. In addition, motivation will decrease, and absenteeism and turnover may become a problem. Eventually, such problems are likely to have a negative impact on output factors. That is, they are likely to result in lower levels of performance, higher costs, and poorer quality work over time. Thus, without going into great detail, we can reasonably conclude that an effective leader is one who has a positive impact on both output and human factors in an organization.

The study of leadership

Early approaches to the study of leadership effectiveness concentrated on the personal characteristics of the leader. Psychologists studied individuals who were considered to be effective leaders and compared them to ineffective leaders. They reasoned in the following way. Some people are good leaders, others are not. If we study leaders and compare their personal characteristics, we should be able to identify characteristics which distinguish good from poor leaders. Some of the characteristics psychologists predicted effective leaders would possess included:

- Aggressiveness,
- Self-confidence,
- Ego strength,
- Strong desire to achieve,
- Intelligence,
- Public-speaking ability.

After years of studying leaders in all types of organizations, however, psychologists were forced to conclude that their predictions were incorrect. Some effective leaders were aggressive, others were not. Some ineffective leaders were just as intelligent as effective leaders. In short, no personal characteristics were found which consistently distinguished between effective and ineffective leaders.

Thus, the attempt to understand how people become effective leaders changed focus. Researchers decided to study the behavior of leaders rather than search for personal characteristics. They thought that by examining what leaders did—how they behaved—they could find out why some leaders were more effective than others.

Leadership behavior

One of the earliest attempts to analyze leader behavior began in the mid-1940s at Ohio State University.[1] The researchers wanted to identify different leadership behaviors and analyze the effects of those behaviors. Two broad types of leadership behavior were identified: initiating structure and consideration. **Initiating structure** refers to the leader's behavior in structuring the job of the follower and establishing well-defined patterns of organization and communication. **Consideration** is leader behavior showing mutual trust, respect, and friendship.

They found that these two types of leadership behaviors were independent. Some leaders structured follower activities, but provided little consideration. Others were considerate, but provided little structure. Many leaders, however, did not fit into either of these two categories. They used a fairly even mix of initiating structure and consideration, spending a lot of time using both types of behavior. Still other leaders spent very little time using either initiating structure or consideration behaviors. They were relatively uninvolved with their subordinates. Thus the use of different amounts of these two types of leader behavior can result in four different leadership styles. Figure 7.1 shows the four styles of leadership identified by the **Ohio State studies.**

The Ohio State researchers originally proposed that the most effective leadership style would be high in initiating structure and high in consideration. After nearly twenty years of research and hundreds of studies, however, they were forced to conclude that there was no "one best" leadership style. Each of the four styles could be effective and each could be ineffective, depending on the situation in which the leader was functioning.

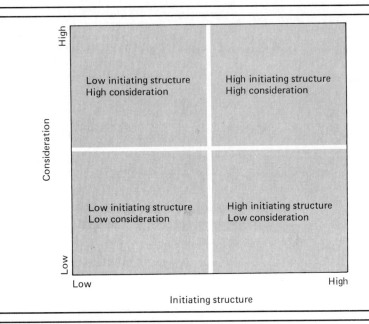

Figure 7.1   Four styles of leadership identified
by Ohio State studies.

Another view of leadership—the **Managerial Grid**—has been
developed by Robert Blake and Jane Mouton.[2] As indicated in Fig.
7.2, the Managerial Grid is based on various combinations of concern for production and concern for people. Five leadership styles
were identified:

- **1,1**— Minimum concern for both production and people, exer-
  tion of minimum effort to get required work done.

- **1,9**—Maximum concern for people, minimum concern for production. Thoughtful attention to needs of people leads to a comfortable, friendly organizational atmosphere and work tempo.

- **9,1**—Maximum concern for production, minimum concern for
  people. Efficiency in operation results from arranging the conditions of work so that human elements interfere to a minimum
  degree.

- **5,5**—Moderate concern for both production and people. Adequate organizational performance is possible by balancing the
  necessity to finish work while maintaining satisfactory morale.

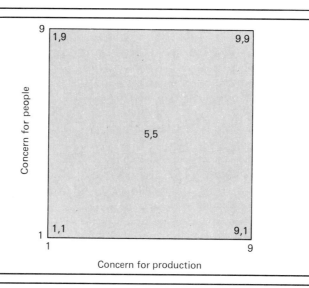

Figure 7.2 The Managerial Grid.

- ■ **9,9**—Maximum concern for both production and people. Work is accomplished by committed people; interdependence through a "common stake" in organizational purpose leads to relationships of trust and respect.

Blake and Mouton argue that 9,9 is the best leadership style. They feel that leaders should have a maximum concern for both people and production if they are to be effective. According to this view, concern for production results in attention to output factors and concern for people assures attention to human factors.

A more recent view of leadership has been developed by Paul Hersey and Kenneth Blanchard.[3] Hersey and Blanchard view leadership styles by examining two dimensions: task behavior and relationship behavior. **Task behaviors** are actions taken by the leader to organize and define the jobs and activities of subordinates. Task behaviors include explaining what people are to do, how they are to do it, and when they are to do it, as well as following up to make sure they progress satisfactorily. **Relationship behaviors** are actions taken by the leader to recognize people for good work (reinforcement), open channels of communication, provide emotional support, and involve workers in job decisions.

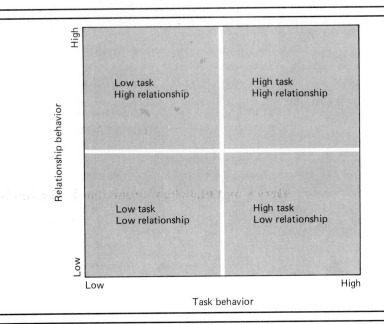

Figure 7.3   Leadership styles identified by
Hersey and Blanchard.

Depending on the level of task and relationship behavior a leader uses, Hersey and Blanchard have identified four separate styles of leadership. As shown in Fig. 7.3, these include:

- **Style 1—High task and low relationship.** The leader uses an above-average amount of task behavior and a below-average amount of relationship behavior. The leader tells followers when, how, and what they are to do. Followers provide little, if any, input.

- **Style 2—High task and high relationship.** The leader uses an above-average amount of both task and relationship behavior. The leader makes decisions, but then discusses them with the followers. There is two-way communication between leader and followers. The followers may influence the leader to alter plans and actions.

- **Style 3—High relationship and low task.** The leader uses an above-average amount of relationship behavior and a below-average amount of task behavior. The leader and followers discuss ideas and problems and make decisions together. The leader does not structure decisions; they are as much a product of the followers' ideas as of the ideas of the leader.

- Style 4—**Low relationship and low task.** The leader uses a below-average amount of both relationship and task behavior. Decisions are delegated to the followers. They independently decide when, what, how, and where, with little input from the leader. The leader provides help and assistance as requested by the followers.

Hersey and Blanchard argue that leadership is situational. The leadership style that will be effective depends on the situation in which the leader is functioning.

As the preceeding discussion indicates, there is some disagreement over which leadership style or styles are most effective. Some authors, such as Blake and Mouton, argue that there is one best leadership style. They believe that leaders should use one particular style, regardless of the situation. Others such as Hersey and Blanchard theorize that leaders should modify their style to fit the demands of the situation. They argue that a leader should not use the same style at all times.

Research on leadership seems to support the argument that leadership is situational. Numerous studies identify different styles as being effective in different situations. Based on their experiences most supervisors tend to agree with this conclusion. They indicate they do not approach all workers in the same way at all times. When supervising workers performing different jobs or working in different organizations, they function accordingly.

Supervisory leadership styles

If there is no one best way to lead in all situations, how can you determine which style to choose? Few supervisors approach all people and situations the same way. Rather, they tend to ask themselves, "How should I handle this situation? How can I best treat my workers so they will expend effort to do a good job?" Planning how you will work with your people is just as important as planning the use of money, equipment, and materials.

There are three steps to selecting a supervisory leadership style. These include:

1. Analyzing the situation;
2. Choosing the leadership style that best meets the needs of the situation;
3. Reviewing results to determine whether or not the leadership style is working. If not, reanalyze the situation and, in light of the additional information, modify your style.

Gathering the information gained from previous studies of leadership, we can identify four basic leadership styles: (1) directing, (2) consulting, (3) participating, and (4) delegating. These leadership styles range from **supervisor-centered styles** (directing) to **worker-centered styles** (delegating).

Directing

When using a **directing style,** you closely structure the activities of your workers. You set goals, tell workers what to do, and how and when to do it. You may or may not tell them why. Your instructions to workers are very clearly stated and are often quite detailed. When you are using a directing style you are exercising very close supervision. You carefully observe workers to make certain they are performing the job as you have directed. If they are not, you take corrective action.

The directing strategy is very similar to what is often called autocratic supervision. Autocratic supervision, however, involves forcing or threatening workers. Under a directing style you are just giving workers specific instruction and using very close supervision.

Consulting

When using the **consulting style** you obtain more input from workers. You ask them for their ideas and opinions and give them a chance to express their feelings about how things should be done. While you consider their ideas, you still make the decision. You will provide clear instructions regarding the work to be done. However, a consulting style requires that you also explain why. You attempt to persuade, or sell, your workers on the proposed course of action.

Thus, the consulting style differs from the directing style in two important ways: (1) you are attempting to get and use the workers' ideas and opinions, and (2) you are attempting to persuade workers to agree with the instructions you give them. The consulting style is similar to the directing style in that you still decide and provide final instructions.

Participating

Workers have considerably greater influence in the **participating style.** You share decisions with your workers; you discuss problems with your workers. Together you decide what is to be done and how and when it is to be done. You express your ideas and opinions and your workers express theirs. Together, you attempt to decide on a course of action acceptable to everyone. This process is sometimes difficult and time consuming. Not everyone will always agree on a single course of action. Your role is to attempt to minimize differences and get a commitment from the workers before taking action.

Delegating

In the **delegating style,** you give a worker, or group of workers, the authority to make a decision or determine a course of action. Within the limits of the authority you give them, they structure their own activities. The workers have the freedom to determine how they will approach an activity, when they will do the work, and in some cases, even what they will do. They may consult with you, but you are not directly involved in making the decision.

This is sometimes called laissez-faire or free-rein leadership. These terms are often interpreted to mean that the leader is not "leading." This is not true. Sometimes you may let workers decide only how a task will be performed. You indicate what needs to be done and when it must be accomplished, but let them decide how to accomplish it as they see fit. You are still responsible for the activities of your workers. Even though you have delegated authority to them, you should still agree with their chosen course of action. You must still check on their activities. So, the workers make decisions, check with you to be sure they are acceptable, and then carry them out.

Situational factors

Which of these styles should you use? There is no one answer to this question. You will not use the same style all the time. Instead, you need to analyze the particular situation, consider a number of factors, and then determine which style is most appropriate. Among the factors you should consider are: (1) the nature of your workers, (2) the amount of time available, (3) what is to be accomplished, and (4) the expectations of your boss.

The nature of your workers

The nature of your workers is one of the most important factors for you to consider. They are the individuals you are attempting to influence. You are expecting them to accomplish a task or perform a job. Thus the way they react to your leadership style is very important. How can you determine how they will react to your style? Hersey and Blanchard have suggested two factors to consider:[4]

- The ability level of the worker.
- The motivation level of the worker.

Ability and motivation need to be considered relative to the specific job. A worker may have the ability to do one job but not a different one. Likewise, a worker may be very motivated to perform one job and turned off by another job.

When analyzing the worker in order to select a leadership style, you should first consider what you want the worker(s) to accomplish and then ask yourself the following two questions:

- Is the worker able to perform the task on his or her own initiative?
- Is the worker willing to be responsible (motivated) for performing the task?

If your workers are very able *and* very motivated to perform the job, you can give them a considerable amount of freedom. You can use a participating style or a delegating style, since your workers have the necessary abilities. In some cases they may even know more about the job than you do. You will not need to spend much time giving them instructions. Also, you will not need to check to be sure workers are doing their jobs because you know they are willing to take the responsibility and carry out their tasks. Thus, you can allow them to participate in determining what is to be done and how it will be done. Or you can agree on what must be accomplished and delegate the job to them.

You need to be much more involved if your workers are not capable or motivated to do the job. If your workers lack the ability to perform a specific task, you have to provide more direction. You must devote considerable time to telling them what to do and explaining how they are to perform the task. You need to supervise these workers closely, giving them clear and fairly detailed instructions. If your workers are unwilling to accept responsibility for a job, you also have to exercise fairly close supervision. You need to provide clear instructions, follow up carefully to be sure the job is being done properly, and take corrective action if necessary. Thus, if your workers lack the ability or the motivation to perform a particular task, you need to use either a directing style or a consulting style.

The amount of time available

When ample time is available, any of the supervisory leadership styles may be used. This is not always the case, however. In some situations little time is available to accomplish a task. These situations might include emergencies or tight deadlines.

When very limited time is available, the leadership styles you can use are also limited. The participating style requires a considerable amount of time for discussion with all concerned, as an attempt is made to get everyone to agree on a course of action. As a result, when time pressures are tight, you would have difficulty using a participating style.

It is also unlikely you would use a consulting style when time is limited. While it doesn't require as much time as a participating style, it does take time to consult with workers and get their ideas and opinions before you decide how to approach the task.

You would generally use a directing style when there are time pressures. In some cases, however, you might use a delegating style. If a task requires one worker or a small group of workers, and if you have workers who are very capable and motivated to perform the task, you might delegate and let them handle it on their own. However, you still would keep in close contact to be certain that the task is accomplished promptly.

What you want to accomplish

It is unclear how the job your workers perform affects which supervisory leadership style you should use. The general assumption has been that if the job to be performed is complex and requires creativity, a participating or delegating style would be most effective. These styles allow considerable discussion regarding the job and use the workers' talents to the fullest extent.

You need to be cautious, however. A participating or delegating style will work in this situation only if you have the right workers. The workers must have the ability to handle complex jobs, and they must be highly motivated. If your workers are somewhat underqualified you need to use a more supervisor-centered style.

Similarly, it is often suggested that you need to use a directing or consulting style when jobs are highly specialized and very routine. This strategy assumes, however, that workers will not perform these jobs adequately without close supervision. This is not always the case. While some workers dislike routine jobs, others are quite happy working at a regular pace and produce acceptable work. In this latter instance, you would be better off using a delegating style, letting them do their work and checking with them now and then to make certain no problems arise.

As you can see, you cannot look at the nature of the job alone. As we indicated earlier, you need to consider your workers at the same time. The important factor is the "fit" between the worker and the job.

Your boss's expectations

Your boss's expectations and the styles he or she uses to lead you also influence the style you can use. If your boss is very directive, you may have trouble giving freedom to your workers. If you are given specific instructions regarding what to do and how it is to be done, you may have little choice but to pass along those specific instructions to your workers. If your boss expects you to have detailed information regarding the activities of your unit, you may have to supervise closely so that you can be up-to-date at all times on those activities.

Your boss may also encourage other styles. For example, a number of organizations encourage participation. As we discussed in

Chapter 2, some organizations are implementing Quality of Work Life programs and quality circles in an attempt to improve productivity.

These programs are consistent with a participating leadership style. If your organization is involved in such efforts, you will be expected to use participating leadership.

In summary, the supervisory leadership style that will be most effective depends on your situation. You should use a more supervisor-centered style (directing or consulting) if:

■ Your workers lack the ability to perform a specific task.

■ Your workers lack the motivation to perform a specific task.

■ Time to accomplish the task is limited.

■ Your boss uses or expects a supervisor-centered style.

You should use a more worker-centered style (participating or delegating) if:

■ Your workers have *both* the ability and motivation to perform a specific task.

■ Sufficient time is available.

■ It is consistent with your boss's expectations.

DEVELOP SUBORDINATES

Power and supervisory leadership

"It is one thing to lead, it is another to get people to follow." This anonymous quote reflects a realistic concern shared by many supervisors. As we indicated earlier, leadership is the process of influencing the activities of workers in their efforts to perform their jobs. Why do workers accept the supervisors influence? The answer is because their supervisors have power.

Power is a term that often has a negative connotation. Some people believe that power is bad. In their view, "power corrupts and absolute power corrupts absolutely." Their criticisms, however, are not directed to power as such but to the way it is used.

Power refers to a supervisor's influence potential. It stems from all the resources a supervisor has available for influencing workers. A number of different sources of power are available to supervisors.

- **Coercive Power.** This power is based on the workers' fear that, if they do not conform to what the supervisor expects of them, they will be punished in some way.
- **Connection Power.** This is power based on the "connections" the supervisor has, enabling him or her to obtain rewards for workers.
- **Expert Power.** This power comes from the respect workers have for the knowledge, skills, and ability of the supervisor.
- **Information Power.** This power stems from the supervisor who has information, or has access to information, that is valuable to workers.
- **Legitimate Power.** This is power based on the supervisor's position in the organization and the formal authority asociated with that position.
- **Referent Power.** This is charismatic power based on the personal traits of the supervisor. This includes the extent to which workers like and want to be liked by the supervisor.
- **Reward Power.** This power is based on workers' feelings that the supervisor is able to provide rewards, either tangible or intangible, that are meaningful to them.

Some people have expressed considerable concern that the supervisor's power has been eroded. They argue that the following factors have served to decrease a supervisor's power to direct workers.

- Government laws and regulations govern the treatment of workers in many areas. Equal employment laws and safety regulations stemming from the Occupational Safety and Health Act are examples.
- Labor contracts generally specify discipline procedures that limit the use of coercive power by the supervisor. They set wages and conditions of work which also limit the reward power of the supervisor.
- Organization policies and procedures often govern the actions of both supervisors and workers. They often limit the supervisor's authority and ability to reward and punish workers.

While limitations to the power a supervisor has do exist, the picture is not necessarily bleak. The sources of power that are generally limited are coercive power, legitimate power, and to some extent, reward power. There are other sources of power, however, and you can work to increase your power in these areas. For example:

- **Connection Power.** You can work to develop better connections with people in the organization. As we discussed in Chapter 3, this is a part of organizational politics. To build this source of power, you must use your connections to benefit your workers as well as yourself.

- **Expert Power.** You can make certain you keep up-to-date on the technical aspects of your workers' jobs so you can provide direction and advice to your workers when they have work-related problems. You can also continue to improve your supervisory skills through personal development and training.

- **Information Power.** Be sure you keep up-to-date on all information relative to the organization. If a worker asks a question, know where to get the answer as soon as possible. Communicate information effectively. Share all the information you can with your workers and share it as soon as you can. Be a person who is "in the know."

- **Referent Power.** You can't change your personality but you can be friendly with your workers. Walk around and chat with them. Make certain you get to know them as individuals and reflect a genuine concern for them in your behavior.

- **Reward Power.** You may not be able to expand your tangible reward power, but you can expand the use of intangible rewards. When someone does a good job, let them know that you are aware of it and show your appreciation. Getting recognition for doing a good job is important to most people, and it's very easy for you to give them such feedback.

A final word about power: use it. Power grows when you use it and withers from disuse. Be sure that you provide assistance when workers request it, you share information with your workers, and you offer rewards whenever possible.

The supervisor as a leader

Thus far we have discussed supervisory power. But, we have left out one very important factor—you! As a supervisor, your background, experience, and personality influence your use of the different styles. In particular three factors affect the styles you can choose.

- **Your value system.** Do you feel that workers should have input in decision making whenever possible or that you (the boss) are paid to assume responsibility and therefore should assume the burden of decision making? In what order of importance do you rank factors like company profits, personal growth of your workers, and organizational efficiency?

- **Your confidence in your workers and your confidence in uncertain situations.** Supervisors vary greatly in the amount of trust they have in other people. This attitude affects the leadership styles they use with their workers. Supervisors also vary in their tolerance for ambiguity. If you use a delegating or even a participating style, you are relinquishing a certain degree of control. The situation becomes less predictable. If you have strong needs for predictability and stability and find loosening up difficult, you will have problems using worker-centered styles (participating and delegating).

- **Your flexibility.** Various situations call for different leadership styles. However, you may feel more comfortable and function more effectively as a task-oriented leader. You may be a problem-solver by nature and inclined to be directive. On the other hand, you may be a team operator. You may thrive on sharing ideas and stimulating give and take among your workers.

Different situations require different styles. You need to be flexible. If you have trouble being flexible, you have two alternatives:

1. You can attempt to become more flexible through some type of training or self-development.

2. You can attempt to work in a job setting where the situational factors match your tendencies.

Summary

☐ Supervisors must be effective leaders. Leadership is the process of influencing the activities of individuals or groups toward goal accomplishment. You are leading whenever you attempt to influence your workers while they perform their jobs.

☐ Effective supervisory leadership is determined by two factors: output factors and human factors. An effective leader has a positive impact on both.

☐ Early studies of leadership reviewed personal characteristics of leaders. When no characteristics distinguishing effective leaders from ineffective leaders were found, the focus shifted to studying how effective leaders behave.

☐ The Ohio State studies identified two independent leadership behaviors: initiating structure and consideration. Four styles of leadership, each involving these two behaviors to varying degrees, were developed. After twenty years of studying leaders, these researchers had to conclude each style could be effective or ineffective.

☐ Blake and Mouton's Managerial Grid is based on various combinations of concern for production and concern for people. It identifies five leadership styles. Blake and Mouton suggest 9,9 (maximum concern for production and people) is the best style.

☐ Hersey and Blanchard define four leadership styles in terms of two dimensions: task behavior and relationship behavior. They argue that the effective leadership style depends on the situation.

☐ Research supports the argument that leadership is situational. Supervisors must approach situations and workers in different ways. Supervisors can determine which style to use by following three steps: (1) analyze the situation, (2) choose the style that best meets the needs of the situation, and (3) review results to determine if your approach is working. If it is not, modify your approach.

☐ Previous work on leadership has identified four basic leadership styles: directing, consulting, participating, and delegating

☐ Deciding which style is appropriate requires analyzing the situation. Factors to consider are (1) the nature of your workers, (2) amount of time available, (3) goals to be accomplished, and (4) the expectations of your boss.

☐ Most supervisor-centered styles are appropriate when the situation involves workers who lack the ability and/or motivation to perform the task, limited time to accomplish the task, and a boss who expects you to use supervisor-centered leadership. Work-centered styles are appropriate in situations where workers have the ability and motivation to perform the task, sufficient time is available, and these styles are consistent with your boss's expectations.

☐ Workers accept a supervisor's influence because the supervisor has power. Power is the supervisor's influence potential and arises from a number of sources. A supervisor's coercive, legitimate, and reward powers are generally limited. Supervisors can, however, increase their connection, expert, information, and referent powers. Reward power as related to intangible rewards can also be enhanced.

☐ Characteristics of supervisors themselves also affect the way they lead their workers. Their values, need for security in uncertain situations, and flexibility will influence which styles they will be comfortable using.

Questions for review and discussion

1. How can you determine whether or not a supervisor is an effective leader?

2. Discuss the Ohio State studies. What leadership styles were identified? Which one(s) was most effective?

3. What is the Managerial Grid? What leadership styles were identified by the Grid? Which was found to be most effective?

4. How did Hersey and Blanchard approach leadership behavior? What do they argue is the most effective leadership style?

✗5. Describe directing, consulting, participating, and delegating leadership styles. *about multi choice*

6. What factors must be considered when analyzing the leadership situation? How does each influence the appropriate leadership style?

✗7. What are the sources and types of power? Which ones can supervisors control? Why is power necessary for effective leadership?

8. How do your personal characteristics affect the leadership styles you can effectively use?

Key terms

Coercive power	Managerial Grid
Connection power	Ohio State studies
Consideration	Output factors
Consulting style	Participating style
Delegating style	Power
Directing style	Referent power
Expert power	Relationship behaviors
Human factors	Reward power
Information power	Supervisor-centered styles
Initiating structure	Task behaviors
Leadership	Worker-centered styles
Legitimate power	

Cases for discussion and practical exercises

1. You are a new supervisor working in a small department store. Your staff includes three sales clerks. All have a minimum of ten years working experience. Cooperation among the sales clerks has been decreasing. Recently, sales in your department have been declining and you have noticed that the sales clerks are slow about waiting on customers.

    Which of the following four actions best describes the way you would approach the situation? Why?

    a) Leave the sales clerks alone.

    b) Discuss the situation with the sales clerks and then initiate necessary changes.

    c) Take steps to direct the sales clerks toward maintaining good relations with customers and high levels of sales.

    d) Work with the sales clerks to determine how better performance can be obtained.

2. You have been promoted from supervisor to general supervisor. The previous general supervisor was usually uninvolved in the daily activities of the subordinate supervisors. However, if requested by a supervisor, she would readily visit any area. The supervisors have run their own departments adequately. Interrelationships among the supervisors are good.

    Which of the following four actions best describes the way you would approach the situation? Why?

    a) Let the supervisors direct their own activities.

    b) Make yourself available for discussion without pushing.

    c) Clarify your feelings about productivity and do all you can to help goal achievement.

    d) Redefine goals and supervise closely.

3. Think back over your work experience. Identify the supervisor you feel was the most effective leader with whom you have worked. Describe the types of workers he or she supervised and any other important situational factors. Why was the supervisor effective? Identify the least effective supervisor you have worked with and perform the same analysis. Compare the two supervisors and decide why one succeeded while the other failed.

Notes

1. Ralph Stogdill and Alvin E. Coons, eds., *Leader Behavior: Its Description and Measurement*, Research Monograph No. 88 (Columbus, Ohio: Bureau of Business Research, Ohio State University, 1957).
2. Robert R. Blake and Jane S. Mouton, *The Managerial Grid* (Houston, Texas: Gulf Publishing, 1964).
3. Paul Hersey and Kenneth H. Blanchard, *Management of Organizational Behavior*, 3rd ed. (Englewood Cliffs, New Jersey: Prentice-Hall, 1977).
4. Ibid.

8

Developing positive discipline

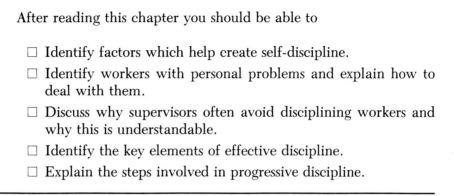

Objectives

After reading this chapter you should be able to

☐ Identify factors which help create self-discipline.

☐ Identify workers with personal problems and explain how to deal with them.

☐ Discuss why supervisors often avoid disciplining workers and why this is understandable.

☐ Identify the key elements of effective discipline.

☐ Explain the steps involved in progressive discipline.

Discipline is a topic that many supervisors would like to ignore. It cannot and should not be ignored, however, because it is an integral part of every supervisor's job. Moreover, discipline need not be viewed in strictly negative terms, as is often the case. Typically, when people hear the word discipline, they are inclined to think of the use of authority or force. However the best discipline—self-discipline—comes from within.

In this chapter we will discuss self-discipline, focusing on what supervisors can do to encourage it. To be realistic, however, we must recognize that some workers will not exhibit self-discipline. For a variety of reasons, rules will be broken and conflict will arise. Accordingly, this chapter will also discuss personal problems affecting job performance and guidelines for effectively administering discipline.

Self-discipline

Self-discipline arises from a natural tendency on the part of most employees to meet reasonable standards of acceptable behavior on the job. Employees who know what is expected and view the organization's rules as reasonable will usually observe them. They are likely to come to work on time, generally follow their supervisor's instructions, and refrain from stealing, fighting, or drinking on the job. In short, most people in an organization tend to obey most of the rules most of the time. If they didn't do so, the supervisor's job would be intolerable. Supervisors would spend three-fourths of their time and energy spotting and correcting unacceptable behavior.

Employees don't exhibit self-discipline spontaneously, however. As a supervisor you cannot just assume that the natural good will and positive moral character of most employees will automatically produce self-discipline. While most employees will "meet you half way," you have to devote effort to building a self-disciplined work group. How can you do this? First, as discussed in Chapter 6, you can create a positive motivational climate in your unit. Employees who see that they can achieve goals that are important to them, while in the process of achieving the organization's goals too, are more likely to exhibit self-discipline.

Our discussion of work groups in Chapter 3 is also relevant here. Cohesive groups with positive norms represent the essence of self-discipline. A cohesive group with positive norms will exert considerable group pressure on possible dissenters, thus establishing self-discipline on the part of group members.

Effective communication, as presented in Chapter 5, is also vital to establishing and maintaining self-discipline. Employees need to know what is expected of them before, not after, they have made a mistake or violated a rule. Also, when new rules are introduced, supervisors must be certain to convince employees of the purpose and reasons for the rules.

Finally, supervisors cannot expect employees to practice self-discipline unless it starts at the top of the organization and continues down through management and supervisory ranks. If employees are expected to be on time, dress and behave in an appropriate manner, and observe safety and other rules, supervisors should comply with these requirements too. Employees cannot be expected to exhibit self-discipline if supervisors do not set a proper example.

When discipline is necessary

As we have said, most employees tend to exhibit a considerable degree of self-discipline. Unfortunately, every supervisor eventually will encounter employees who will fail to observe the established rules and standards or will behave in an unacceptable manner. For one reason or another, these employees simply will not accept the responsibility of self-discipline. In response, supervisors cannot afford to ignore workers' behavior. Some type of action is necessary to correct the situation. If left unchecked, the generally accepted norms of responsible employee behavior will be undermined.

In the course of their work experience most supervisors are likely to encounter a variety of behaviors requiring disciplinary action. Those most frequently encountered include:

- Breaking rules concerning rest periods and other time schedules;
- Violations of safety standards;
- Excessive tardiness or absenteeism, especially around weekends or holidays;
- Shoddy workmanship or abuse of equipment, supplies, or raw materials;
- Argumentative, uncooperative, or aggressive behavior toward co-workers, which negatively affects the quality and/or quantity of work produced;
- Open insubordination, such as the refusal of an employee to carry out clear and legitimate work assignments.

To complicate matters, many on-the-job problems stem from personal problems faced by workers off the job. Alcohol abuse, for example, has created problems for supervisors for years. Increased availability and usage of drugs in the last ten years has given rise to yet another set of problems. Whatever their source, when an employee's off-the-job conduct has an impact on performance on the job, you must be prepared to take action.

While we are most familiar with uncooperative workers who are persistent rule-breakers, problems arising from alcoholism, drugs, and other emotional stress may be more difficult to detect. Further, these workers should be handled differently from uncooperative, persistent rule-breakers.

Personal problems affecting job performance

Workers are human beings and bring to work the same problems that trouble them away from the job. Since these problems can have a significant impact on job performance, they are of great concern to supervisors.

It has been estimated that at least 10% of all workers experience personal problems that have measurable effects on their job performance.[1] These problems include (1) emotional stress resulting from family, marital, financial, health, and legal problems, (2) alcoholism, and (3) drug abuse. In the past, organizations disciplined workers whose performance was hindered by personal problems just like they disciplined rule-breakers. Today, the trend is to counsel these workers and attempt to help them resolve their problems before disciplinary action is invoked.

Counseling workers

Counseling troubled workers is an important supervisory function. Some organizations provide formal counseling programs in which supervisors play a critical role. Where such services do not exist, supervisors must provide assistance on their own.

The objective of **counseling** is to provide troubled workers with a way to solve the problems affecting their job performance before more drastic action is taken. It is intended to help workers help themselves. Counseling involves:

1. Identifying the problems troubling the employee;
2. Taking action to resolve the problems;
3. Following up to see that the problem is solved.

Identifying problems

A number of indicators can alert supervisors to the existence of personal problems which may affect a worker's performance. They include: (1) sudden decreases in quantity and quality of work, (2) sudden personality changes, (3) increased errors or accidents, (4) erratic work performance, (5) excessive absenteeism or tardiness, (6) unexplained absences from work, (7) leaving early, and (8) listlessness, irritability, and irresponsibility. There are a wide variety of specific personal problems. Three problems, however, are relatively widespread and will be discussed in more detail. They are alcoholism, drug abuse, and emotional stress.

Detecting alcoholism Alcoholism is a disease suffered by approximately 5% of the total work force. However, studies have revealed that over half of all workers with performance problems suffer from alcoholism.[2] It is estimated that alcoholic workers cost American industry over $25 billion a year. As a result, performance problems resulting from alcohol abuse cannot be ignored.

Alcoholics are not as easily detected as we once thought they were. Jack Halloran has described the stages alcoholics pass through in terms of their work behavior. These stages are presented in Table 8.1.

Table 8.1

Stages of alcoholism at work

STAGE A	STAGE B	STAGE C	STAGE D
Work performance is inconsistent: sometimes excellent and other times really poor. Worker behavior is inconsistent: sometimes nervous, irritable; avoids supervisor; sometimes arrives at work late, often leaves early, and often takes long lunches. Worker may show signs of economic and family problems.	Worker seems fine in the morning but often doesn't return after lunch. Unreported absences or calling in sick increase. Worker may arrive at work with a hangover, bloodshot eyes, or may seem unusually depressed and untalkative.	Worker is arrested or hospitalized for drinking. Evidence of drinking on the job surfaces. When confronted with problem, worker promises to quit drinking but doesn't.	Worker is fired for drinking problem and loses self-respect.

Source: Adapted from Jack Halloran, *Applied Human Relations* (Englewood Cliffs, N.J.: Prentice-Hall, Inc., 1978.)

Supervisors should be on the watch for behaviors described in Table 8.1, including careful observation of:

- Absences and tardiness;
- Sudden changes in quality and quantity of work;
- Physical changes: bloodshot eyes, flushed face, nervousness, irritability, slurred or sloppy speech, and the smell of alcohol;
- Changes in behavior: sudden mood changes, argumentative attitude, impaired judgment, fluctuating performance, and avoidance of supervisor.

Detecting drug abuse   The extent of **drug addiction** on the job is not really known but is probably at least as common as alcoholism. Marijuana, heroin, cocaine, barbiturate, and amphetamine usage all surface on the job. As with alcoholism, drug abuse is found throughout organizations. Drug abusers may exhibit nervousness, physical tremors, confusion, impaired judgment, as well as dangerous, aggressive behaviors, which result in poor performance.

Workers on drugs exhibit many of the same signs alcoholics do. Unfortunately, drug abusers seem to be far less easily detectable than alcoholics. That is, drug usage goes undetected for longer periods of time than does alcohol abuse.

Detecting emotional stress   Workers experiencing stressful situations tend to behave in a fairly predictable manner. Troubled people attempt to hide their problems and, as a result, behave in an exaggerated fashion. That is, in trying to act like everything is normal when it clearly is not, they become even more loud and boisterous than usual or more quiet and withdrawn.

Typically, emotionally upset people are unable to concentrate and are more likely to be upset or startled by events. They also begin to show physical signs of stress resulting from lack of sleep and food. Another indicator of an emotionally disturbed worker is a radical change in behavior. **Emotional stress** often causes people to react irrationally. They may fly off the handle over a passing comment. Or they may suddenly attack the most trivial activity with such force that co-workers are amazed.

To be able to detect these symptoms of emotional stress, supervisors must know how their workers typically behave. They must also consciously be aware of behavior deviating from the usual pattern.

Take action

When personal problems have been identified, assistance should be offered to the troubled worker. Organizations with formal counseling programs have staff specialists who handle counseling activities. In recent years, many organizations have adopted **employee-assistance programs.** These programs provide specialized services for workers which are directed at resolving any personal problems hindering job performance. While company policies differ, supervisors are responsible for identifying problems and referring workers to the counseling service.

If no internal program is available, supervisors must confront the troubled workers themselves. You need to be very cautious however, remembering that you are not an expert psychologist. Trying to play amateur psychologist can create more problems than it solves. Sympathetic listening might be helpful, but be careful in recommending actions to the disturbed worker. Your best alternative is to assist the worker in obtaining professional help available in the community. Many outside agencies provide services to troubled workers, such as Alcoholics Anonymous. Know the services available so you can help workers when the need arises.

Identifying the problem, bringing it to the worker's attention, and providing direction for assistance is not enough for counseling purposes. The consequences of continued unsatisfactory performance must be made clear to worker. While every attempt should be made to support and assist the worker in resolving the problem, the supervisor's main concern is job performance. If a worker cannot perform the job satisfactorily, action must be taken.

Follow-up

Counseling is designed to help workers help themselves before disciplinary action is taken. However, once you have talked with the worker and assistance has been made available, you must continue to observe his or her performance on the job. If the worker chooses not to seek help or does not respond to the help received, action must be taken. The fact that the worker is undergoing treatment should not influence your evaluation of his or her job performance. If performance is not improving within a reasonable time, disciplinary action should and must follow.

Administering discipline

Situations involving disciplinary action usually are not pleasant. They must be dealt with, yet many supervisors try to avoid disciplinary issues by pretending to ignore them or "passing the buck" to someone else in higher management. Why do many supervisors avoid disciplinary issues? According to Wallace Wohlking there are a variety of reasons, including:[3]

- **Lack of training.** Some supervisors lack the necessary skill and knowledge to handle discipline problems.
- **Perceived lack of support.** Many supervisors fear that higher-level management will not support disciplinary action. They are afraid that management will "pull the rug out from under them" once they have taken an unpopular or controversial stand.
- **Desire to avoid being the "heavy."** Some supervisors do not want to take disciplinary action because other supervisors in the organization seem to be avoiding it. According to this view, "No one else is disciplining employees, so why should I?"
- **Fear of lost friendship.** Supervisors may fear that a disciplinary action will damage a friendship with an employee.
- **Concern about draining away valuable time.** Discipline takes time and many supervisors feel hard-pressed for time already.
- **Fear of emotional outbursts.** Some supervisors are afraid that disciplinary action might "set off" an employee. Others are fearful that they might lose control of themselves once they start talking about a rule violation.

Trained and experienced supervisors can cope with all the factors just cited. In addition to removing these barriers and inhibitions concerning discipline, remember the positive results of disciplinary action. According to Dowling and Sayles, the supervisor who disciplines a subordinate accomplishes four things:[4]

- The supervisor strengthens the rule and expresses confidence in it by enforcement. As Dowling and Sayles put it, "Rules, like muscles, atrophy through disuse."

- The supervisor corrects the employee's breach of the rules and serves warning that rules must be followed in the future or more serious consequences will result.
- The disciplined employee's co-workers are reminded of the existence of the rule and of its seriousness and importance. In Dowling and Sayles' view:[5]

  Occasional reference to the possibility for discipline helps some people to obey the rules of the game. As one man put it, "If you can sneak nuts and bolts out of the plant in your lunch box, you start trying to take spare parts and accessories next. It's much better if you know that they are going to check your lunch box every night and you can't take out the smallest thing. Then you don't get into bad habits."

- Supervisors who take disciplinary action reassure the majority of employees who are self-disciplined. Most of us have been in a situation where we have seen a supervisor let some else "get away with murder." Whether we really wanted to break the rule or not, a bad example is promoted when a fellow employee is not disciplined for misconduct.

The key elements of effective discipline

Most organizations of any size have established disciplinary policies. These policies are often included in an employee handbook or, in unionized organizations, in a labor–management contract. No matter how well-written the discipline policy is, however, it is only as effective as its implementation. And the implementation stage is where most organizations' efforts at discipline collapse or are less than a complete success. What are the key elements of effective discipline? There is no sure-fire formula or specific set of steps. Effective **discipline,** however, generally has the following characteristics:

- The "rules of the game" should be clear to all.
- Supervisors should take a problem-solving approach to discipline, not a punitive one.
- Disciplinary action should be taken as soon as practical.
- Discipline should be impartial, consistent, and fair.

■ Disciplinary action should not be viewed as an isolated event; follow-up is important.

Let's examine each of these characteristics in more detail.

The "rules of the game" should be clear to all. As mentioned earlier, the importance of complete and accurate communication for effective discipline cannot be overstated. Just as all employees are expected to know what kind of job performance is required of them they also have a right to be informed concerning the rules which determine acceptable behavior on the job. Understandably, discipline which comes as a surprise is nearly always viewed as unfair. Consequently, you should take steps to assure that (1) disciplinary rules are communicated and clearly understood by new employees; (2) changes in rules are made clear to all, preferably both orally *and* in writing; and (3) the organization's position on the severity of any disciplinary offense should be clearly stated. Also, if an organization has been negligent in applying its rules and decides that it now intends to enforce them rigorously, employees should be given advance notice of the organization's change in policies.

Supervisors should take a problem-solving approach to discipline, not a punitive one. The fundamental idea here is that discipline should not be used as a substitute for effective supervision. The first step in approaching what seem to be employee-caused difficulties should be problem solving. This means, for example, that if an employee has trouble getting to work on time, your first response should not be an oral reprimand or any specific disciplinary action. Instead, using the problem-solving approach, you need to explore the reasons for tardiness and help the employee develop a plan for eliminating it. If the tardiness stems from difficult transportation, you may be able to identify an alternative mode of transportation which will remedy the problem. Or if the problem is lack of reliable child care, you may be able to suggest a reputable babysitter or nursery.

Using the problem-solving approach, you do not merely react to an employee's behavior problem with disciplinary action. Instead, you attempt to understand the cause of the behavior problem first and, along with the employee, identify a workable means for dealing with it. A problem-solving approach does not restrain you from expressing concern over an employee's unacceptable behavior. In some cases, a problem-solving effort may be part of a warning discussion. In other cases, however, you may want to approach the problem in a counseling format initially without tying it in any way to a disciplinary action.

While problem-solving efforts can and have eliminated or significantly minimized employee behavior problems, they do not always work. If they do not, disciplinary action is necessary.

Remember that the primary purpose of an organization's disciplinary policy is to prevent future problems, not to get revenge for employee wrongs which have already been committed. All organizations are concerned with accomplishing work and providing goods and/or services, not the moral rehabilitation of employees. Therefore, discipline should focus on preventing the reoccurrence of problems as well as preventing new ones from arising, not on administering punishment.

Disciplinary action should be taken as soon as practical. A supervisor should not delay disciplinary action. Generally, the longer the delay between an infraction of the rules and the supervisor's action, the greater the resentment of the employee. During the delay the worker rationalizes and justifies the behavior. The need for promptness, however, must be tempered by two important concerns.

First, gathering adequate facts about the alleged offense takes time. In addition to collecting information to determine whether the employee misbehaved and why, you should document the offense and the facts surrounding it. This preparation may take some time, but is usually well worth it, especially in cases where a supervisor's disciplinary actions may be challenged by a union, for example. In these situations, authorities recommend that supervisors investigate the circumstances of an alleged offense thoroughly. The employee should be told the nature of the offense and interviewed by the supervisor and one other manager (usually the personnel director). These people should obtain the employee's version of the circumstances surrounding the alleged offense. They should ask the reasons for the employee's actions and the names of others whom the employee feels will be supportive. The company's decision concerning discipline should take no longer than 72 hours to reach. An employee whose position is found to be valid should be put back to work and paid for the time off. The employee should understand this in advance, but should also be told that if the company disagrees with actions in question, appropriate discipline will be imposed.

The second concern is the need to consider emotions. Obviously, when tempers are heated a brief cooling-off period is necessary. Emotions frequently can cloud the judgment of one or both parties. A hasty reaction in an emotionally-charged situation may provoke abusive or even aggressive and violent behavior on the part of the employee, a situation which in its extreme has even resulted in loss of life.

Disciplinary action should be impartial, consistent, and fair.   The surest way to undermine the effectiveness of dicipline is to discipline some employees but not others. It is an understandable and perfectly normal instinct to be more lenient with some employees, particularly those who are good and reliable workers. However, employees quickly spot inequities in the handling of disciplinary matters. If friendship is seen as the cause of favoritism, the employees' resentment will be particularly strong. For example, many supervisors know of good workers who are allowed more leeway in being late, for example, than average workers. This leniency is often viewed as unfair by other employees who suspect that there are two sets of rules, one for favorites and one for everyone else.

In addition to being impartial, discipline should be consistent, not only within a particular unit, but across units of the organization as well. Discipline in a unit may be consistently administered, but if it is handled differently in another department, the grapevine soon spreads the word. Lack of consistency across units in approaching discipline problems is a particularly thorny problem for the individual supervisor. It requires great tact and diplomacy, but is a problem that cannot be ignored.

Disciplinary actions should also be fair. Put simply, the punishment should fit the crime. The severity of discipline must bear a reasonable relationship to the nature of the employee's offense and work record. A minor violation does not justify imposing severe disciplinary penalties unless the employee has committed the same violation several or many times in the past.

While the employee's work record provides valuable information for determining the severity of disciplinary action, it should never be used to determine whether the employee is likely to have committed a recent infraction. In the interest of fairness the work record should only be used as background information in determining the severity of discipline, once it is determined that the employee actually did commit the violation.

Maintaining fairness does not mean, however, that each employee should be subject to exactly the same penalties for identical violations. Wallace Wohlking has illustrated this in the following example:[6]

If a maintenance worker arrives late several times a month, he or she is likely to receive one or more oral warnings. If another worker who has the responsibility for opening the work premises, arrives late the same number of times in the same period, the disciplinary actions might be more severe—possibly one oral warning followed by one or more written warnings. This is because the actions of the second worker will cause others lost work time since these employees are unable to go to their work places. In other words, differences in job responsibilities and failure to execute these responsibilites can lead to differences in response by management to rule infractions.

Discipline should not be viewed as an isolated event; follow-up is important. When a minor disciplinary problem prompting an oral warning has occurred, follow-up action is not always necessary. However, if a pattern of problems emerges—say repeated absenteeism or tardiness—you should inform the employee that a discussion will be conducted in the near future to determine progress on the problem. This also tends to motivate the employee to avoid committing the violation again. When the review discussion is held, if progress has been made and the problem has been remedied, the employee can be commended for improved behavior. If the problem persists, the discussion can be used to explore the difficulty further, and you can consider more severe disciplinary measures.

Taking disciplinary action

Let's look now at the mechanics of taking disciplinary action. No specific set of steps is used in all situations. However certain guidelines can be established. Disciplinary actions should be taken in private whenever possible. Public disciplinary actions, such as reprimands, are likely to create resentment on the part of the employee. Public disciplinary actions can also lead to other complications. If the disciplined employee's co-workers view a disciplinary action as too harsh for the violation, the disciplined employee is likely to emerge as a martyr. At the very least, public disciplinary actions are subject to second guessing by every employee in the unit. Even worse, if the disciplined employee is humiliated in public, great damage to the morale of everybody in the unit can occur. These and other factors have given rise to the maxim, "discipline in private, praise in public."

One important exception to this general rule are situations where a supervisor's authority is challenged directly and publicly by a worker. If an employee is drunk or fighting on the job or in cases of clear and blatant insubordination, you may have to take disciplinary action quickly and publicly in order to regain control. Failure to act decisively may cause other employees to lose respect for you. Fortunately, such situations are relatively rare.

Progressive discipline

Progressive discipline is a problem-solving approach which calls for instituting penalties appropriate to the violations (or accumulated violations). The steps typically used in progressive discipline are discussed in the following sections. They are not the only steps that might be used, nor are they necessarily the best for every type of organization or situation. They are, however, representative of the progressive disciplinary steps adopted by many companies. The steps include:

1. Informal talk
2. Oral warning
3. Written warning
4. Disciplinary layoff
5. Demotion
6. Discharge

Informal talk   If the violation is relatively minor and if the employee's work record reflects no previous disciplinary problems, an informal talk will resolve most issues. During this discussion you should attempt to discover the causes for the employee's behavior problem. At the same time the employee's basic worth and previous good work record should be acknowledged. Usually the informal talk will resolve minor problems. If such an approach is unsuccessful, or if the violation is not minor, the oral warning is necessary.

Oral warning The **oral warning** should be viewed as a dialog or discussion, not a speech or an opportunity to "chew out" or "read the riot act" to the employee. You should encourage the employee to relate his or her view of the problem. Employees should be urged to provide a reasonably concise statement of the facts as they see them. You will want to question the employee during the discussion but should avoid interrupting. During the discussion you attempt to obtain all the relevant facts and solicit the employee's views and opinions.

Once you have obtained and evaluated the facts, the employee should be informed of your decision. You should be certain to tell the employee the following:

- Expected changes in the employee's future behavior;
- Any assistance that you intend to give the employee in correcting the problem;
- An indication of further official disciplinary action that will be taken if there is no improvement;
- Follow-up action that will be taken and a timetable for the action.

The tone and atmosphere you set for the oral warning often play a big role in determining its results. Handled properly, most employees will recognize the error of their ways and improve. A poorly handled oral warning, however, may produce a sullen, uncooperative employee and lay the groundwork for future problems. Anger, sarcasm, and personal judgments about the employee's character should be avoided at all costs. The emphasis should be kept on the employee's behavior, not on the employee as a person. This does not mean, however, that you need to be lax. A firm, straightforward approach is almost always more effective in achieving the real goal of the oral warning: changing the employee's behavior so that the problem is resolved and no further action is necessary.

Depending on organizational policies, at the end of the discussion you may want to make a notation in the employee's personnel record. Among the factors noted should be the date, purpose, and results of the discussion. The employee should also be informed that such a notation is being made.

Written warning   The written warning is usually the next step in progressive discipline. It is generally preceded by a discussion similar to that in an oral warning. The main difference is that the employee is told at the conclusion of the discussion that a written warning will be issued.

According to Wallace Wohlking, several key points should be included in the **written warning:**[7]

■ A clear statement of the problem and an indication of the rule which has been violated;

■ A statement of the consequences of continued violation;

■ An indication of the employee's commitment to changed behavior (if any);

■ A statement of follow-up to be taken.

A threatening or punitive tone should be avoided in the written statement. When writing the warning you should strive for clarity so that a newly-hired supervisor could read the warning and understand the particular problem on the employee's discipline record.

Also you should request that the employee sign and return a copy of the warning memo upon its receipt. This documents that the employee has understood the warning. This signed copy may then be placed in the employee's file. Should the employee refuse to sign the warning memo, a notation to that effect may be included in the file.

Disciplinary layoff   A **disciplinary layoff** is in order if the employee has committed repeated violations and previous steps were ineffective in correcting the behavior. It may also be appropriate without such a record if a major violation has occurred. A disciplinary layoff may be used as an alternative to discharge when management believes the employee may still be salvaged. Some employees who fail to respond to a written warning may be jolted by a disciplinary layoff without pay. The enforced idleness may convince the employee that the supervisor is really serious and may restore a sense of the necessity to comply with rules and regulations.

A disciplinary layoff is normally instituted only after careful investigation and discussion with the employee. Obtaining all the facts is critical, regardless of the disciplinary action being considered.

Once a decision has been made, the circumstances and the disciplinary action taken must be documented. Disciplinary layoffs normally range from one day to several weeks. In some organizations, repeated violations call for successively longer layoff periods. After oral and written warnings an employee may be suspended for one day without pay. A subsequent similar violation may result in a suspension of three days without pay.

Demotion   **Demotion** is the next step in some progressive discipline procedures. Many supervisors have seriously questioned the value of demotion, however. The usual result of demotion is dissatisfaction and discouragement on the part of the affected employee, since loss of pay and status over a long period is a form of constant punishment. These negative attitudes may easily spread to the demoted employee's co-workers. As a result, demotion is not considered a workable step in progressive discipline in a number of organizations.

Discharge   **Discharge** is the last and, obviously, most drastic step in progressive discipline. It is instituted only for the most serious violations or for a prolonged series of violations which have not been affected by prior disciplinary action. Due to its seriousness it is an action which should be taken only when absolutely necessary. Sometimes, however, discharge may be the only realistic alternative available.

Because discharge decisions are so significant, many organizations allow only higher-level managers to make them. This is particularly true in many unionized organizations, where supervisors are allowed to suspend employees only pending further investigation. The discharge decision, if supported by the investigation, is then made. Other organizations require that any discharge initiated by a supervisor must be reviewed and approved by higher levels of management and/or by the personnel department.

Where employees are represented by a union, any discharge action is likely to be appealed to arbitration. Consequently, when a discharge action is taken as a consequence of a series of minor disciplinary violations, complete and accurate documentation is critical. A detailed record of prior oral and written warnings as well as disciplinary layoffs must be available. If the employee is being discharged for a single serious violation, the supervisor must be certain that the reason for discharge is consistent with the organization's standards for a major disciplinary violation and that this fact is well known to all concerned. Such issues are crucial should the case be pursued to arbitration. This consequence is discussed in greater depth in Chapter 15.

Summary

☐ Disciplining workers is an integral part of the supervisor's job. Most workers exhibit self-discipline. Supervisors must strive to build a self-disciplined work group.

☐ When workers behave in an unacceptable manner, corrective action must be taken. Workers whose performance is unacceptable because of personal problems should be handled differently than uncooperative, persistent rule-breakers.

☐ Workers with personal problems should be counseled in an attempt to resolve their problems before disciplinary action is taken. Several indicators identify workers with personal problems. Supervisors should be alert to these indicators so as to detect such workers as soon as possible.

☐ Over half the workers having performance problems suffer from alcoholism. Drug abuse is also widespread. Alcoholics are difficult to detect but drug addicts are even more difficult to identify. Both dependencies result in behaviors supervisors can observe. Emotionally distressed workers tend to behave in an exaggerated fashion or undergo a radical change in behavior.

☐ When supervisors detect personal problems, they should see that assistance is provided to the worker. If the organization has no formal assistance program supervisors must take action on their own. This usually involves directing troubled workers to professional help.

☐ Disciplinary action is required when troubled workers do not improve and for other workers behaving in an unacceptable manner. Although there are many reasons why supervisors avoid discipline, positive results are gained from effective discipline.

☐ Effective discipline requires: clearly stated "rules of the" game; the use of a problem-solving approach; quick, impartial, consistent, and fair actions; and follow-up. In most situations, disciplinary actions should be handled privately.

☐ Progressive discipline uses a problem-solving rather than punitive approach. It involves increasingly harsher penalties which fit the violation or accumulated violations. The steps typically included are (1) informal talk, (2) oral warning, (3) written warning, (4) disciplinary layoff, (5) demotion, and (6) discharge. At each step the supervisor attempts to help the worker improve performance or behavior. *Document action taken*

Questions for review and discussion

1. How can supervisors build a self-disciplined work group?

2. What on-the-job behaviors typically require disciplinary action?

3. How have organizations changed their dealings with workers who experience personal problems which affect their job performance?

4. How can supervisors identify workers suffering from alcoholism, drug abuse, and emotional stress?

5. What should supervisors do when they have a troubled worker in their unit?

6. Why do supervisors tend to avoid disciplining workers? What are the positive results to be gained from meeting disciplinary responsibilities?

 7. Discuss the characteristics of effective discipline.

8. When might disciplinary action be required in public? Why is it undesirable to discipline workers publicly in most cases?

9. How should each step in progressive discipline be handled?

Key terms

Alcoholism	Drug addiction
Counseling	Emotional stress
Demotion	Employee-assistance programs
Discharge	Oral warning
Disciplinary layoff	Progressive discipline
Discipline	Written warning

Cases for discussion and practical exercises

1. Tom Jackson, general construction supervisor for Small Homes Construction Company, was trying to assess a problem he was having with his lead carpenter, Gene West. Gene had worked for Tom for about five years and had always been one of his best

carpenters. Since Gene was made lead carpenter last year, Tom had relied on him to help direct the other carpenters. Gene was supposed to arrive at the construction site first each morning and, using the prints Tom provided, start the carpenters working. Gene had been very reliable and capable in his work with the carpenters until recently. Now there seemed to be a problem. Twice during the last month, Gene's wife called Tom early on Monday morning saying Gene was sick and wouldn't be coming in to work. Last week one of Tom's friends said he saw Gene, obviously very drunk, leaving the Golden Slipper late Sunday night. But today Gene really caused trouble. One of the carpenters called Tom about 10:00 A.M. to ask what they should be doing. Apparently Gene hadn't shown up for work yet and Tom hadn't received a call from either Gene or his wife. No one was at the site to get the carpenters started to work. After Tom returned from giving directions to the carpenters he sat down to decide what to do about Gene. What steps would you recommend that Tom take to handle the problem with Gene?

2. You have just returned from a meeting of supervisors called by the General Manager. The purpose of the meeting was to inform supervisors of the results of a recent study of lost time conducted by a systems analyst. The study revealed that too many work hours per year were lost because workers abused the break policy. The policy provides for two 15-minute breaks, one in the morning and one in the afternoon. However no one really paid attention to these time limits and 20 to 25 minute breaks appeared to be the norm. This resulted in 10 to 20 minutes each day during which workers were not performing their jobs but were being paid. You have been instructed to go back to your department and see that the abuse stops. How would you handle this situation?

3. Assume you are a supervisor in your community. What particular personal problems would you anticipate confronting with your workers? Which ones should you deal with directly? Which ones are beyond the scope of your responsibility and expertise? What outside resources are available in the community for helping workers with the problems identified? What services do they offer? How would you make this information available to your workers?

Notes

1. M. Jane Kay, "Employee Counseling," in Dale Yoder and Herbert Heneman (eds.), *ASPA Handbook of Personnel and Industrial Relations* (Washington D.C.: Bureau of National Affairs, 1979), Chapter 5.4, pp. 5–79.

2. *Ibid.*, pp. 5–99.

3. Wallace Wohlking, "Effective Discipline in Employee Relations, *Personnel Journal*, September 1975, p. 489.

4. William F. Dowling, Jr. and Leonard R. Sayles, *How Managers Motivate: The Imperatives of Supervision* (New York: McGraw-Hill Book Company, 1971), p. 134.

5. *Ibid.*

6. Wohlking, "Effective Discipline," p. 491.

7. *Ibid.*, p. 493.

Cases for section II

Howard Atkins and Joseph Wexler—Part 1

The Brainerd Instrument Company manufactured instruments for the aircraft and electronics industries. By 1973, the company had several sizable contracts, but the major growth during its 20 years' existence had occurred largely because of its ability to handle small orders. Also, Brainerd was able to meet new and often unique conditions for the use of its products. Indeed, one of the executives said that the company's success was due to its personnel's ability to meet new situations "with flexible thinking from the top down." The company had recently moved to a new building with room for future expansion.

The company had a small machine shop, where many of the heavier parts needed in some of its instruments were made. Although the company subcontracted more than half of this kind of work, the management was considering enlarging its own production. Currently, fourteen people worked there under the direction of a supervisor, Howard Atkins. Eight of them were skilled machinists and six unskilled. All except one had completed high school and four had one or more years of college work. An outside observer, studying supervisory and employee problems in the company, noted that among the workers, Bill, a skilled machinist, was the person most often called on for help by the other workers.

In the machine shop, work lots were small as a rule and the processing steps for different jobs varied considerably in sequence. After job orders and parts were delivered to Atkins, he assigned them to the workers according to the tasks required and the completion dates scheduled on the orders. When workers finished their jobs, they went to Atkins for others.

Howard Atkins spoke of himself as an "old-timer" among machinists. He seldom asked his superiors for equipment for the machine shop, even when it would not have been expensive. Howard knew that the company's special advantage in its field lay in the cost-conscious, but imaginative, contributions its management had made to the design and assembly of the delicate instruments it manufactured. Consequently, he preferred to work out problems which arose in the machine shop, using his own ingenuity and the existing equipment, rather than making what he considered might be costly or unreasonable demands on the company's resources. Except for the contacts required by his job, Howard did not spend much time with his workers. During breaks he usually sat alone at his desk drinking coffee, checking orders, blueprints, and time tickets. He left the shop only occasionally, to attend supervisors' meetings and talk with the superintendent to whom he reported. Also, when outsiders, usually staff engineers or accountants, came to the shop, he took care of them.

At the first meeting with the observer, Howard talked about one of the skilled machinists, Joseph Wexler. Joe was single and about 40 years old. In mentioning him, Howard called the observer's attention to several notices pinned on the wall near the entrance to the shop. Some of them described chess problems and their solution; two quoted material from a textbook on machine shop practice. The latter emphasized that carboloy cutting tools should be used for machining heat-treated and hard metals. At the bottom of these notices, printed in large letters, was the following:

WHY DON'T WE HAVE CARBOLOY TOOLS IN THIS SHOP?

In referring to Joe, Howard said, "There is one person around here who is a problem to me. That's Joe. He won the city chess championship. You may have noticed the wall with all those chess notices. Well, they were put up by Joe. He's even got some of the workers around here playing the game. He may be surly or rude to you when you speak to him. If he is, just walk away and forget about it. You may approach him on another day, and he'll be all right. You just can't tell about Joe, so don't let him bother you."

Actually, the observer found Joe friendly and eager to talk about himself. After they had been introduced and the observer had answered a few questions Joe had about her study, Joe spoke as follows.

> *JOE:*   Let me give you a problem and see if you can answer it. Perhaps you've noticed the things I put up on the bulletin board. Now, those things go up for a purpose. Right now I'm

writing a paper on inventory. Here, let me show it to you. (He stepped over to a stand near his lathe and extracted a few sheets of paper from the middle of a folded newspaper.) Here, read these and tell me what you think.

The paper was entitled "What Is an Inventory? Part I." It posed the question: "To whom does an inventory belong: the management, the stockholders, or the workers who use the inventory?"

JOE: Let me explain what I'm trying to get at. Under the present scheme, with the existing hierarchy, things have to fall into designated places, little boxes in the organizational chart, or management is unhappy and becomes suspicious. Items are ordered. This person is in charge of costs, or that person is in charge of inventory. That's the way things are organized. But here I am, a worker, who uses the machine or the materials. When I go over to a machine, I should see near it all the equipment that goes with this machine. Why should I be kept in the dark? After all, to whom is this information more important than to the person who has to work at the machine?

Or take the stockroom. In drawing out supplies, why shouldn't I know what is available? After all, I'm the one who has to use the supplies. But no, this inverts the hierarchy; it destroys the order that has been established. Even the very act of bringing my ideas to my supervisor or someone else in management can be taken only as a criticism of the way they introduce the ideas. If I do so, then it implies they are not carrying out their function. Do you see you are stuck?

That's why I take the trouble to write out these papers and post them on the bulletin board. Because once the idea is publicized, it becomes generally known, and it can't be ignored. But even then, you see, this goes counter to the system and it must be taken as an implied criticism of management and the supervision. But because it has been publicized, the idea cannot be ignored. That's the one thing that must be maintained, publicity.

Here, let me show you other things that I'm going to post on the bulletin board. (Joe reached into his newspaper and pulled out several sheets of paper. One quoted from a poem by Yeats and another from a poem by Ogden Nash.) They're beautiful, aren't they? I also put up chess problems. I post these to give people something to think about and appreciate. There's more to life than what we see here, and anything I can do to broaden horizons helps.

As you can probably see, I'm somewhat of a maverick. I'll be leaving this job soon. It's bound to happen. Just like at the ____ Company, my last job, and others. Because I introduce ideas counter to the expectations of the hierarchy about what a worker should be doing, I can't last long anywhere.

A few days later the observer saw that the notices had been removed from the wall. When she had an opportunity to talk with Joe, Bill joined them and spoke first.

BILL: Howard called me over and told me that he didn't have anything to do with the removal of your things from the bulletin board. He said the superintendent took them down, and he (Howard) wanted me to tell you that he didn't do it. (Joe shrugged and smiled.) Why don't you go over to the superintendent and ask him why he took them down?

JOE: What good would that do?

BILL: Well, go over anyway and ask him.

Later Joe went to see the superintendent; he described the conversation to the observer as follows.

JOE: I asked the superintendent why he had taken the notices from the wall. He said to me, "We can't have the walls getting cluttered up. The next thing you know, we'll be having pictures of naked women up on the wall." Can you imagine that? So what I've done is make my own bulletin board that I've put right next to my machine. I'll put my notices up here and get them publicized that way. (Joe showed the observer a crude bulletin board on a stand which he had built and placed next to the lathe on which he worked. No notices had been posted as yet.)

On the observer's following visit to the plant, a few days later, Joe spoke to her again.

JOE: Say, let me ask you something. What do you think? Do you think this bulletin board of mine is going to drive management nuts? (He laughs.) The management believes that it has the ideas and that a person in a worker's position shouldn't be expected to have ideas. That's not a worker's job. It's just like this business with the inventory. That's supposed to be none of my business. All I'm supposed to do is just stick to my job.

That's what's wrong with this new merit-rating thing they just put in. It's based on the assumption that the worker is responsible for the output. After all, output is based on a lot of things and largely on supervision. It is based on the condition of the machine, the material, and the kind of supervisor you have, but the supervisors here aren't being rated. I wonder what the management would think if we turned it around and rated them. I bet they wouldn't like that one bit. You'll probably disagree with my ideas, but I think things should be just the reverse of the way they are. The saying goes that workers should be paid a standard rate and that management should get the results of output. I think that's just the reverse of the way things should be. What we should have is the workers getting the results of output, a continually increasing wage, and management getting a going rate or a standard pay. That's a different idea, I know, but it's what I believe.

Questions

1. What are the problems at Brainerd Instrument Company?
2. If you were Howard Atkins, how would you describe the problems?
3. If you were the observer, how would you describe the problems?

Source: Copyright © 1956 by the President and Fellows of Harvard College. Reproduced by permission. This case was prepared by Abraham Zaleznik and is based on material from his book, *Worker Satisfaction and Development* (Boston: Division of Research, Harvard University, Graduate School of Business Administration, 1956).

Valpo Industries

Doug Slater, plant supervisor in charge of the evening and midnight turns at Valpo Industries in New Haven, Tennessee, closed the door of his small office and eased into the soft leather chair behind his cluttered desk. The 10:30 whistle had just signaled the midnight turn employees to their work stations, and Doug anticipated that the time remaining before 12:00 would be uneventful. He recalled that there had been problems in the past. When production orders started to back up on the big welders five months ago, the main office decided to put in an extra eight-hour shift at the plant. This necessitated an overlap of an hour and a half between the second and third shifts, and it created a few scheduling difficulties at first. However, the overlap period had been operating rather smoothly during the last month as the workers became accustomed to doubling up on their machines.

When the phone rang, Doug hissed a silent curse to himself. "Doug here."

"Doug, this is Gus. You better get down here to 15. We've had some big trouble."

"What is it, Gus?"

"I'll have to fill you in once you're here. All I can say is hurry!"

Department 15 was situated at the north end of the building and was the largest department in the plant. It was in Department 15 that six giant welding machines fabricated steel parts of various shapes and sizes that were cut and assembled in the other sections of the plant. When Doug arrived he noticed a crowd gathered at one of the large doorways that led to the oil supply area outside. Gus Hoffman, second shift supervisor for 15, approached Doug.

"Darn it all, Doug, another problem with one of those third-shift boys! I just don't see how poor Tom can put up with all this . . ."

"Hold on, Gus. Settle down. Now tell me what happened so we can get something done about it."

"Jack Metcalf, that big maintenance man, reported to Tom that someone was snooping around outside with a flashlight. Tom went out to the yard to check while Jack went up to the front gate to back Tom up. I had just picked up the phone to call you when I heard Tom yell. I ran outside and saw Tom rubbing his head. Jack had grabbed that huge chain we use to lock up the gate to the yard and cornered the guy before he could run out."

"Jack didn't have to use the chain on the guy, did he? And who is the guy anyway?"

"Jack would have taken the man's head off if he hit him with that twenty-pound chain. The guy just froze in his tracks when he saw Jack. The man's name is Richard Johnson; he's one of the welders from the third shift. He didn't report in at 10:30. Johnson said that he was just trying to get in through the side door by the employee's locker room. He said he forgot his safety glasses and didn't want to walk through the plant. Jack and Tom are holding him now waiting for the police to arrive. Johnson looks pretty drunk to me."

"Why did you call the police in on this; was Tom hurt?"

"No, he was just stunned. It seems Tom caught Johnson by surprise. Johnson panicked and threw his flashlight at Tom. The flashlight glanced against Tom's head and knocked him down. He said he was feeling all right and told me he wanted to get the police here so he could press assault charges against Johnson."

"Okay, Gus, get these men back to work. I'll try to talk Tom into going to the hospital and getting his head checked. I suppose he'll be tied up most of the night if he's going to file a complaint. How about staying on a few extra hours, Gus, and I'll get a first-shift supervisor to come in and relieve you around 3 A.M."

"Well, I don't like the idea of working third shift, but I guess there's no way out of it. You just make sure you get someone in here. I don't want to be in here all night."

"Don't worry, Gus, and thanks a lot. Send Tom and Jack up to my office as soon as they're finished with the police. I've got to get a report started on this."

Doug sullenly walked back to his office. He was concerned about Tom. It seemed a shame that this should happen to such a nice guy. Ever since Tom took over third shift he's had problems with absenteeism and drinking on the job. It just seemed that those inner-city men that personnel hired never worked out for Tom. But Tom wanted to work midnights. He felt it would give him more time to work on his farm.

As Doug entered his office and got a stack of forms out of his desk, he started to wonder whether Tom would think of leaving the company because of tonight's incident. It didn't seem likely, but it might happen. Doug hoped not. Tom had been with Valpo for nearly twenty years. Before he had been made supervisor, Tom had been one of the ablest workers in the plant. In fact, he had a couple of records for parts produced on the welders. He was a good supervisor too, and when he was on the second shift last year his department had the highest production level in the company. Some local competitors had tried to lure Tom away recently, and Doug began to worry that Tom might decide to accept one of those offers after what happened.

The next day, Doug received the latest production reports for the previous month. He noticed that the third shift was still rated far behind the other shifts in parts per hour. He began to wonder whether a piece-rate wage would bring production up, but then he remembered that both management and the union opposed the idea.

Doug was just beginning to put the finishing touches to his report of the previous night's incident when the phone rang. It was Jim Mitchell, the plant manager, calling from the main office.

"Doug, Watkins in personnel just briefed me about the trouble you had with Johnson last night. Have you got a report on it yet?"

"I've just about finished it up, Jim. It should be on your desk before you leave the office this afternoon."

"How about Tom, is he all right?"

"The X-rays were negative, but the doctor advised him to take things easy for a few days."

"I imagine we'll be hearing from the union on this. I understand that Johnson joined the union a couple of months ago."

"We shouldn't have to worry about the union. Johnson was late for work; he didn't report in that he would be late; he was drunk, and he assaulted a foreman on company property. The company rules are pretty clear in calling for discharge. I told the shop steward of Johnson's dismissal last night. I waited until this morning to tell Johnson. He wasn't in any shape last night to really understand what was going on. When I talked to him this morning he didn't show any surprise at being discharged."

"I just hope that's the end of it, Doug. You realize I've got to go into bargaining with the union over a new contract in three months. I'd like to be sure our relations are pretty good by then. I've also been looking at the latest production report. I'm beginning to think opening up a third shift for Department 15 was a bad idea. We just barely cover our operating expenses, not to mention the beating we've been taking in personnel losses. We just can't seem to get good people to work midnights. I'm seriously thinking of shutting down the third shift and telling our salespeople we can't handle any more new orders for a while. Look, Doug, I've got to go out of town for the rest of the week, so check into that for me. I'll expect your opinion when I get back."

Doug heard a knock on the door as he was hanging up the phone. It was Bill Benedict, the shop steward for third shift.

"Yeah, Bill, come on in. What brings you in so early?"

"Well, Doug, it's about last night."

"The union's not going to try to get Johnson reinstated, are they!"

"We don't think so, Doug. It seems that it would be a losing battle. We talked about it at a meeting we just had, and the consensus was that there is something more important at issue here."

"What are you trying to say, Bill?"

"Let me ask you something first, Doug. Do you believe that a rule is fair only if it is applied equally without exception?"

"Of course! A rule is reasonable only if it can be used fairly. That's what I try to do all the time. So, what's your point? Are you going to tell me that it was unfair to dismiss Johnson because the rules are unreasonable?"

"Doug, that's exactly where the union disagrees with you. Company rules state that any employee who assaults or physically threatens to do bodily injury to another employee on company property is subject to immediate discharge. The union feels that Jack Metcalf violated that rule when he threatened Johnson with a chain. We decided to file a grievance against Metcalf. We want him discharged or we'll push for Johnson's reinstatement with back pay."

"You've got to be kidding, Bill! You were there last night and you saw Johnson's condition and what he did to Tom! What should Jack have done, stand there and let Johnson run off? Besides, Jack had no way of knowing it was Johnson out there. It was pretty dark last night. What did Jack have to say about all this at your meeting?"

"He wasn't there, Doug. Metcalf's not a union member. Look, Doug, now is not the time to argue about it. We'll have plenty of time to hash things out at the grievance meeting next week. I've got to get home and get some sleep before work tonight, so I'll see you later."

Bill half slammed the door on his way out. Doug got up to get some aspirin. He felt a tremendous headache building up in the back of his neck. He wondered whether he should call Jim Mitchell up and give him the bad news now or wait until Jim came back from his trip. Either way, he thought, his neck would still be in a noose.

Questions

1. What are the problems at Valpo?
2. What are the causes of the problems?
3. Does the leadership have anything to do with the problems? Communication? Interpersonal relationships? Group behavior?
4. If you were Doug, what would you do about the problems?
5. If you were Gus, what would you do about the problems?

Source: Adapted from *Management*, 2nd ed., by William F. Glueck. Copyright © 1980 by the Dryden Press, a division of Holt, Rinehart and Winston Publishers. Reprinted by permission of Holt, Rinehart and Winston.

A Case of Misunderstanding

In a department of a large industrial organization, seven workers (four men and three women) were engaged in testing and inspecting panels of electronic equipment. In this department one of the workers, Bing, was having trouble with his immediate superior, Hart, who had been a worker in the department.

Had we been observers in this department we would have seen Bing carrying two or three panels at a time from the storage racks to the bench where he inspected them together. For this activity we would have seen him charging double or triple set-up time. We would have heard him occasionally singing at work. Also, we would have seen him usually leaving his work position a few minutes early to go to lunch and noticed that other employees sometimes accompanied him. And had we been present at one specific occasion, we would have heard Hart telling Bing that he disapproved of these activities and that he wanted Bing to stop doing them.

However, not being present to hear the actual exchange that took place in this interaction, let us note what Bing and Hart said to a personnel representative.

What Bing said   In talking about his practice of charging double or triple set-up time for panels which he inspected all at one time, Bing said the following:

"This is a perfectly legal thing to do. We've always been doing it. Mr. Hart, the supervisor, has other ideas about it, though; he claims it's cheating the company. He came over to the bench a day or two ago and let me know just how he felt about the matter. Boy, did we go at it! It wasn't so much the fact that he called me down on it, but more the way in which he did it. I've never seen anyone like him. He's not content just to say clearly what's on his mind, but he prefers to do it in a way that makes you want to crawl inside a crack on the floor. What a guy! I don't mind being called down by a supervisor, but I like to be treated like a person and not humiliated like a school teacher does a naughty kid. He's been pulling this stuff ever since he's been promoted. He's lost his friendly way and seems to be having some difficulty in knowing how to manage us employees. He's a changed man over what he used to be like when he was a worker on the bench with us several years ago.

"When he pulled this kind of stuff on me the other day, I got so damn mad I called the union representative. I know that the thing I was doing was permitted by the contract, but I was intent on making some trouble for Mr. Hart, just because he persists in his sarcastic ways. I am about fed up with the whole situation. I'm trying every means I can to get myself transferred out of his group. . . . He's not going to pull this kind of kid stuff any longer on me. When the union representative questioned him on the case, he finally had to back down, because according to the contract an employee can use any time-saving method or device in order to speed up the process as long as the quality standards of the job are met.

"You see, he knows that I do professional singing on the outside. He hears me singing here on the job, and he hears the people talking about my career in music. I guess he figures I can be so cocky because I have another means of earning some money. Actually, the employees here enjoy having me sing while we work, but he thinks I'm disturbing them and causing them to goof off from their work.

Occasionally, I leave the job a few minutes early and go down to the washroom to wash up before lunch. Sometimes several others in the group will accompany me, and so Mr. Hart automatically thinks I'm the leader and usually bawls me out for the whole thing.

"So, you can see, I'm a marked man around here. He keeps watching me like a hawk. Naturally, this makes me very uncomfortable. That's why I'm sure a transfer would be the best thing. I've asked him for it, but he didn't give me any satisfaction at the time. While I remain here, I'm going to keep my nose clean, but whenever I get the chance, I'm going to slip it to him, but good."

What Hart said   Here, on the other hand, is what Hart told the personnel representative.

"Say, I think you should be in on this. My dear little friend, Bing, is heading himself into a showdown with me. Recently it was brought to my attention that Bing has been taking double and triple set-up time for panels that he is actually inspecting at one time. In effect, Bart's cheating, and I've called him down on it several times before. A few days ago it was brought to my attention again, and so this time I really let him have it in no uncertain terms. He's been getting away with this for too long and I'm going to put an end to it once and for all. I know he didn't like my calling him on it because a few hours later he had the union representative breathing down my back. Well, anyway, I let them both know I won't tolerate the practice any longer, and I let Bing know that if he continues to do this kind of thing, I'm going to take official action with my boss to have the guy fired or penalized somehow. This kind of thing has to be curbed. Actually, I'm inclined to think the guy's mentally deficient, because talking to him has actually no meaning to him whatsoever. I've tried just about every approach to jar some sense into that guy's head, and I've just about given it up as a bad deal.

"I don't know what it is about the guy, but I think he's harboring some deep feelings against me. For what, I don't know, because I've tried to handle that bird with kid gloves. But his whole attitude around here on the job is one of indifference, and he certainly isn't a good influence on the rest of my group. Frankly, I think he purposely tries to agitate them against me at times, too. It seems to me he may be suffering from illusions of grandeur, because all he does all day long is sit over there and croon his fool head off. Thinks he's another Frank Sinatra! No kidding! I understand he takes singing lessons and he's working with some of the local bands in the city. All of which is O.K. by me, but when his outside interests start interfering with his efficiency on the job, then I've got to start paying closer attention to the situation. For this reason I've been keeping my eye on that bird and if he steps out of line any more, he and I are going to part ways.

"You know there's an old saying, 'You can't make a silk purse out of a sow's ear.' The guy is simply unscrupulous. He feels no obligation to do a real day's work. Yet I know the guy can do a good job, because for a long time he did. But in recent months he's slipped, for some reason, and his whole attitude on the job has changed. Why it's even getting to the point now where I think he's inducing other employees to 'goof off' a few minutes before the lunch whistle and go down to the washroom to clean up on company time. I've called him on it several times, but words just don't seem to make any lasting impression. Well, if he keeps it up much longer, he's going to find himself on the way out. He's asked me for a transfer, so I know he wants to go. But I didn't give him an answer when he asked me, because I was steaming mad at the time, and I may have told him to go somewhere else."

Questions
1. What steps can be taken to solve the problem?
2. How might Hart have handled the situation differently?

Source: Adapted from Henry L. Sisk, *Management and Organization*, Copyright © 1977, pp. 372–373. Reprinted by permission of South Western Publishing Co., Cincinnati, Ohio

Moving the Beta assembly department

The Halston Company's plant at Peoria, Illinois, is the key component in the manufacture of electronic subassemblies. After being manufactured, the subassemblies are sent to the company's other plants for synthesis into the finished products. The Peoria plant became a division of Halston when the parent company, a large manufacturer of private-label electronic equipment, undertook a concerted effort to acquire all of its key suppliers. This consolidation occurred after the company had experienced difficulties acquiring tuners for one of its crucial products and had endangered its relationship with its major customer, a large retail chain. With increasing competition from Japan, Taiwan, and Korea, Halston occupies a tenuous place in a cost-conscious and extremely competitive industry. To some extent Halston relied on its fast and accurate delivery times to compensate for its somewhat higher prices.

The Peoria plant manufactured nine subassemblies, each of which was sufficiently unique so that a separate assembly line or production room was in operation for each. The Beta assembly, a component for the company's 19-inch color portable television set, was produced by seventy assemblers, packers, and support personnel in a large room sixty feet by eighty feet. The room was divided so that the product moved through eight distinct operations before it was packed. Seven employees worked on each of the operations and four worked in packaging. Two employees were in charge of the stock room, and eight were "runners" who carried the subassemblies from one work place to another and kept the various work places supplied with parts that were added to the total subassembly. The following figure shows the department's production layout.

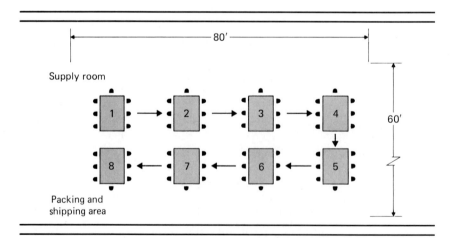

Each production employee worked on only one of the processes involved in the subassembly. After finishing the task on a piece of work, the production employee placed the product in a basket at his or her right side and took a new piece from a similar basket at his or her left side. The runners had the responsibility of moving the finished work on one worktable to the next worktable, where the next process would be applied to the product. Thus the runner became the supplier to the next assembly table. The runners also had the responsibility of keeping their assigned areas supplied with the parts and components, which were to be added to the subassemblies at the stations. These parts were drawn from the supply room as needed.

Most of the work at the various stations involved relatively simple tasks such as soldering, bolting together parts, or adding "plug-in" parts. Qualifying for the work required little training, and most of the skills could be taught in one day or less. The chief problem was that of teaching new workers to solder and to avoid "cold joints."

Most of the employees adjusted well to the system. Although each employee at a work station did exactly the same work as the others at that station, enough repartee and camaraderie developed to relieve any boredom that might be expected from working on a simple repetitive operation. Workers almost always met the production standards demanded of them.

For one month, however, industrial engineers from the central engineering staff had been studying all of the operations at the Peoria plant with an eye toward increasing production. Rumors were rife throughout the plant that the "slide-rule boys" were going to turn the place upside down. No official communication of the staff's purposes was delivered to the production employees.

The plant closed for its annual three-week vacation in July. When the workers returned, they found that the "slide-rule boys" had indeed been working. The group working on the Beta assembly were sent to a new home, and the production workers were routed to a long room forty feet by eighty feet on the second floor. Four of the runners were told to report to the personnel office, where they were informed that they were no longer needed at the plant.

The new plant layout for the Beta assembly section was composed of four long tables, with eight workers seated on each side.

Each side of each table was a complete assembly unit, with parts starting with the first person and being completed by the last person. The four remaining runners kept the table supplied with the parts and then took the finished assemblies to the packing area. The following figure illustrates the new arrangement for Beta.

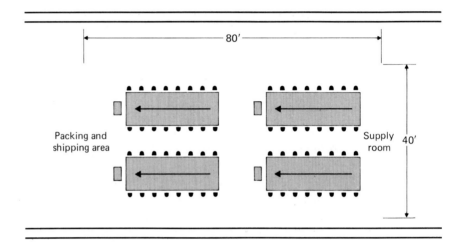

Very few of the workers were ecstatic about the new layout. A few went home on the first day, but returned later in the day. Most loafed for about two hours before starting work. All grumbled about the "brain child" of the "slide-rule boys." "They didn't tell us anything about this change" was the least vulgar of the many remarks made about the new system. The supervisors on the assembly line tried to explain the promised efficiency of the new set-up, but the workers were not easily convinced.

For the first four months, production levels never approached the previous ones under the old system, although the central staff engineers were convinced that output would be one and one-half times the level under the old system, with less direct labor cost.

Questions

1. What problems do you see with the move of the Beta assembly department?

2. How should the changes have been made?

Source: Arthur Elkins, *Management: Structure, Functions, and Practices,* © 1980, Addison-Wesley Publishing Company, Inc., pp. 235–238. Reprinted with permission.

Supervisory management functions

9

Solving problems
and making decisions

Objectives

After reading this chapter you should be able to

☐ Describe a systematic approach to problem solving and decision making.

☐ Use the Kepner-Tregoe process to describe problems and determine their causes.

☐ Explain how alternative actions can be developed and how the best alternative is selected.

☐ Explain how you can decide which decision-making approach to use.

Solving problems and making decisions are important activities for all supervisors. While decisions facing supervisors may not involve as much money as those facing top managers of large organizations, they are often no less difficult to make. Supervisors continually face both major and minor problems. All of these problems, however, require decisions to be made about what is wrong and how it can be corrected.

Many supervisors make decisions on the basis of intuition or past experiences. However, as their jobs have become increasingly challenging and complex, more supervisors have begun to rely on systematic approaches to problem solving and decision making.

In this chapter we will examine a systematic framework for solving problems and making decisions. We will then compare the effectiveness of individuals versus groups in decision making. Finally, we will examine some of the pros and cons of involving workers in decision making and identify situations where their involvement is appropriate.

The problem-solving and decision-making process

Solving problems and making decisions are not simple matters and cannot be reduced to formulas. A systematic approach to the **decision-making process,** however, can be helpful. Such an approach includes the following steps (see Fig. 9.1):

1. Identify the problem and determine its cause.
2. Develop alternative solutions to the problem and select the best alternative.
3. Put the decision into action and follow up.

Identifying problems and determining their causes

As a supervisor you are often faced with many problems, more than you can possibly handle at any given time. These problems are sometimes brought to your attention forcefully. But to be really effective, you can't wait for problems to arise. You need to take the initiative and analyze your operations, looking regularly for problems and potential problems.

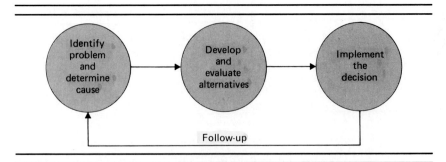

Figure 9.1   The decision-making process.

How do you identify a problem? How do you know when a problem exists? A problem exists when a difference or *deviation* exists between what *should be* happening and what *actually is* happening (see Fig. 9.2). For example, if the production rate on a process is supposed to be sixty units per hour and the actual production rate is fifty units per hour, there is a problem. A deviation exists between what should be (sixty units per hour) and what actually is (fifty units per hour) being accomplished.

Once you identify a problem, you need to analyze it to determine the cause, which is difficult unless the problem is clearly described. To describe a problem, you must collect information. Kepner and Tregoe have suggested an approach to describing problems that can help you collect and organize information.[1] They suggest four questions that you should ask about any problem.

1. What is the deviation?
2. Where is the deviation located?
3. When did the deviation appear?
4. What is the extent of the deviation?

Further, they suggest that in answering each of these questions, you describe what *is* true about the problem and what *is not* true about the problem.

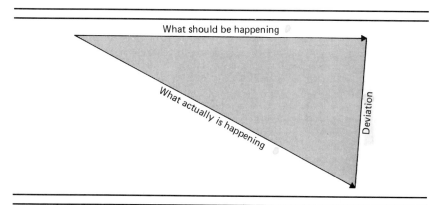

Figure 9.2 A problem is a deviation.

To illustrate how the **Kepner-Tregoe process** works let's look at the case of the Jones Door Company.[2] The Jones Door Company first learned of a problem through a phone call from Mrs. Cunningham, the wife of a Jones Door customer. Mrs. Cunningham had been furious. "Look, that garage door came down last night and almost killed my husband! Come and get your door. I'm reporting you to the Better Business Bureau and telling everyone I know how lousy Jones Doors are."

Wow! thought Henry Jones as he hung up the phone. What an earful. Mr. Jones was the owner of the Jones Door Company, a small company that manufactured and sold garage doors. At the present time, they operated only in the Plains City area. The company had been growing, however, so marketing the garage doors in a wider area had been discussed.

One of their most successful recent products was an automatic garage door. The automatic door was electronically powered and operated by a tiny radio transmitter carried in the car. The transmitter had a short range so the signal would not raise all doors in the area. Since about the first of September, however, they had received about thirty complaints. In each case the customer complained that the door would go up or down for no reason. Many were quite irritated and threatened to take some type of action.

Mr. Jones was very concerned about the problem. Jones Doors was a relatively young company that appeared to have a good future. But the company's future could be ruined if the automatic garage door problem wasn't solved.

Mr. Jones called in Herb Swenson, the production manager, and Marge Crow, the manager of sales. "We're getting more and more complaints on the automatic doors. This takes top priority. If we don't do something, our sales could be ruined. We have to find the cause of the problem and decide how to solve it."

Identifying the problem was relatively easy for Mr. Jones. A garage door should open or close only when activated by the owner, when actually, doors were opening and closing when they were not activated by the owner.

To attempt to determine the cause of the problem, Mr. Jones decided to use the Kepner-Tregoe process. A sample of Jones door customers in Plains City were interviewed to get information to answer the four questions suggested by Kepner and Tregoe. The answers are summarized in Table 9.1.

Table 9.1

**Analyzing Jones Door's
problem**

	IS	IS NOT
What	Garage doors going up and down randomly.	Any other quality problem with the doors.
Where	On Bermuda Peninsula between 6th and 18th streets.	Any other location.
When	Early fall; early evening; only some days.	Any other time of year; any other time of day; all days or any specific pattern of days.
Extent	Most Jones doors in the area.	A few Jones doors in the area.

What is the deviation?   The only deviation found was that some of the doors would open and close for no particular reason. They did not find any other major quality problem.

Where is the deviation occurring?   The only place the deviation occurred seemed to be on Bermuda Peninsula between 6th and 18th Street. People interviewed in other areas of the city indicated that they never had the problem.

When did the deviation occur?   Those with the problem indicated that it had started during the early fall. They had not had the problem during the summer or last winter. Further, it only happened occasionally, during the early evening. No one recalled the door opening or closing during the day or later at night. Nor did they notice any particular pattern, such as always on Saturdays and never on Sundays.

What is the extent of the problem?   Practically all people with Jones doors in the problem area reported the problem. It was not a problem for only a few customers.

In searching for the cause of the problem, you must look for distinctions, that is, what are the differences between what is true about the problem and what is not true. What could cause the exact effects of the problem and not cause any other effects?

For the Jones Door Company, the answers to the where and when questions provided distinctions that led to the cause of the problem. What was different about the Bermuda Peninsula between 6th and 18th Street? Mr. Jones, an Air Force Reserve pilot, remembered that this area was in the glide path for the final approach to the longest runway of the local air base. What was different about early evenings in the early fall? Mr. Swenson, whose hobby was sailing, noted that during this time of year heavy fogs were a frequent occurrence. He also pointed out that the fog rolled in during the early evening.

Thus, they identified two major distinctions between is and is not: (1) foggy weather conditions, and (2) planes crossing the area on the final approach to the longest runway. A check with the air station found that during periods of heavy fog, air controllers guided the aircraft onto the longest runway by radar, using a special radio frequency. This was the same frequency that was used to operate the garage doors. Every time the air controller and the pilot talked during the approach, their radio frequency would cause the doors to open and close, the cause of the problem for Jones Doors!

As a supervisor you are often faced with many problems and must decide how to allocate your time. Problems need to be arranged in some order of priority. To do this, it is helpful to ask two questions: (1) How urgent is the problem or, in other words, is immediate action required? (2) How serious is the problem or is a great deal of difficulty being created?

Answers to these questions will help order the problems according to importance. Then, you can start work on the highest-priority problems, those that are the most urgent and/or serious. For the Jones Door Company, for example, the automatic garage-door problem had the highest priority and demanded immediate action.

You must also distinguish between symptoms and causes of problems. Causes, not symptoms, must be treated. In many instances, a problem has a chain of causes. The immediate problem may be only a symptom of a deeper problem. Once you determine the cause of the immediate problem, you can work backwards to find the root cause.

For example, a general supervisor in a local company recently discovered a production problem. After describing the problem and determining its cause, the general supervisor concluded that high absenteeism was causing low productivity. But the process didn't stop with that conclusion. There was a new problem to deal with, absenteeism. The general supervisor had to analyze that problem and determine its cause, which was traced to a newly hired supervisor. The workers were unhappy with their treatment, as they were being pushed to work harder and reprimanded in public. What would have happened if the general supervisor had only treated the surface cause? Absenteeism could have been reduced by requiring a doctor's excuse or offering prizes for perfect attendance. But the workers' dissatisfaction with the new supervisor would have shown up in other ways, such as more quits or poorer quality work.

Developing and evaluating alternatives

After determining the cause of a problem, you need to take steps to solve it. To do this, you develop several possible actions, consider the merits of each, and finally select the best alternative among them.

When considering how to solve a problem, most people think of one possible solution and move quickly to implement that action. Such haste often leads to a poor decision. Looking at several alternative solutions generally increases the chance of making a sound decision.

How might you devise a variety of possible actions? Developing alternative actions is a creative process: nothing mysterious or magical is involved. As Thomas Edison observed, creativity is 99% perspiration and only 1% inspiration.

One way of getting new ideas is to ask for others' opinions. Gathering ideas from people of different backgrounds often helps you develop different viewpoints. Another approach is **brainstorming.** The basic idea behind brainstorming is to think of as many alternatives as possible, without pausing to evaluate them. If you stop to evaluate each alternative as you think, the "creative juices" don't flow as freely and you are not likely to develop as many alternatives.

Even though some of the alternatives may have little value, you should keep developing ideas to maximize creativity. Brainstorming can be done individually or in a group. In other words, you can brainstorm alternatives alone or gather a group of people to help you.

The people at Jones Door developed four possible alternative actions:

1. Do nothing.
2. Offer to replace all automatic doors with manual doors at no cost and sell only manual doors in the future.
3. Change the frequency of the radio signal that operated the electronic door.
4. Develop a new technology (light, laser) for opening automatic doors.

After developing a number of alternatives, you select the "best" alternative. To do this, each alternative must be evaluated on the basis of expected results. Kepner and Tregoe recommend classifying objectives—desired results—under two headings: **must objectives** and **want objectives.**

Must objectives are outcomes the alternative action has to achieve. They are constraints on your actions that have to be met. If an alternative does not meet a must objective, it is eliminated. In the Jones Door Company, for example, one must objective was to stop the doors from opening and closing because of airplane landings. Any alternatives that did not meet this objective would have to be eliminated.

Want objectives are desirable, but not necessary, outcomes from the decision. Want objectives for Jones Door were to correct the problem: (1) at the lowest possible cost; (2) in the shortest possible time; and (3) with a minimum of customer inconvenience.

The best alternative is the one that meets the must objectives and the most want objectives. As shown in Table 9.2, Jones Door decided to change the frequency of the radio signal. Doing nothing did not meet the must objectives and was therefore rejected. Using manual doors was more inconvenient for customers. Developing a new technology would take too much time and would be too costly.

Table 9.2

Evaluating alternatives facing
Jones Door

ALTERNATIVES	MUST OBJECTIVES	WANT OBJECTIVES		
	Stop doors from opening and closing randomly	Low costs	Short time	Minimum customer inconvenience
Do nothing	No			
Sell manual doors	Yes	Yes	Yes	No
Change frequency	Yes	Yes	Yes	Yes
Develop new technology	Yes	No	No	No

Selection of the best alternative requires careful analysis. You need to be thorough and make certain that no unexpected, undesirable outcomes will result from the selected alternative.

Implementing the decision

The end result of the decision-making process is action. After you decide on the best alternative, the decision must be implemented. Then follow-up is necessary to make certain the problem has been solved.

As a supervisor, you are not the only person involved in the process. Other people often implement the decision. So, all involved should accept the decision and agree with the action to be taken. Thus, the ultimate effectiveness of a decision is affected by both the quality of the decision itself and the acceptance of the decision by those who must implement it.

SPEND A BUCK

In some decisions, quality is much more important than acceptance. This may be true of decisions requiring a high degree of technical expertise, for example. The selection of the steel girders used in the construction of a high-rise building requires technical knowledge. Presuming the girders chosen are safe, the acceptance of a particular type by those who put them up is not critical. The type of girder they are using is unlikely to cause resentment.

In other decisions, acceptance is more important than the quality of the decision. Consider the office supervisor who needed two of the clerks in her group to work overtime on Sunday. Each of her clerks was asked and claimed to have a prior commitment. The office supervisor did not care which of her clerks worked on Sunday, since they all could do the work. The decision was quite important to the clerks, however. In this case, the supervisor let the clerks make the decision and they reached a solution all could accept.

In many decisions however, both quality and acceptance are important. You want to be sure a good decision is made and that it is implemented effectively. In such cases, the question of who should make the decision is important. Should you make the decision and try to persuade others to agree? Should the workers who will be affected by the decision be allowed to participate? Should some other approach be used? In the next two sections, we will discuss some ideas that will help answer these questions.

Group decision making

Supervisors often do not make decisions entirely on their own. Frequently, they consult with others to get information or test ideas before reaching a final decision. At times, they call together a group of people to make the decision.

In recent years, more attention has been directed toward **group decision making,** including decisions made through informal participation between supervisor and workers and those made in formal committees. Do groups make better decisions than individuals? There are advantages as well as disadvantages to group decision making.

Advantages of group decision making

Groups can bring more resources to decisions than a single individual could. Different people bring a variety of information, ideas, and views. Theoretically, if these resources are used effectively, the group should be able to arrive at a better decision than could any individual within the group. In the Jones Door Company, as you recall, Mr. Jones was a pilot and Mr. Swenson a sailor. The different information each possessed helped solve the problem. Even when decisions require technical knowledge, groups of experts often make decisions. A doctor, for example, may ask other doctors for consultation on a difficult case.

Group discussion can also increase the creativity of decisions. One person may present an idea that sparks ideas in others' minds. This "piggybacking" of ideas can lead to alternatives that no individual would develop. As indicated earlier, this interaction is the basis of brainstorming as a creative technique.

Finally, group decision making can lead to increased acceptance of the decision and consequently to more effective implementation. If people participate in making a decision, they tend to be more committed and more motivated to putting the decision into action. This is particularly important when accepting the decision is critical to implementing it effectively. Remember the office supervisor who needed two clerks to work on Sunday? If the supervisor had arbitrarily made the decision, one or both of the clerks selected quite likely would have been unhappy. Since the clerks made the decision, they accepted it, and two clerks were willing to work on Sunday.

Problems with group decision making

There are also problems with group decision making. Some of these cannot be avoided, while others are the result of ineffective group functioning.

Some critics of group decision making have argued that groups take more time to make decisions than individuals. They say an individual can collect information, analyze a problem, and select an alternative action faster. The time necessary for group discussion of different points of view is not required when an individual makes a decision alone.

According to Norman Maier, this assumpton is not necessarily true.[3] As shown in Table 9.3, if a supervisor makes a decision alone, the decision-making time is short. Implementation may take longer, however. The supervisor must communicate the decision and persuade others to accept it. If a group makes the decision, the decision-making time is longer, but communication time and persuasion time are quite brief. Thus, in many decisions, action may come just as quickly through group decision making.

Another major problem with group decision making has been noted by Irving Janis.[4] He calls it "groupthink." When people are deeply involved in a close-knit, cohesive group, there is a danger of groupthink developing. Group members try very hard to maintain friendly relations and to avoid conflict. This effort reduces the group's ability to evaluate realistically alternative courses of action. Having a happy group becomes more important than making good decisions. An overemphasis on group harmony produces the following symptoms of **groupthink:**

- Group discussion is limited to a few possible courses of action (often only two).
- The group does not thoroughly examine the initially preferred course of action for risks and drawbacks.
- The group does not thoroughly examine the advantages of initially rejected courses of action.
- The group makes little or no effort to get information from outside experts.
- The group shows interest and discusses opinions that support their initially preferred course of action. They ignore conflicting facts and opinions.

Janis gives a good example of groupthink from history, what he calls the Bay of Pigs Fiasco. On April 17, 1961, 1,400 Cuban exiles invaded the coast of Cuba at the Bay of Pigs. They were aided by the U.S. Navy, Air Force, and the CIA. Nothing went as planned. By the third day, 1,200 invaders had been captured and led off to prison camps.

Table 9.3

Time requirements for decisions
made by supervisor and group

	DECISION-MAKING TIME	COMMUNICA-TION TIME	PERSUASION TIME
Supervisor makes decision	Short	Long	Long
Group makes decision	Long	Short	Short

The idea for the invasion was born in March 1960. President Eisenhower directed the CIA to organize Cuban exiles in the United States into a unified political movement against Castro. They were to give military training to those willing to return and engage in guerilla warfare. In late 1960, the CIA began to assume that they could carry out a full-scale invasion using the Cuban exiles.

President Kennedy first learned of the plan two days after his inauguration. He and several other members of his new administration were briefed by Allen Dulles, head of the CIA. During the next eighty days they discussed the plan at regular meetings. In early April, the plan was formally approved.

The results were totally unexpected by the President and his advisors. It was a military disaster. People in Castro's Cuba did not join the exiles in revolt. The United States government's attempts to avoid responsibility were discredited. Friendly Latin American countries were outraged, and European allies joined in the condemnation. Protest meetings were held to denounce the United States for its illegal aggression. The Soviet Union was encouraged to set up nuclear missiles only ninety miles from Florida.

Afterward, those who participated in the decision recognized that they should have anticipated the results. Information was available that indicated the Cubans would not support the revolt. The United States' involvement could not be kept secret. Yet these factors were ignored. Why? Groupthink was at least part of the problem.

Participants later said that the discussions took place in an atmosphere of assumed agreement. It seemed that the plan was accepted by the group as whole. Individuals thus did not raise questions because they did not want to risk the disapproval of their associates.

Two examples make the point. Secretary of State Dean Rusk had doubts about the plan, yet he said little in the meetings. Because of his silence, Kennedy and the others assumed he was in agreement with the plan. Arthur Schlesinger had expressed his doubts. At a private party, Robert Kennedy took Schlesinger aside and asked him why he opposed the plan. After listening, Kennedy said, "You may be right or you may be wrong, but the President has made his mind up. Don't push it any further. Now is the time for everyone to help him all they can." Schlesinger conformed.

The participants in the Bay of Pigs decision were members of a very cohesive group. They tried very hard to maintain friendly relations within the group. They did not, therefore, raise questions that might have created conflict, but also might have led to a more realistic evaluation of the plan.

Improving group decision making

As we discussed earlier, there are advantages to group decision making. In some cases, groups make better quality decisions. Decisions are also generally more acceptable to the implementors if they have helped to make the decision. On the other hand, some groups get bogged down in petty bickering and game playing. Excessive conformity and groupthink are an ever-present danger.

What can you do to maximize the advantages of group decision making and minimize its disadvantages? While there is no formula for effective group decision making, people who have spent a lot of time analyzing decision-making groups offer several suggestions.

Consider the importance of group size and setting for group decision making. If the group has too few members, it may not have enough views represented. On the other hand, as groups get larger, it becomes harder for each member to participate freely. Likewise, a meeting in the supervisor's office may have a different atmosphere than one held in a "neutral" setting, such as a conference room.

Avoid conflict-reducing techniques such as majority vote, coin flips, and bargaining. Differences of opinion are natural and expected. Seek them out and try to involve everyone in the decision process. Disagreements can actually help improve the group's decision. With a wide range of information and opinion, there is a greater chance that the group will arrive at a good decision. Also, when a disagreeing member finally agrees, do not feel that the person must be rewarded by having his or her own way on some later point.

Preplanning for group meetings is important. Goals should be formulated explicitly to guide the group's effects. Agendas may be helpful, but flexibility is important so that the group maintains its ability to handle new issues.

Be aware of the roles people play in groups. As you observe decision-making groups, you can usually see group members assuming a variety of roles. Some of these are helping roles; they help the group function more effectively. Others are hindering roles; they disrupt group functioning and generally lead to poorer decisions. Some of the more common helping and hindering roles people play in groups are described in Table 9.4. Try to identify the roles group members, including yourself, are playing. Do what you can to discourage hindering roles and encourage helping roles.

Table 9.4

Helping and hindering roles in decision-making groups

HELPING ROLES	HINDERING ROLES
Initiators are fountainheads of ideas. They express a variety of ideas for discussion and different approaches to solving problems. They often stimulate the group to be more creative. Initiators help the group by expressing ideas.	*Aggressors* present ideas and then stubbornly refuse to consider any other view. As others present different ideas, aggressors try to discredit their suggestions by being louder and more persistent. They may even attempt to discredit the individual making the suggestion. Aggressors discourage communication and create a tense atmosphere in the group.

(continued)

Table 9.4 (continued)

HELPING ROLES	HINDERING ROLES
Clarifiers probe for meaning and understanding of all opinions. When they feel they understand an idea, they restate it to make certain that all group members understand. In addition, they often give relevant examples from their own experience. Clarifiers help the group develop a common understanding of all ideas.	*Withdrawers* are present, but only physically. They do not participate in the discussion unless forced to by the group. They may take notes, but this is done to appear involved. Withdrawers cheat the group by withholding ideas and opinions.
Harmonizers help reduce conflict between group members. If conflict is hindering the group, they help the group resolve the problem. They keep the group from ignoring conflict or from letting it interrupt group relations. Harmonizers help maintain good relationships between group members, so they can work together effectively.	*Recognition seekers* try to impress others with their own importance by continuous boasting. They love to talk about their own experiences and accomplishments, even when these are unrelated to the subject being discussed. Their favorite expression is, "That reminds me of the time I. . . ." They take up time and add little to the discussion.
Summarizers are integrators. They bring together the ideas that have been expressed on a particular topic. As they summarize ideas, they test to see if the group is ready to come to a decision. This role is vital. It is through the efforts of summarizers that the group decision is reached.	*Dominators* talk a lot and try to take over the meeting. They like to be looked at as the leader of the group. They enjoy going to the chalkboard and writing out an idea as they are talking. This focuses the attention of the group on their idea. They can also direct the discussion by controlling communication. The danger is that dominators can railroad ideas, opinions, and decisions.

Decision-making approaches and situations

We have seen that both individuals and groups can make effective decisions. There is no one "best" decision approach, nor is there any specific answer to the question of who should make the decision.

A recent analysis of decision situations provides some guidelines, however.[5] This analysis identifies four different decision-making approaches and the situations in which each is likely to be effective. The approaches are:

1. **Directive decision making.** The supervisor collects information, analyzes the problem, and makes the decision. It is then communicated to those who implement the decision.

2. **Consultative decision making.** The supervisor shares the problem with workers. Their ideas and suggestions are obtained. The supervisor then makes the decision and communicates it to workers.

3. **Participative decision making.** The supervisor shares the problem with workers. Together they analyze the problem, generate alternatives, and make the decision.

4. **Delegative decision making.** The supervisor delegates the authority to make the decision to one or more workers. The supervisor is still responsible for resolving the problem but allows the workers to make the decision. The supervisor is, of course, informed of the decision.

Each of these approaches can be used effectively. In order to determine which approach will be most effective in a given situation, you must evaluate several situational factors. One is the nature of the decision itself. Does it call for a choice between several equally desirable (or undesirable) alternatives? If so, the "quality" of the decision, the alternative chosen, is not crucial. Or must you decide between alternatives that vary widely in their potential impact? Here quality is critical.

A second situational factor is the importance of acceptance of decision by workers. If they have a stake in the decision or will be strongly affected by it, acceptance will probably be necessary for effective implementation. On the other hand, workers may not really care what decision is reached. In such situations, acceptance is not an issue.

Your knowledge and capabilities and those of your workers are also important factors. Do you have sufficient information to make the decision alone? Or must you seek out workers for advice and information?

Various combinations of situational factors and preferred decision approaches for each are shown in Table 9.5. Let's look at these in more detail.

In the first two situations, decision quality is important; acceptance is not. If you have the information to make the decision, the directive approach is preferable. Since the workers' acceptance is not important, involving them in the decision process would be a waste of time. If you do not have the information and workers are capable, however, they need to be involved. You can consult with workers to get their information, bring them together for a participative group decision, or delegate the decision to them.

In situations 3 and 4, acceptance of the decision is more important than its quality. When workers have the capability, delegation is the best approach when the decision directly affects the workers. If you have information not available to workers, however, a participative approach could also be used.

Situations where both quality and acceptance are important are probably more common. If worker capability is low, a consultative approach is preferred. Since acceptance is important, you need to get ideas and reactions from workers before the decision is finalized. This consultation can help gain their acceptance. In situation 5, where you lack information, consulting people outside the immediate work group is necessary to get information.

If worker capability is high, either participation or delegation can be used. In situation 7, when your information is low, delegation is more likely. If you have information, however, participation may be used more often. In both situations, workers have the capability to make the decision and their active involvement in the decision process will probably increase acceptance of the final decision.

Table 9.5

Situational factors to consider when determining the preferred decision approach

SITUATION	QUALITY IMPORTANT	ACCEPTANCE IMPORTANT?	SUPERVISOR INFORMATION	WORKER CAPABILITY	PREFERRED DECISION APPROACHES
1	Yes	No	High	High or Low	Directive
2	Yes	No	Low	High	Consultative Participative Delegative
3	No	Yes	Low	High	Delegative
4	No	Yes	High	High	Participative Delegative
5	Yes	Yes	Low	Low	Consultative
6	Yes	Yes	High	Low	Consultative
7	Yes	Yes	Low	High	Participative Delegative
8	Yes	Yes	High	High	Participative Delegative

The situational analysis we have discussed provides only general guidelines. Not all possible situations are considered, nor are all situational factors. For example, you could be confronted with a crisis situation in which immediate action is necessary. Even though acceptance is important and worker capability is high, you would probably use a directive approach because of time pressures.

Generally, however, the situational analysis can be quite useful. It helps you analyze each decision situation and rationally determine which approach is probably the best.

Summary

☐ Supervisors must continually make decisions to resolve problems. A systematic approach to decision making involves: (1) identifying the problem and determining its cause, (2) developing alternative solutions and selecting the best one, and (3) putting the decision into action and following up.

☐ Problems exist when there are deviations between what should be happening and what is actually happening. Once a problem is identified its cause must be determined.

☐ Kepner and Tregoe offer an approach to help describe problems. Four questions are asked about the problem: (1) What is the deviation?, (2) Where is it occurring?, (3) When did it occur?, and (4) What is the extent of the problem? In answering these questions, what is true and not true about the problem should be identified.

☐ Supervisors must allocate their time among problems. Problems can be arranged in order of importance by determining the urgency and seriousness of each one. Causes not symptoms of problems must be identified and treated.

☐ Once the cause of the problem is identified, you develop a variety of alternative actions to solve it. You select the "best" alternative by evaluating each in terms of its expected results. The best alternative is the one that meets all must objectives and the most want objectives.

☐ The decision-making process results in action, or implementing the alternative decided upon. The effectiveness of a decision depends on the quality of the decision and the acceptance of the decision by those affected by it. Quality may be more or less important than acceptance. In many decisions both may be important.

☐ Group decision making involves informal participation by supervisors and workers as well as decisions made by formal committees. Groups can generate more different ideas, information, and views than a single individual can. Group discussion can increase creativity. When people participate in making a decision, they tend to be more motivated to implement it.

☐ Group decision making may require more time. It also may result in groupthink. Groupthink occurs when group members overemphasize group harmony, which may reduce the quality of the decision.

☐ Group decision making can be made more effective. The size of the group and the decision-making setting are important. Differences of opinion should be encouraged. Group meetings should be planned in advance. Hindering roles should be discouraged and helping roles encouraged.

☐ Both individual and group decision making are effective. Four different decision-making approaches can be identified: directive, consultative, participative, and delegative. Each is effective in different situations. Situational factors that influence which approach will be most effective include the nature of the decision, importance of acceptance by workers, and your knowledge and capabilities as well as those of your workers.

Questions for review and discussion

1. What are the three steps in the decision-making process?

2. What questions should be asked when describing problems? Why do we distinguish between causes and symptoms?

3. How do Kepner and Tregoe suggest alternatives can be evaluated? Which alternative should be selected?

4. What are the advantages of group decision making over individual decision making? What are its disadvantages?

5. What is "groupthink?" What symptoms are associated with "groupthink?"

6. Using situational analysis, what situational factors are considered in determining which decision-making approach is likely to be most effective?

7. Define the four decision-making approaches and the situations in which each is most likely to be effective.

8. Do you see any relationship between the decision-making approaches discussed in this chapter and the leadership styles discussed in Chapter 7?

Key terms

Brainstorming	Groupthink
Consultative decision-making	Kepner-Tregoe process
Decision-making process	"Must" objectives
Delegative decision making	Participative decision making
Directive decision making	"Want" objectives
Group decision making	

Cases for discussion and practical exercises

1. Think of a problem you are confronting at the present time or one that you have had recently. State the problem specifically. Using the Kepner-Tregoe approach, describe the problem thoroughly and identify the most likely cause of the problem. Then identify alternative actions that could be taken to solve the problem. Set the "must" and "want" objectives that any action should meet and select the best alternative action.

2. Think of a time when you have worked with a group of people in solving a problem or making a decision. Identify the helping roles and hindering roles that different people were playing. The next time you are in a group discussion do the same thing.

Notes

1. Charles Kepner and Benjamin Tregoe, *The Rational Manager* (New York: McGraw-Hill, 1965).

2. This case is based on an example from Kepner and Tregoe, *The Rational Manager*.

3. Norman R. F. Maier, *Psychology in Industry* (Boston: Houghton Mifflin, 1965).

4. Irving Janis, *Victims of Groupthink* (Boston: Houghton Mifflin, 1972).

5. Victor Vroom and Philip Yetton, *Leadership and Decision Making* (Pittsburgh: University of Pittsburgh Press, 1973).

10

Planning and controlling

After reading this chapter you should be able to

- [ ] Identify the four stages in the planning and control process and distinguish between the involvement of top managers and supervisors.
- [ ] Explain how planning can help supervisors be more effective.
- [ ] Identify the three steps in the control process.
- [ ] Describe the characteristics of successful control systems.

In this chapter, we will examine how supervisors direct the work of their units to ensure coordination with the rest of the organization—the planning and control process. In the next chapter we discuss some techniques used in planning and control. The planning and control process helps people in an organization know their aims, how they are doing in relation to those goals, and what changes, if any, are needed to keep performance on target.

In many books the topics of planning and control are discussed separately. In reality, however, the difference between planning and controlling is not clear. In planning, you set performance objectives and determine how these objectives will be achieved (plans). In the control process, the objectives become standards against which actual performance is checked. If there are differences between actual performance and standards, you take corective action. This action may include revising plans and setting new standards. Because of the close relationship between planning and control, we will discuss them as part of the same process.

The planning and control process

There are four stages in the **planning process** and the **control process.** As shown in Fig. 10.1, these stages are (1) establishing objectives, (2) developing plans, (3) taking action, (4) measuring and evaluating progress, and (5) taking corrective action.

Establishing objectives

The first stage in the planning and control process is establishing objectives. **Objectives** are the goals, aims, or purposes which executives, managers, and supervisors want the organization, or organizational unit, to achieve over a period of time. They are the targets toward which the organization or unit is moving. The importance of establishing specific objectives cannot be overstated. Unless members of the organization know what the objectives are—where they are going and what they are expected to accomplish—they will not know what to do.

Often we think of an organization as having only a single objective. In business it might be to make a profit, in schools to help students learn, or in hospitals to help the sick become well. In reality, however, most organizations have a number of objectives. In fact, Peter Drucker, a noted management consultant, recommends that a business organization establish concrete objectives in all the different areas on which its survival depends. He feels that businesses should have objectives in at least eight areas.[1] These areas are (1) market standing, (2) innovation, (3) productivity, (4) physical and financial standing, (5) profitability, (6) manager performance and development, (7) worker performance and attitude, and (8) public responsibility.

There are also differences in the degree of specificity of objectives. Some objectives are broad targets and apply to the organization as a whole. Others are quite specific. Top management generally sets broad objectives which give direction to the whole organization. Each department within an organization then sets more specific objectives consistent with the broad, organizational objectives. Finally, each individual may be guided by even more specific objectives related to particular department objectives.

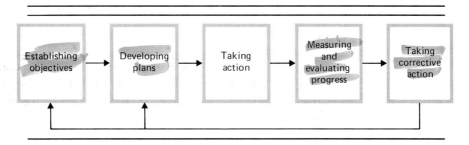

Figure 10.1 Four stages in the planning and control process.

Developing plans

The second stage in the planning and control process is developing **plans.** Once you have decided what you want to accomplish (setting objectives) you must determine how you will accomplish these objectives (developing plans.) When developing plans, you should remember that you are looking into the future. You are predicting what needs to be done to accomplish an objective based on what you know today. However, since conditions may change, you may not have complete information when developing plans. Thus, you should keep your plans somewhat flexible. Then, if necessary, you can change the plan and still accomplish your objective.

Measuring and evaluating progress

The third stage in the planning and control process is measuring and evaluating progress. This is done by measuring actual performance and comparing it to your objective (standard) to determine if activities are progressing as you planned.

In determining how to measure performance you need to remain aware of several factors. First, performance should be measured in the same units or terms in which objectives have been set. If you set an objective in terms of dollars, then you need to measure performance in terms of dollars. Second, you should decide how accurate your performance measurement needs to be. High degrees of accuracy can be quite costly and may be unnecessary. At the other extreme, however, "ball park" figures may be almost useless.

Taking corrective action

The final stage in the planning and control process, taking corrective action, is invoked if actual performance is not meeting standards. But before you "grab the bull by the horns," you need to check the facts. What caused the problem? What are the reasons for the deviation? As we discussed in the last chapter, a problem exists and you need to solve the problem.

Remember, both objectives (first stage) and the plan (second stage) were based on certain assumptions about the future which may or may not have held true. Only after you have analyzed carefully the reasons for any deviations will you be able to take meaningful corrective action. As the "feedback" line on Figure 10.1 shows, this action may involve replanning or even changing your objectives.

Planning and control at different levels

All levels of management are involved in the planning and control process. There are, however, variations in involvement at different levels. The planning and controlling done by a first-line supervisor in a large corporation differs from that done by the president of the corporation. Likewise, the planning and controlling activities of a nursing supervisor in a hospital differ from those of the hospital administrator.

One major difference concerns the length of time to be covered. Top-level managers in organizations typically are more involved with long-range planning. They are concerned with objectives and activities to be carried out and met six months, two years, or even five years in the future. For example, think of all the activities necessary to introduce a new car model: product design, production process design, and the marketing plan. Top management makes plans regarding these activities four years before the new car is introduced. Lower-level managers are more concerned with planning and controlling activities for the day, week, or month. Supervisors, for example, plan work activities for the day or week. Then they follow up to make certain their people do the work.

A second major difference concerns the emphasis placed on planning and control. Top managers generally spend more time on the planning part of the process. They are more concerned with establishing objectives and developing overall plans to meet those objectives. In addition, they become involved in replanning when information indicates objectives are not being met. Supervisors are more involved in the control part of the process. They are primarily responsible for activating plans and monitoring performance. When results are not "up to par" they take corrective action themselves or inform higher-level management so that corrective action can be taken.

The benefits of planning

The statement "failing to plan is planning to fail" applies to nearly all areas of life. If we don't have a good idea of where we are going and how we will get there, our chance of success is slim. This maxim is particularly true for you as a supervisor. You are responsible for the work of other people. Unless you establish objectives and develop plans for meeting those objectives, directing the efforts of your people will be difficult.

If you do not plan adequately you ultimately may spend a major portion of your time solving crises. You may find yourself trying to solve problems that probably would not have occurred if you had planned more carefully. While good planning does not eliminate all problems, it certainly can reduce them. Supervisors find good planning helps them perform their jobs more effectively.

Planning helps you deal with change.   Change is a fact of organizational life. Fluctuating demands, worker turnover, government regulation, and energy problems are just a few examples of changes with which supervisors must cope. Organizations must adapt to change if they are to continue functioning effectively. The planning process involves forecasting or anticipating the changes likely to occur which will affect the organization and its units.

Planning gives you and your workers a sense of direction. Without plans, you can only react to the events of the moment. Your reactions may or may not be consistent with the overall direction of the organization. Plans provide guidelines for today's actions, guidelines which ensure that today's actions contribute to the accomplishment of long-run objectives.

Planning focuses your attention on results.   Too often people tend to be activity-oriented rather than results-oriented. We concentrate on what we are doing rather than focusing on the results of our activities. Planning defines "why" we are performing an activity. By focusing on the goals or objectives established in planning, you can see how the results of your activities contribute to the accomplishment of organizational objectives.

Planning helps guide you in day-to-day decision making.   All decisions are future-oriented. Decisions you make today will influence how your unit will function in the future. When you make decisions within the framework of well-developed plans, the chances of making poor decisions or decisions inconsistent with organizational objectives are reduced.

Planning helps you coordinate work.   You must coordinate the efforts of your workers and the use of resources if your departmental objectives and the organizational objectives are to be accomplished. No organization can survive when people work in a haphazard manner. In the planning process, you identify activities necessary to accomplish department and organization objectives. Then, you can determine the resources necessary to perform these activities. As the plan is implemented, activities within the organization are coordinated by following the developed plan.

Types of plans

There are two different types of plans in most organizations. **Strategic plans** provide the long-run direction for the total organization and are the responsibility of top management. **Operating plans,** based on the strategic plan, are then developed within the organization. Operating plans cover a shorter period (one year or less) and provide more specific guidelines for action.

Tactical Plan – Day to Day

Supervisors typically are more involved in the development and implementation of operating plans. They are seldom involved in the strategic planning process. However, since operating plans flow from the strategic plan, supervisors are directly affected by the strategic plan. Therefore, you, as a supervisor, should have some understanding of the strategic planning process.

Strategic planning

Strategic planning involves all the activities which lead to the determination of objectives and the strategies the organization will use to accomplish those objectives.[2] The process involves anticipating changes in the external environment of the organization and planning how the organization will adapt to those changes. The strategic plan charts a course for the organization over the next three, five, or even ten years. It identifies products, services, and/or activities that will be emphasized as well as those that will deemphasized.

The strategic planning process begins with focusing on the external environment of the organization. Are trends or changes occurring which will affect the organization? Will these changes affect the organization's customers/clients? In particular, changes in technology, economic conditions, and social factors are examined for possible impact on markets served currently or potential markets.

Competitors are also analyzed. Are they particularly strong or weak in certain areas? Have they captured the major portion of the market in any areas? Comparing competitors' strengths with trends in markets helps identify areas of opportunity. Areas where market demand is growing and competitors' positions are weak are areas of greatest opportunity.

Once areas of opportunity have been identified, the organization is analyzed. What are its particular strengths and weaknesses? Strengths may include products or services that have a particularly good position in the market, particular capabilities of people in the organization, or specific facilities, equipment, or distribution channels.

A comparison of the organization's strengths and weaknesses and the areas of opportunity provides the basis for establishing strategies. The strategic plan would emphasize areas where the organization is strong, the market is growing, and the competition is weak. These areas would offer the greatest potential for future growth. Areas where the market is growing, the competition is weak, and the organization is weak should also be considered. To move into these areas, however, would require the addition of substantial resources. The organization would have to build a base capable of taking advantage of the potential opportunity, but risks are involved in this gamble. Other organizations might develop strength and be able take advantage of the opportunity more rapidly.

Areas where the organization is weak and the market is declining are areas to ignore. If the organization has an investment in these areas, it should attempt to draw resources from these areas and use them. But if competition is weak, the market is declining, and the organization is strong, it should not necessarily withdraw from that market to use the resources in some other area. While the organization would make no new investment in this area, it could use any remaining profits in the market to invest in other areas.

On the basis of this strategic analysis, the organization determines what products or services to provide to particular customers or markets. Further, it determines where resources will be added to develop products or markets and where these resources will be obtained. Objectives are then established for each product, service, and market. Plans are developed to indicate how these objectives will be accomplished.

This is the completed strategic plan: the overall objectives and the plans for accomplishing the objectives. It is a map of the organization's future direction, indicating the "business" it is in and specifying the mission of the organization.

Operating plans

Operating plans are developed within the framework of the strategic plan. These operating plans include programs, policies, procedures, and rules.

Programs   Programs are single-use plans. That is, they are plans for action designed to accomplish a single objective. Once the objective is accomplished, the plan will not be used again. Examples would be a plan (program) to build a house or a program to reduce absenteeism among workers. Likewise, the game plan developed by a football coach for a specific opponent would be a program.

Basically, programs answer the question, "What must be done to accomplish the objective?" The program may be quite general in nature, allowing for last-minute changes. General programs are best if the conditions of the particular planning situation are not too well known. The football coach, for example, would not make a game plan too detailed without being familiar with the opposing team. Likewise, the program might be quite specific, presenting in detail each step to be taken. In the next chapter, you will be introduced to techniques used in program planning.

Policies, procedures, and rules   Policies, procedures, and rules are standing plans. They serve as guides to action in day-to-day operations. They remain in force until they are changed.

Policies are the least specific of the standing plans. They are general statements that guide decision making. Policies define the boundaries within which decisions can be made and direct decisions toward the accomplishment of objectives. Another way of regarding policies is that they specify the range of acceptable behavior.

For example, a company may have the objective of obtaining market leadership in sales volume. The management of the company might develop a policy prescribing that only television advertising be used to increase sales volume. Note that the policy does not specify the nature of the advertising. It does, however, indicate that managers cannot advertise through newspapers, radio, or other media. Likewise, some organizations have a policy stating that they will hire only high school graduates. The policy does not specify who should be hired, but it does specify that people who are not high school graduates cannot be hired.

As you can see, a policy does not tell a supervisor specifically what to do in a situation. It does, however, clearly indicate action that should not be taken. Policies provide guidance by limiting decisions that can be made.

Some policies are established by top management and apply to all parts of the organization. Policies are, however, also developed by lower-level managers and apply to specific parts of the organization. Individual supervisors may develop specific policies for their sections only. To illustrate, colleges frequently have admission policies that apply to all students seeking admission to any program, while individual instructors might have attendance policies for their own classes. These latter policies would apply only to students in those classes and might differ from instructor to instructor.

Procedures are courses of action arranged in a sequence and designed to meet specific work objectives. In other words, procedures list the steps to be performed in a sequence to accomplish a specific task. The steps to be used in handling orders in a sales department or invoices in accounting are example of procedures.

Procedures are used to provide consistency of action among similar tasks within an organization. Without procedures, individuals performing the task might do things differently, leading to confusion and disorganization.

Rules are specific statements of what may or may not be done. Once it has been determined that a rule applies in a situation, little freedom of choice is left to the individual. An example would be "no smoking" rules. As we move from policies to procedures to rules, narrower, more specific guides to action are given.

The control process

The control process follows directly from the planning process. Once objectives are established and plans are developed to accomplish the objectives, the plans are put into action. Follow-up should occur to verify that actual performance is progressing according to plans and that the objectives are being accomplished. This involves the control process.

The purpose of the control process is not always to ensure that plans are being followed. Sometimes the control process indicates that plans must be changed. Remember, plans are established on the basis of forecasts and assumptions about the future. If those forecasts and assumptions turn out to be inaccurate (and the control process should provide that information), following the established plan would be foolish. Rather, the plan should be changed in light of new, more accurate forecasts or assumptions. Three steps are involved in the control process. They are (1) establishing standards, (2) measuring results and comparing them to the standard, and (3) taking corrective action when necessary. Let's look at each of these in more detail.

Establishing standards   This is the bridge between planning and control. Establishing standards is actually a part of the planning process. Standards are derived from objectives and are really statements of objectives for the activity being controlled. Standards are targets representing desired or expected performance for a given activity. Without standards no basis for comparison exists and no effective control process can be executed. For the control process to be effective, standards need to be clearly and specifically stated. Standards for any given activity should be related also to the larger objectives of the unit.

Comparing actual performance to standard   This is the information phase of the control process. Information is collected on the actual performance of an activity and is channeled to the supervisor responsible for the performance of the activity. The supervisor then compares actual performance with the established standard. If actual performance compares favorably with the standard, the activity is in control and no corrective action is required. If, however, actual and standard performance differ, corrective action may be necessary.

Taking corrective action   This is the action phase of the control process. If actual performance differs from standard, the first question to be asked is "Why?" The responsible supervisor begins the problem-solving process by attempting to determine the reason for the difference. Once the reason is identified and the cause is determined, action is taken to bring actual performance in line with standard performance. Remember however, that this can involve changing the plan or standard as well as changing actual performance.

When we examine organizations we find both formal and informal control systems. Formal control systems have explicitly stated standards of performance. Performance is systematically observed and measured. Written and documented reports of measurements and comparisons are compiled. Informal control systems are just the opposite. Performance is observed and measured in a nonsystematic manner. Oral, informal reports are used.

As a supervisor, you will do a great deal of informal controlling. Your daily work routine will involve checking casually to make certain your people are performing their work appropriately. You will also be involved in formal control systems. You will forward information on actual performance and receive reports on cost, performance, quality, and/or other significant factors.

What determines whether or not a formal control system should be established? Generally the importance of the activity is the determining factor. Since formal control systems are costly to establish and operate, organizations try to make certain that the benefits they obtain are worth the costs of the system. Thus, activities that are central to the accomplishment or organizational objectives are generally covered by formal control systems.

Characteristics of effective control systems

What are the characteristics of effective control systems? Peter Drucker provides the following guidelines for successful control systems.[3]

Controls should be economical. It is best to minimize the number of controls. Too much control and more elaborate control systems not only cost more, but create confusion rather than control.

Controls should be meaningful. Formal control systems should be applied to only key activities, or those that have a major impact on performance and results. Trying to control all the activities that only marginally contribute to results generally leads to a loss of control and confusion.

Controls should be simple. Complicated controls don't work. If people can't understand a control system they can't use it. Or, at best, they must spend their time trying to comprehend what the control system is and how it works. For control systems to be used effectively, they should be as simple as possible.

Controls should be operational. Controls should focus on action. The standards and information received on actual performance must be designed to lead to corrective action. Thus, if controls are to be operational, the information should reach the manager or supervisor who is responsible for the activity being controlled and who can take corrective action. Information given to top management does not help supervisors control their units. Likewise, giving information to supervisors is of no value unless they have the authority to take action.

Controls should be timely. Not only should the right people receive information, they should receive it at the right time. Information indicating that there is a cost overrun on a project is of no value to the supervisor after the project is completed. No action can be taken. Thus, control information should get to the individual who can take action in time for the action to affect the results.

Problems in planning and control

We have now discussed the planning and control process. Unfortunately, it is not as easy to plan and control effectively as it is to talk about it. You are likely to encounter problems in actually developing and using planning and control systems. Discussing these problems will not provide any easy answers, but it can point out some things to anticipate.

Planning and control involves looking into the future and making judgments about future conditions. Objectives are set and plans are made based on a combination of predictions and assumptions. In a changing world, however, some or many of these predictions and assumptions will prove inaccurate. Thus, if planning and control is to be effective, it must be part of a continuous process. As changes occur, you need to adjust your plans accordingly.

There is a tendency for planning and control systems to become unnecessarily complex and difficult to understand. Drucker has provided a good example of the importance of simple, understandable planning and control systems.[4] In the 1960s major New York banks devoted considerable effort to developing planning and control systems. A great deal of time and money was spent to develop detailed control manuals. According to Drucker, the manuals actually were being used in only one of these banks.

When Drucker asked an executive at a bank that was using the manual to explain why. He said "I have two teenage kids. They know nothing about banking and are not terribly good at figures. But they are bright. Whenever I had worked out an approach to controlling an activity, I took my intended procedure home in draft form and asked my kids to let me explain it to them. And only when I had it so simple that they could explain back to me what the procedure intended to accomplish and how, did I go ahead." Thus, for a planning and control system to be effective it should be understandable.

Too often planning and control systems provide information too late for it to be of any real value. Remember, planning and control systems are forward-looking by nature. Since you cannot control the past, the sooner you are aware of deviations in performance from objectives and plans, the sooner you can take corrective action.

Thus, reporting deviations from objectives and plans quickly is often more desirable, even if only approximations are available, than waiting a long time for exact information.

How often you make and report comparisons of actual performance and plans depends on what you are controlling. If you are the project manager for the installation of equipment on a company's premises and you have a tight time schedule for completion, you might want to plan the project down to a day-by-day basis and receive daily progress reports. On the other hand, the proper planning and control time span for a research and development manager would certainly not be daily or even monthly. He or she would be involved in much longer planning and control time spans.

Finally, planning and control systems sometimes cost more than they are really worth. A complex planning and control system that may be necessary for a large corporation is not needed in a small business. The need for planning and control exists in both situations, but the degree of complexity required is different. More complex planning and control systems do not necessarily make for better planning and control. They do cost more money, and sometimes the only result is increased confusion. Thus, while planning and control systems are necessary, they should not be overly complex and costly.

Summary

☐ The planning and control process helps direct the work of a supervisor's unit and ensure it is coordinated with the rest of the organization. Planning involves setting performance objectives and determining how they will be achieved (plans). Control involves comparing actual performance with standards (objectives) and taking corrective action when deviations occur.

☐ There are four stages in the planning and control process: (1) setting objectives, (2) developing plans, (3) measuring and evaluating actual performance, and (4) taking corrective action. All levels of management engage in the planning and control process. There are variations in involvement at different levels.

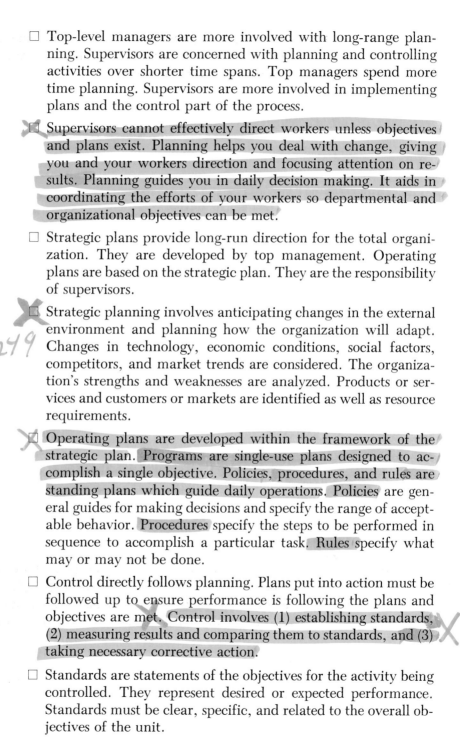

☐ Top-level managers are more involved with long-range planning. Supervisors are concerned with planning and controlling activities over shorter time spans. Top managers spend more time planning. Supervisors are more involved in implementing plans and the control part of the process.

☐ Supervisors cannot effectively direct workers unless objectives and plans exist. Planning helps you deal with change, giving you and your workers direction and focusing attention on results. Planning guides you in daily decision making. It aids in coordinating the efforts of your workers so departmental and organizational objectives can be met.

☐ Strategic plans provide long-run direction for the total organization. They are developed by top management. Operating plans are based on the strategic plan. They are the responsibility of supervisors.

☐ Strategic planning involves anticipating changes in the external environment and planning how the organization will adapt. Changes in technology, economic conditions, social factors, competitors, and market trends are considered. The organization's strengths and weaknesses are analyzed. Products or services and customers or markets are identified as well as resource requirements.

☐ Operating plans are developed within the framework of the strategic plan. Programs are single-use plans designed to accomplish a single objective. Policies, procedures, and rules are standing plans which guide daily operations. Policies are general guides for making decisions and specify the range of acceptable behavior. Procedures specify the steps to be performed in sequence to accomplish a particular task. Rules specify what may or may not be done.

☐ Control directly follows planning. Plans put into action must be followed up to ensure performance is following the plans and objectives are met. Control involves (1) establishing standards, (2) measuring results and comparing them to standards, and (3) taking necessary corrective action.

☐ Standards are statements of the objectives for the activity being controlled. They represent desired or expected performance. Standards must be clear, specific, and related to the overall objectives of the unit.

☐ Comparing results to standards is the information phase. It indicates whether or not the activity is in control. When differences occur, corrective action may be needed.

☐ Supervisors must determine why actual performance differs from standard. Corrective action may involve changing actual performance, the plan, or the standard.

☐ Formal and informal control systems exist in all organizations. Supervisors spend much time informally controlling the daily activities of their workers. They also are involved in formal control. Formal control generally exists for activities important to accomplishing organizational objectives.

☐ Planning and control are difficult because they involve predicting the future. As conditions change, plans must be adjusted. Planning and control systems tend to become too complex to be understood. Information is often provided too late. Sometimes planning and control systems cost more than they are worth.

Questions for review and discussion

1. What is planning? What is control?

2. Discuss the four stages in the planning and control process.

3. Distinguish between the involvement of top managers and supervisors in the planning and control process.

4. How can planning make supervisors more effective?

5. What are the two types of plans in organizations? How do they differ? How are they related?

6. Describe the strategic planning process.

7. Discuss the types of operating plans found in organizations.

8. Discuss the three steps involved in the control process.

9. How do formal control systems differ from informal control systems? When are formal controls desirable?

10. What are the characteristics of an effective control system?

Key terms

Control process	Policies
Formal control systems	Procedures
Informal control systems	Programs
Operating plans	Rules
Objectives	Standards
Planning process	Strategic plans
Plans	

Cases for discussion and practical exercises

1. Think of an activity that you must perform in the next month to six months. Establish specific objectives that you want to accomplish relative to the activity. Develop a plan detailing how you will perform the activity and accomplish your objectives.

2. Consider the process used at your school to register for classes. Write a procedure statement detailing each step in the registration process. Also, identify five policies that affect you at your school. Identify three rules. Analyze the differences between the identified policies, procedures, and rules.

Notes

1. Peter Drucker, *Management* (New York: Harper and Row, 1974).

2. A. A. Thompson, Jr., and A. J. Strickland, III. *Strategy and Policy* (Dallas: Business Publications, Inc., 1978).

3. Drucker, *Management*.

4. Ibid., p. 503.

11

Techniques for planning and controlling

Objectives

After reading this chapter you should be able to

☐ Explain the management by objectives (MBO) process.

☐ Explain how bar charts and networks are used in work activity planning and control.

☐ Discuss the supervisor's use of budgets.

☐ Explain how supervisors can use break-even analysis.

☐ Explain how supervisors can determine when to reorder inventory.

Much of the planning and controlling you do as a supervisor is informal. You determine the tasks to be accomplished and assign jobs to workers. Then you observe how workers are progressing. Is the work getting done on time? Does the quality of work seem acceptable? Are there any problems?

There are, however, more formal planning and control techniques which can be useful. Generally, these techniques are used for more complex planning and control when considerable resources and/or a substantial amount of time are involved. In this chapter we will discuss a number of these techniques.

Management by objectives

Management by objectives (MBO) is a popular approach to planning and control. MBO formalizes the informal planning and control process that occurs in an organization. With this approach goals and deadlines are determined, and follow-up occurs to ensure goals are accomplished. *Set new objectives.*

Ideally, MBO begins at the top of the organization with the establishment of specific organizational objectives. Then, at the next level of the organization, managers, working with their bosses, establish objectives for their departments. The departmental objectives flow from and are consistent with organizational objectives. This procedure is repeated down through all levels of the organization.

The central factor in the MBO process is the objective-setting discussion between manager and subordinate. During the discussion they decide (1) the objectives to be accomplished, (2) the time required to accomplish each objective, and (3) the basis on which progress will be judged. When the established time has lapsed, they meet again. During this second discussion they review accomplishments and set further objectives for the future, thereby starting the process again.

The results of the discussion between manager and subordinate are usually summarized in a formal document, such as that shown in Fig. 11.1. Column one lists the agreed-upon objectives. Column two indicates the date by which the objectives are to be accomplished. Column three will be completed when they meet again to review accomplishments.

OBJECTIVE	DATE	ACCOMPLISHMENTS
To reduce waste to 4% of raw materials used	1/15/82	
To reduce lost time due to accidents to 5 person-days per year	6/15/82	
To reduce operating costs to 5% below budget	6/15/82	
To complete the Ohio University supervisory development program	5/1/82	

Dean Jones   6/4/81

Position: Production Supervisor

Figure 11.1   A sample management-by-objectives form.

Two factors are quite important if the MBO process is to work effectively.

■ The objective-setting meeting should involve a thorough and complete discussion between manager and subordinate. The subordinate should participate fully in determining his or her objectives. Further, each objective should be completely discussed, since the purpose is not just to set objectives. Rather, the purpose is to ensure that there is a common understanding of and agreement on objectives.

■ The established objectives should be stated clearly and specifically. Each person should state exactly what is to be accomplished. Note the differences between the following two objectives: **Objective 1:** Improve quality in the department as much as possible as soon as possible. **Objective 2:** Decrease daily rejects in the department by 50% by March 1, 1983. The first objective is unclear and could be interpreted differently by different people. In contrast, the second objective states the quality of performance sought (decrease rejects), the desired level of improvement (50%), and the date by which the improvement should be accomplished (March 1, 1983).

An effective MBO system has several advantages for any type of organization. Most importantly, it requires that clearly stated objectives be set and helps ensure that objectives are consistent throughout the organization. Developing objectives consistent with the overall organizational plan ensures that people and departments are working cooperatively rather than at cross-purposes.

In the MBO process, subordinates are actively involved in setting objectives for their areas. This involvement can encourage higher levels of work motivation. If they help set their objectives, subordinates generally will be more committed to the objectives and work harder to accomplish them.

MBO also encourages a more objective evaluation of performance. Performance is evaluated on the basis of the degree of accomplishment of specific objectives. This is generally better than evaluating performance on the basis of personal characteristics or other subjective factors. Evaluating performance on the basis of general traits or characteristics, such as leadership, initiative or judgment, provides little basis for concrete feedback. It also fails to provide an indication of changes needed to improve performance. MBO provides tangible feedback and clearly indicates improvement opportunities.

The use of MBO can cause difficulties. Some supervisors report that they feel MBO is just a paper-shuffling exercise. They feel the emphasis is on neatly completing all the forms, getting the proper signatures, and making certain the forms suit their boss. No real discussion with the boss occurs and often, after the forms are submitted, the process is forgotten until review time. The MBO process becomes an end in itself rather than the means to an end. These problems need not occur. If the emphasis is on reaching agreement about what is to be accomplished, the MBO process can function effectively. Rather than being merely an exercise, MBO can be a useful tool for planning and controlling.

Planning and controlling work activities

Any organization, whether it makes a product or provides a service, needs to resolve such questions as who is going to do what, in what order, and in how long a time. Work activity planning and control systems use techniques that are designed to deal with these questions. We will look at two of these techniques: bar charts and network techniques.

Bar charts or, as they are sometimes called, Gantt charts, are useful for repetitive projects or projects involving relatively few activities. For more complicated projects with many interrelated activities, network techniques are often used.

Bar charts

To develop a bar chart, you first determine the activities or operations that comprise a particular job or project. Then you determine the order in which the activities should take place and the duration of each activity. Once these estimates have been made, each activity can be represented by a bar on the chart.

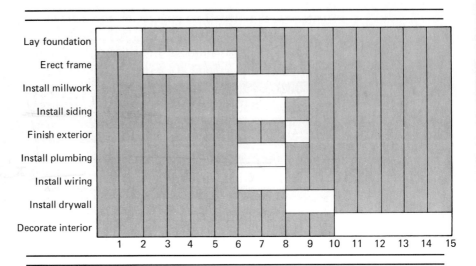

Figure 11.2 Bar chart for building a house.

Figure 11.2 is an example of a bar chart showing the plan for the construction of a house. The activities involved in building the house are listed on the left side of the chart. Along the bottom of the chart is a time scale. The length of the bars on the chart indicate the estimated amount of time each activity will take, as well as when the builder plans to start and complete each activity.

The bar chart shown in Figure 11.2 is developed before the construction of the house begins. Once the project is activated, the progress of each activity can be monitored and shown on the chart. Figure 11.3 shows the bar chart for the same construction project at the end of eight weeks. The amount of progress for each activity is indicated by the shaded part of the bar. The time elapsed since the beginning of the project is shown by the arrow on the time scale of the chart.

According to the bar chart in Figure 11.3, everything appears to be going well. All activities, except wiring, are on schedule. However, a delay in wiring may not be a problem. The project still has seven weeks to run and the chart shows only one week of wiring to be completed.

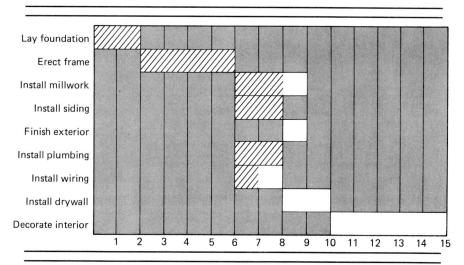

Figure 11.3   Updated bar chart.

Although bar charts are quite useful for relatively simple projects, they do have a serious weakness. They do not show the relationships among the activities, or which activities must be completed before others can be started.

For example, look at the bar chart in Figure 11.3 again. As we noted before, the one-week delay in wiring does not seem to be a problem, since the project still has seven weeks to go. But what the bar chart does not show is the very important fact that dry walling cannot begin until the wiring is completed, and interior decorating cannot start until the dry walling is completed. In other words, it is doubtful that the house will be completed on time unless some corrective action is taken.

Network techniques

Like a bar chart, a network shows the activities to be done and the time required for each activity. In addition, it shows the relationships among the activities, or which activities must be completed before others are begun.

PERT

Program

Evaluation

and

Review

Technique

Is used for new projects

Thus, although network techniques require more thorough planning, they permit greater accuracy in evaluating progress. For example, a builder using a network for the house construction project would have known that wiring must be completed before plastering could start and that the building project was running behind schedule. Networks are constructed around two elements: activities and events. An activity is the work necessary to complete a particular event. An event is an accomplishment at a particular time. In networks, an event is represented by a circle and activities are indicated by arrows.

Five basic steps are involved in constructing a network. These are:

1. Determining each activity that must be done to complete the project.
2. Determining which activities must be completed before others are begun.
3. Estimating how long each activity will take.
4. Constructing the network, making certain that it shows each activity that must be completed before another activity can be started.
5. Finding the **critical path:** the series of activities that takes the greatest amount of time from the beginning event to ending event. FIG 11.4

A network shows all the events and activities necessary to complete the project and the relationships among these activities.

Table 11.1 is a network development worksheet showing the activities and their sequence for the house construction project. Using this worksheet the network shown in Fig. 11.4 is developed.

To find the critical path, it is first necessary to identify each path or series of activities in the network. Then, the activity times for each of the paths are totaled. The path that takes the greatest amount of time is the critical path. The time required for the critical path is the estimated completion time for the project.

Properly constructed networks are useful in two ways: (1) they permit improved planning, and (2) they ensure better control. Networks help plan the best use of resources within overall time limits. Because they indicate the relationships among activities and the estimated times of completion, networks facilitate planning an optimum schedule before starting work. If, for example, the builder

Table 11.1

Network development
worksheet

	ACTIVITY	IMMEDIATELY PRECEDING ACTIVITIES
A	Lay Foundation	
B	Errect Frame	A
C	Install Millwork	B
D	Install Siding	B
E	Finish Exterior	D
F	Install Plumbing	B
G	Install Wiring	B
H	Install Drywall	F, G
I	Decorate Interior	H

wanted to complete the house in a shorter time, more people could be added to work on activities on the critical path.

Once the network is completed and the project started, the networks may be used for control. By keeping track of actual versus scheduled times for each activity, you can determine when and where time "slippage" is occurring. Action then can be taken to correct the problem. If, for example, the builder found that wiring was taking longer than originally planned, more workers could be added to complete the interior decorating in a shorter time so the house would still be completed in fifteen weeks.

Budgets

In most organizations, budgets are the primary financial planning and control technique. While most organizations generally prepare and use several types of budgets, the operating budget is the most basic. An operating budget shows projected revenue, costs, and profits for a fixed time into the future.

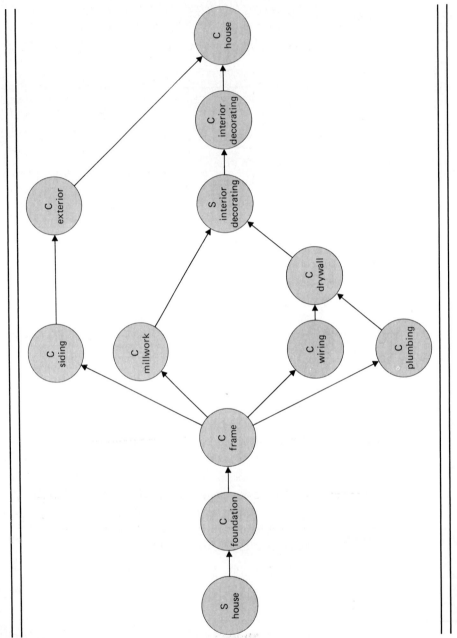

Figure 11.4   Network for building a house.

As an example of how an operating budget is constructed, let's look at Robert's, a small manufacturer of fashion jeans. The first task in constructing an operating budget is forecasting revenue for the year. After talking with their salespeople and estimating economic conditions, Robert's forecasted that they could sell 10,000 dozen jeans at a price of $100.00 per dozen.

Based on past experience and estimates of future conditions, Robert's also projected the expenses that would be incurred to meet their forecasted sales volume. They estimated that the fabric and other materials would cost about $50.00 per dozen of finished jeans. Labor costs were estimated to be $24.00 per dozen.

Revenue and expense projections were combined to arrive at the operating budget for Robert's shown in Table 11.2. This budget shows the planned financial results and provides a standard against which actual results can be compared.

Table 11.2

**Robert's Fashions Inc.
operating budget**

		BUDGET
Net Sales	10,000 dozen @ $100/dozen	1,000,000
Expenses		
Materials	@ $50/dozen	500,000
Direct labor	@ $24/dozen	240,000
Selling expense		40,000
Shipping		15,000
Management and office salaries		88,000
Rent		20,000
Utilities		15,000
Depreciation		12,000
Repairs		10,000
Total expenses		940,000
Operating profit		60,000

During the first eight months of the year, the operating results of Robert's were surprisingly close to the budget. Trouble began to emerge in October. Poor economic conditions decreased retail sales so reorders did not come in as anticipated. To move its growing inventory of jeans, Robert's decided to cut prices to retailers. Even then, sales were below the budget forecast. The actual revenue and expense figures for the year are compared with budgeted figures in Table 11.3.

The difference between budgeted and actual profit is primarily the result of lower-than-budgeted sales. There is more to the picture, however. Actual labor costs were $1.56 per dozen higher than budgeted costs. Variations in other expenses were minor. This compari-

Table 11.3

Actual revenue and expenses
compared to budgeted:
Robert's Fashions Inc.

	BUDGET		ACTUAL		DIFFERENCE
Net sales	10,000 dozen @ $100/dozen	1,000,000	9,000 dozen @ $98/dozen	882,000	– 118,000
Expenses					
Materials	@ $50/dozen	500,000	@ $50/dozen	450,000	– 50,000
Direct labor	@ $24/dozen	240,000	@ $25.56/ dozen	230,000	– 10,000
Selling expense		40,000		36,000	– 4,000
Shipping		15,000		14,000	– 1,000
Management and office salaries		88,000		88,000	0
Rent		20,000		20,000	0
Utilities		15,000		16,000	+ 1,000
Depreciation		12,000		12,000	0
Repairs		10,000		12,000	+ 2,000
Total expenses		940,000		878,000	– 62,000
Operating profit		60,000		4,000	– 56,00

son indicates that sales volume and direct labor costs are areas where improvements must be made if Robert's is to become more profitable.

Many supervisors are involved only in the expense side of budgets. In this situation, supervisors can neither plan nor control the level of work activity. They can, however, plan and control the expenses incurred while obtaining a required level of work activity.

A supervisor of an assembly department, for example, does not plan the number of units assembled. The number to be produced is determined by higher-level management or a staff department such as production control. Knowing how many units are to be produced, however, the supervisor can budget the amount of labor, materials, supplies, and so forth required to meet production requirements. An example of a month's budget for the sewing room of Robert's is given in Table 11.4.

Table 11.4

Sewing room budget for Robert's: Month 1

MATERIALS

Cut fabric	4000 doz. halfs @ 20.00	80,000
Thread	1000 spools @ 0.50	500
Labels	25,000 @ 0.10	2,500
Zippers	25,000 @ 0.20	5,000
		88,000

DIRECT LABOR

20 Sewing Machine Operators @ 5.00	16,800
4 Inspectors @ 6.00	4,032
1 Maintenance person @ 10.00	1,680
	22,500

Note: Production requirement: 2000 dozen

Expense budgets are used for control purposes. The supervisor may or may not be involved in establishing the budget. But the supervisor is accountable for meeting the budget. The budget provides the standard and, if there is deviation from the budget, the supervisor is expected to determine the cause and take corrective action.

In using budgets, you should keep in mind that you are dealing with estimates. If budgets are to be useful, estimates of revenues and expenses should be as accurate as possible. It is unlikely, however, that any budget will be totally accurate. For example, changes in economic conditions, such as those experienced by Robert's, can make initial estimates unreasonable. Similarly, changes in costs of material or supplies can make a budget inaccurate. Thus, actual versus planned estimates of revenues should be reviewed on a regular basis such as weekly, monthly, or perhaps quarterly. If deviations are apparent, it can be determined if they are controllable. If controllable, corrective action can be taken. If uncontrollable, budgets can be revised to be more accurate.

Break-even analysis

Break-even analysis is a technique for studying relationships between level of output (i.e., the number of products sold or units of service provided), revenues, costs, and profit or loss. It can provide answers to questions such as (1) What level of output is necessary to avoid losing money?; (2) What amount of profit or loss can be expected at various levels of output?; and (3) What level of output is necessary to achieve a desired level of profit?

Break-even analysis may be performed using either a break-even chart or a formula. Figure 11.5 depicts a typical break-even chart. The vertical scale on the graph represents dollars of revenue and cost, while the horizontal scale represents volume or activity in units of output. On the chart, four different lines are plotted: fixed costs, variable costs, total costs, and total revenue lines.

Fixed costs are constant regardless of the level of output. For example, a firm anticipating the need for warehouse space may have purchased a warehouse. However, because of present production levels, it may not be using the space completely. Yet the warehouse is insured for period of time and the fixed insurance premium must be paid regardless. Other examples of fixed costs are rent, and administrative salaries. Because they are the same for all levels of output, fixed costs are represented by a horizontal line.

Variable costs are those costs directly attributable to the level of output. If output goes up, so do these costs. If output declines, these expenses decrease proportionately. In a production organization, direct labor and materials are examples of variable costs. The more units produced, the more direct labor and materials costs will be incurred. Since there are no variable costs unless there is output, the variable costs line is zero at zero units of output. As the level of output rises, the level of variable costs increases.

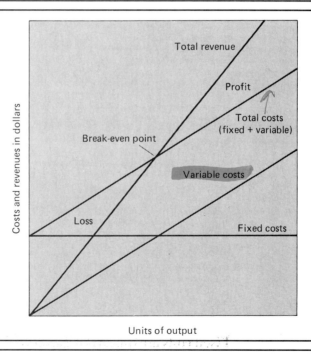

Figure 11.5   An example of a break-even chart.

Total costs represent the sum of fixed and variable costs.

Total revenue is the product of unit sales price and the level of output. The relationship between total revenue, price, and output volume can be expressed mathematically as:

$$TR = Q \times P$$

where TR designates total revenue; P designates unit sales price; and Q designates unit volume of output.

On the chart shown in Fig. 11.5 the point at which the total revenue line and total costs line intersect is the break-even point. To the right of this point, the spread between total revenue and total costs represents profit potential; to the left, it represents the loss potential.

Break-even analysis can be determined more quickly and accurately (but not as vividly) by using a formula. The following symbols are generally used:

BE = break-even point,
P = selling price per unit,
VC = variable cost per unit,
TFC = total fixed costs,
Q = number of units of output.

Using the symbols cited above, we can derive the break-even formula. First we define the equation for total costs:

$$TC = (VC \times Q) + TFC.$$

Then we define total revenue:

$$TR = P \times Q.$$

At the break-even point the total costs equal the total revenue. Therefore, equating these two equations yields:

$$P \times Q = (VC \times Q) + TFC,$$
$$P \times Q - VC \times Q = TFC,$$
$$(P - VC) \times Q = TFC,$$
$$Q = \frac{TFC}{P - VC}.$$

Thus, the formula for calculating the break-even point (in units of output) is:

$$BE = \frac{\text{Total Fixed Costs } (TFC)}{\text{Selling price per unit } (P) - \text{Variable cost/unit } (VC)}.$$

To illustrate the use of the formula, let's consider a hospital administrator who is trying to decide whether to add a family practice center. An adjacent building can be purchased for $160,000 and will entail a $200,000 remodeling expense. The following cost and revenue figures have been projected.

A service charge of $10 per patient is contemplated. This is the charge made by the organization and does not include the doctor's fee, which is billed separately. Thus, the hospital's revenue per unit of service (output) will be $10.

The annual fixed costs are as follows: (1) depreciation at 10% of the building acquisition and remodeling costs (straightline depreciation over ten years) or $36,000 per year ($360,000 × .10); (2) heat and electricity averaging $6,000 per year; (3) the depreciation of equipment acquired and periodic replacement of equipment averaging $6,000 per year; (4) salaries for two registered nurses and one clerk receptionist totaling $44,000; and (5) maintenance service fee of $4,000. The variable costs for disposable supplies used with each patient will be $2.00 per patient served.

Using the costs and revenue data, the break-even point can be calculated as follows:

$$TFC = \$96,000 \ (36,000 + 6,000 + 6,000 + 44,000 + 4,000),$$
$$P = \$10,$$
$$VC = \$2.$$

Solving for the break-even point:

$$BE = \frac{96,000}{10 - 2}$$
$$BE = \$12,000.$$

Thus the family practice center would have to serve 12,000 patients a year in order to break even.

There are limitations to break-even analysis. Precise estimates of costs, either fixed or variable, are often difficult to obtain. In addition, costs can change rather quickly. Finally, in an organization that produces a variety of products or services, allocating fixed costs is difficult.

Break-even analysis can, however, provide you with additional insight for planning and control. It can help you analyze the effect of changes in costs or prices on profitability. Therefore it can be helpful in determining appropriate courses of action.

For example, what if the hospital administrator in our example felt there would be a utilization rate of only 10,000 patients per year? What could be done? Several possibilities are open. The price of each visit could be raised. He or she might try to obtain the building at lower cost. A cheaper source of disposable supplies might be available. Or, he or she might decide that it was not feasible to add the family practice center. In any case, the use of break-even analysis can make the administrator aware of the relationship among demand for the service, price of the service, and costs of providing the service. Without such an analysis, the family practice center might have imposed a severe financial drain on the hospital.

Supervisors are affected by many decisions made using break-even analysis. They are more likely, however, to use an application of break-even analysis that considers only costs. In particular, they often need to determine what volume of operation is necessary to justify an increase in fixed costs that leads to a decrease in variable costs. Consider the following example. Jim Jones is a supervisor of an office services area of a firm. He is responsible for all longer-run copying done by his firm. They now use a machine that has a rental cost of $100 per month and a per-copy charge of $0.05. The copy machine salesperson is proposing that they switch to a slightly larger and more sophisticated machine. The monthly rental on the proposed machine is $200, but the per-copy charge is only $0.03. Jim is trying to decide whether or not he should recommend changing to the proposed machine.

Jim can use a type of break-even analysis to help make his decision. Considering only costs, he can determine how many copies per month he must run for the costs of both the present machine and the proposed machine to be equal. Using the symbols we used before:

$$\text{Present machine} = TC = VC \times Q + TFC = 0.05Q + 100,$$
$$\text{Proposed machine} = TC = VC \times Q + TFC = 0.03Q + 200.$$

To determine the number of copies that must be made per month for the costs of the two machines to be equal, set the total costs equal and solve for Q.

$$0.05Q + 100 = 0.03Q + 200,$$
$$0.02Q = 100,$$
$$Q = 5000.$$

Knowing the break-even point can help Jim decide whether or not to recommend renting the proposed machine. If his section processes more than 5000 copies per month on average, the proposed machine will save his company money. A variable cost that is $0.02 per copy lower will more than offset the $100 increase in fixed costs. If the average monthly volume were less than 5000 copies, it would be cheaper to keep the present machine.

Inventory planning and control

Planning and controlling inventory levels is an important function in many organizations. In a clothing store, for example, a sufficient amount of stock in different styles, sizes, and colors must be kept on hand. Hospitals need to plan and control their supply of drugs. McDonald's must ensure that they have sufficient hamburgers and buns. And, of course, manufacturing organizations need to control the amount of raw materials and parts available for making their products, as well as the amount of finished goods produced but not yet sold.

Several decisions are necessary to plan and control inventory effectively. For each part, product, or unit of raw material, a maximum inventory level, a minimum inventory level, a reorder point, and an order size needs to be determined. As can be seen in Fig. 11.6, over time, usage will cause the amount of stock on hand to decline. Before the minimum inventory level is reached, an order for additional stock should be placed. The inventory level at which an order is placed is called the reorder point.

To determine the **reorder point**, you consider the usage rate, lead time, and safety stock level. The formula is $R = U \times L + SS$.

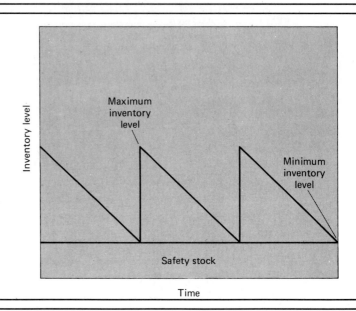

Figure 11.6   Inventory levels.

Usage rate (U) is the number of units used per unit of time. Lead time (L) is the time that is required to obtain additional units. Safety stock (SS) provides protection if there is a change in either usage rate or lead time. Both usage rate and lead time are estimates based on past experience. Thus, the usage rate may increase or it may take longer for an order to be received. If so, units available in safety stock can keep you from running out of inventory.

Let's try an example. Assume that you are the supervisor of a small specialty printing department in an organization. A key inventory item you need to plan for and control is a special type of paper. You use 10 cases of the paper each working day. Each case contains 10 reams and each ream contains 500 sheets. Your past experience indicates that it takes 1 week (5 working days) to receive the paper after the order is placed. Since usage rate is very constant and the supplier of paper has been reliable, you maintain a fairly low safety stock—30 cases. What is the reorder point?

First identify your terms:

U = usage rate = 10 cases/day,
L = lead time = 5 days,
S = safety stock = 30 cases.

Then use the formula:

$$R = U \times L + SS$$
$$= 10 \times 5 + 30$$
$$= 50 + 30$$
$$= 80.$$

Thus the reorder point is 80 cases. When your inventory reaches 80 cases, you place an order with the expectation that the order will be received in 5 days when your inventory is 30 cases.

This raises another question. How many cases should you order? To help answer this question you can use the economic order quantity technique.

Economic order quantity

Economic order quantity is a technique that helps minimize two kinds of costs: those associated with obtaining and with carrying inventory. Ordering costs are the costs associated with ordering goods, obtaining them, and placing them in inventory. Carrying costs include the interest on money invested in inventory, the taxes on inventory, the costs of storage space, rent, obsolescence, insurance, and losses due to theft, fire, and deterioration. The ordering costs occur each time an order is placed and received. The carrying costs are ongoing and are generally expressed as a percentage of the average value of the inventory. Organizations attempt to minimize inventory costs by minimizing ordering costs and carrying costs. These costs, however, are inversely related as shown in Fig. 11.7.

How do we determine order costs? The number of orders for a given period of time is equal to the demand (D) for that period divided by the number of units ordered each time (Q). The total ordering costs per period (week, month, year) are equal to the costs of placing each order (C) multiplied by the number of orders placed per time period (D/Q). As the size of each order increases, fewer orders are required to meet the demand for the period. Thus, ordering costs for the period decrease. This is shown graphically by the downward sloping order–cost curve in Fig. 11.7.

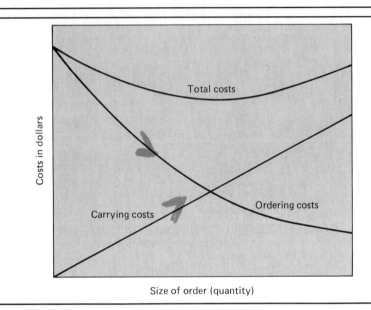

Figure 11.7   Inventory costs.

How do we determine carrying costs? The cost of carrying one item in inventory is calculated by multiplying the value of the item (V) by the percentage value of inventory associated with carrying costs (P). The total carrying costs are equal to the cost of carrying one item ($P \times V$) multiplied by the average inventory size ($Q/2$). As shown in Figure 11.7, carrying costs increase as order size increases because with larger orders, there is a larger average inventory.

To illustrate, let's return to our previous example. Since you work 240 days per year, your yearly demand for paper is 2400 cases. Further, you know that the cost of placing and receiving each order is $75. The carrying costs are 20% of the average inventory value. The value of a case of paper is $20. Thus the components involved are:

D = yearly demand = 2400 units/year,
C = ordering costs = $75/order,
P = carrying costs = 20%,
V = item value = $2/unit.

As shown in Table 11.5, total costs decrease as order size decreases, up to a point. Then total costs start to increase with decreasing order size. To minimize inventory costs, the economic order quantity formula can be used to calculate the order size.

Referring back to Fig. 11.7, we can see that the minimum inventory cost is at the point directly above the intersection of the carrying cost curve and the ordering cost curve. Thus, to derive the economic order quantity (EOQ), we first want to balance carrying costs and ordering costs:

$$Q/2 \times (V \times P) = D/Q \times (C).$$

Solving for Q:

$$Q(V \times P) = 2(D \times C)/Q,$$
$$Q^2(V \times P) = 2(D \times C),$$
$$Q^2 = 2(D \times C)/(V \times P),$$
$$Q = \sqrt{2(D \times C)/(V \times P)}.$$

Table 11.5

Inventory costs for varying numbers of orders and order sizes

NUMBER OF ORDERS	ORDER SIZE	AVERAGE INVENTORY UNITS	AVERAGE INVENTORY VALUES	ORDERING COSTS	CARRYING COSTS	TOTAL
1	2400	1200	24000	75	4800	4875
3	800	400	8000	225	1600	1825
6	400	200	4000	450	800	1285
8	300	150	3000	600	600	1200
12	200	100	2000	900	400	1300

Using this formula to find the best order size for paper in this example we find:

$$Q = \sqrt{2(2400)\ 75/20\ (0.20)}$$
$$= \sqrt{36000/4.00}$$
$$= \sqrt{90000}$$
$$= 300.$$

Thus, 300 cases of paper should be ordered each time to minimize the costs of ordering and carrying inventory in our example.

There are limits to the use of the economic order quantity formula. The formula is based on the assumption that the demand for the item is known with certainty. Further, it is assumed that the inventory is depleted at a constant rate. Estimating demand can be quite difficult. Many factors, such as economic conditions and competitive prices, can influence demand. Seldom is the demand constant; it fluctuates over time. In addition, estimates of costs, such as order costs and carrying costs, may not be completely accurate. They are generally based on historical information and, particularly in inflationary times, may not be accurate estimates for the future. Despite these limitations, however, the economic order quantity formula can help you make more effective decisions when attempting to minimize inventory costs.

Summary

☐ Management by objectives (MBO) formalizes the informal planning and control process. It involves an objective-setting discussion between managers and subordinates. This discussion results in joint decisions regarding objectives to be accomplished, when they will be accomplished, and how progress will be evaluated.

☐ Advantages of MBO include (1) clearly stated and consistent objectives, (2) subordinates' participation, and (3) systematic evaluation of performance. Difficulties arise when MBO is viewed as a paper-shuffling exercise and real discussion does not occur.

☐ Work activity planning and control systems determine who does what, in what order, and in what time period. Bar charts are useful for repetitive projects and projects involving few activities. They do not show relationships among the activities.

☐ Network techniques are used for more complicated projects with many interrelated activities. Like bar charts, they show the activities to be done and the time required. They also show which activities must be completed before others are started.

☐ Networks involve two elements: activities and events. Activities are the work necessary to complete a task. Events are accomplishments at a point in time. Each series of activities forms a path. The critical path is the path that takes the greatest amount of time.

☐ Operating budgets show projected revenue, costs, and profits for a fixed time in the future. Supervisors typically are involved in planning and controlling expenses necessary to obtain an established level of work activity. They do not usually plan or control the level of work activities.

☐ Budgets provide standards. Supervisors may not develop budgets but they are accountable for meeting them. Remember that budgets are based on estimates of the future which may be inaccurate.

☐ Break-even analysis relates the level of output, revenues, costs, and profits. It indicates the expected level of profits or losses at various levels of output, and the level of output necessary to achieve a desired level of profit.

☐ Break-even analysis may be performed using break-even charts or a formula. Fixed costs remain constant at all levels of output. Variable costs increase or decrease with the level of output. Total costs equal the sum of fixed and variable costs. Total revenue is the product of unit sales price and the level of output. On a break-even chart, the point where the total revenue line intersects the total costs line is the break-even point. Using the formula, the break-even point is:

$$\frac{\text{Total Fixed Costs } (TFC)}{\text{Selling Price per Unit } (P) - \text{Variable Cost per Unit } (VC)}.$$

☐ Inventory planning and control involves determining the maximum inventory level, minimum inventory level, reorder point, and order size for each part. The reorder point is influenced by the usage rate, lead time, and safety stock level for the part. Order size can be determined by using the economic order quantity technique. This technique minimizes ordering and carrying costs.

Questions for review and discussion

✗ 1. What is MBO? Describe the purpose of the objective-setting discussions. What advantages and problems are associated wth MBO?   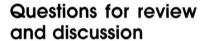 MOTIVATION

2. Distinguish between bar charts and network techniques.

3. How are networks constructed? How can they be used in planning and controlling work activities?

4. What are operating budgets? What is the nature of the supervisor's involvement with budgets?

5. What is break-even analysis? How is it used by supervisors? What are its limitations?

6. What are the four lines found on break-even charts and what do they represent? What is the break-even point and how is it determined?

7. What are the key decisions required in inventory planning and control?

8. How can supervisors determine the reorder point?

9. Explain the economic order quantity technique. What does it involve? What are its limitations?

Key terms

Bar charts	Management by objectives (MBO)
Break-even analysis	Network techniques
Budgets	Reorder point
Critical path	Total costs
Economic order quantity	Total revenue
Fixed costs	Variable costs

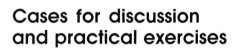

Cases for discussion and practical exercises

1. Donna Rose decided to open a specialty submarine sandwich shop. She has identified two possible locations. Location two is near a local college, while location one is several blocks away from campus. There is a higher estimated sales level for location two, but the rent for location two is higher. Donna is trying to decide which location she should select to make the most profit. Revelant information is given as follows:

	LOCATION 1	LOCATION 2
Estimated number of customers per month	6000	7000
Average sale per customer	$2.50	$2.50
Average variable cost per sale	$1.75	$1.75
Fixed costs per month (including rent)	3000	4000

a) Which location should Donna select? Why?

b) What if Donna has underestimated the average number of customers per month at location two? Assume that 7500 per month is a better estimate. Does this figure change your recommendation?

c) Determine the break-even point for each location.

2. Refer back to the plan you developed to accomplish an objective in the practical exercise in the last chapter. Develop a bar chart, showing each activity in the plan and scheduling when the activity will begin and end. Develop a network showing the same thing.

3. Develop an operating budget for your own personal finances for the next month. Estimate your revenues and expenses. Assume that any profit goes into savings.

Cases for section III

Mr. Maynard's Dilemma

Jean Morrison had started her retail career as a clerk at Maynard's during the summer of her sixteenth year. She liked being in the store much more than going to school, and because her family needed the extra income, they encouraged her to continue working after school and on Saturday, even when it became obvious that Jean would have a hard time passing. She did fail that year and was very happy to accept a full-time job at Maynard's.

In those days, Maynard's carried ladies', men's, and children's clothing, but the store was small enough for the salespeople to sell in all departments. As Maynard's grew, however, Jean began to take charge of the ladies' accessories. She would tell Mr. Maynard when they lacked certain items, interview travelers to see whether they had anything interesting and if they did, she would show it to Mr. Maynard who would then decide whether to order it.

As the store continued to expand, Mr. Maynard became more involved in administrative duties and Jean, of necessity, began to make a greater number of decisions regarding her area (which had now expanded to include sportswear) without consulting Mr. Maynard. He was content to let her take charge of these merchandise sections and only complained if the sales figures dropped or when Jean made an obviously poor buy. Eventually it became known that Jean was "in charge" of the ladies' accessories and sportswear department. However, this recognition had no effect on her duties, responsibilities, or salary. It was simply a referral procedure, and one that afforded Mr. Maynard an opportunity to criticize Jean and the two other employees who were "in charge" of the men's and children's departments. Mr. Maynard retained full control of the coat and dress departments.

The "key" employees decided what they could do by themselves and what required Mr. Maynard's attention. Eventually, these employees were provided with comparative sales figures and end-of-year inventory totals, which they received sometime in August, although the merchandise was counted before January 31.

As the store grew in physical size, merchandise diversification, and organizational complexity, Mr. Maynard realized that he was less and less aware of what was happening in every department but the coats and dresses for which he still bought and over which he still exercised complete control.

Therefore, whenever he had time, he would visit ("snoop" was the word the staff used for his actions) the other departments and ask questions of the department head and of the salespeople. He would quickly find fault with the merchandise and the housekeeping, and when he left the department to look after his duties, he always felt that if he could have stayed a bit longer, he would have discovered more areas to criticize.

One aspect that worried Mr. Maynard most was the store's inventory situation. The only guide he had for establishing the value of the merchandise was the cost and retail code that appeared on each price ticket. These told him whether the retail price was attractive to his customers and whether the item gave him sufficient markup.

In more instances than he cared to remember, the retail price on certain items seemed too high because the merchandise looked old, shopworn, or out of style. Yet when he questioned the person in charge, he usually had trouble obtaining a satisfactory answer as to its age and customer acceptance. When the clearance seasons arrived, Mr. Maynard would go through the store and tell his department heads to mark down everything they thought was selling poorly. Yet, when he examined the merchandise outside his own departments, he still found many items that, in his opinion, should be reduced, but which showed the original retail price on the ticket.

"It is still a good number, Mr. Maynard" the person in charge would say, defending the judgment. "Why should we reduce it when it will sell at regular prices?" Occasionally Mr. Maynard would say, "Never mind, mark it down to cost," but usually he was too busy to do more than look quizzically at the employee and move on.

Mr. Maynard also knew that the inventory taken at the end of his fiscal year was improperly recorded and priced. The employee in charge of each section made his or her own decisions as to the total merchandise figure against last year's and adjusted the current total so as to bring it "into line" with the net sales figures. This meant Mr. Maynard would arbitrarily raise or lower the inventory total to have it work out to a set gross margin percentage. He would then give the auditor this figure for statement purposes.

But while Mr. Maynard worried about his lack of inventory knowledge, he did nothing to rectify it until the beginning of one fall season when his bank manager refused to extend the store's credit limit. Mr. Maynard pointed out that sales had been showing a steady yearly increase and so had the dollar gross margin. He did admit that Maynard's liquid position had worsened but claimed this was because his accounts receivable had increased, and the store had paid out a great deal of cash for new fixtures. Maynard's required extra credit from the bank for that reason.

The bank manager advanced another theory concerning Maynard's poor capital condition. She said that from her reading of Maynard's statements, she had come to the conclusion that the store had been accumulating more and more inventory, which tied up capital and made no profit as long as it remained on the shelves. If this merchandise could be turned back into cash, the bank manager thought Maynard's would recoup enough liquid capital to conduct its operations without increasing its credit limit.

Mr. Maynard was surprised and unhappy with the bank manager's reasoning. He made an appointment with his auditor who, in more diplomatic language, agreed with the bank manager, and then went on to explain the advantages inherent in good merchandise turnover. He suggested that Mr. Maynard could control his store's stock by installing the retail inventory method, six month plans, stock aging, and other merchandise control systems.

Mr. Maynard went back to the bank manager and eventually succeeded in extending his credit limit. But the experience frightened him sufficiently to investigate merchandise control procedures and to reach a decision to install them in the store. These systems necessitated establishing a true departmental structure and the appointment of definite department buyer–managers who would be responsible for the operations.

As a result of these changes, Mr. Maynard decided he required more time to perform his administrative functions, but he still wanted to do some buying. Therefore, he took Jean out of the sportswear and lingerie departments and moved her into dresses. This left him free to merchandise the coat department. To replace Jean, he hired Mary Coles as his new sportswear buyer and made Susan Palmer, Jean's former assistant, the new lingerie buyer.

Jean was frightened by her new responsibilities. She had to buy from strange vendors; the office kept giving her figures that she could not use because she could not understand them, and she was beside the coat department, and so directly under Mr. Maynard's eye.

Installing merchandise controls and a better store organization proved so successful that Mr. Maynard decided to undertake a major store expansion. He devoted so much of his time to planning and executing this project that he could not supervise his buyers properly, and they soon began to run their departments as though they were separate specialty shops.

This was particularly true of the dress department. Jean felt that Mr. Maynard trusted her because he spent very little time in her department and seldom criticized her merchandise. She began to buy more and more dresses that pleased her rather than Maynard's customers, paid no attention to the rest of the store, and never looked at the figures that the office sent her because she could not understand them and they only made her uncomfortable.

Part of the store alterations consisted of enlarging the dress department and moving it to a better traffic area than it formerly occupied. When this section was completed, Mr. Maynard set higher sales and profit quotas for the department. In spite of running a larger and better-located department, Jean's method of buying and operating did not lead to increased dress sales. In fact, shortly after the effects of the opening promotions had passed, dress sales compared to the previous year began to fall off. This worried Mr. Maynard but he was so busy with his own department and the problems in the rest of the store, he kept postponing the talk he knew he should have with Jean. Aside from occasional outbursts of annoyance, he let her use her own methods.

On the other hand, his regard for Mary Coles was quite different from his feelings toward Jean. Mary had come from another town where she had been trained in the use of merchandise controls. Besides being a disciplined buyer, Mary had good taste and a better knowledge of vendors than Jean. Unlike Jean, she bought for Maynard's customers and ruthlessly reduced merchandise as soon as she believed it would not sell otherwise.

It was not long before Jean revealed that the relationship between Mr. Maynard and Mary Coles was not to her liking. Spicy stories about Mary's past and present conduct as well as her after-store-hours activities began to circulate in the store. These emanated from Jean who made certain that they reached Mr. Maynard. Because he had prided himself on the type of help he employed, these rumors disturbed him so much that he decided to have them investigated. He was soon convinced that they had no substance and so he dismissed any further stories which came his way.

Shortly after Mr. Maynard's fears about Mary Coles had been dispelled, Susan Palmer, the lingerie buyer, left and and Mr. Maynard asked Mary Coles whether she thought she could manage the lingerie as well as the sportswear department.

Mary Coles thought that she could, providing she was permitted to have Jim Kurtz, her assistant, order staple sportswear. She told Mr. Maynard that she had been training Jim for just such an emergency. Mr. Maynard was very pleased and gave his approval and even suggested that Mary find a bright person to assist her in lingerie as Jim Kurtz did in sportswear. If this could be accomplished, said Mr. Maynard, Mary Coles would have more time to be on the floor and supervise the sales personnel of the two departments.

When Jean heard of Mary's new promotion, she was beside herself with rage. At the buyers' meetings she began to make snide remarks about the lingerie and sportswear departments, but Mary held her tongue, leaving Jean even more frustrated than ever.

The same sales and profit pattern began to develop in the lingerie department as it had in sportswear, and Mr. Maynard became very overt in his satisfaction with Mary Coles' efforts.

His pleasure did not extend to Jean. For some months he had watched the dress department figures with annoyance. Since the alteration, sales had increased not only in the sportswear and lingerie departments, but in every section in the store except the dress department.

Finally Mr. Maynard had his talk with Jean. When he asked her what was wrong with her department, Jean rationalized her drop in sales by giving such reasons as this was not a dress season, the styles were poor, and merchandise was too expensive. When Mr. Maynard pointed out that the dress department figures he had obtained from outside sources showed a substantial increase in sales at dress departments of other stores, Jean repeated her arguments and then burst into tears. That ended the interview.

She then began to carry cheaper and cheaper merchandise in the hope that her volume would increase. But the rest of the store was trading up, and so fewer customers were generated to Miss Jean's department. She soon found that she was not only selling fewer dresses per day but those sold were at lower prices.

She therefore shifted her strategy and upgraded her department, but because she had no knowledge of the customers who came into the store, she bought dresses that were too extreme in style and price. Moreover, as she did not have the right salespeople to sell this type of merchandise, sales and transactions fell still further.

Mr. Maynard became very anxious about the dress department, particularly when he saw the physical inventory figures. These now aged the merchandise and Mr. Maynard could see that the dress department had accumulated a very large amount of old stock. He confronted Jean with the figures and asked her for an explanation. She gave him the same excuses as she had in the first interview, and then burst into tears.

But this time Mr. Maynard was too disturbed himself to worry about Jean's feelings. He told her to group the dresses into three categories, based on how long they had been in the store. When this was done, he went through the groups, and with much sarcastic commet, told Jean what prices each group should have. Shortly afterwards, Jean disappeared into the washroom and stayed there for the rest of the afternoon.

Mr. Maynard was in a quandry. He felt he could not fire Jean because by this time she had worked in Maynard's longer than any other employee. Besides, he could see she was loyal to him and to the store and that she meant well. It was not her fault that the job he had given her was too complex for her abilities.

He believed the proper move was to put Mary Coles in charge of the dresses but he hesitated to make this appointment. It would be difficult enough to demote Jean but it would be almost impossible to place Mary over her. Nevertheless, he knew the situation was so serious he could not afford to let the dress department deteriorate any further.

In desperation he decided to join a buying office that had a reputation for centrally merchandising the kind of dresses he thought his customers wanted. After arrangements had been completed, he called Jean into his office, patiently reviewed the dress department figures, and then asked her what she thought could be done about them. Jean protested loudly. Mr. Maynard disregarded the outburst and went on to tell her about the buying office and what he hoped it would do for her department. He said it would relieve her of her buying functions and thus give her more time to look after the department and do more personal selling, which, after all, was what she could do best. This would raise the dress sales volume and make everybody happy.

Jean cried all through the interview but she knew her only alternative to accepting the buying office was to look for another job. She was too disheartened to make the effort, and so she decided to stay where she was and see what would happen.

For some weeks she avoided Mr. Maynard and the rest of the staff as much as possible and stayed in the store as little as she could. Everyone was kind to her, except Mary Coles, who simply ignored her.

Mr. Maynard insisted that she meet Grace Piersen, the resident buyer who was to merchandise Maynard's dress department and to shop the market with her. It was a very humiliating experience for Jean, but by then she knew she had no alternative but to endure it. Thus, although Grace constantly asked for Jean's opinion as they reviewed the market, Jean was as noncommittal as possible without being insulting.

From then on, the dresses that arrived at Maynard's were already ticketed. Jean's job was simply to see that they were hung in their proper places, to sell them, and be sure each day's sales stubs were forwarded to the resident buying office. For some time Jean's obvious curtailment of her powers made her very unhappy, and she would burst into tears at the slightest provocation. But eventually she began to brighten up and take some pride in her department and her ability to sell. Because she was a good salesperson and helped her staff, the department's sales figures began to improve.

However, after four months had passed, Mr. Maynard decided that the buying office was not for him. It began to pay less and less attention to his store's requirements, particularly after Grace Piersen left, and the new resident buyer was unable or unwilling to visit the store. Dress sales fell rapidly, and the stock aged.

During this period Jean began to hear rumors that Mr. Maynard was planning to replace her with Mary Coles and demote her to salesperson or assistant buyer. Furthermore, she noticed that Mary Coles had hired an intelligent woman for her lingerie department and was teaching her to run the department as she had already trained Jim Kurtz in sportswear.

Jean became very unhappy. She wanted to ask Mr. Maynard about the rumors but was afraid to confront him directly in case they were true. She made a few half-hearted attempts to look for other work, but by this time she had lost confidence in herself as a buyer. Besides, her salary plus her accumulated fringe benefits were much too high for any other employer to meet. Anyway, she really did not want to move, since she had spent the greater part of her life at Maynard's. She hoped the rumor was untrue and that Mr. Maynard would protect her status.

Mr. Maynard, too, was unhappy. As the buying office idea was not working out, he decided not to renew the contract when it expired. This would put him back in the same position he was in before he engaged the office. He knew he must stop Jean from buying dresses but he hesitated to take any action because most of the alternatives would be very embarrassing and painful to Jean as well as to him.

Eventually, however, the condition of the dress department became so alarming that he was finally forced to make a decision. This was to promote Mary Coles to buyer–manager of the dress department and to move Jean into the coats department as assistant buyer. He knew the step would be very unpleasant for Jean but it would save her from working under Mary. Besides, there was a certain amount of logic to the move as Jean was a good salesperson and could help the other coat sales personnel to sell as well. He also felt she could do the routine buying and reordering. But would she accept the position, and if not, was he prepared to let her continue to buy dresses or to let her go?

In order to give both Jean and himself a breathing spell, he called her into his office and told her he understood she was not well and that he wanted her to take a two-week holiday with pay. Jean burst into tears and said she was not feeling well, but what would happen to the dress department if she was absent for two weeks? He assured her that he would look after it himself and that she was not to worry, but to have a good rest instead.

When Jean had been away a week, Mary Coles took over the dress department as buyer–manager. She now controlled three departments and was the most influential executive in the store. A few days later, one of Maynard's employees told Jean about the move. Jean phoned Mr. Maynard at his home. She asked him whether it was true that he had put Mary Coles in charge of the dress department. Mr. Maynard said, "Yes, but that is not the whole story," that he needed Jean more in coats than in dresses, and he promised to tell her about the move when she came back the following week. He stressed that the whole thing was too complicated to discuss over the phone.

Miss Jean said, "I should think so," burst into tears, and hung up.

Questions

1. What is the cause of Mr. Maynard's dilemma?
2. What should Mr. Maynard do?

Source: Adapted from Frank Greenwood, *Casebook for Management and Business Policy: A Systems Approach.* Copyright © 1968 by Harper & Row, Publishers, Inc. Reprinted by permission of the publisher.

IV

Supervisory staffing

12

Selecting and orienting workers

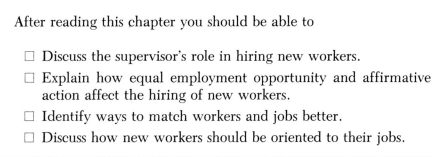

Objectives

After reading this chapter you should be able to

☐ Discuss the supervisor's role in hiring new workers.
☐ Explain how equal employment opportunity and affirmative action affect the hiring of new workers.
☐ Identify ways to match workers and jobs better.
☐ Discuss how new workers should be oriented to their jobs.

Supervisors, as seen in Chapter 1, perform a vital function in organizations. However, they do not actually produce computers, process insurance claims, or make airline reservations. From the organization's standpoint, supervisors do not exist to do these tasks. The supervisor's position is created to see that others get these things done. So supervisors are responsible for ensuring their workers successfully produce computers, process insurance claims, and make reservations.

In organizations, employees are evaluated on how well they carry out the responsibilities of their jobs. Supervisors are evaluated on how well their workers perform, since this is their primary responsibility. Thus, to be effective, supervisors must ensure their workers function satisfactorily. In Chapter 6, we identified the factors which influence how well workers do their jobs. They must have the ability to do the work as well as the motivation to do it well.

Whereas in Chapter 6 we focused on motivating workers to do their jobs, here our focus is on ability. In this chapter we will look at ways supervisors can select and orient new workers. We will discuss how supervisors can hire workers who are capable of performing their jobs well. Then, in Chapter 13, we will discuss ways supervisors can develop their workers' abilities to function effectively. Finally, in Chapter 14 we will look at how supervisors determine whether or not a worker's performance is satisfactory.

These activities together represent the **staffing process.** Through properly hiring and training workers and then reviewing their job performance, supervisors can increase their chances of achieving positive results from their workers.

Objectives of selection

When supervisors need to hire new workers their primary objective is to assure a good fit between the worker and the job. A good fit exists when the worker has the ability to do the job and likes doing the job. Obviously, hiring people who are not capable of performing the job can result in problems. These workers may require additional training. Even worse, they may not be able to master the job and eventually will quit or be dismissed. In either case when workers do not have the ability to perform their jobs, they become frustrated, as do their supervisors, and co-workers.

Hiring people who will like doing the work is also important. The selection process is a two-way street. While supervisors want to hire people with certain skills and abilities, job applicants also have expectations regarding jobs they would like to have. They are looking for jobs which provide certain rewards and opportunities. Pay, overtime demands, working conditions, and opportunities for advancement are examples of requirements people have for jobs they would consider. When people accept jobs based on unrealistic expectations of what is being offered, they often become dissatisfied. They may adopt a "turned off" attitude toward their jobs or eventually quit.

While assuring a good fit between the worker and the job is important, one other important objective must be met. The various laws and regulations that guarantee people equal employment opportunity must be followed. Today more than ever, supervisors must understand these laws and ensure their hiring decisions do not violate them. As we will discuss later, this objective does not conflict with the goal of matching people and jobs.

How workers are hired depends on the organization and the particular job. Larger organizations tend to have more formal selection processes than smaller organizations. Higher-level jobs are typically filled through a more formal selection process than lower-level jobs. Figure 12.1 shows the typical steps in selecting new workers. In some instances, all the steps shown in Fig. 12.1 will not be followed. The order of the steps may also vary.

The supervisor's role in selection

The supervisor's role in the **selection process** varies from organization to organization. In smaller organizations supervisors may have almost total responsibility for selecting their workers, receiving assistance only from a receptionist or the manager's secretary. In larger organizations the personnel department often takes responsibility for

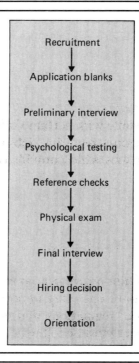

Recruitment

Application blanks

Preliminary interview

Psychological testing

Reference checks

Physical exam

Final interview

Hiring decision

Orientation

Figure 12.1   The selection process.

some of the steps in the selection process. Figure 12.2 shows the typical division of selection responsibilities in larger organizations. As shown in Fig. 12.2 supervisors are generally responsible for the following activities:

1. Notifying the personnel department when a job vacancy occurs;
2. Providing the personnel department with information about the duties and responsibilities of the vacant job (job description) and the type of person needed to fill the job (job specification);
3. Conducting final interviews with a narrowed-down list of candidates to determine who will actually be hired (final interview and hiring decision);
4. Orienting the new worker to the job and department.

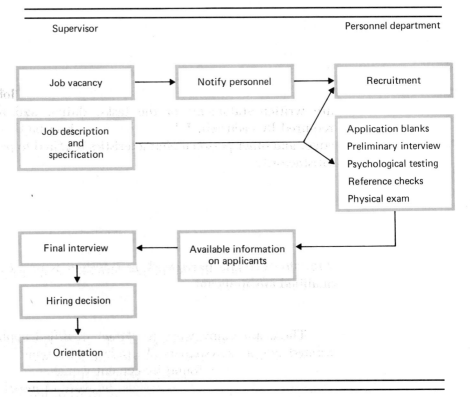

Supervisor   Personnel department

Figure 12.2   Supervisory responsibilities in selecting new workers.

Supervisors typically become more involved during the later stages of the process. Normally the personnel department uses a variety of techniques to narrow the initial pool of applicants. This weeding-out process is accomplished by comparing applicants' qualifications with job requirements. At various points in the selection process, unqualified applicants are eliminated. The pool is narrowed to a relatively small number of applicants who all possess at least the minimum qualifications for the job. At this stage the remaining applicants are interviewed by the supervisor, who then makes the hiring decision. Once the new worker is hired the supervisor is responsible for orienting him or her to the job and department.

Before we look more closely at the supervisor's role in selection and orientation, let's examine the basic steps in the selection process.

Steps in the selection process

Job description and specifications Job descriptions and specifications play a critical role is the selection process. **Job descriptions** are written statements of the tasks, duties, and responsibilities required by each job. **Job specifications** describe the skills, knowledge, and other personal characteristics required to perform the job satisfactorily. This information describes the kind of person needed to fill the job vacancy. As a result, it directs recruitment efforts and guides decisions made during the selection process. Examples of job descriptions and specifications for a clerk typist and a heavy-duty mechanic are found in Figs. 12.3 and 12.4.

Recruitment The purpose of recruitment is to attract a pool of qualified job applicants. The more qualified people who apply for a particular job, the better are the chances of finding the right person for the job.

There are many ways to attract qualified applicants. Help-wanted ads in newspapers or trade publications are often used. Many applicants are found by current workers who know of a vacancy and pass on the information by word of mouth. In addition placement agencies can be used to find qualified applicants. Some of these agencies are private while others are government sponsored.

CLERK TYPIST III

DESCRIPTION OF WORK:

General Statement of Duties: Performs a variety of clerical and typing work requiring the exercise of some independent judgment.

Supervision Received: Works under general supervision of a clerical or technical superior.

Supervision Exercised: Exercises supervision over personnel as assigned or full supervision incidental to the other duties.

EXAMPLE OF DUTIES: (Any one position may not include all the duties listed nor do the listed examples include all tasks that may be found in positions of this class.)

Types correspondence, reports, and other office forms requiring some independence of judgment as to content, accuracy, and completeness. Reviews correspondence and reports; determines what information is to be cross-filed and/or included in other files or reports so that a ready and complete history or file is available; determines routing and filing.

Compiles, computes, and tabulates data for reports requiring judgment as to content.

Locates source material, edits, and coordinates material for inclusion into research-and-development reports, recognizing variations and verifying completeness of report.

Furnishes the public with information and advice in areas where the public is generally uninformed (such as auto theft, and in cases where time is of the essence), requiring a working knowledge of both agency policies and procedures and applicable laws.

Determines and collects amount of fees, where some degree of personal judgment is involved in the decision, issues receipts, keeps records of transactions.

Performs related work as required.

REQUIRED KNOWLEDGE, SKILLS, AND ABILITIES:

Considerable knowledge of grammar, spelling, and punctuation. Working knowledge of office practices and procedures. Skill in operating a typewriter. Ability to follow written or oral instructions. Ability to make mathematical computations. Ability to establish and maintain effective working relationships with employees, the public, and other agencies.

QUALIFICATIONS FOR APPOINTMENT:

Education: High-school graduation or equivalent.

Experience: Two years experience in general clerical work involving typing or any equivalent combination of education and experience.

Figure 12.3   Job description and specifications: Clerk typist
Source: Adapted from Richard W. Beatty and Craig Eric Schneier, *Personnel Administration: An Experiential Skill-Building Approach.* © 1977, Addison-Wesley Publishing Company, p. 231. Reprinted by permission.

HEAVY-DUTY MECHANIC
DESCRIPTION OF WORK:

General Statement of Duties: Performs skilled work in the repair and maintenance of automotive and heavy-duty equipment.

Supervision Received: Works under the guidance of a supervisor.

Supervision Exercised: None

EXAMPLES OF DUTIES: (Any one position may not include all of the duties listed nor do the listed examples include all tasks that may be found in positions of this class.)

Overhauls, repairs, and maintains cars, trucks, earth-moving, road-construction, and heavy-duty equipment.

Performs major repairs on gasoline, semi-diesel, and diesel engines; transmissions; differentials; drive units; brakes; suspension systems, chassis; front and rear ends; cooling systems, fuel systems; instruments; electrical systems; hydraulic systems; and accessory power equipment.

Rebuilds engines, carburetors, ignition systems, and radiators.

Performs general tune-up, using testing machines.

Performs emergency road service.

Performs welding as required.

Performs related work as required.

REQUIRED KNOWLEDGE, SKILLS, AND ABILITIES:

Considerable knowledge of the standard practices, methods, materials, and tools used in the automotive mechanic trade. Working knowledge of the hazards and safety precautions peculiar to the trade. Working knowledge of the design, operation, and repair of light- and heavy-duty equipment. Skill in the use of mechanic's tools, materials, welding equipment, and testing equipment. Ability to diagnose mechanical defects and determine parts and adjustments necessary to put equipment into proper operating condition. Ability to follow written and oral instructions. Ability to establish and maintain effective working relationships with employees and the public.

QUALIFICATIONS FOR APPOINTMENT:

Education: Eighth-grade completion or equivalent.

Experience: Four years experience in the repair and maintenance of automotive equipment, including one year on heavy-duty and construction equipment *or* any equivalent combination of education and experience.

Figure 12.4   Job description and specifications: Heavy-duty mechanic
Source: Adapted from Richard W. Beatty and Craig Eric Schneier, *Personnel Administration: An Experiential Skill-Building Approach.* © 1977, Addison-Wesley Publishing Company, p. 230. Reprinted by permission.

Many colleges, trade schools, and professional associations also provide placement services which aid in recruiting. In organizations that use a job bidding and posting system, recruitment occurs internally. The job requirements and qualifications are posted and interested workers who feel they meet the qualifications apply for the job. In some cases, such as in the construction industry, labor unions are responsible for recruiting applicants.

Recruiting efforts usually result in many interested applicants. Some will be more suited for the job than others. A help-wanted ad, for instance, may result in anywhere from 10 to 200 responses from people with varying qualifications. Consequently a "weeding out" process is necessary.

Application blanks Application blanks provide a good starting point for determining who is qualified for the job and who is not. They are a convenient method for obtaining information regarding the applicant's education and work experience. This information provides an idea of the skills and abilities a person has, as well as his or her background.

Preliminary interview The preliminary interview is for remaining applicants, once applicants who are clearly not qualified have been eliminated on the basis of the application blank. Usually conducted by the personnel department, this interview is short and to the point. Again, the objective is to eliminate those applicants who are obviously not qualified. The preliminary interview is sometimes conducted in conjunction with the completion of the application blank.

Testing Testing is designed for applicants who on the surface appear qualified for the job. They may be given tests to assess further their suitability for the job. These tests are designed to measure characteristics which cannot be accurately assessed through application blanks or interviews. Applicants whose test scores do not meet minimum ability or skill requirements can be eliminated from the selection process. A variety of tests to measure many different characteristics have been developed.

- **Performance Tests.** These require applicants actually to perform a sample of the job. Examples are typing and shorthand tests for secretarial positions and driving tests for forklift operators.

- **Performance Simulations.** These are designed to measure abilities required on the job but do not require the applicant to actually perform the job. Instead the applicant's ability is evaluated in a simulated environment.

- **Paper and Pencil Tests.** These are designed to measure general mental abilities. An example would be a test of mathematical ability given to applicants for the job of bank teller or sales clerk.

- **Personality Tests.** These are designed to measure personality characteristics such as aggressiveness, drive, ambition, and adaptability. They have generally proven to be the least effective in helping select good workers.

- **Polygraph Test.** As a result of large increases in on-the-job crime, some organizations use polygraph tests to double-check information about the applicant. The use of these tests is highly controversial. Some evidence suggests that the polygraph labels people as liars who respond emotionally to questions.[1] There are also legal issues such as rights to privacy and bans against self-incrimination as well as concerns about individual dignity. However, it has been estimated that dishonest workers cost organizations around $5 billion per year.[2] As a result, polygraph tests may be used for certain jobs.

Reference checks These allow you to check into the applicant's background. Talking to personal and business references may provide useful insights about the applicant's past behavior. It also provides a check on the accuracy of information given by the applicant. A commonly asked question is whether or not past employers would rehire the applicant.

Physical exam For some jobs, certain health standards may be required. As a result, the selection process may require applicants to complete a medical questionnaire or physical exam.

Final interview At each successive step, unqualified applicants are eliminated until only those who appear to possesss the minimum requirements remain. At this stage, applicants are interviewed in depth. Because of the supervisor's involvement in this step, it will be discussed in detail in a later section.

Hiring decision   After all the information gathered during the selection process is collected for each remaining applicant, the final decision is made as to who will be hired. This assumes more than one person is qualified. Unfortunately, none of the applicants may be satisfactory. In this instance, if the job requirements and qualifications are accurate and realistic, hiring the best unqualified person may not be the best decision. Instead, it may be better to begin the selection process again.

Orientation   The final step in the selection process is orientation. The new worker must be oriented to the job, co-workers, the department, and the organization. Here again, since supervisors play an important role, the orientation process will be discussed in detail in a later section.

The supervisor and EEO

In recent years **equal employment opportunity (EEO)** laws and affirmative action have become increasingly important to supervisors. These laws govern all aspects of an organization's relationship with its workers, including determination of pay rates and pay increases, job assignments and promotions, disciplinary procedures, and of course, hiring practices.

1971
Griggs vs Duke Power Co

Title VII of the Civil Rights Act, originally passed in 1964, was amended by the **Equal Employment Opportunity Act of 1972**. This law prohibits discrimination in all terms and conditions of employment on the basis of race, color, national origin, religion, and sex. The law applies to private employers with more than fifteen employees, unions, employment agencies, state and local governments, and educational institutions. Thus coverage under Title VII is very broad.

1978 Bakke
1979 Kaiser Steel
vs Weber

The law also created the **Equal Employment Opportunity Commission (EEOC)**, which is responsible for enforcing Title VII and several other anti-discrimination laws. The EEOC is a separate federal agency reporting to the President. Under the law, the EEOC may investigate a charge of discrimination. Normally the EEOC investigates charges to determine whether there is reasonable cause to believe discrimination has occurred. If the evidence supports discrimination, the burden then shifts to the employer (or union or employment agency) to prove that discrimination has not occurred.

Extended to state & local govt.
EEOC can go directly to court

The **Age Discrimination in Employment Act** was passed in 1967 and prohibits discrimination on the basis of age. It specifically covers individuals between the ages of 40 and 70. Under the jurisdiction of the law are private employers of twenty or more persons, public employers, employment agencies, and unions.

The **Vocational Rehabilitation Act of 1973** prohibits discrimination against individuals on the basis of their physical and mental handicaps. It further requires that employers develop specific programs aimed at increasing employment opportunities for the physically and mentally handicapped. All organizations doing more than $2500 worth of business with the federal government are covered.

Remedies and penalties   If the courts find an organization guilty of discrimination under any of the laws, several types of remedies and penalties are possible. These include reinstatement of employees, back pay awards (up to two years prior to filing of the charge), and payment of attorney's fees for the plaintiffs. In addition, the courts may require the employer to set up a specific plan for increasing the employment opportunities for members of the complaining class (e.g., women, blacks, or Hispanic Americans). Organizations that have contracts with the federal government face an additional penalty. Their contracts may be withdrawn, and the organization may be barred from doing additional business with the government if its management violates the law.

These penalties and remedies can be costly. For example, AT&T has had to pay $15 million to a large number of women and minority-group men in settlement of discrimination charges. A number of companies in the steel industry agreed jointly to pay over $30 million in the settlement of a discrimination suit. Many other organizations have also been forced to spend substantial amounts of money, not only for settlement costs but also for preparation and defense of cases.

Affirmative action plans are required for certain companies. Organizations covered by EEO laws are required to be neutral in making employment decisions. Supervisors must make hiring decisions based solely on the applicant's ability to perform on the job.

Organizations doing business with the federal government must also engage in affirmative action. Affirmative action requires more than nondiscrimination. It requires that positive action be taken to seek out, hire, and promote qualified members of groups previously discriminated against.

Affirmative action plans are usually developed by the personnel department. These plans must establish goals and timetables for hiring women and minority workers. Organizations with affirmative action plans often require that hiring decisions be approved by the personnel department to ensure affirmative action goals are being pursued.

The impact of EEO on supervisors

EEO laws and regulations affect supervisors in a variety of ways:

- Supervisors cannot refuse to hire someone because of their race, religion, color, national origin, sex, age, or handicap *if* these characteristics do not affect their ability to perform the job. Hiring decisions must be based on job-related factors.
- Supervisors are not required to hire unqualified people. They may, however, have to hire people who possess the minimum qualifications for the job even though there are others more qualified.
- Regardless of whether or not the supervisor intends to discriminate, if discrimination occurs, the law is violated. Results, not intent, are what count under the law.

The objective of selection is to make a hiring decision. This means certain applicants will be hired and others will be rejected. EEO laws are concerned with *how* applicants are selected or rejected and they attempt to eliminate unfair discrimination in this process. They require the hiring decision to be made on the basis of job-related factors.

We stated in the beginning of this chapter that supervisors play a critical role in specific stages of the selection process. They have considerable input in defining the requirements of the job and they make the final hiring decision. These two activities are critical to determining whether or not the organization will meet its obligation to provide equal employment opportunity. Equally important, how well these activities are performed can determine whether or not a good hiring decision will be made.

Preparing job descriptions and specifications

Job descriptions and specifications are vital for ensuring a good fit between people and jobs. Typically supervisors write and update job descriptions for the jobs they supervise with the help of personnel specialists. Doing so is good practice because supervisors are generally much more knowledgeable about actual job requirements.

Unfortunately, not all organizations have job descriptions and specifications. Or, if they do have them, they may be horribly out of date. This situation hinders your ability to hire good, qualified workers. Without accurate job descriptions and specifications, how do you know what kind of worker to hire? It also causes you to play Russian roulette with EEO legislation. The job description and specifications define the characteristics you will use to make hiring decisions. If you cannot demonstrate that the factors you are using are related to actual job performance requirements, and rejected applicants happen to be women or minorities, you may find yourself in trouble.

If you use inaccurate, out-of-date job descriptions and specifications to hire workers you are probably not hiring the best people for the job. You also may be scaring off qualified applicants with misleading descriptions.

Because supervisors are so familiar with the jobs they supervise, it is their responsibility to ensure accurate, up-to-date job descriptions and specifications exist. Job descriptions and specifications should be periodically reviewed with special attention paid to the following areas:[3]

- **Are the duties and responsibilities included still part of the actual job?** Automation and computerization have greatly altered the nature of many jobs. In many cases, they have reduced the skill level required. In other cases, skill requirements have been changed. New technology may reduce physical skill requirements while increasing mental skill requirements.

- **Are all aspects of the job included?** If the total job is not reflected in the job description, people may think they have been misled when they learn later they must perform additional duties.

■ **Is the job described in a distorted way?** For a variety of reasons, jobs often appear more glamourous, prestigous, and difficult on paper than they really are. This inflation may satisfy current workers' status needs but it also may keep out qualified women and minorities. It also may lead to hiring people whose expectations cannot be met by the job. Figure 12.5 provides an excellent example of this situation. Included is the inflated description found in a help-wanted ad for an "Editorial Assistant" compared to the actual job duties. In its actual form, the job is really secretarial in nature.

■ **Can the required skills, knowledge, and abilities be measured in more than one way?** Quite often, expertise can be gained outside school or without special training. People often learn how to do things through a combination of talent, interest, and personal drive. If knowledge, skills, and abilities are required and not education or specific training, make sure the job specification reflects this.

Employment interviewing

The **final employment interview** is designed to meet two main objectives: (1) to provide an opportunity for the supervisor to meet and evaluate the remaining candidates, and (2) to provide candidates with a chance to meet their prospective supervisor and ask questions. The general guidelines discussed in Chapter 5 apply to employment interviewing. Additional topics aimed specifically at making the employment interview more effective will be discussed here.

Preparing for the interview

Effective interviews require careful planning. You need to review job descriptions and specifications, as well as information received about applicants during earlier steps in the selection process.

■ **Review the job description and specifications.** In order to evaluate each applicant, you must know the skills, abilities, and knowledge required to perform the job. A thorough review of the job description and specifications can provide you with questions and points to look for during the interview.

HELP-WANTED: EDITORIAL ASSISTANT

Handle broad contact with authors, rewrite, edit, some research. Work under deadline pressure. Typing and shorthand required.

JOB DESCRIPTION	ACTUAL JOB
Editorial Trainee	Secretary
"broad contact with"	Talking to authors on the phone simply to give or take messages, or set up or verify appointments; typing letters to authors; filing correspondence from them.
"rewrite"	Compose a business letter from someone's scribbled message.
"edit"	Catch boss's typos, mispellings, etc.
"research"	Check addresses or company/client names in phone directory.
"work under deadline pressure"	Getting out letters, collating manuscripts by certain times. The deadline pressure exists, but the "trainee's" part in it is strictly secretarial.
"typing, shorthand required."	The heart of the job; what the individual will spend 99% of the time doing.

Figure 12.5 Impact of inflated job description.
Source: Adapted from Stephen Sahlein (Jeff Baron, ed.), *The Affirmative Action Handbook: Dealing with Day-to-Day Supervisory Problems* (New York: Executive Enterprises Publications, Inc., 1979), p. 6. Reprinted by permission.

■ Review other information on applicants. If information has already been obtained from the applicants during the earlier stages of the selection process, you should carefully review it as well. Typically, application blanks are completed prior to the interview. You should look for any responses which seem incomplete or unclear. The interview gives you a good opportunity to probe more deeply and ask each applicant to explain certain areas in greater detail. For example, an applicant may appear to have the qualifications needed to perform the job, but the application blank may indicate a long period of unemployment between jobs. Most supervisors would like to know why the applicant was not working during that "off" time. The reason may or may not be acceptable, but in any event, it needs to be clarified.

- **Develop a checklist.** Combining the information received from a review of the application blank and job description, you can outline key areas that need to be covered during the interview. The planning phase should result in developing an interviewing checklist. Using a checklist, like the one illustrated in Table 12.1 helps ensure that you ask all applicants the same questions. It also helps you remember to ask important questions.

Table 12.1

Interview checklist

TOPIC	QUESTIONS ASKED	WHAT YOU SEEK
Introduction	■ General greeting ■ Inquire how applicant learned of job opening	■ Appearance and mannerisms ■ Ability to express self ■ Responsiveness
Work experience	■ Duties of past jobs ■ Which liked best? Least? ■ Major accomplishments? ■ Problems faced? How were they handled? ■ Reasons for changing jobs? ■ Earnings? ■ What was learned from jobs? ■ What is applicant looking for in a job? From an organization?	■ Relevance and sufficiency of work experience ■ Skills and competencies ■ Motivation and initiative ■ Ability to work with people ■ General attitude toward work ■ Does job fit what the applicant seeks?

(continued)

Table 12.1 (continued)

TOPIC	QUESTIONS ASKED	WHAT YOU SEEK
Education	■ Schooling or special training ■ Best subjects? Worst subjects? ■ Favorite subjects? Least-liked subjects? ■ Relations with teachers ■ Special achievements? ■ Extracurricular activities? Leadership activities? ■ How was education financed? ■ Why did applicant take courses chosen? Relation to job or career?	■ Relevance and sufficiency of schooling/training? ■ Intellectual ability ■ Broad/narrow knowledge ■ Level of accomplishment ■ Motivation ■ Initiative ■ Reaction to authority ■ Team work ■ Sense of responsibility ■ Management of time
Present activities	■ Special interests? Hobbies? ■ Civic or community involvement? ■ How is spare time spent?	■ Vitality ■ Management of time ■ Maturity and judgement ■ Diversity of interests ■ Basic values and goals

Conducting the interview

Interviews are effective only if you obtain the information needed to make a good fit between the applicants and the job. So, you must receive information regarding each applicant's suitability. On the other hand, each applicant must receive information regarding how well the job fits him or her. Three areas must be considered if interviews are to be effective. Supervisors must ask the right questions.

The questions must be asked so the applicant can provide the right information. And, finally, supervisors must provide the right information for applicants.

Asking the right questions   Obviously, the questions asked during the interview determine the information you receive. This is important for two reasons. If questions pertaining to job-related characteristics are not asked, how will you have the information you need to decide which applicants are suitable for the job? At the same time, EEO legislation requires that interview questions be related to the applicant's ability to do the job. Many questions that were asked in the past are now illegal. A guide to help you determine what can and cannot be asked during interviews is provided in Fig. 12.6. This guide also applies to questions that appear on application blanks.

The interview should focus on the applicant's personal qualities and past experiences. Qualities such as poise, ability to deal with people, and ambition are more easily detected through interviews than other selection devices. You can observe the applicant's behavior. For example, if the job requires the ability to get along with people, you should observe how the applicant relates to you. Is he or she friendly, polite, and attentive? Or is the applicant withdrawn, shy, or even defensive while talking to you?

You can predict how someone will behave by looking at what they have done in the past. For this reason, most of the interview should deal with the past history of the person being considered. What courses were studied at school? Which subjects were most interesting? What about activities other than school or work? Specifically, what were the applicant's responsibilities and duties in past jobs? What are his or her present goals and ambitions? Such questions can give insight into what type of worker the applicant would be if hired for a particular job. Performance in school may indicate the quality of work to be expected. When trying to determine whether or not the applicant has the ability to learn technical job skills, a detailed description of past job duties is more meaningful than knowing the length of time worked in a particular job.

How questions are asked   Good interviews take time. You should give applicants enough time to understand and respond fully to your questions. You should not turn over the interview to the applicant, however. You must control the interview to ensure only job-related topics are discussed.

Race or Color

You may not ask about complexion or color of skin.

Religion or Creed

You may not ask about the applicant's religious practices.

National Origin

You may not ask about the applicant's nationality.

Sex

You may not ask questions related to the applicant's sex.

Marital Status

You may not ask if the applicant is married or has children.

Age

You may ask if the applicant is between 18 and 70 years of age.

You may not ask the applicant's age.

Disability

You may ask applicants if they have any disability that would hinder their ability to do the job.

You may not ask if applicants have disabilities or if family members have had any diseases.

Citizenship

You may ask if applicants are citizens of the United States and, if not, whether they have the legal right to remain permanently in the U.S.

You may not ask if applicants are native-born citizens or when citizenship was acquired.

Character

You may ask applicants if they have ever been convicted of any crime.

You may not ask whether they have ever been arrested.

Figure 12.6 Questions that can and cannot be asked.

Too often supervisors talk too much or too little during interviews. Important information can be forfeited if you rattle off a list of questions permitting applicants only to make specific responses. On the other hand, if your questions are too general and you let applicants ramble about whatever topics they choose, you probably will obtain much useless information.

Structured interviews can help you derive enough useful information from each applicant. In a **structured interview**, you ask all applicants a set of predetermined questions in an open-ended, general manner. The applicant is allowed to talk freely about specific topics. By asking all applicants a common set of job-related questions, you will obtain comparable information. Letting applicants answer each question enables you to obtain much more information than would result from a simple yes or no answer. For example, the response to the question, "Did you like your last job?" provides less insight than would a similar but open-ended question, "What things did you like best about your last job?"

Too often supervisors are overly concerned with the questions they want to ask and give applicants little time to make comments freely. Unsolicited comments often contain valuable information and should be encouraged.

Giving the right information to applicants   You should use the interview to answer any questions applicants may have about the job and organization. The job and its requirements should be explained in enough detail so the applicant can make the decision to accept or refuse if an offer is made.

For many reasons, supervisors often describe the job inaccurately, making it sound much more appealing than it really is. While their intentions may be decent (persuading good applicants to accept jobs), the results clearly are not desirable.

An experiment conducted by a New England telephone company with applicants for the job of operator demonstrates the problems found when jobs are sugar-coated.[4] Half of the applicants were told the operator's job was exciting, important, challenging, and very satisfying. The other applicants heard a description that was more realistic. The operator's job was described as rather easy and routine, involving close supervision and little recognition for doing good work. Contrary to what might be expected, the sugar-coated description did not result in more applicants who accepted job offers than did the realistic description. However, those new workers who had been told the job was exciting, challenging, and satisfying were less likely to stay on the job. After three months, 50% of the workers who heard the sugar-coated description had quit while only 38% of the workers given realistic information quit. Since supervisors are concerned with hiring good workers who will stay on the job, accurately describing the job during the interview is vital.

As the interview ends, you should summarize the discussion. Encourage any further questions the applicant may have. Close the interview on a friendly note. By that time, you probably have a fairly good idea of whether the applicant is suitable for the job. The closing remarks should reflect this judgment. If an applicant clearly is not qualified, this should be pointed out tactfully. Certainly the unqualified applicant should not be told lies. This practice only creates negative feelings about the organization. Qualified candidates should be told when a decision will be made and how they will be notified.

Evaluating interview results

The suitability of applicants should be judged by comparing their responses and behavior during the interview to those characteristics identified as necessary to perform the job. Using the structured interview, you can compare each applicant's answers. Here again a checklist may prove helpful. Checklists allow you to record information as soon as it is received and present information on all applicants in a standardized form.

As discussed in Chapter 5, you need to be careful not to let personal prejudices, stereotypes, and the halo effect influence your evaluation. Impressions are gained in the first few minutes of the interview and often remain regardless of the applicant's qualifications. Similarly, certain stereotypes are difficult to ignore. Viewing a woman as qualified to do what has traditionally been a man's job is difficult for many people. Knowing these problems exist and attempting to be as objective as possible can help to reduce ill effects on hiring decisions. You need to look for facts and information revealed during the interview to support your evaluation of each applicant.

Orienting the new worker

The hiring process is not complete until the new worker is fully ready to function on the job. Such readiness is not achieved just by hiring the worker. All new workers, regardless of their backgrounds, need to be oriented to their new jobs, co-workers, and the organization.

As a supervisor, you may not be responsible formally for orienting new workers. However, you must make sure they know and understand enough about their new jobs to perform them effectively. Newly hired workers are ready for advice, open to suggestions and direction, and eager to become a part of the work group. In fact, during this time you can probably have greater influence over workers' attitudes than at any other time. Use this advantage, because positive attitudes created early during employment can pay dividends later.

For a variety of reasons, supervisors cannot depend on new workers to approach them with problems or questions. New workers do not want to appear "stupid" in front of their bosses. In some cases your own manner many inhibit new employees. Consequently, they may not feel free to ask questions or discuss problems with you.

Problems with orienting workers and how to avoid them

Typical problems which arise during the **orientation process** include:

■ Informal, haphazard handling of new employees;
■ Lack of preparation of other workers;
■ Reluctance to let new workers spend time away from the job to attend personnel-sponsored orientation programs;
■ Overwhelming the newcomer with too much information in too short a time.

As a rule, successful orientation programs are carefully planned and executed. You may find a checklist helpful to ensure that all the necessary information is provided. Figure 12.7 illustrates a typical checklist including areas that should be covered in orienting new workers.

New workers are often given employee handbooks and procedures manuals and told to read them. This may or may not contribute much to the orientation process. Handbooks are sometimes outdated, inaccurate, or, even worse, written at a reading level new workers find hard to understand. Also, new workers may not take the time to read through the material. Even if they do, reading about how things are supposed to be done is never as effective as discussing how and why.

From the organizational perspective, include

1. The objectives and philosophy of the organization.
2. An explanation of the organization's operations, the levels of authority, and how they relate to each other.
3. A brief history of the organization.
4. What is expected of the new employee: attitude, reliability, initiative, emotional maturity, and personal appearance.
5. Job functions and responsibilities.
6. Rules, regulations, policies, and procedures.
7. Why the organization needs the new employee.
8. City, state, and federal laws, if applicable.
9. Functions of management.
10. Telephone techniques.

From the new employee's perspective, include

1. A welcome.
2. Introduction to his or her department and fellow workers.
3. General office practice and business etiquette.
4. Skill training.
5. Job responsibilities.
6. Performance evaluation criteria.
7. Promotional opportunities.
8. Conditions of employment: punctuality, attendance, conduct, hours of work, overtime termination.
9. Pay procedures.
10. Benefits: salary, job security, insurance, recreational facilities, employee activities, rest periods, holidays, vacation, sick leave, leave of absence, tuition refund, pension.
11. Safety and fire prevention.
12. Personnel policies.
13. Techniques for learning.
14. Encouragement.

Figure 12.7 Orientation checklist.

Source: Adapted from Joseph Famularo, ed., *Handbook of Modern Personnel Administration,* © 1972. Used with permission of McGraw-Hill Book Company.

Another often overlooked problem is that supervisors rarely prepare other workers for the arrival of the newcomer. Employees should be told someone has been hired and when the new worker will start. They should also be told what job is being filled and be given general information about the new person's background. More importantly, you should encourage co-workers to assist the newcomer.

When personnel departments have orientation programs, the supervisor should allow the new worker to attend. The time spent away from the job during the first few days will pay off later. In a study at Texas Instruments, for example, one group of newcomers spent two hours away from their jobs at a personnel-sponsored orientation program covering general information. Another group attended the same two-hour seminar but also spent the rest of the day in a special seminar focusing on the job, their supervisors, typical new-worker pranks, and other useful information. The extra time spent away from their jobs paid off. The second group outperformed the first group in both work and attendance after four weeks on the job.[5]

It is interesting to note that nearly half of all worker turnover occurs during the first six weeks of employment. Almost all worker turnover occurs during the first six months. Much of this "early" turnover may be caused by poor selection techniques resulting in a mismatch of people and jobs. However, even the best matches can quickly turn sour if new, eager workers are left to their own devices to discover how to succeed on the job.

New employees are usually deluged with information when they first begin working. The handbooks, operating procedures, policies, rules and regulations, co-worker's names and duties are all necessary but may contribute to confusion if not properly presented. The best approach is to discuss whatever is presented in written form and encourage the new worker to ask questions before leaving each topic.

In conclusion, some key points to remember when orienting new workers are:

- Give the worker a friendly welcome and ensure the first impression is a good one.
- Make the worker comfortable. If possible assign a relatively new worker to talk with the newcomer. This person can relate to the problems the new worker faces or will face and can help minimize any concerns.

■ Make sure the worker is aware of your desire to help.

■ Stress the importance of safety where hazards exist. Explain and demonstrate what needs to be done to avoid danger. Then ask the worker to repeat your instructions.

■ Stress that you know the worker can do a good job.[6]

Summary

☐ Selection is concerned with establishing a good fit between people and jobs. Problems may result if supervisors don't hire people whose abilities, skills, interests, and experience match the job. Applicants look for certain characteristics in jobs.

☐ The supervisor's role in selection varies across organizations. They are generally responsible for notifying personnel of job vacancies, providing personnel with job descriptions and specifications, conducting the final interview, making the hiring decision, and orienting the new worker.

☐ Job descriptions are written statements of the tasks, duties, and responsibilities required on the job. Job specifications describe the skills required to perform the job. Qualified applicants are recruited in a variety of ways. Various combinations of selection devices are then used to weed out unqualified applicants until the hiring decision is finally made.

☐ Hiring new workers is influenced by equal employment opportunity legislation. These laws require people be hired on the basis of job-related characteristics. Organizations doing business with the federal government are required to take affirmative action. This means they must actively seek to hire members of groups previously discriminated against.

☐ Supervisors have considerable input into job descriptions and specifications. Accurate job descriptions and specifications are essential for complying with EEO legislation.

☐ Nearly all supervisors conduct the final interview. The interview should meet two objectives: (1) enable supervisors to meet and evaluate remaining applicants and (2) enable applicants to meet their prospective supervisors and ask questions. Supervisors should carefully prepare for the final interview. The questions asked must be related to the job. The way questions are asked influences the information received from the interview. Supervisors should describe the job and its requirements accurately.

☐ At the close of the interview, unqualified applicants should be informed about their status and qualified applicants should be told when the hiring decision will be made. Supervisors make the hiring decision by comparing information received from all applicants. Using a checklist helps make this comparison.

☐ The hiring process is not over until the new worker is ready to function on the job. New workers must be oriented to the job, co-workers, and the organization. Supervisors must be sure new workers receive proper orientation.

Questions for review and discussion

1. What are the goals of selection?
2. What steps are typically involved in the selection process? What is the supervisor's role? *Request + Final Interview Hiring decision*
3. What laws influence selection? How do they affect how supervisors hire workers?
4. Why are accurate job descriptions and specifications necessary for effective selection? What should supervisors do to ensure they are accurate?
5. What is the purpose of the final interview? How should supervisors prepare for the final interview?
6. How do supervisors decide whom to hire?

7. Why is orienting new workers important? What problems are typically encountered?

8. How can supervisors ensure workers receive proper orientation?

9. What should the role of government legislation be in determining who is hired in an organization?

Key terms

Affirmative action plans	Job specifications
Age Discrimination in Employment Act	Orientation process
	Preliminary interview
Application blank	Reference checks
Equal employment opportunity (EEO)	Selection process
	Staffing process
Equal Employment Opportunity Commission (EEOC)	Structured interviews
	Testing
Final interview	Title VII of the Civil Rights Act
Job descriptions	Vocational Rehabilitation Act

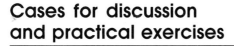

Cases for discussion and practical exercises

1. I began working at Mohawk Communications as a credit analyst just three weeks after graduating from college. I had one interview before I was offered the job with Mr. Hall, the supervisor of the credit department. Before talking to him, the vice

president's secretary had given me the application to complete. After waiting a few minutes, I was taken to Mr. Hall's office and my interview began.

When I first met Mr. Hall, he was pleasant but acted as if he had other things on his mind than hiring a credit analyst. I sat silently as he looked over my application blank. After a few minutes, he opened his desk drawer and pulled out a piece of paper. He began asking questions and writing down everything I said in response. He focused mainly on areas already covered on the application blank. He seemed very impressed with my grades and the fact that I had worked every chance I had while I was in school. Then he asked me if I would relocate. When I said no and explained I was getting married in two months, I knew I had no chance of getting the job. Shortly thereafter, the interview ended.

I was pleasantly surprised when Mr. Hall called four days later and offered me the job. When I reminded him I couldn't relocate, he reassured me it wouldn't be necessary. He said that applicants were always asked that question.

Mohawk had a good reputation as a place to work. The pay and benefits were better than the other offers I had received. I was really excited about my new job. Mr. Hall had told me to report to his office at 8:30 the following Monday morning.

The first day, Mr. Hall took me back to the vice president's secretary. She gave me a copy of the employee handbook. She explained that she was responsible for handling the personnel work at the regional office. From there, Mr. Hall showed me where I would be working. He introduced me to the other analysts (there were three). As he left he explained, "Just look through the files on your desk. You can learn the accounts you are responsible for. As orders come in, one of the other analysts will show you how to handle them. You'll catch on in no time." With that, Mr. Hall disappeared. I never did see him again that day.

There I was, sitting at a desk piled with file folders. Each had a tab of either blue, red, or yellow coloring; what the colors meant, I wasn't sure. I turned to the analyst seated closest to me. Before I could open my mouth she reassured me that it really wasn't as confusing as it all seemed. She told me that all the job entailed was keeping up with the salespeople.

"We are each assigned to about five salespeople. All you have to do is check their orders to make sure the customer's credit is good. If not, they are put on C.O.D. You also have to check the discounts. Lots of times the salespeople are trying to make quota and they come up with all kinds of tricks to do it," she said.

At that moment my phone rang. I answered it only to find an angry voice yelling about a credit hold placed on an order from General Electric.

"They're a yellow account. When will you people up there realize General Electric is not a credit risk? How we can be expected to sell anything when our own people are working against us is beyond me," the angry salesperson yelled.

As the phone slammed on the other end, I sat back in my chair. It was only 10:00 in the morning. All I knew was that I shouldn't interfere with the yellow accounts. My spirits were sinking slowly as I eagerly waited for lunchtime to come.

a) How would you evaluate the hiring process used in this case?

b) What might have been done differently to make the first day a better experience for the new worker?

c) What type of orientation was the new worker given? Would you have handled it differently? How?

2. Think back to a time you were hired for a job. What steps in the selection process did you go through? If you did not go through all the steps in the selection process described in this chapter, why do you think some steps were omitted? What recommendations would you have to improve the selection process?

Notes

1. Burke M. Smith, "The Polygraph," *Scientific American*, Vol. 216, January 1967, pp. 25–31.

2. Bruce Gunn, "The Polygraph and Personnel," *Personnel Administration*, Vol. 33, May 1970, pp. 32–37.

3. Stephen Sahlein (Jeff Baron, ed.) *The Affirmative Action Handbook: Dealing with Day to Day Supervisory Problems* (New York: Executive Enterprises Publications Co., Inc., 1979), pp. 4–6.

4. J. P. Wanous, "Tell It Like It Is at Realistic Job Previews," *Personnel*, Vol. 52, No. 4, 1975, pp. 50–60.

5. Earl R. Gomersall and Scott Myers, "Break-Through in On-the-Job Training," *Harvard Business Review*, Vol. 44, July–August 1966, pp. 64–65.

6. Gary P. Latham and Kenneth N. Wexley, *Increasing Productivity Through Performance Appraisal* (Reading, Mass.: Addison-Wesley, 1981), pp. 161–162.

13

Training and developing workers

Objectives

After reading this chapter you should be able to

- [ ] Explain how task analysis is conducted and used to identify training needs.
- [ ] Identify the factors influencing the presentation of the job in training.
- [ ] Explain how supervisors can determine the best arrangement of practice sessions.
- [ ] Explain the JIT process.
- [ ] Describe how the coaching process helps develop job skills.

Training has become an increasingly important part of the supervisor's job. Although supervisors may not do all of the training, they are ultimately responsible for their workers' performance and must see that their workers have acceptable job skills. Particularly as jobs become technologically more complex, workers need more training to master their tasks. Also, changing technology has affected workers' jobs, requiring that the workers be retrained.

However, we should not overemphasize the importance of training, since several other factors affect job performance. The skill or ability to perform the job is only one factor. The level of motivation to perform, the availability of tools, equipment, and materials, and effective planning also affect workers' performance. Training, of course, is directed primarily at the development of job skills.

In this chapter we will discuss the supervisor's training function. We will examine how people learn and how to determine training needs, plan for training, and conduct training sessions. We will also discuss an approach to informal training—coaching.

Training and learning

The primary purpose of **training** is to develop workers' skills. This statement implies, of course, that workers learn. Thus before developing plans for training workers, you should have an understanding of how people learn. There are no hard and fast rules for learning, but there are some guidelines that should be helpful.

Motivation to learn   You cannot force people to learn. They must want to learn; they must be motivated to involve themselves in the learning process. Several factors influence a worker's **motivation to learn.**

■ Workers are more motivated to learn when they see that the material being presented is relevant to them. Thus, workers should understand the objectives of the training and see how the training will help them perform their jobs more effectively.

■ Workers are more motivated to learn when they see that the learning benefits them. You need to link the training and resulting job performance to rewards that are meaningful.

■ Workers are more motivated to learn when the training is, in and of itself, interesting and stimulating. Using techniques that involve the worker and varying your training methods generally make training more interesting.

Modeling   **Modeling** is one of the basic approaches to learning a skill. From the earliest age we observe people behaving and copy their behavior. Modeling is not necessary for learning, but it makes learning easier. Think of how difficult it would be to learn how to swim by reading a description of swimming. If you can see someone demonstrate how to swim, you can understand what you must do more easily.

When training workers, you should use models. Demonstrate how the worker is to perform the job. Let them observe another worker performing the job correctly. Show a movie or videotape, if appropriate. In some way, give them a model they can copy.

Practice People learn best by doing. Skills are developed slowly and a person must practice to develop the skill. Think of our swimming example again. Can you imagine learning how to swim without ever practicing?

When training workers, you need to give them plenty of opportunities to practice. The amount of practice needed may vary from worker to worker. Generally, however, they should be able to practice until overlearning occurs, or, until the task becomes second nature.

Feedback and reinforcement Feedback is necessary for learning to occur. The worker must receive a response, or **feedback,** to know whether he or she is performing the task correctly or incorrectly. Positive feedback also serves as positive reinforcement. It is a reward that increases the probability that the worker will perform the task correctly.

Therefore, while workers are practicing, you should observe them. Let them know when they perform the job incorrectly and tell them what was wrong. Also, look for every opportunity to provide positive reinforcement. Tell them when they did the job right or let them know when they are improving.

Learning rates Learning is not a standardized, clear-cut process. What happens in the workers' mind between the time a task is taught and the worker actually learns is a mystery. We do know, however, that people learn at different rates. In addition, each worker's rate of learning differs over time. Usually, they begin learning at a rapid rate, after which learning levels off. Learning rates continue to fluctuate and level off until the worker becomes competent.

Leveling-off periods and periods of slow learning can be extremely frustrating to both workers and supervisors. If they are not handled correctly, learning can stop. You need to be supportive when workers are on a plateau, keeping them from getting frustrated and discouraged.

Transferring learning No training occurs in exactly the same environment in which the job is performed. If the training environment differs a great deal from the actual job environment, it may be difficult for the worker to transfer the learning. Thus the training situation should resemble the job situation as much as possible.

Training needs analysis

Before you actually begin training you need to determine whether it is necessary and, if so, what specific training is needed. Two methods of identifying training needs are often used, task analysis and performance review. Let's look at each in more detail.

Task analysis

Task analysis involves analyzing the job and describing the tasks which are involved in its performance. Performance standards indicating minimally acceptable levels of performance on each task are also defined. The result of task analysis is a detailed **job definition**. Figure 13.1 is a useful guide to use in developing job definitions. Thus, the job definition serves as a framework for training new workers. It defines each task required to perform the job. It describes how each task is performed and defines the level of competence workers must achieve on each task.

Task analysis is used to design training for new workers and workers who have changed jobs. It specifies exactly that workers need to learn and what level of competence is expected. It may also be used to review expected performance with workers who are having performance problems.

On paper, task analysis looks easy. However, carefully conducted task analysis can easily result in pages and pages of detailed description. To reduce the number of tasks to a more manageable size, you should classify each task into one of three categories:

- ■ Those tasks which are critical: unless performed properly they would cause injury or great financial loss.
- ■ Those tasks which must be performed frequently: hence, great cost benefit results from ensuring they are done correctly.

Knowledge Items (Excluding Job Methods). These are items to be explained to the trainee. They include

Where tools, equipment, machinery, and information used in performing tasks are usually located.

Definitions of terms peculiar to the job.

The mechanical features of the equipment or machinery used to perform the job. The organization of information used to perform the job.

Safety hazards, quality requirements, housekeeping, waste standards, information on supplies, and supply usage relevant to the job.

Standard (required) times for performing each task, machine cycle time, schedules (for tasks such as cleaning, lubricating, patrolling, reporting), and priorities of tasks relevant to the job.

Statement of Task Pattern. These are descriptions of tasks to be performed, including

Sequence of motions or activities comprising the task.

What motions or activities are involved in performing the tasks (reaches, moves, grasps, compiling information, reports)?

What hand and finger positions are required in making the motions?

What specific information is needed to complete the activities?

Signals. These are items trainees must be aware of that indicate something needs to be done or indicate some task or activity is being done well or poorly.

Signal to begin a particular task. What indicates that something must be done by the worker? What conditions or situations indicate the Task A must be performed rather than Task B?

Indicators that the task has been performed correctly. Standards regarding proper position, distances, amounts, tolerances, tensions, appearance, features, number of complaints, volume sales, etc.

Reference points or attention points that can be used to determine if worker will achieve required standards.

How can workers check progress? Do they look, listen, or feel? In what other ways can they check?

Figure 13.1 Guide to developing job definitions.
Source: Adapted from James E. Gardner, *Helping Employees Develop Job Skills: A Casebook of Training Approaches* (Washington, D.C.: Bureau of National Affairs, Inc., 1976), pp. 44–46.

■ Those tasks which are noncritical and nonfrequent: these tasks do not merit the same degree of training effort as those in the first two categories.[1]

Task analysis would be performed only on tasks that fall in the first two categories. Noncritical, infrequently performed tasks can be learned through the use of performance aids.

Performance aids are simple, graphic descriptions of how to perform a task. Figure 13.2 illustrates a performance aid for valve assembly. When posted at the work site, they are readily available for workers to review when the task must be completed.

1. Place stamped brass valve bodies in assembly fixture and close toggle clamp on fixture to hold value bodies upright and steady.

2. Place greased stems in valve bodies two at a time and start them by hand. Continue until all valve bodies have stems.

3. Slide brass packing glands over stems. Flat side should face down toward threads.

4. Slide greased packing washers over stems into bodies until they are snug. Do not overtighten.

5. Use the air wrench to tighten stems into bodies until they are snug. Do not overtighten.

6. Place packing nuts (bonnets) over stems and thread into bodies by hand. Use preset torque-controlled air driver to tighten packing nuts (bonnets). Remove valves from fixture and place in crate.

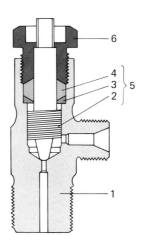

Figure 13.2   Major assembly steps: valve assembly.

Source: Stanley J. Holden, "Manufacturing Training—A Two Step Process." Reproduced by special permission from the September, 1980 *Training and Development Journal.* Copyright 1980 by the American Society for Training and Development, Inc.

Performance review

A second approach to determining training needs, **performance review,** is generally used in upgrading workers' skills. Unlike task analysis, this method is used when workers' actual job performance does not meet performance standards. By detecting important individual or group performance problems and discovering why they exist, you can determine whether training is needed.

You should be careful in determining the causes of performance problems. Remember that training is not a cure-all for every performance problem. Poor performance is caused by many factors. Workers capable of satisfactory performance may not be properly motivated. Factors outside the workers' control may prohibit them from achieving good performance. Inadequate equipment or tools, for example, may be causing poor performance. People may have personal problems or they may not have the basic ability to perform the job under any circumstances. Training is not the answer when poor performance results from these factors.

You should consider training to resolve important performance problems when:

■ Poor performance is caused by a lack of knowledge, skills, or ability.

■ The unsatisfactory performers are capable of performing the job satisfactorily.

Unless these two conditions exist, training will probably result in wasted time, effort, and money.

Once training needs have been identified, they are translated into specific training objectives. The training objectives specify expected performance capabilities. If a task analysis has been performed and a job definition developed, the job definition gives the specific training objectives. If training needs were identified through performance review, the level of performance you expect workers to achieve must be stated.

Training objectives should be specifically defined and measurable, indicating the exact job skills required and expected level of performance. General statements such as, "Develop the ability to perform the job," provide little guidance. This statement does not specify the steps required to perform the job, the skills needed, or the expected performance level. A more appropriate training objective would use the following format: "Produce 30 units per hour, meeting quality standards, using the following steps." The objective statement would go on to describe the skills necessary at each step of the job.

Planning for training

Effective job skills training requires planning. As we indicated in the section on training needs analysis, you need to know exactly what you will teach the worker. Also, you need to make some additional decisions. These include where the training will take place, how the job should be presented, and how practice sessions should be arranged.

Where should the training be done?

Training may be done on the job or away from the job. **On-the-job training** occurs at the regular job station using the normal tools and equipment. Off-the-job or **vestibule training** occurs away from the actual work station. This training method involves recreating the work place in a training room or facility. Trainees learn how to perform their jobs in separate but similar facilities. They are taught the required tasks while using equipment, machinery, and tools exactly like the ones found in the work setting.

Learning in vestibule settings offers certain advantages. Unlike the work setting, there are no distractions. The training occurs without the noise, confusion, and operating pressures found in the work place. Mistakes made by trainees and the slow work pace typical during the learning process do not interfere with normal operations. Special expert trainers whose sole purpose is to work with the trainees are available also.

Vestibule training has disadvantages, however. Transfer of learning is sometimes a problem. The setting approximates but is not identical to the actual work setting. As a result, some trainees have difficulty adjusting to the regular job pressures. In addition, vestibule training is expensive. The equipment and tools used and the specialized trainers incur additional costs not found in on-the-job training.

On-the-job training may be less expensive but it is not without costs. During the training period, the time supervisors spend training the worker is time spent away from their normal job duties. Workers also perform at less than satisfactory levels during the training period. Furthermore, since workers are learning how to perform the job, the potential for damaged equipment or poor quality production or service is increased.

The environment where on-the-job training occurs is its greatest advantage. Training workers while they actually perform their jobs minimizes the problem of transferring skills learned in training to the job environment.

How should the job be presented?

Determining how much workers should be taught at one time is important. Learning conditions are best when the material taught is challenging enough to prevent boredom, but not so difficult as to prevent successful learning.

Jobs can be taught in their entirety (**whole learning**). They can also be broken down into parts, teaching workers one task at a time (**part learning**). Which approach is best depends on the abilities of the workers. Quick learners learn better when the job is presented as a whole. Slower learners succeed when exposed step-by-step to each part of the job.

The type of job is also a factor. Jobs should be taught as a whole if they are short, simple, or involve highly related activities which join together in a meaningful sequence. Part learning is better for jobs that are long, complex, or involve loosely related activities that are meaningful by themselves.

How should workers practice?

Practicing what they have learned is necessary if workers are to retain job skills. Again, how much practice is needed depends on the kind of worker doing the learning and what is being taught. **Massed practice** over long, uninterrupted periods tends to work best with quick learners. **Distributed practice** sessions that are shorter and occur more frequently are better for slower learners.

Similarly, if the task to be learned is complex and difficult, distributed practice sessions are advisable. Simple, short tasks are are best learned using a massed practice session. In all cases, workers should be given enough practice so they are able to perform each task readily, without thinking about it.

Although practicing tasks on the job may interfere with normal operations, advantages are apparent. In particular, the costs of short-run losses in production as a result of practice sessions usually are less than costs resulting from poor learning.

Conducting the training

The most commonly used training approach for developing job skills is **Job Instruction Training (JIT)**. JIT was used to teach supervisors how to train new workers during World War II. It is based on the learning principles discussed earlier and can be used for on-the-job training or off-the-job-training. There are four steps in the JIT process.

1. **Prepare the worker for training.** First you need to put the worker at ease. Workers frequently are rather anxious and nervous when they are being trained. This nervousness can hinder learning. Talk with workers and help them relax before beginning. Help them understand that the training is not threatening but is designed to help them learn. At this time, try to influence the worker's motivation to learn. Discuss the objectives of the training with them. Explain how the training will help the worker meet job requirements and how they will benefit.

2. **Present the job.** You have already decided whether you should present the job as a whole or use part learning. Now, using the selected approach, explain each task that comprises the job. The following guidelines can help you present the job effectively.

   ■ Present each step in the job in a logical, orderly manner, emphasizing the important points.

   ■ If you have a written job specification or a checklist, share this with the workers and let them review it with you.

   ■ Go slowly and repeat important information. What may seem easy to you may be quite confusing to workers unfamiliar with the job.

■ Make certain workers understand the explanations. Ask questions periodically to check their learning progress.

■ Demonstrate each step in the job to the workers. Present a "model" so they can see how to perform the job correctly. You may need to demonstrate each step in the job a number of times.

■ Explain why the job should be performed as it is presented and why the specified results are necessary.

3. **Have the worker practice.** First, let the worker try out the task after you have explained and demonstrated how to do it. Ask the worker to explain each step as he or she performs it. Give the worker feedback, correcting any mistakes and positively reinforcing correct performance. Frequently, after the worker tries to perform the job, you will have to go back and give another demonstration and explanation. After the basics have been mastered, you can put the worker on a practice schedule. You should have decided already whether massed or distributed practice is appropriate. You may not need to be present constantly while the worker is practicing, but you should check back frequently. Observe how the worker is progressing and give the worker a chance to ask questions. Identify correct performance and incorrect performance. Indicate how incorrect performance should be corrected.

4. **Follow-up.** After the worker has developed minimally acceptable skills and is doing the job, you should continue to follow-up. To really master most job skills requires some time, so the worker may need periodic help and reinforcement. Slipping into some bad habits shortly after training is easy. You should help the worker transfer learning effectively from the training situation to the normal job environment. As the worker masters the skill you can taper off and eventually let the worker perform on his or her own.

Coaching

Coaching involves all the informal instruction, questions, and discussions supervisors have with workers regarding job performance. It is a method of providing workers with feedback on their performance and providing instruction to improve performance. While this type of discussion frequently occurs during the formal training period, it is also important after workers are on their own in their jobs.

Separating coaching from the day-to-day interaction of supervisors with their workers is difficult because it is informal. For poor performers it often involves corrective action. For good performers it involves encouraging continued development.

If you determine that a worker's performance is slipping and the problem is job skills, coaching is appropriate. It provides an approach for taking immediate action to solve the problem. With coaching, you discuss the performance problem with the worker and provide instruction. The JIT approach can be used to provide the instruction. However you should remember you are not starting from the beginning. The worker has some skill and has slipped into some bad habits. Thus, the first step is for the worker to recognize a problem exists so that he or she becomes receptive to instruction. The following guidelines are useful in coaching poor performers.[2]

- Be honest with the worker about the problem. However, keep the worker's self-image separate from the problem. What you say can influence how effective your coaching will be in improving performance. Don't say "Why are you messing up?" Instead tell the worker production has decreased and seek his or her suggestions for possible solutions. This approach reduces the potential for excuses and justification. It focuses on the problem, not the worker.

- Seek and pay attention to workers' ideas and suggestions. Learning and changed behavior is more likely to occur if the worker is involved. In addition, you may discover the cause of unsatisfactory performance is beyond the worker's control.

- Make sure the performance objectives or plans that are discussed are mutually accepted. Repeat what you believe them to be before ending your conversation with the worker.

- Follow up the conversation. This should involve establishing a time by which you expect the worker to have corrected the problem.

Coaching poor performance does involve criticism. However, you should use criticism carefully. You do not want to cause the worker to develop a negative work attitude. The key is to keep emotions out of your conversation with the worker.

- Explain the behavior you have seen and why it concerns you. Explain why the behavior cannot continue.

- Ask why the behavior is occurring and listen. That is the only way you can get all the facts.

- Keep to the issue. Don't let the discussion wander onto unrelated topics.

- Seek the worker's advice on how the problem can be solved. Offer your ideas and suggestions. Convey your sincerity in helping the worker solve the problem. Don't appear to be eager for an excuse to take disciplinary action. You are not a police officer. You are attempting to encourage productive, contributing workers.

- Agree on the steps each of you will take to resolve the problem and the timetable for ensuring it will be solved.[3]

Supervisory development

In Chapter 2, we presented an overview of the challenges supervisors face on the job. The fact that change and complexity are a reality of supervisory work cannot be overstated. Supervisors also must cope with increasing demands from their superiors. But meeting these responsibilities without adequate training is difficult. Just as workers must continually develop on their jobs, supervisors must too.

Many organizations encourage supervisory development. In a survey of organizations it was found that 86% used on-the-job coaching, 81% offered tuition assistance for college courses, and 75% offered in-house supervisory training programs.[4] Many organizations also send supervisors to training programs sponsored by universities or professional training groups.

Individual supervisors can do much to enhance their own development. Different supervisors have different development needs. These needs may be met in part through company-sponsored programs. However, supervisors must take the responsibility to ensure they continue to develop in their jobs. This requires you to assess your performance objectively and determine where you are weak or strong. In both cases, you should seek improvement. Further develop your strong skills and improve in your weak areas.

Supervisors can engage in self-development in a variety of ways. They can seek the help of an experienced superior or mentor. It is also helpful to keep abreast of current developments and to find out how other supervisors handle certain problems. You can get this information by reading regularly publications with articles geared toward supervisors' problems.

Summary

- [ ] Training has become an increasingly important part of the supervisor's job. Job performance is affected by several factors. Having the skill to do the job is only one factor. Training is necessary to develop job skills.
- [ ] Several factors can help increase learning. These include workers' motivation to learn, the use of models, opportunities for practice, feedback and reinforcement, knowledge of learning rates, and transfer of learning.
- [ ] Training needs can be identified by task analysis or performance reviews. Task analysis should be performed only on tasks that are critical or performed frequently. It results in a job definition. Task analysis is appropriate for training workers on new jobs.
- [ ] Performance review is used to identify training needs of current workers with performance problems. Training can resolve performance problems only in certain situations.
- [ ] Training needs must be translated into specific and measurable objectives. They should indicate clearly job skills to be learned and the expected level of performance.
- [ ] Training may occur off the job. Vestibule training involves training workers away from the job in similar facilities. There are advantages, but transfer of learning is a problem. Vestibule training can also be expensive.
- [ ] On-the-job training is more common. Transfer of learning is not a serious problem as training occurs in the actual job environment.
- [ ] Jobs can be taught as a whole or broken into parts. The choice depends on the ability of the workers and the nature of the job.

Train the trainer
Identify the trainer
Pay to train
Follow up or test

☐ Practice is necessary for learning to occur. Massed practice occurs over long, uninterrupted periods. Distributed practice sessions involve shorter, frequently occurring opportunities for practice. The way practice sessions should be structured depends on the workers and type of job.

☐ Job Instruction Training (JIT) is the most common, formal on-the-job training technique. Developed during World War II, JIT involves four steps: (1) preparing the worker for training, (2) presenting the job, (3) having the worker practice, and (4) following up.

☐ Coaching involves all the informal instruction, questions, and discussions supervisors have with workers about job performance. For good performers it involves encouraging continued development. For poor performers it involves taking corrective action.

Questions for review and discussion

Problems
1. Best worker may not be best trainer. TRAIN PEOPLE to TRAIN
2. Worker passes bad habits to trainee
3. Production not training emphasized,
4. worker dislikes training
5. Personality conflict
6. Deliberate under-training, FOLLOW UP TRAINING
7. Not workers job to train. PAY TO TRAIN

1. Why is training an important part of a supervisor's job?
2. What guides to learning can help make training more effective?
3. Discuss how supervisors can identify training needs.
4. What is vestibule training? What are its advantages and disadvantages? What are the advantages and disadvantages of on-the-job training?
5. What factors must be considered in determining whether whole or part learning is the best way to train workers? How can supervisors determine whether to provide massed practice or distributed practice sessions?
6. Describe the JIT process.
7. What is coaching? What guidelines should supervisors follow when coaching poor performers?
8. How can you be sure criticism will not result in a negative work attitude?

9. On-the-job training is the most common form of training for nonsupervisory workers, yet in many cases, little effort is devoted to planning formal on-the-job training. Why do you think this is the case? What problems may arise as a result.

Key terms

Coaching	On-the-job training
Distributed practice	Part learning
Feedback	Performance aids
Job definition	Performance review
Job Instruction Training (JIT)	Task analysis
Massed practice	Training
Modeling	Vestibule training
Motivation to learn	Whole learning

Cases for discussion and practical exercises

1. Jane Braddock, supervisor of claims, was proud of her new training system for newly hired claims processors. She spent at least three months ironing out all the rough spots.

    A little over a year ago, her company had decided to do something about the bad publicity they were receiving as a result of the inordinate amount of time it took to process claims. Once they were processed, many of them were released with mistakes. As a result of this problem, the company established a committee to study the claims department.

The committee determined that part of the problem was that many workers were careless in processing claims. Others, they learned, really didn't know what they were doing. As a result, some of the more difficult claims were often left sitting in a file for extended periods.

In an attempt to resolve the problem, top management decided to implement an incentive system for claims processors. They were to receive a bonus based on the number of correctly processed claims per month. Workers would be able to sizeably increase their earnings under the new bonus plan. With regard to training, supervisors were held responsible for ensuring their workers were trained well enough to process the claims. As the supervisors too received a bonus based on how well their groups did, they had an incentive to prepare workers adequately to perform their jobs.

Jane's system involved a mixture of on-the-job and off-the-job training. New employees were given a manual on their first day at work. The manual described how various types of claims were to be processed, the information needed, and so forth. Jane prepared the manual herself. Having been a claims processor for four years prior to being promoted to supervisor, she was careful to include things she found troublesome at first.

In addition to receiving the manual, each new worker was assigned to one of the more senior workers for the first month of their employment. During this time the new worker was to serve as an "assistant to," watching the senior employee perform the job. The senior employee was responsible for training the new worker, demonstrating exactly how each type of claim was to be handled. Jane had decided that within a month's time, the new worker would have gained enough exposure to the various types of claims to be allowed to work independently. At the end of the first month, new workers were to be put on the bonus system.

After the first six months of operation, the results were somewhat dismal. Jane couldn't understand what had gone wrong. She had hired four new processors during this time and only one was still on the payroll. And, he was the only one out of the group who had had prior experience in the area. The others had quit during the first month of employment or shortly thereafter.

Jane made it a habit to talk to workers when they quit to discover their reasons for quitting. Some of the comments she had received from these workers included:

"Hey, I got sick of sitting around watching the minutes tick by on the clock all day. Having an easy job is one thing, but being bored to death is ridiculous."

"The job is too confusing. I never did figure out what information went where. When my sister told me about the opening at her company, I couldn't pass it up. I was so frustrated. I knew there wasn't that much to the job but for some reason, I couldn't do anything right."

"No, the guy who was working with me was good. I mean he really tried. He just had too much to do. He couldn't spend the time I needed to explain everything and show me how to do it. After two weeks on my own, I knew I'd never break standard."

a) What has gone wrong?

b) If you were Jane, what changes would you make in an attempt to correct the problem and why?

2. Recall a time when you have been trained to perform a task. It could have been either a work task or a nonwork task. How was the training conducted? Did it follow the JIT process? What things did the trainer do particularly well? What things were handled poorly? What recommendations would you make to improve the training you received?

3. Think of a task you perform on a regular basis. Once again, if you are not now working, select a nonwork task. Do a task analysis. Develop a job definition for the task. Develop a plan for training another person to perform the task.

Notes

1. Stanley J. Holden, "Manufacturing Training—A Two-Step Process," *Training and Development Journal*, Vol. 34, September 1980, p. 25.

2. Gary P. Latham and Kenneth N. Wexley, *Increasing Productivity through Performance Appraisal* (Reading, Mass.: Addison-Wesley, 1981), pp. 162–167.

3. Ibid.

4. *Management Training and Development Programs*, PPF Survey No. 116, (Washington, D.C.: Bureau of National Affairs, March 1977).

14

Reviewing worker performance

Objectives

After reading this chapter you should be able to

☐ Identify ways formal reviews can help supervisors become more effective.

☐ Explain the relationship between informal and formal performance reviews.

☐ Identify the characteristics of successful review discussions.

☐ Explain how to handle recurring performance problems.

Performance reviews

In Chapter 13, you saw that supervisors regularly observe and evaluate workers' performance during their coaching activities. These daily informal discussions require you to recognize good performance and discuss areas where improved performance is needed. Periodically you may be asked to review formally the overall performance of each worker. Informal performance reviews are scattered among the day-to-day conversations you have with your workers. **Formal performance reviews** involve conferring with your workers and specifically evaluating their performance. The outcome of the performance review generally affects the employment status of workers. Whether they will be retained, promoted, demoted, transferred, terminated, or given a salary increase may be determined by the outcome of these formal performance reviews. More important, formal performance review can serve as a way to improve job performance.

Many supervisors find evaluating the performance of their workers an uncomfortable task. Confronting workers with performance deficiencies can be unpleasant. Unfortunately, few workers, if any, are without need for improvement in the way they do their jobs. The situation becomes even more uncomfortable when we realize we are often uncertain as to what is really being reviewed—job-related or non–job-related characteristics.

A poor performance review system can damage an organization or one of its units. If you felt your performance was evaluated unfairly wouldn't you react negatively? All too often the real objective of performance review—improved job performance—is forgotten. The evaluation aspect tends to be overemphasized, reducing the positive effects performance review can have on job performance.

As a result of these problems, some organizations don't use performance review information in making employment decisions. They use seniority instead. Even worse, many organizations continue to use meaningless, time-consuming review systems. Frustration over performance review has increased recently since it is subject to EEO regulations when used to make employment decisions. If a worker is denied a promotion on the basis of his or her performance on the job, you must demonstrate that you accurately measured the worker's job performance.

Unfortunately, eliminating performance review means the organization will not have an accurate assessment of whether workers are doing their jobs well. Many arguments can be made for why this information is important. Supervisors must be concerned with who is and who is not performing satisfactorily.

In this chapter you will learn how effective performance reviews can help you be more successful in your job. We then will discuss some common techniques used in reviewing workers' performance. Finally we will shed some light on the problems frequently encountered by supervisors during the review process. We will suggest how you can reduce these problems and develop the ability to review your workers' performances effectively.

The use of performance review

The **performance review process** involves the formal and systematic evaluation of workers' performance. Typically, the evaluation is conducted once a year, although sometimes it occurs more frequently. If you supervise office workers, you are more likely to conduct formal performance reviews than supervisors of production workers. Both large and small organizations use formal performance reviews.

The information resulting from a formal performance review can help you in several ways. With few exceptions, you can use performance review information to help increase the productivity of your workers. In fact, reviewing workers' performance is fundamental to productivity improvement. By evaluating each worker, as well as counseling and developing workers, they will maintain or increase their productivity on the job.

Planning   More and more supervisors are finding themselves responsible for improving the productivity of their work group. As discussed in Chapter 10, good planning requires obtaining information on which objectives and plans for meeting these objectives can be based. Planning for workers' development involves this same process. The information gathered during the review process is used to establish performance goals and to outline the ways workers can achieve these goals. The formal review process provides an excellent vehicle for involving workers in the planning process.

Control   As also discussed in Chapter 10, the control process involves setting standards, monitoring actual performance to detect deviations from standards, and then taking corrective action to bring performance up to par. The performance review is a control system, requiring supervisors to determine who is performing the work correctly. A good review system will identify where specific performance problems exist and will aid in determining what corrective action must be taken. As a method of providing feedback to workers regarding their work performance, you can use performance reviews to counsel (motivate) and develop (train) your workers.

Reward decisions   When supervisors determine workers are performing above standard, a good review system should provide for formal recognition of their accomplishments. In addition to recognizing good performers, many supervisors find themselves responsible for awarding merit pay increases. If workers' performance is systematically evaluated, these decisions can be made more fairly on the basis of individual performance. Finally, an effective performance review system can help identify workers deserving promotion into higher-level jobs.

Communication A good review system facilitates communication between supervisors and their workers in several ways. During the review discussion, supervisors have the opportunity to clarify their expectations. In addition, they can make sure performance standards are understood. In an effective review discussion the supervisor will inform workers about their status, their progress on the job, their strengths and their weaknesses, and the changes expected in their performance.

A good review system also will help supervisors get to know their workers better. They can understand more clearly what motivates their workers, their frustrations and their triumphs on the job, and their attitudes toward their work, co-workers, and the organization. Given the hurried atmosphere of the average work day, the formal review may be one of the few opportunities supervisors have to concentrate solely on the needs and feelings of workers as individuals. In this respect, the review process can help enhance relationships with workers. If conducted effectively, supervisors can use the review process to build a helping and trusting relationship.

Documentation An effective performance review system will provide an accurate record to be used in making decisions about wage increases, promotions, layoffs, or discharges. This record also will serve as proof of the fairness of these actions. If these decisions are made on the basis of accurate and valid performance data found in the worker's file, challenges of discrimination or arbitrary treatment are more easily countered. Basing employment decisions on information obtained from a good review system helps to ensure fair and equitable treatment of all workers.

Informal and formal performance review

Most supervisors are involved in **informal performance review** programs. As indicated before, some organizations do not use a formal review system; they rely only on informal performance review. But even the best formal review system will be ineffective if a good informal review process does not exist. How can you expect a once-a-year discussion with your workers to affect their performance? Performance feedback, goals, plans for improvement, and direction must occur regularly. These functions are effectively handled through informal review or coaching.

The role of formal performance review is not reduced where good informal review exists. The formal review serves as a summary of each worker's performance during the review period. It occurs out of the context of daily work activities. Formal performance review is gaining importance in most organizations, in part, because of increased concern about workers' productivity. EEO requirements that employment decisions be based on job-related information are also a factor. However, at no point will a good informal review or coaching process cease to be critical.

Reactions to performance review

The mere mention of performance review brings mixed reactions. Top management complains that managers and supervisors do not take reviews seriously. Managers and supervisors dread the red tape and burdensome paperwork and feel their time is being wasted. Workers grudgingly participate, pointing out at every opportunity the subjectivity of the process.

While the advantages of a good performance review system are difficult to discount, the fact remains that the typical review system often falls short. A major problem is found in the psychological effect performance reviews have on both workers and supervisors.

How workers react

For the most part, workers naturally are uncomfortable having their job performance evaluated. No one openly welcomes having their record subject to challenge. If the review affects the worker's employment status, this fear is even more understandable. Worst of all, workers traditionally do not trust the performance review system. They believe supervisors too easily may allow personal likes or dislikes to influence their evaluations.

When evaluating your workers, you should remember several factors about workers' views of appraisals.[1]

- Being identified as an "average," "outstanding," or "below average" worker carries with it certain consequences. Workers rated as average may perceive limits on their opportunities and future pay increases. Below-average workers may fear losing their jobs. Furthermore, people tend to overrate their own job performance. As a result, evaluations tend to make workers defensive unless, of course, they are evaluated positively.

- Workers differ in their views on performance evaluation. Workers who are succeeding on the job are more willing to be evaluated. On the other hand, workers who are failing on the job tend to be more fearful of their supervisor's opinion.

- Workers anticipating evaluation often feel threatened. They may believe the resulting evaluation will be unrelated to their performance. Workers with low self-esteem tend to feel more threatened than those with high self-esteem.

- Workers are more likely to accept the evaluation if they feel they have influence on the evaluation. As a result, the quality of supervisory relationships with each worker is a critical factor. Workers tend to be more accepting of evaluations from supervisors whom they like, respect, and recognize as competent.

- Workers are more likely to accept evaluations similar to those received in the past.

How supervisors react

Much of the resistance to formal review stems from a fear of confronting workers. Sitting down face-to-face with a worker to discuss his or her strengths and weaknesses places supervisors in an uncomfortable, judgmental position. Typical reactions to the process that may hinder your ability to evaluate your workers include:[2]

- The majority of my workers feel they are at least average if not above-average performers. How can I tell them otherwise?

- If I evaluate workers as below-average performers, they will dislike me. They may do even less work and then I'll look bad. Besides, they probably will challenge my evaluations.

■ If I differentiate among my workers on the basis of their performance, the resulting jealousy, rivalries, and hostilities will cause more trouble than it is worth.

■ It's difficult to ignore the knowledge that "this worker has a family to support" when he or she is performing poorly on the job, and a negative review could be devastating.

Given the negative psychological environment surrounding formal performance reviews, it is understandable that many people would like to abolish them. However, effective performance reviews are critical and necessary. As a result, supervisors must confront the review process directly. A good system can eliminate many of the negative feelings discussed so far.

The performance review process

In light of this discussion, if formal performance reviews are to be effective, they must be seen as fair and trustworthy by workers and they must be viewed as important and useful by supervisors. In larger organizations, the personnel department is usually responsible for establishing the review technique to be used.

The best review process will fail to reach its objectives, however, if it is not implemented correctly. Since the supervisor typically carries out the review process, we will discuss briefly the factors involved in a formal review system. Then we will concentrate on your role in reviewing workers' performance.

Conducting the review

Typically, formal performance review includes a standard technique to evaluate the level of performance and then a review discussion. In any formal review system, someone must evaluate the worker. The timing of the evaluation must also be decided. These decisions are usually made by upper management in conjunction with the personnel department.

Who should review performance? The individual responsible for the formal review of performance should be the one who is best able to obtain the needed information. Since reviews generally require specific performance-related information, immediate supervisors are the obvious choice. Supervisors are the only people who have intimate knowledge of what the jobs in their units involve. They are in a prime position to observe workers performing these jobs on a daily basis. Further, workers feel more comfortable discussing performance-related issues with their supervisors than with other individuals. Therefore, in practice, supervisors usually are responsible for evaluating the performance of their workers.

When should review occur? Many new workers initially are placed on probationary status. The purpose of a **probationary period** is to determine whether the worker can perform the job. Where probationary periods are used, formal review generally occurs at least once during the initial employment period prior to granting the new employee permanent status. For other workers, common practice is to review performance formally once a year or at most twice a year.

It is difficult to understand how consulting with each worker once a year can have a significant impact on job performance. Nor can it aid supervisors in the day-to-day direction of workers. Further, if performance is formally reviewed only once a year, supervisors are not likely to remember accurately all job performance behaviors of all workers over the twelve-month period.

For these reasons, the distinctions and interrelationships between formal performance review and informal daily coaching and counseling (Chapter 13) are important. As we suggested earlier, a good performance review system incorporates regular feedback sessions (coaching) regarding performance during the review period. These sessions should communicate to workers how they are doing and any desired performance changes. Coaching is an informal version of the more formal review method.

The formal performance review then serves as a summary evaluation regarding performance over the entire appraisal period. The ongoing coaching and counseling activities provide information used by supervisors when making the summary evaluation.

Performance review techniques A variety of techniques to measure workers' performance are found in organizations. Some of the more common techniques will be discussed here. While supervisors usually do not devise the review technique, they must use it to review their workers. Therefore, an understanding of the available techniques is helpful.

Rating scales are by far the most popular method of evaluating workers' performance. They appear in a variety of forms but all are designed to indicate the worker's relative strengths and weaknesses in specific aspects of performance. Typically, for each aspect of performance, supervisors are asked to place the worker along a continuum of performance levels ranging from outstanding to poor.

Comparison evaluations may be used. These involve comparing each worker to all other workers in the group. Ranking techniques require supervisors to rank workers from highest to lowest on a performance dimension. Under the forced distribution technique, a fixed percentage of the workers must be placed in each of the performance-level categories. Another technique called paired comparisons involves determining who is the better worker for all possible pairs of workers.

Some supervisors may find their organization uses other methods to evaluate workers' performance. The essay appraisal may be used in conjunction with a rating scale or employee comparison method. This technique requires you to describe each worker in written form, on each performance dimension. Critical incidents, checklists, and behaviorally anchored rating scales are other techniques used by some organizations.

Problems in measuring performance

All performance review techniques are designed to measure how well a worker is doing on the job. Regardless of the method used, the result is the supervisor's opinion or judgment. If performance review is to achieve any of the purposes discussed earlier, accurate judgments are necessary.

Several errors are made typically by supervisors when evaluating their workers. If you are aware of these errors and try not to commit them, your evaluations will be more accurate. Some of these errors were discussed in Chapter 5. Here, examples related to performance reviews are given.

- **Halo Effect.** This occurs when a worker is rated higher overall than actually is deserved because of good performance areas. For example, a worker who is extremely dependable but doesn't really have a good grasp on the job may be overrated on job performance as a result of his or her dependability.

- **Central Tendency.** Supervisors who rate all workers as average performers are guilty of central tendency error. Evaluating workers as average is much easier than explaining why one is below average or why others are superior. Improving job performance is not made any easier, however.

- **Strictness–Leniency.** Supervisors differ in their expectations of workers. Some are never satisfied, while others are satisfied too easily with their workers' performance. These expectations carry over to the review process. Finding workers who are evaluated as average by one supervisor, but who would probably be evaluated higher by another supervisor, is not uncommon.

- **Recent Behavior Bias.** A significant amount of time and job behavior is covered in the formal review process. It is understandable that supervisors are prone to evaluate workers on the basis of their most recent performance. But when the review period covers performance over six months or a year, this bias clearly is inappropriate. Maintaining a log or diary of observed behaviors is one way of reducing this type of error.

- **Spillover Effect.** Supervisors often are influenced by previous performance review results. If a worker has received good evaluations in the past, there is a tendency to give good evaluations in the present—even when actual performance is not satisfactory.

- **Friendship.** Supervisors get to know and like some workers better than others. It is sometimes difficult to separate your role as a supervisor who directs and reviews a worker from that as the worker's friend. Clearly, if performance reviews are to be perceived as fair, questions of friendship should not enter into the process.

- **Stereotypes.** Stereotyping also can affect performance reviews. The effect can be both positive or negative. In both cases, it introduces bias into the evaluation. For example, a woman working in a job traditionally held by men may be underrated because of the supervisor's stereotype of women.

■ **Contrast Effects.**   Here supervisors evaluate a worker in relation to other workers rather than the actual performance requirements. In a work group where workers are generally below standard, the tendency may be to evaluate the best "below-standard" worker as outstanding. But if that worker doesn't meet the performance requirements, this ranking is inappropriate. On the other hand, if you have a clearly superior worker, evaluating the other workers in comparison to this superstar is just as absurd. Focus on whether performance requirements are being met by each worker individually.

■ **First Impressions.**   Impressions of workers formed during their first few weeks of employment must be held in check. Often these impressions are lasting, regardless of whether they are warranted.

■ **Similar-To-Me-Effect.**[3]   Supervisors tend to evaluate workers who are similar to them in attitudes or background more favorably than those who are not.

Regardless of the type of evaluation technique used, the potential for error exists. As supervisors, it is to your advantage to ensure the reviews you give are as fair and accurate as possible. Becoming aware of these errors and attempting to ensure you do not commit them is the first step to eliminating them. Keeping a record of your workers' performance during the review period is helpful. Further, when evaluating a particular worker on any performance dimension, be sure you can justify your rating with several concrete examples of actual job behavior.

Higher-level review

One method organizations have used to reduce errors in appraisal is to require supervisors to justify their evaluations to their superiors or members of the personnel department. Some supervisors react negatively to this requirement. They feel their authority is being reduced or even worse, their decisions questioned. The intent of **higher-level reviews** is to force supervisors to base their evaluations on performance-related information. Rarely do higher-level managers actually evaluate the workers.

Worker review

In many instances, the review process is not complete until the worker has signed the review form. Understandably workers' approval is not as good a barrier to error as higher-level review, since few workers feel comfortable challenging their supervisors. However, supervisors must actually present their evaluations to the workers. A problem may result to the extent supervisors avoid rating workers as poor to avoid negative confrontations.

The accuracy of evaluation ratings, then, can be increased when supervisors:

- Observe and are familiar with the performance to be evaluated.

- Document job behaviors between formal evaluations.

- Know the performance dimensions to be evaluated and have a clear idea of what is good and poor performance on each dimension.

- Make themselves aware of their own personal biases and try to minimize their effect on evaluations.

- Can justify their ratings with examples of actual job performance.

- Focus attention on performance-related behaviors.[4]

Up to this point, we have been concerned with the mechanics of the performance review process. The real heart of the process lies in the review discussion. During this discussion supervisors typically discuss their evaluations with the worker. The success of the discussion largely determines the success of the review system.

The performance review discussion

The **review discussion** should meet several objectives. First, it should provide supervisors with information that helps them better understand their workers. It should result in plans to improve future performance. Last, it should help link rewards to actual performance.

Preparing for the discussion

Successful performance review discussions are planned in advance to determine where you will meet with the worker, how long the discussion will last, and what issues will be discussed.

- **Where Will the Discussion Be Held?** Due to the nature of the conversation, the performance review discussion must take place in a private area free from interruptions. Few workers feel comfortable knowing others can hear your comments regarding their performance. They will be even more apprehensive about making comments themselves when privacy does not exist. When the discussion is interrupted by phone calls, secretaries, or passing conversations, little satisfactory discussion can continue.

- **How Long Should the Discussion Last?** Supervisors undoubtedly have many demands on their time, only one of which is conducting performance reviews. The advantages of spending an hour or so with each worker, however, far outweigh the disadvantages of hurriedly relating the evaluation to the worker.

- **What Should Be Covered?** Effective supervisors prepare an outline or agenda to be covered during the discussion. Sometimes they give the worker an opportunity to add topics for discussion to the agenda. If possible, you should explain beforehand to the worker what the review session will involve. This clarification helps in making an already anxiety-ridden situation a little less uncertain.

In general, you should be sure you have gathered and analyzed all information relating to each worker's performance over the review period. Also, you should determine beforehand what information you are seeking in the interview. Although the review is not completed until after this session, you should begin with a fairly clear perception of the worker's performance and have specific observations as evidence. This information then forms the basis for the major content of the discussion.

Conducting the discussion

The manner in which the discussion is conducted is a critical consideration. Six major characteristics of successful performance review discussions can be used as guides to follow:[5]

- When workers are able to participate and express opinions in the review discussion they tend to be more satisfied with the process and their supervisors. As a result, they will accept their supervisor's observations regarding their performance more readily than if they have no involvement in the review process.

- Workers' acceptance of the review process and their satisfaction with their supervisor increase when supervisors are supportive.

- When specific performance goals are established during the review process, workers improve performance up to twice as much as when the discussion centers around general goals.

- Discussing problems that may be hindering the worker's performance and working out solutions have an immediate effect on productivity.

- Criticism can have a negative effect. The number of times you criticize workers influences how defensive the worker is during the discussion. Criticism often leads to defensive behavior and results in little or no change in a worker's performance.

- Work performance improves when the worker believes rewards are based on performance.

Incorporating these characteristics in your review discussions can serve only to make them more effective. Keeping them in mind, we will now talk about the key considerations when conducting the review discussion.

How will the discussion be structured?

You can discuss performance with each of your workers using three methods.[6] You can tell them your evaluation and persuade them to improve (**tell and sell approach**). This approach requires a minimum of your time. While it may work in some cases, more often than not more harm than good will result. You place yourself in a superior position and can easily strain your relationship with the worker.

The second approach is to tell workers what you see as their strengths and weaknesses and then give them the opportunity to respond (**tell and listen approach**). While workers are given the opportunity to express opinions, no specific goals for improvement are established. As a result, improved performance is unlikely.

The **problem-solving approach** is the third way to discuss workers' performance. This approach enables the worker to become involved in discussing performance, resolving problems, and setting goals. Thus, it is generally the preferred approach.

Using the problem-solving approach while discussing the worker's performance places you in the role of a supportive helper rather than a critical judge. The following guidelines can help you use the problem-solving approach.[7]

Put the worker at ease

The worker should have had advance notice of what this meeting will involve. Even so, you should immediately restate that the purpose of the discussion is to recognize areas of good performance and discuss any problems the worker may be experiencing on the job.

The worker should be prepared, having had time to analyze the job and any problems prior to the meeting. If not, you must clarify or restate just what you believe the job responsibilities and performance standards to be. You must be sure the two of you are comparing apples with apples, or in other words, that you both agree on what good performance on the job entails.

Recognize good performance

Early in the discussion, specifically describe what the worker has done that deserves recognition and explain why. Specific praise is important. You should use concrete examples of job behavior to justify your praise and to clearly indicate exactly what type of performance you expect. Merely saying "keep up the good work" is not enough. Not only may this seem insincere, but also, the worker will not know what he or she is doing right.

Seek out problem areas

Ask workers whether they are experiencing any problems on the job. See whether you can provide any assistance and be sure your workers understand that you are there to help them. Workers are more open and frank with supervisors if they trust them and believe they are supportive. This attitude is not developed overnight, but is the result of the daily experiences workers have with their supervisors.

Even in the best of relationships, workers still may not confide in you openly. It is particularly difficult to admit personal weaknesses. At the same time, unwritten codes of work behavior often inhibit workers from "ratting on" any co-workers who may be affecting their work performance.

Focus on areas where improvement is needed When workers do not bring out the weaknesses you have observed, you are faced with this task. This is perhaps the trickiest part of the review discussion. Failure to handle this aspect of the discussion effectively can result in undesirable consequences, since describing weaknesses involves criticizing the worker's performance. The effects of criticism are potentially negative, so focusing on weaknesses must be handled carefully. Several guidelines can help you improve the chances the situation will have a positive outcome.

First, discuss no more than two general performance areas where weaknesses exist. Remember, the number of criticisms determines the number of defensive reactions made by the worker. Being overwhelmed with negative comments about one's performance is threatening and should be avoided. If you are doing an effective job of informal review in your daily coaching efforts, no worker should have major weaknesses in many more areas. Along the same lines, the weaknesses you present should not surprise the worker. How can you have an impact on workers' performance if you only point out areas where corrective action is needed only once or twice a year? The formal review should summarize your observations of the worker's progress in areas brought out during informal coaching.

Focus on performance problems and not on personalities Constructively criticize what the worker does, not the worker as a person. The concern here is making a conscious effort to avoid rating errors. Contrast effects, first impressions, and the "similar-to-me effects" are particularly crucial. Aside from being potentially discriminatory, personal attacks only serve to create a more threatening situation. Defensive unconstructive behavior is the sure result.

Last, come right out and explain what you have observed that has caused you to believe the weakness exists and why it concerns you. Be specific and give examples of actual behavior. The review discussion is more anxiety-ridden when the behavior discussed is fuzzy. Don't beat around the bush and hope the worker can figure

out what areas need improvement. When the performance requirements are well known by both the supervisor and worker and actual
performance is discussed openly, you can be more frank and comfortable.

Encourage worker response and listen   When focusing on problem areas, ask workers to give their opinions. Be prepared for emotional outbursts—remember the worker will inherently be defensive.
You must encourage workers to feel free to express their concerns.
While excuses do not justify poor performance, they may point out
specific areas where corrective action is needed. Discussing the
"why" of poor performance and doing something about it can help
build better relationships with workers.

Once emotions have been spilled out it is often easier for workers to see the situation more objectively. The guides to effective
listening presented in Chapter 5 are appropriate here. The key is to
get the worker to see that a problem exists and to help determine
how to solve it.

Agree on a plan of action to resolve the problem   Once the problem has been recognized, you must ensure that both of you agree on
how it will be resolved. This involves establishing goals, determining
what you and the worker must do to reach the goals, and finally,
deciding on period within which improvement is expected. Again,
offer whatever assistance you can. Once the goals and plan have
been established, be sure to follow up through informal coaching.
Then you and the worker will know what progress is being made
and when the problem has been resolved.

Recurring
performance problems

Up to this point, our discussion of both formal reviews and informal
coaching has assumed workers performance problems are not long
established ones. When your daily observations indicate serious performance problems exist and your coaching efforts are fruitless, further action is necessary. Appropriate action does not include waiting
until the formal performance review and then pulling out an endless
list of work deficiencies to justify firing the worker.

Once a performance problem has been identified and is not resolved, you must immediately talk to the worker again. While you should help resolve any problems causing poor performance, if a worker cannot meet the requirements of the job, further action must be taken. Your concern is with job performance.

If when following up you find a worker is not improving as planned, you should meet with the worker. Clearly define the problem. For example, little or no progress made in getting to work on time. Restate your concern and carefully explain why tardiness cannot be tolerated. You should not merely restate a company rule. Make sure the worker understands why his or her tardiness is unacceptable. Once again ask the worker why the problem has yet to be resolved. Listen carefully so you can learn all the facts and make a good decision as to what to do next.

Many organizations have rules governing workers behavior and performance as well as disciplinary action to be taken when rules are violated. This is particularly true in unionized organizations. If disciplinary action is required, explain carefully what it will be and why you are disciplining the worker.

Make sure the worker understands he or she is responsible for eliminating the problem. Although you will and should help, the worker should understand that performance problems must be corrected. Never act eager to discipline workers. Rather, objectively point out why discipline is necessary and improvement is required. Also you should explain the consequences of failure to resolve the problem.

Summary

☐ Supervisors often are responsible for formally reviewing performance. The outcome of performance review often affects the worker's employment status. Reviewing workers' performance is important because supervisors must be concerned with who is and who is not performing their jobs satisfactorily.

☐ Effective performance review helps supervisors plan and control human resources. It also can improve supervisor–worker communication and provide accurate records to support employment decisions.

☐ An effective informal review process must support the formal review process. The formal review is a summary review occurring out of the context of daily work activities.

☒ Formal reviews usually involve a standard technique used to evaluate the worker's level of performance and a discussion between the worker and supervisor regarding performance. Standard techniques that may be used include rating scales, comparison evaluations, essay appraisals, critical incidents, checklists, and behaviorally anchored rating scales.

☐ Regardless of the review technique used, the rating each worker receives is influenced by the supervisor's opinion. Supervisors should be careful not to commit common errors which distort evaluations. Higher-level review is one way organizations try to reduce rating errors.

☐ Review discussions should help supervisors better understand their workers, result in plans for improved performance, and relate rewards to performance. They should be planned in advance.

☐ How the discussion is conducted influences its effectiveness. Supervisors can use one of three approaches: tell and sell, tell and listen, or problem solving. The problem-solving approach is generally the preferred approach.

☐ The contents of the discussion should include putting the worker at ease and clarifying job responsibilities and standards. Good performance should be recognized. Try to identify any problems the worker may be having. Supervisors should focus on areas needing improvement, but criticism should be minimized and handled carefully. Encourage the worker's participation in the discussion and listen to what the worker has to say. Finally, agree on a plan of action to resolve performance problems.

☐ Recurring performance problems cannot be left unattended until the formal review. When workers are not improving as planned, supervisors must make sure workers understand performance problems must be corrected.

Questions for review and discussion

 1. Why is an effective formal performance review system important in organizations? *Performance goals, detect performance problems,*

2. Distinguish between informal and formal review systems. How are they related to each other?

3. How do workers and supervisors generally react to the performance review process? How do these reactions influence the effectiveness of performance review?

4. How can supervisors prepare for the review discussion?

5. What are the characteristics of effective review discussions? How are these characteristics incorporated in the three ways to structure the discussion? Which approach is usually best? *Problem solving*

6. How can supervisors reduce the negative effects of criticism?

7. How should supervisors handle recurring performance problems?

8. Some supervisors say that the informal performance review is more important than formal review. Why might this be true?

Key terms

Central tendency	Higher-level review
Comparison evaluations	Informal performance review
Contrast effects	Performance review process
First impressions	Probationary period
Formal performance review	Problem-solving approach
Halo effect	Rating scales

Recent behavior bias	Stereotypes
Review discussion	Strictness-leniency
Similar-to-me effect	Tell and listen approach
Spillover effect	Tell and sell approach

Cases for discussion and practical exercises

1. "That was lousy," thought Bill Devlin as he left his supervisor's office. Bill, who had been employed as a drafter for six months, had just finished discussing his performance review with Laura Jackson, his supervisor.

   Actually, Bill had been looking forward to the performance review discussion. When he first took the job, he knew he had a lot to learn. But, he felt he had made considerable progress. Laura had not indicated that there were any problems with his performance. Of course, Laura hadn't said much about his performance one way or the other. Laura wasn't the type of supervisor who talked much with her workers.

   "I guess maybe that was why I looked forward to the discussion," Bill thought as he sat back at his desk. "I was hoping to get a pat on the back for my progress as well as some suggestions on what I could do to improve my performance even more."

   "That sure wasn't the way it worked out. Laura just handed me the completed performance review form, asked me to look at it and sign it." Bill saw that his performance was evaluated as average on all categories and that there were no comments. When Bill started to ask what he could do to improve, Laura seemed nervous and said he did not need to worry. "You're new on the job and your ratings will go up as you get more experience," Laura had said. She then indicated that if Bill didn't have any other questions, he should check on a job that was behind schedule.

a) What mistakes did Laura make in handling the performance review discussion?

b) Had she made any mistakes relative to performance review prior to the discussion?

c) What effect do you think this experience will have on Bill's performance? Why?

2. Recall a time when your performance has been reviewed and discussed with you. If you have not received a performance review on a job, think of a time when you have been evaluated in school or some other nonwork activity. How was the performance review discussion conducted? What did the person reviewing your performance do that was effective? What was done poorly? What changes would you recommend in the way the performance review discussion was conducted?

Notes

1. Richard Henderson, *Performance Appraisal: Theory to Practice* (Reston, Va.: Reston Publishing Co., Inc., 1980), pp. 7–8.

2. *Ibid.*, pp. 8–9.

3. K. N. Wexley and W. F. Nemeroff, "Effects of Racial Prejudice, Race of Applicant, and Geographical Similarity on Interviewer Evaluations of Job Applicants," *Journal of Social and Behavioral Sciences*, 1974 (20)66–78.

4. Richard Henderson, *op. cit.*

5. R. J. Burke, W. Weitzel, and T. Weir, "Characteristics of Effective Employee Performance Review and Development Interviews. Replication and Extension," *Personnel Psychology*, 1978(31) 903–919.

6. Norman R. F. Maier *The Appraisal Interview* (La Jolla, Calif.: University Associates, Inc., 1976). pp. 4–20.

7. Gary P. Latham and Kenneth N. Wexley, *Increasing Productivity Through Performance Appraisal* (Reading, Mass.: Addison-Wesley, 1981), pp. 153–154.

Cases for section IV

Zappa Grain and Seed Company

Zappa Grain and Seed Company is a well established seed packaging and sales company. Company sales and revenue transactions in 1978 were well over $25 million. The firm is headed by Walter Zappa, who founded the company nineteen years ago. He is assisted by the plant superintendent and six departmental supervisors. The organizational chart of the management hierarchy follows.

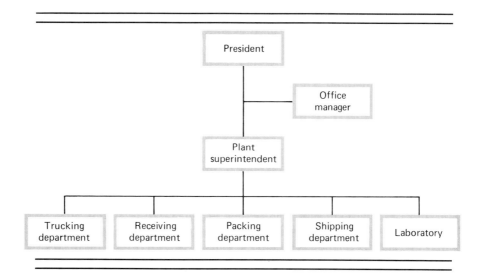

Fescues, bluegrass, and ryegrass are some of the types of seeds handled by the Zappa plant. Although grains are purchased and sold, the majority of business is in seeds. Shipments of seeds are made throughout the continental United States and to several Latin American countries. Zappa's largest customers are seed houses and operators of large farms. Some customers pick up the seeds themselves; however, the firm has three large trucks for regional delivery and a rail spur for long-distance shipping. Latin American orders are shipped by ocean vessels.

Seeds are purchased from large mill houses in the United States and processed at the Zappa plant. Upon receipt of seeds, samples are taken and tested by the company in cooperation with requirements of the United States Department of Agriculture. After verification of purity and germination, the seeds are packaged in 50 and 100 pound bags.

The packing department has the largest number of workers. Under the supervision of Bob Ewell, thirty-four employees in the department work without representation from a union. Because of the hard manual labor involved and the low pay, the turnover of packers is high. Generally, packers remain with the firm less than one year. In a recent attempt to find out why there is such a high labor turnover in the department, Mr. Zappa was told by employees who were called into his office for an interview that they had nothing to look forward to in coming to work. Several employees indicated they stayed on the job only because they probably could not find work elsewhere. Four packers noted that people do not like to be treated as though they cannot think for themselves and make appropriate decisions concerning their work. In summarizing the packer's comments, Mr. Zappa noted to himself that employees do not remain loyal to an organization that treats them as something less than human.

Two months after the interview session, Betty Whittier complained that another person had been hired for a position for which she felt she was qualified. The following conversation occurred:

WHITTIER: Mr. Ewell, I have been a packer here for six months, and I thought that I would be promoted to shipping clerk as soon as there was an opening. Yesterday, a person was hired for that job without having first served as a packer.

EWELL: Well, Whittier, who told you that you would be promoted?

WHITTIER: Mr. Zappa did, about two months ago when I talked to him about why people are so prone to leaving the packing department. He said that I was a good worker and would be the next packer promoted.

EWELL: You go back to work for now, and I will go talk to the plant superintendent. I will talk with you later.

After Ewell had explained the above conversation to the plant superintendent, he was told, "I really don't care what you do about this, it is your problem. Zappa never said anything to me about promoting Whittier. Why don't you go tell Zappa about it; he is the one who sets policies around here." Ewell's conversation with the superintendent ended at this point. Further, Ewell did not talk with Zappa nor did he discuss the situation with Whittier. In one instance, Whittier mentioned the promotion to Ewell, but he was cut off when Ewell said he was going for a cup of coffee.

Three weeks after these discussions, another opening occurred in the shipping department. The following day Ewell informed Whittier that if she was interested in the position she would get it. Overjoyed with the good news, Whittier told the other packers about her promotion and that she would miss working with them. Another packer, however, who had been employed by the company for a little over a year complained to the plant superintendent that he should be transferred before Whittier since he had seniority. The plant superintendent then called Ewell to his office and informed him that transfers within the plant had always been based on who had been with the company the longest. Ewell did not say anything and returned to the packing department. The following conversation then occurred:

EWELL: The plant super just told me that the one who has been with the company the longest will get the promotion.

WHITTIER: But you told me yesterday that the opening in the shipping department was mine if I was interested. You know how much I want that job. I have done a good job as a packer and I feel that I can do a good job in shipping.

EWELL: I am sorry, but you know the policy we follow if there is a transfer from one department to another.

WHITTIER: I am not talking about a transfer, but a promotion. What kind of runaround am I getting?

EWELL: Look here, Whittier, you don't seem to be very happy with your job. Why don't you just collect your paycheck and go home?

Questions

1. Why did Mr. Zappa tell Whittier that she would receive the next promotion, but not inform the plant superintendent?
2. Is there any inconsistency in the policy statements?
3. Is Whittier being unreasonable in her demands? What should she do now?
4. List the problems that you feel are causing the present difficulty and indicate some alternative solutions to prevent similar incidents in the future.

Source: From Robert L. Trewatha and M. Gene Newport, *Management: Functions and Behavior.* © *Business Publications, Inc., 1982.*

The education of Greg Horning: March 4

Greg's call to Ed Briscoe hadn't proved anything one way or the other, but it had made Greg aware of something new. Those knobs could loosen up by themselves sometimes, Ed said, but whatever it was, he wasn't going to let his crew get stuck with the blame. They had too much to do so they couldn't be expected to run all over the plant every time a knob rattled. Ed's loyalty to his crew struck Greg. He'd been expecting his group to support him; now, he suddenly saw that it could work both ways. Still, if he reversed his decision, he'd look awfully foolish. Maybe he should check with Ann Sykes, head of personnel.

By the time Sykes finished raking him over the coals, Greg conceded he deserved it. "You just don't pick someone who's been with the company for over thirty years as a scape goat," Sykes told him. "Not when there's a union in the shop. These people stick together, and with the amount of proof you had, you'd have to be out of you mind to think you could make it stick. You'd better do something to get yourself out of this mess and fast."

So the morning after the accident, Greg had called Kilpatrick at home. He admitted to being hasty in his judgment and apologized for accusing Kilpatrick of being drunk. He told Kilpatrick to forget about the layoff, but since his machine wasn't functioning he might as well take the day off. Kilpatrick surprised Greg by saying no, he'd rather come in than do odd jobs around the house.

The reactions of the others suprised Greg, too. They'd pitched in to make up the time on that rush order and they'd only lost a half day getting it out. Greg had appreciated that effort and he'd told them so. During the next few days, Helen had called him over a few times to check pieces with him. They talked a little and she told him about her son who was majoring in business administration at college. "He's just about as pigheaded as you," she'd said, and they'd both laughed. Then there was that morning when he came in with a wild, new tie with red, white, and blue stripes. Jeannette had called out to him on the floor, "Hey, boss! You getting Rick to buy your clothes for you?" He blushed and grinned and they all had laughed.

Gradually the crew was becoming more friendly and relaxed. Greg found that he was relaxing too. Furthermore, he was beginning to see that there were better ways of tackling his big, unsolved problem, increasing production by 25%.

As the crew was starting back to their machines after the midmorning break, Greg came out on the floor. "Before you get back to work, I thought we might have a talk." He felt a little nervous, remembering the other "talks" he had had with his crew, but they had interested expressions on their faces and some of them were looking around for a place to sit.

"Sure, Greg. What'd you have in mind?" Phil Martello said.

"Well, Phil, I'll tell you. You all know the pressure I'm getting for more production from this department, and I thought you people might have some worthwhile ideas about how we can get more out." He looked around the group, waiting. Martello was the first to speak.

"Gee, Greg. I don't know, I just don't know. We work very hard. Now I don't know what more we could do. Of course, the materials they give us these days aren't what they used to be and there's always something going wrong with the machines. I mean, look at what happened with Ted's a couple of weeks ago. . . ."

"And what about the materials handlers?." Helen cut in. "You know how they're always putting the tote boxes in the wrong place. And can you ever find one of those people when you need them?"

"Well, you know I've tried to talk to them, Helen," Craig said. "They just won't cooperate. Now that I think of it, the mixing department does whatever they can to mess things up for us, too. Like you say Phil, the plastic they've been sending us is lousy."

"Okay. Let's back up a minute," Greg put in with evident exasperation. "So far all the complaints have been with other departments. What about what goes on right here? Everything can't be the fault of another department. What can we do ourselves to get more work out?"

"Well, as I was saying, Greg," this was Phil again, "we do a fair day's work for a fair day's pay. In fact, we probably do a lot more than we get paid for right now. I don't see how we can do any more."

"Besides, Greg," Jeannette added, "what's the good of turning out more pieces when Helen and I get backed up with the flashes and the sorting and packing and all that. If you put too much pressure on the workers, they get careless, and that means more work than we can handle. See what I mean?"

"Now wait a minute Jeannette," Phil broke in. "Don't you start blaming us. As I say, we do a fair day's work. And if we're more careful about the rough edges we'd have to slow down. Henry and Rick, now, it'd be easier for them to turn out more since they've got the larger machines."

"Hold on, now, Phil," Greg said. "No one is blaming anyone. We're just trying to figure out where our problems are so we can get rid of them. As far as the other departments go, I'll get to work on them and see what I can do. But what about us? That's the big point. We've got to cooperate too. Right?" He looked around the group. Craig and Alfred shrugged their shoulders, but the rest nodded or smiled.

The crew went back to work and Greg returned to his office, but he didn't forget about the meeting. For the rest of the day the same questions about the crew's complaints kept recurring. How much of it had been shifting the blame and an attempt to duck the pressure? How much of the griping was legitimate? And even if it were, what could he do about it? Most important, under these conditions, could they really do anything to speed up output without sacrificing quality? The situation seemed difficult to resolve.

Questions

1. Most employees can convince themselves (and to try to convince others) that they are working very, very hard (regardless of how hard they are working) and that their supervisor doesn't realize how conscientious they are. Is Greg helping to give his people an overinflated view of their own accomplishments?

2. How can Greg positively reinforce their accomplishment of getting out that rush order without agreeing with everything they say?

3. Are there any "internal" incentives on these jobs that Greg is not conscious of which either encourage or discourage good performance?

4. Given the nature of this work group and the work they are doing, what elements of employees' performance should be discussed only with individuals and what elements should be discussed with the group as a whole?

Source: From William F. Dowling and Leonard R. Sayles, *How Managers Motivate: The Imperatives of Supervision*, 1971, McGraw-Hill, New York. Reprinted with permission.

V

Special supervisory topics

15

Supervisors
and unions

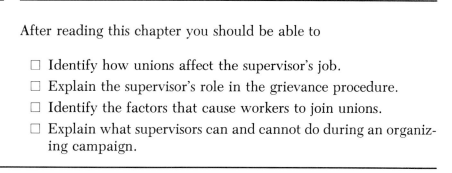

Objectives

After reading this chapter you should be able to

- ☐ Identify how unions affect the supervisor's job.
- ☐ Explain the supervisor's role in the grievance procedure.
- ☐ Identify the factors that cause workers to join unions.
- ☐ Explain what supervisors can and cannot do during an organizing campaign.

Unions are a fact of work life for many supervisors. The existence of a union significantly affects the way supervisors work with their employees. When there is a union, many of the decisions that might be made regarding employees are governed by the labor contract. While this constraint is not necessarily bad, the actions that supervisors can take are limited.

Not all supervisors, of course, work in a unionized organization. Unions represent only about 22% of the workers in the labor force. As can be seen in Table 15.1, the extent of unionization varies widely among industries. Not reflected in Table 15.1, however, is the fact that union organizing is increasing rapidly in some areas that now have little unionization such as fast foods, state, county, and municipal government, retailing, and health care.

Whether you have a union in your work place or not, you should have some understanding of labor law, the collective bargaining process, and grievance handling. You will be influenced by unions whether you are working directly with one or working to retain nonunion status. These topics will be discussed in this chapter.

Table 15.1

Prevalence of unions by industry

INDUSTRY	PERCENTAGE OF WORKFORCE BELONGING TO UNIONS			
	0–25%	25–50%	50–75%	75% or more
Agriculture & fishing	X			
Apparel			X	
Chemicals		X		
Contract construction				X
Electric utilities	X			
Electric machinery				X
Fabricated metals			X	
Federal government			X	
Finance	X			
Food & kindred products			X	
Furniture		X		
Gas utilities		X		
Instruments	X			
Leather		X		
Local government	X			
Lumber		X		
Machinery		X		
Mining			X	
Nonmanufacturing	X			
Ordinance				X
Paper				X
Petroleum			X	
Primary metals			X	
Printing and publishing		X		
Rubber			X	
Service	X			
State government	X			

(continued)

Table 15.1 (continued)

INDUSTRY	PERCENTAGE OF WORKFORCE BELONGING TO UNIONS			
	0–25%	25–50%	50–75%	75% or more
Stone, clay, and glass products			X	
Telephone and telegraph			X	
Textile mill products	X			
Tobacco manufacturers			X	
Trade	X			
Transportation				X
Transportation equipment				X

Source: Adapted from U.S. Department of Labor, Bureau of Labor Statistics, *Directory of National Unions and Employee Associations, 1973* (Washington, D.C.: Government Printing Office, 1974), p. 81.

Legal status of unions

A **union** is an organization chosen by workers to represent them in dealings with their employers. Also called employee associations, unions bargain with management to establish the terms of employment, wages, hours, and the conditions of work.

American workers have not always had the right to belong to unions. Even though the first labor union was formed in 1792, it wasn't until 1935 that employers were legally required to recognize and bargain with unions. Prior to that, employers could establish wage rates, hours of work, and working conditions unilaterally, as long as workers would take jobs. While many employers did not abuse the power they held over the individual worker, some did. In these situations, workers often had little choice but to continue working since work was necessary to survive. Whatever conditions existed, some pay was better than no pay. Efforts by workers to improve conditions often resulted in firings, or worse, being blackballed from other employment.

Wagner Act (1935)

Bitterness on the part of workers and the adamant refusal of employers to recognize their unions led to much strife in the early part of this century. In an attempt to bring stability and peace to industry, Congress passed the Railway Labor Act in 1926. The act enabled workers in the transportation industry to join unions and required employers to bargain with these unions.

In 1935, similar rights were given to other workers in private industry by the National Labor Relations Act, more commonly called the **Wagner Act.** This law applies to all nonmanagerial workers employed in the private sector. Supervisors, government employees, and the transportation industry are excluded. The Act gave workers three basic rights:

- The right to join unions;
- The right to bargain collectively with the employer over hours, wages, and working conditions;
- The right to strike.

The Wagner Act requires employers to recognize and bargain with a union that has the support of a majority of the workers in the bargaining unit. In addition, the Act outlaws certain **unfair labor practices** by managers and supervisors. Specifically, managers and supervisors are prohibited from:

- Coercing or interfering with workers' rights to form or belong to a union;
- Supporting a union or creating a union for workers to join;
- Discriminating against workers because of their union activities.

The Wagner Act also created the **National Labor Relations Board** (NLRB), a federal agency responsible for enforcing the law. When someone is accused of commiting an unfair labor practice, the NLRB investigates the charge and determines whether the law has been violated. If a violation is found, the NLRB may take corrective action. It also is responsible for conducting elections to determine whether a union will represent a group of workers.

Taft-Hartley Act (1947)

The Wagner Act resulted in a trememdous surge in union membership and the power of unions. Prior to the passage of the Wagner Act, unions and workers were definitely the underdogs in dealing with employers. While the Wagner Act was intended to equalize union power relative to management's power, many felt it put employers at a disadvantage.

In 1947, Congress once again attempted to balance the power of union and employers. The **Taft-Hartley Act** (Labor Management Relations Act) amended the Wagner Act. It restricted union activities much as the Wagner Act had done for employers. Union **unfair labor practices** specifically prohibited by the Act include:

- Encouraging employers to discriminate against workers to encourage or discourage union membership;
- Forcing an employer to bargain with a union when another union is already the workers' elected representative;
- Engaging in secondary boycotts, that is forcing employer A to stop doing business with employer B when the union has a dispute with employer B;
- Conducting jurisdictional strikes, or forcing employers to assign work only to members of a particular union rather than members of other unions;
- Engaging in featherbedding by forcing the employer to pay for work that is not performed.

Again, the NLRB investigates charges of unfair labor practices by unions and determines whether unions have violated the law.

Landrum-Griffin Act (1958)

While the Taft-Hartley amendments appeared to balance union power relative to the power of employers, it soon became evident that in certain situations individual workers needed protection from excessive union clout. Reports of certain unions affiliations with Communist groups and underworld criminals began to surface, as did indications that unions did not necessarily bring democracy to the work place. In response to these abuses, Congress passed the **Landrum-Griffin Act** (The Labor-Management Reporting and Disclosure Act) in 1959.

This act governs internal affairs and regulates leadership elections and financial reporting procedures of unions. The law also contains a workers' "bill of rights." Union members are guaranteed freedom of speech, voting rights, control over increases in union dues, the right to sue the union, and the right to have copies of the labor contract.

Although many attempts have been made to amend the laws governing labor relations, only one has been successful. In 1974, federal labor laws were extended to cover workers in private nonprofit hospitals.

Collective bargaining and supervisors

When there is a union, the process of **collective bargaining** occurs. In collective bargaining both the union and management are involved in four subprocesses. These are:

- Negotiating the labor contract;
- Interpreting the labor contract;
- Applying the labor contract;
- Enforcing the labor contract.

Supervisors are rarely involved in negotiating labor contracts. Typically, representatives from the personnel department or lawyers hired to represent management sit down at the bargaining table and negotiate with the union. **Negotiations** result in the **labor contract** which establishes procedures for making certain decisions. After negotiations are over, however, supervisors play a critical role in administering the contract.

Many supervisory decisions may be covered by labor contracts. While labor contracts often restrict supervisory actions, many people argue that contracts help supervisors "clean up their act." Generally, the contract is an attempt to assure that workers are treated fairly and consistently on the job and that they are guaranteed some level of security. Let's look at some of the key supervisory actions that are influenced by the union.

Promotions, transfers, and work assignments Through promoting or transferring workers, you seek to place qualified workers in available jobs. Unfortunately, favoritism and other unfair considerations have sometimes influenced placement decisions. Labor contracts attempt to limit favoritism and arbitrary treatment.

Labor contracts generally require that job vacancies be posted. Interested workers having the minimum qualifications for the job may bid (sign up) for the job. The worker must then be selected to fill the higher-level job on the basis of seniority and ability to perform the job.

In most labor contracts **seniority** is the determining factor in promotion decisions. Seniority refers to the length of time a worker has been employed. It may be determined on the basis of the company as a whole, a particular department, or even a particular job classification. If you promote a less senior worker, you probably will be challenged by the union. You will have to demonstrate that the senior bidder is clearly not capable of performing the higher-level job. The fact that the senior bidder is somewhat less capable is usually not a reason to justify promoting a junior worker. Some contracts even require that unqualified senior bidders be given an opportunity to learn and perform the job before a junior worker can be considered.

Scheduling Contracts also typically spell out methods for determining shift schedules and assigning overtime. Seniority is usually the determining factor in scheduling shift work. Workers are able to bid for shift assignments on the basis of their years of service. Generally overtime work also is assigned on the basis of seniority.

Dicipline and discharge Labor contracts set disciplinary procedures for employees. These procedures usually involve **progressive disciplinary action,** which gives workers a chance to improve performance or behavior. If the union believes the correct procedure has not been followed, it can, and probably will, challenge the supervisor's actions. Even when discipline is justified, if the procedure has not been followed, the discipline stands a good chance of being revoked.

It is often claimed that unions prevent workers from being discharged. While discharging workers may be more difficult in unionized settings, it is not impossible. The labor contract requires that all disciplinary decisions, including discharge, be objectively based and that attempts to improve the worker are made when possible.

Layoffs Just as seniority is used in promotion decisions, it is used to determine who will be laid off when production demands fall. Most contracts follow the principle "last hired, first to leave" in laying off workers. When business picks up again, the most senior workers are recalled first. In some cases, senior workers laid off from their jobs may be able to claim ("bump") less senior workers' jobs rather than being laid off.

Performance of work assigned to union workers In an attempt to protect the jobs of their members, many union contracts prohibit supervisors from performing any work assigned to the workers. Also, contracts generally forbid workers from working outside their job classifications. Workers can perform only those tasks assigned to their job and not those tasks belonging to another job.

Supervisors working under a labor contract face constraints not found in nonunion settings. It is interesting to note however that, with one important exception, many nonunion organizations tend to follow procedures much like those established in labor contracts. The exception is that supervisors in nonunion organization have the advantage of flexibility in assigning tasks not found in union settings.

Critical supervisory actions governed by the labor contract arise daily. As a result, supervisors find themselves constantly interpreting and applying the contract. Their actions are always subject to evaluation by union stewards who have their own interpretations of the contract terms. **Union stewards** are locally elected or appointed leaders. Their function is to serve as a "watchdog," seeing that the contract is enforced. In the contract administration process, supervisors make decisions with the union steward constantly watching to see that their actions do not violate the contract. At this point supervisors become intimately involved with collective bargaining. This involvement is most apparent in the grievance process.

Grievance handling

Nearly all labor contracts establish grievance procedures to resolve disagreements over what the contract means and how it should be applied. These disagreements are called grievances. **Grievances** can arise over any decisions made in the areas discussed so far as well as other situations covered by the contract.

Grievances exist whenever workers feel they have not been fairly treated. Grievances may be "real" (there may be a violation of the contract) or they may just be gripes. While both types of grievances are of concern, grievances resulting from potential contract violations should be handled differently than those arising from general dissatisfaction.

To distinguish between **"real" grievances** and **general gripes** we need to determine what has caused the grievance. Grievances that involve contract-related problems should be resolved through the formal grievance procedure. Those that are not potential contract violations however, should be resolved directly through informal means. Noncontract-related problems should not be allowed to become formal grievances.

Handling problems so they do not become grievances

Many problems, if handled immediately and effectively, do not need to become formal grievances. Let's look at the sources of grievances and determine when problems should become formal grievances.[1]

Human nature. People evaluate a particular situation in terms of how it affects them. For example, a supervisor may announce a new rule requiring workers to wear hard hats on the job with the penalty of a fine for disobedience. The workers may see this rule as arbitrary and resent the discomfort of wearing a hard hat. Their general dissatisfaction easily may result in a "gripe" which could be resolved if the supervisor realizes they do not see the need for such a rule. Otherwise this gripe may become a formal grievance.

Misunderstood communications also can result in unnecessary grievances. For example, a supervisor may be in a bad mood and respond to a worker's question in a gruff manner. Later, the supervisor cites the worker for breaking for lunch 15 minutes early. In view of the earlier incident, the worker may grieve the discipline even though it was fair because "my supervisor was out to get me." Another unnecessary grievance may arise.

No one likes to have their actions questioned. Often supervisors handle situations on the basis of their initial gut reactions. Once a decision has been made, they often find it difficult to admit they were wrong. They defend themselves and justify their actions at the expense of unnecessary grievances. Admitting and correcting mistakes may be difficult, but can be the best course of action.

Finally, no one gets along with everyone equally well. When supervisors find workers they just can't get along with, they must be on guard to ensure grievances do not result from personality conflicts.

The worker   Workers themselves are often the source of unnecessary grievances. Unfortunately, workers are sometimes overqualified or underqualified for their jobs, and their dissatisfaction may make them poor performers. If they don't challenge reprimands given for poor performance, their resentment, frustration, and dissatisfaction with their jobs may cause them to initiate grievances. These unnecessary grievances can be prevented by improving job placement. Overqualified workers can be guided to more challenging jobs. Underqualified workers pose a different problem. Just reprimanding them for unsatisfactory work may result in their feeling picked on. Instead, you should determine why the performance is below standard. If poor performance results from a basic lack of skills, termination or transfer may be the only answer. But you should try first to help these workers improve their performance through special instruction or training.

Good workers can also become a source of unnecessary grievances. For example, your best forklift driver suddenly begins making mistakes. You talk to him about it, stating that you'll have to write him up if he doesn't improve. Later that day he drives the forklift into a pillar, dislodging part of the ceiling of the plant! For his benefit as well as the safety of the others, you suspend him for a week. A grievance over his suspension is filed. During the grievence hearing, you learn his wife recently left him and their three children.

Frequently, good workers experience personal problems that affect their performance at work. As discussed in Chapter 8, before disciplining workers who have performed satisfactorily in the past, you should try to discover what has caused the change in performance. Disciplining workers who usually perform well not only may result in unnecessary grievances, it also may cause resentment and low morale among other workers.

Finally, some workers are naturally "problem workers," that is, they have trouble accepting authority. When directing or disciplining this type of worker, you should be careful to explain why they are being disciplined. You must try to seek their cooperation in the work effort. If you don't formal grievances surely will arise.

In summary, you can prevent many formal grievances by being alert to potential problems workers may have. If left unattended, these problems may easily become grievances. As a rule, problem workers can be identified before there is trouble. Signals to watch for include:

- Decreased interest in work;
- Negative statements about the job, co-workers, supervisors, and the company;
- Less willingness to cooperate;
- Higher absenteeism than usual;
- Poor job performance;
- Spending excessive time away from the work station.[2]

The union steward Union stewards are elected by the members of the union. As a result of their political position, they may encourage formal grievances so they appear to be helping the workers. Obviously, supervisors have no control over how stewards behave. Although they are workers, they are the supervisors' equals in their union activities. Understanding the political nature of the steward's job may be helpful. It may be useful to help stewards "look good" to the workers. Strong stewards have fewer political battles to fight and as a result, can devote more time to improving conditions at work.

The supervisor   Supervisory mistakes and poor decisions often cause unnecessary grievances. Workers file more grievances against supervisors who do not make decisions objectively, fairly, and impersonally. Supervisors have a responsibility to ensure that their actions are based on facts and not emotions or personal preferences. They must ensure that their actions are consistent.

Failure to eliminate minor sources of irritation also may result in grievances. When something irritates a worker, a grievance may not follow automatically. However, if the irritation continues and is added to other general dissatisfactions, it finally breaks open like a festering wound. A problem that could have been easily resolved at earlier stages becomes a formal grievance.

Failure to communicate with workers—not keeping them informed and clarifying rumors—can lead to many unnecessary grievances. In one instance, a company purchased a new crane and assigned its use to the crane operators. The maintenance workers, having heard inaccurate rumors that their unit was being reduced, immediately filed a grievance over the use of the new crane for "maintenance purposes." The company had to spend a lot of time proving the work was not maintenance work. The supervisor could have avoided this grievance easily by explaining to the maintenance crew why the crane was purchased and correcting the rumors that some of their jobs were in jeopardy.

A recent problem at the Chrysler plant in Trenton, Michigan, illustrates what can happen when supervisors fail to consider the workers' best interests and their view of a particular situation. The contract provided that work would be halted when the temperature inside the plant reached 100° F. One day a group of workers, now known as the "Trenton 7," complained to their supervisor that it was too hot to work. The supervisor refused to suspend operations since the temperature had only reached 98° F. The workers walked out and the Trenton 7 were disciplined for their disobedience. Had the supervisor looked at the situation from the workers' point of view (the high humidity made the 98° F heat intolerable), he might have considered other action and the resulting two-week wildcat strike, grievances, and several years in court might have been avoided.

Finally, many grievances occur because supervisors do not know the contract. As a result, they may violate it when dealing with their workers, and grievances will result. These grievances, like informal gripes, could and should have been avoided. Grievances should only arise because there is an honest disagreement over how a contract provision should be interpreted and applied to a situation. They should not arise because the supervisor has not taken the time to read and understand the contract.

In summary, supervisors can prevent many unnecessary grievances. To minimize grievances you should:

- Treat all workers as individuals with dignity;
- Recognize your good performers;
- See issues from the workers' point of view;
- Identify and promptly eliminate sources of irritation to workers;
- Give clear orders and explain your directions;
- Train your workers to perform their jobs;
- Be objective, fair, and consistent in disciplining workers;
- Avoid favoritism;
- Know the labor contract and apply it.[3]

The grievance procedure

Despite attempts to minimize grievances, they will be filed. The supervisor's interpretation of a contract provision often differs from the worker's interpretation. Disagreements over day-to-day contract application are practically unavoidable.

The **grievance procedure** is a formal appeals process established in the contract. Using this process, unions and workers may challenge supervisors' actions if they believe the contract has been violated. Supervisors play an important role in resolving formal grievances as well as informal complaints, as discussed earlier.

Most grievance procedures involve a series of steps. At each step in the process, higher levels of management and union officials attempt to settle the dispute. The last step generally involves bringing an outside neutral person—an **arbitrator**—into the process. The arbitrator has the authority to make a final decision and resolve the grievance for the parties. Figure 15.1 outlines a typical grievance procedure indicating what levels of management and union leadership are involved at each step.

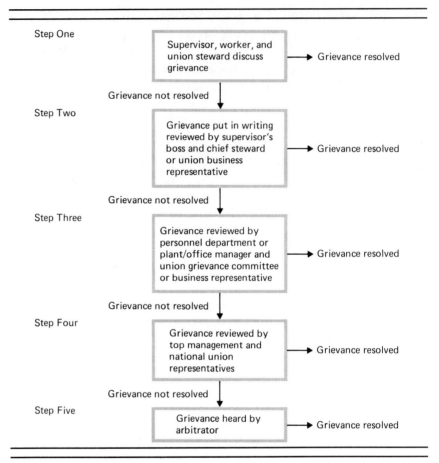

Figure 15.1   A typical grievance procedure.

Step one Step one involves a meeting of the supervisor with the worker and union steward to discuss the grievance. Many grievances can and should be resolved during this step. If a problem has not been detected, this is the time to identify and resolve the problem. After the discussion, supervisors generally have a specific amount of time within which to decide whether the grievance is right or wrong, that is, whether the action that is being challenged by the worker was the right thing to have done.

Typically, the contract requires that workers file grievances within a certain amount of time. This encourages prompt resolution of grievances. Supervisors should make every attempt to resolve grievances as early as possible. The grievance procedure is costly, since it takes supervisors and workers away from their jobs. Further, if the grievance continues through the entire procedure to arbitration, resolution may take as long as a year. A year is a long time to wait to see if Marty's discharge was unfair of if John should have been promoted rather than Susan, for example.

If Marty's discharge was in violation of the contract, she most likely will be reinstated to her job and probably awarded back pay lost while waiting for her grievance to be resolved. Also you must deal with the worker who has been placed in Marty's old job. Similarly, if Susan was incorrectly promoted, John likely will be awarded the job and probably the wages lost as a result of not receiving the job. Susan will have to be reinstated in her old job. In both instances, additional problems arise when grievances are not resolved as quickly as possible.

A number of factors influence the extent to which supervisors settle grievances during the first step. If the supervisor and the union steward do not have a good working relationship, little hope exists that the grievance will be resolved. Further, if the union is using the grievance procedure as a political tool, supervisors can do very little to encourage early settlement. There are, however, some guidelines which may help you settle grievances during the first step. These guidelines are given in Fig. 15.2.

Steps two, three, and four   Grievances that are not resolved during the first step are reviewed by higher levels of management and union leadership. Unresolved grievances are usually put into writing after step one. Depending on the size of the organization, different managers will become involved in the grievance process. Where personnel departments exist, labor relations specialists enter into the picture. For the union, business representatives and grievance committees usually replace the union steward. Business representatives are employed by the union to help local unions negotiate contracts and settle grievances. Grievance committees are usually made up of elected or appointed union members for the purpose of resolving grievances. Smaller organizations tend to have fewer steps involved.

1. Be sincere and listen carefully to what grievants (workers) are really saying. What is the real cause of the grievance? Is it a disagreement over what the contract means or some other problem?

2. Let the grievants "get it off their chest." Be patient and put them at ease. Often letting off steam is all that is needed to settle the grievances.

3. Keep an open mind. Discuss the complaint calmly and without argument. Adequately explain your actions without interrupting the grievant's story.

4. Get the grievant's story and separate the facts from opinions. Clarify any doubtful points.

5. Do not assume the grievant is wrong. Consider the other side of the story fully.

6. Avoid snap judgments. Investigate the grievance completely—talk to every person who may have important information.

7. Evaluate all facts and opinions and then decide if the grievant is right or wrong. If you've made a mistake, admit it and correct it. If you are uncertain, give the grievant the benefit of any doubt.

8. Be as fair as possible in making your decision. Give it to the grievant as soon as possible.

9. If your decision is against the grievant, be tactful and explain your decision clearly.

Figure 15.2   Supervisory guidelines for settling grievances.

In some instances, grievances not resolved during the first step may be sent directly to arbitration. This is most common for grievances resulting from discharge and discipline cases.

Processing grievances through these steps takes time. Meetings must be held when managers and union leaders are available. Specific times for conducting these meetings and making a decision are usually stated in the contract and may be as long as two weeks for each step. Just as the supervisor reviews the grievance and decides if the grievant is right or wrong during step one, the management officials involved at each step make a similar decision.

While the decision to accept or reject the worker's grievance is usually made by managers other than the supervisor during these later steps, the supervisor is still involved in the process. Supervisors are called into grievance meetings to explain their story and justify their actions.

The final step, arbitration   Most grievances are settled without going to arbitration. Both the company (management) and the union agree to accept or reject the grievance. However, many grievances still must be resolved by an arbitrator.

The arbitrator listens to both sides of the story. Supervisors play a critical role during the hearing. They are usually the company's key witness and must justify what they have done to the arbitrator and prove the contract was not violated. At the same time, the union's key witness, the grievant, is attempting to convince the arbitrator that the contract was violated. To prepare your case for arbitration, you should ask yourself the questions provided in Fig. 15.3. After hearing all the facts and information provided by both sides, the arbitrator decides whether or not the contract has been violated. Whether the arbitrator decides in the company's favor often depends on how well the case is presented during the hearing. If the arbitrator finds a violation, action is usually required to correct the mistake such as the awarding of back pay lost because a worker was wrongly discharged or the awarding of a higher-level job wrongly denied to a worker. In all cases, the arbitrator's decision is final and binding on everyone concerned: the company, the union, and the worker.

Working with the union

Few topics arouse as much controversy as the question of whether unions are desirable or even necessary. The issue of union representation is an emotional one, with some people strongly for and others strongly against unions. The realities of supervision, however, make this argument meaningless. If you work in a unionized environment, you must accept the fact that the union is there. You can't ignore it and hope it will disappear.

How supervisors react to the union has a major impact on how the union will behave toward them. Supervisors are the critical link

1. **Did you follow all the relevant contract provisions?** Many supervisory activities are covered by more than one contract provision. The arbitrator will evaluate your actions in terms of the whole contract, not just the part you extracted.

2. **Did you follow the procedural requirements set out in the contract?** Regardless of whether your actions are correct, if you did not follow the procedure established in the contract, the arbitrator probably will decide against you. For example, if the disciplinary process requires a written warning to be given before discharging workers, and you failed to give it prior to discharging a worker for good cause, you probably will find the worker reinstated to your unit even if the discharge was appropriate.

3. **Did you apply the contract provision consistently?** If you have enforced the rule only on occasion or have not enforced it for all workers in similar situations, you will lose. The arbitrator will find your actions unfair to the grievant regardless of the situation.

4. **How has the provision been interpreted in the past?** Past experience may make your actions incorrect. If your interpretation of a particular provision is different from that of other supervisors and past interpretations chances are the arbitrator will decide against you. For example, the contract states work begins at 8:00 A.M. and you discipline workers for being tardy—beginning work at 8:10 A.M. In the past, workers have been allowed to punch in by 8:00 A.M., set up, and begin work by 8:10. Your discipline probably will be found unfair, regardless of the contract.

5. **Are your arguments documented?** Merely telling the arbitrator that Worker A was promoted rather than Worker B who is more senior because worker B is unqualified will not be convincing enough. Performance records, performance problems, and other related information must be presented to the arbitrator to document your decision.

6. **Do you know all the facts?** When supervisors testify before an arbitrator and (1) do not know all the facts, or (2) appear not to have tried to get all the facts, they are fighting a losing battle. Arbitrators frown on supervisors who take action without doing their homework.

7. **Do you have good witnesses?** If you use other people to build your case, make sure they are qualified to do so. Arbitrators tend to listen only to witnesses who directly observed the situation or have other personal knowledge about the issues involved. What people "have heard" and their opinions usually are not very helpful.

Figure 15.3   Preparing your case for arbitration: Questions supervisors should ask themselves before arbitration.
Source: Adapted from M. S. Trotta, *Handling Grievances: A Guide for Management and Labor* (Washington, D.C.: Bureau of National Affairs, Inc., 1976).

in developing good or bad relations. Upper and middle-level managers do not regularly interact with the union members. Supervisors do. In fact, supervisory behavior plays a big part in determining how the union sees the company. Just as workers have daily contact with supervisors, union leaders constantly deal with supervisors in the day-to-day administration of the labor contract. As a result, supervisors and their attitudes toward the union can either make or break good union–management relations.

If you approach your dealings with the union from a negative viewpoint, you may create a number of problems for yourself. If you fight the union at every step, you can expect the union leaders to react in the same way. They will become more defensive and fight to convince you of their legitimate right to represent the workers. You may find yourself burdened with unnesessary grievances. Your workers may be less willing to devote any extra effort. In turn, their reaction may cause you to become even more embittered about the union. It's a vicious circle, and no one really wins.

A good relationship requires you to recognize and fully accept the union steward as the representative of the workers in areas covered by the contract. You must gain the steward's trust and respect. He or she can help you be more effective as a supervisor. While it is true stewards "police" your actions, making certain they are in compliance with the contract, they can also police the actions of the workers, assuring they meet their responsibilities as well. Problem workers—chronic "hookey players" or belligerent, ill-tempered people—are difficult for the union as well. If you've established a good working relationship with the steward you can expect to be supported.

Supervisors who have a good relationship with union members often find them helpful in solving problems. The union also has a stake in the organization. When organizations decline, union membership declines. A good working relationship is necessary for both parties.

Remaining nonunion

While unions are a fact of life for many supervisors, many other supervisors work in nonunionized organizations. Normally, organizations that are nonunion prefer to remain that way. Supervisors help the organization remain nonunion in two ways: (1) managing so that workers do not feel a union is needed; and (2) resisting a union organizing drive.

Why do workers join unions?

Why might workers feel a union is needed? Generally, they become interested in unions because they are dissatisfied with their present situation. They feel they are not being treated fairly by the organization. They expect that, by joining together in a union, they will have the power to get management to change the conditions causing their dissatisfaction. With a union, the collective bargaining process is a mechanism for obtaining more acceptable working conditions. Specifically, workers expect that if a union is established to represent their interests, there will be improvements in the following areas:

- Economic factors: higher wages, more company-paid insurance, more paid holidays, and longer vacations;
- Working conditions: more comfortable physical working environment, improved safety conditions, and improved tools and equipment;
- Fairness of treatment: equality of treatment for all employees.

Improvement in these areas is not the only reason that workers establish a union. They are, however, the most common reasons. James Lee has developed a tool to help organizations determine the likelihood that their workers would form a union. (See Fig. 15.4.) An analysis of the questions included in the "Susceptibility Inventory" demonstrates that both economic and social concerns are considered. Look at the scoring system presented in Fig. 15.5. If social considerations are positive (indicating good supervisory practices), the higher the potential number of points awarded for economic considerations, regardless of the level of wages and benefits. That is, wages and benefits will be important considerations, but not as critical if social conditions are desirable. Good social conditions may exist according to the Susceptibility Inventory when:

- Supervisors direct a manageable number of workers so that adequate direct, personal interaction between supervisors and workers can occur (Items 1, 2, and 7).

(Partial) Susceptibility Inventory

1. On the average, the first-line supervisory span of control is   (1) 26 + /1   (2) 21–25/1   (3) 16–20/1   (4) 11–15/1   (5) 0–10/1.

2. Our supervisors can name employees' first and last names and know how many children each employee has for   (1) 20% of his subordinates   (2) 40%   (3) 60%   (4) 80%   (5) 100%.

3. Our average supervisory IQ is around   (1) 95   (2) 100   (3) 105   (4) 110   (5) 115 +.

4. During the last few years, our supervisors have had about   (1) 0 hours of planned training in human relations (grievance handling, communications, or practical psychology)   (2) 10 hours   (3) 20 hours   (4) 30 hours   (5) 40 + hours.

5. Our supervisors   (1) refer most personnel policy interpretation matters to the personnel department   (2) refer some policy interpretation matters to the personnel department   (3) know the policies and handle most matters themselves   (4) have access to written copies of the policies and written implementation procedures   (5) have their own copies of the policies and interpret them for employees.

6. Our supervisors   (1) have no regular desk or place to put paperwork   (2) share a counter or desk with another supervisor   (3) have their own desk in their work area   (4) have both a desk and a convenient private place to talk to employees when needed   (5) have a private office.

7. How often do our supervisors in the regular course of their work have person-to-person contact with each subordinate (estimate an average)   (1) about every week   (2) every 2 to 3 days   (3) every day   (4) about twice daily   (5) several times a day.

8. What is the ratio of average age of *employees* to average age of supervisors   (1) employees 10 + years older   (2) employees 2 to 10 years older   (3) employees and supervisors about same age   (4) supervisors 20 + years older   (5) supervisors 10 to 20 years older.

9. Our turnover (exclusive of layoffs) is   (1) 4% per month   (2) we never calculate it   (3) 3% (national average)   (4) 2%   (5) 1%.

10. Our absenteeism (% of scheduled person shifts unfilled for all reasons except vacations and holidays) is   (1) 5%   (2) 4%   (3) 3%   (4) 2%   (5) 1%.

11. Our wages are in which percentile of those paid in organized shops in our industry   (1) 30th%   (2) 49th%   (3) 50th%   (4) 60th%   (5) 70th%.

12. Our fringes are in which percentile of those in organized shops in our industry   (1) 30th%   (2) 40th%   (3) 50th%   (4) 60th%   (5) 70th%.

Figure 15.4   Susceptibility inventory.

Source: James Lee, Ohio University.

Used with permission.

VALUE

1. Give it the value of the answer number.   _____

2. Give it the value of the answer number.   _____

3. If the answer is 4 or 5, the value is 4, otherwise give it the value of the answer number.   _____

4. Give it the answer number value.   _____

5. If the answer is 3, 4, or 5, give it a value of 4, otherwise give it answer number value.   _____

6. If answer is 4 or 5, give it a value of 4, otherwise give it answer number.   _____

7. Answer number value.   _____

8. Answer number value.   _____

9. Answer number value.   _____

10. Answer number value.   _____

SUBTOTAL   _____

11. If subtotal points for questions 1 to 10 are over 20 and less than 32, multiply answer value by 3. If subtotal is 32 or over, multiply answer value by 4.   _____

12. Score same as for 11.   _____

TOTAL   _____

NOTE: The higher the total number of points *the less susceptible* the organization is to union organizing.

Figure 15.5   Susceptibility inventory scoring sheet.

Source: James Lee, Ohio University. Used with permission.

■ Supervisors are old enough to command their workers' respect and to appear credible and do not make mistakes resulting in loss of respect (Items 3 and 8).

■ Supervisors are capable of handling workers' problems effectively (Items 4, 5, and 6).

■ Supervisors take care of workers' needs on the job, creating a relatively satisfied and secure work force (Items 9 and 10).

Union organizing drive

How does a union become the workers' representative? Both the union and the company engage in an **organizing campaign.** The supervisor's role in the organizing drive can be critical in determining whether the union wins. Further, if the union wins, the way supervisors handled themselves during the campaign can affect their relationship with the new union.

In some cases, workers contact a union indicating they desire representation. In other cases, the union initiates the campaign by contacting workers and trying to convince them it can better meet their needs. In either case, the union must obtain signed authorization cards from the workers it is seeking to represent. **Authorization cards** state the workers support the union as their representative in collective bargaining.

If the union obtains cards from a majority of the workers (more than 50%), it can ask the employer to recognize it voluntarily as the workers' representative and begin negotiating a labor contract. Obviously, employers rarely agree to this. Rather, they usually insist the National Labor Relations Board (NLRB) come in and conduct a representation election.

For a **representation election** to occur, the union must obtain signed authorization cards from at least 30% of the workers. The NLRB then conducts a secret ballot election. If the union wins a majority of the votes cast, the employer must recognize and bargain with the union. If the union does not receive a majority of the votes, it does not become the workers' representative and another election cannot be held for one year.

The supervisor's role in organizing campaigns

Many employers rely heavily on supervisors during union organizing drives. Supervisors are in daily contact with workers. Workers are accustomed to receiving guidance and direction from their supervisors. As a result, supervisors can pass on information regarding the company's position and feed back information regarding employees' reactions.

However, supervisors must be careful not to commit unfair labor practices during the organizing drive. It is legal to express views, arguments, or opinions based on facts, but you cannot threaten or interrogate workers about their union allegiances and activities. Promising workers certain rewards in return for rejecting the union is also illegal. Supervisors' are more likely to commit unfair labor parctices because they interact regularly with workers. They should check carefully all actions taken during an organizing campaign with higher-level management to assure they are not breaking the law. When unfair labor practices are committed, remedies are made available by the NLRB and the courts to the people or union involved. Individuals discharged because of their union activities probably will be reinstated with back pay. Of even greater importance, if serious unfair labor practices are committed, the NLRB can require the company to negotiate a contract with the union without an election. You should be aware of several key areas that typically result in unfair labor practice charges. A wrong move in any of these areas may prove to be a costly mistake.[4]

Organizing activities in work areas   While you may prohibit union organizers who are not employed by the company from entering work areas to build support for the union, current workers are a different matter. Workers cannot be forbidden to campaign during nonworking time as long as it does not interfere with work activities. That is, workers may try to get support for the union during coffee breaks, lunchtime, trips to the restroom, wash-up time, and during downtime caused by equipment failure.

Further, if workers are usually allowed to talk freely while they work, this practice cannot be stopped just because they are talking about the union. This includes passing out authorization cards as well as talk about the union, as long as it doesn't interfere with work.

You cannot prohibit workers from wearing union buttons to work but you can refuse to allow them to put union stickers on company property such as machines, walls, or equipment.

Organizing activities in nonworking areas   In places away from working areas such as lunchrooms, bathrooms, parking lots, and hallways, workers are legally allowed to distribute union literature and campaign for the union. Outsiders may be forbidden from entering nonwork areas if other outsiders are forbidden as well. That is, if the Girl Scouts, American Cancer Society, and other groups are allowed to sell cookies, solicit contributions, and so forth on company property, the union organizers may be allowed to "sell their wares" too.

Antiunion workers   In many situations you might find workers who do not like the idea of unionization. While you can inform them that they may campaign against the union, you *cannot* ask or encourage them to do so. It 1s critical that you do not give these workers special treatment or grant them favors not available to prounion workers. Assigning antiunion workers to better jobs, giving them overtime opportunities, or letting them take an extra half-hour for lunch when prounion workers are denied the same treatment can lead your organization right into an unfair labor practice charge.

Prounion workers   You must be very careful in laying off, disciplining, or discharging prounion workers. If the decision to take action against these workers is not justified by nonunion-related circumstances, you can bet unfair labor practice charges will follow. If layoff, discipline, or discharge is necessary, it must be applied to antiunion workers as well.

Job applicants   If you interview job applicants, the temptation may exist to find out how they feel about the union. As these people will vote in the election once hired, you cannot ask them anything about the union, promise them certain rewards if they oppose the union, or refuse to hire them because they support the union.

Working conditions   You can do very little about working conditions during an organization drive. You cannot promise to make improvements if the union is defeated.

Getting information   Because supervisors are a direct communication link to workers, management often relies on them to forward information on how workers feel about the union. Nothing prohibits you from listening to any information freely volunteered by workers. You may even tell them that while you're not asking any questions, they can tell you anything they want. However you cannot question workers as to whether they've signed authorization cards, attended union meetings, or how they intend to vote. Further, spying on workers directly or indirectly or even giving the impression you're watching them as they campaign for the union is taboo.

Giving information As pointed out earlier, workers are used to looking to their supervisors for guidance and advice. Union campaigns are no exception. If you are asked questions about the union answer them. Give the facts and express your opinions and views as long as they are based on facts. When answering questions be careful not to appear threatening. Calling workers into your office to discuss the union in privacy can get you in trouble. Visiting workers at home is even worse and should not be done at all.

Supervisors are truly caught in the middle of an uncomfortable situation in many cases. On one side they have the workers and their needs and expectations. On the other side are their bosses with equally demanding needs and expectations. While supervisors can exert considerable influence over how satisfied workers are, in many areas their hands are tied. Nowhere is this dilemma more sharply illustrated as when supervisors are relied on to advance a poorly managed company's position during an organizing campaign.

Giving workers the company's side during an organizing drive is a critical strategy that must be used if the company is to have a chance of winning. As we said before, supervisors are the ideal representatives for the company. In fact, they are typically relied on to communicate the company's position. During a campaign you have every right to counter what the union is saying. If you don't, who will?

Problems arise when supervisors are (a) not trusted and respected by their workers, or (b) when they find themselves defending a position they themselves see as inadequate. You must be trusted and respected by workers before they will seek and follow your advice. The second problem is more complex.

As we have said before, workers desire union representation for many reasons. Some of these may fall directly under the supervisor's control while others do not. For example, wage and salary levels and benefits are usually established by upper management, not supervisors. The decision to introduce technological improvements which will displace current workers is made by upper management. Similarly, decisions to lay off workers typically are not made by supervisors. If these or other similar issues prompt workers to seek union representation, you may be hard-pressed to present management's side effectively. This is particularly true if you see your interests being threatened as well.

Most likely, if supervisors are doing their jobs well and upper management is effectively managing the organization, supervisors can communicate the company's position effectively on why a union is not needed. Contrary to what many may think, no company is immune from unionizing drives. Often unions are drawn into situations where only a few disgruntled workers attempt to generate workers' interest in organizing. As a result, you should never assume your workers "know the truth" and couldn't possibly be interested in what the union has to say. If you do not provide information regarding the company's position, workers may have a one-sided picture of what the union can do for them—the union's side.

Summary

- Unions are chosen by workers to represent them in dealings with employers. Supervisors are affected by unions whether or not their organization is unionized.

- Labor laws give nongovernmental workers the right to join unions, bargain with employers over wages, hours, and working conditions, and the right to strike.

- Collective bargaining involves (1) negotiating, (2) interpreting, (3) applying, and (4) enforcing the labor contract. Supervisors primarily are involved in interpreting and applying the labor contract.

- The labor contract affects many supervisory decisions. Supervisory actions that are influenced by a union include: promotions, transfers and work assignments; scheduling; discipline and discharge; and layoffs. When supervisors take action in areas covered by the contract, they can be challenged by the union.

☐ Grievances exist whenever workers feel they have not been treated fairly. Labor contracts establish grievance procedures to resolve grievances. General gripes should be resolved immediately through informal means.

☐ Grievances result from problems associated with human nature and personal characteristics of workers, supervisors, and union stewards. Supervisors should try to minimize grievances. Grievances should occur only when there is disagreement over what the contract means.

☐ The grievance procedure is a formal appeals process. It involves a series of steps during which higher levels of management and union leaders attempt to settle the grievance. Unresolved grievances typically are heard by an arbitrator. The arbitartor's decision is final and binding on all parties.

☐ Supervisors play a critical role in the grievance process. Their actions are often the basis for grievances. Supervisors are involved in the first step of the grievance process. They should attempt to resolve grievances as early as possible because the grievance process takes time and is costly.

☐ When top management and union leaders cannot resolve the grievance, it goes to arbitration. Supervisors must justify their actions while the union and worker attempt to demonstrate that the contract was violated. The arbitrator makes a final decision based on the information provided at the hearing.

☐ Supervisors are the critical link in developing good labor–management relations. They can benefit from good working relations with the union.

☐ Supervisors in nonunionized organizations can influence whether their organization remains nonunion. Many workers join unions because supervisors aren't doing their jobs effectively. When workers are interested in joining a union, an organizing drive occurs. The union tries to get workers to support the union while management campaigns against the union.

☐ Supervisors often are involved heavily in management's campaign. They are in daily contact with workers and can communicate the company's position. They must be careful not to commit unfair labor practices. Particular areas of concern include how supervisors handle organizing activities in work and nonwork areas, antiunion and prounion workers, job applicants, working conditions, and receiving and giving information about the union.

Questions for review and discussion

X1. What is collective bargaining? What is the supervisor's role in the collective bargaining process?

2. Distinguish between real grievances and general gripes. How should each be handled and why?

3. Describe a typical grievance procedure.

X4. Why do workers want to join unions? 3

5. Discuss the procedure followed in a union organizing drive.

6. During a union organizing drive, what can supervisors do in the following areas? What can't they do?

   a. regulate organizing activities in work and nonwork areas;

   b. deal with prounion workers, antiunion workers, and job applicants;

   c. get information from workers about the union;

   d. give information to workers.

7. Many experts have argued recently that unions are no longer needed in our modern organizations. They argue that security and fair treatment are available for workers through legal regulation and more enlightened, sophisticated supervisory practices. What is your opinion?

8. In dealing with unions, supervisors are often described as being caught in an uncomfortable position. Why is this so?

X HISTORY OF LABOR RELATION

Key terms

Arbitrator	Organizing campaign
Authorization cards	Progressive disciplinary action
Collective bargaining	"Real" grievances
General gripes	Representation election
Grievance procedures	Seniority
Grievances	Taft-Hartley Act
Labor contract	Unfair labor practices
Landrum-Griffin Act	Union
National Labor Relations Board (NLRB)	Union steward
Negotiations	Wagner Act

Cases for discussion and practical exercises

1. Jan Van Camp pulled out Sam Adams' file. She was scheduled to meet with Sam and his union steward at 9:30 that morning to discuss Sam's grievance. As supervisor, Jan usually was able to resolve most of the grievances during these meetings. The steward was reasonable and they were usually able to resolve any difficulties to everyone's satisfaction. This time, however, she wasn't so sure she'd be successful.

    On August 3, a little over two weeks ago, Sam had come to her and indicated he was quitting. His last day would be August

17. He told Jan he was moving to Florida to help his brother open and run a night club. Although he was not required to give notice, Sam had told her that he wanted to let her know ahead of time.

Jan was pleased that Sam had notified her in advance. The plant was in the process of laying off workers. While Sam's position would not be affected, someone who would otherwise have been laid off would be able to bid for Sam's job. The labor contract required that all job vacancies be posted for three days so all qualified and interested workers could bid for the job. The most senior, qualified worker would then be chosen to fill the position.

Sam's job was posted according to the contract on August 4. On August 7, Aaron Hall was chosen to replace Sam. Aaron began working immediately so Sam could train him. By coincidence, Aaron's former job also was not affected by the planned reduction in the work force. As a result, his job was posted on August 7 and filled on August 12 by a worker who would have been laid off if she had remained in her old job.

On August 14, the last working day before he was scheduled to quit, Sam came into Jan's office. "I talked to Mitch, my brother, last night, " Sam said. "His loan fell through so the deal's off. I guess I wasn't supposed to be heading for sunny Florida after all. What luck! I sure was looking forward to moving down there."

Jan said she was sorry and hoped something would work out. "By the way Sam," she added, "you've done an excellent job training Aaron. He's doing just fine now, don't you think?"

Sam responded, "Yeah, sure, he's doing great. Now that I'm not leaving, I sure hope he doesn't get sore over having to go back to his old job."

Jan stared at Sam in disbelief. "Why Sam, you've quit. We've posted and filled two jobs because of your decision. I can't pull those people out of their jobs just because you've changed you mind. Aaron would never understand. And the woman that took his job would have been laid off a few days ago. What would I tell them? It just wouldn't be fair!"

"Fair, who's talking fair? Sam retorted. "It's my job until I quit or get fired. Don't you read the labor contract? You have no reason to fire me. And I'm not quitting. It's not my fault my brother messed everything up."

Jan hadn't been able to get Sam to understand her position. Sam and the steward would be in her office in exactly 20 minutes. She quickly glanced over the information she had compiled in Sam's file.

■ Sam was 24 and had been employed by the company for 6 years. He had a few minor infractions on his record such as unexcused absences and tardiness. His work was marginal. At his peak, Sam was an average worker.

■ Company records showed that in the past, two other workers had quit their jobs only to change their minds later. In both cases, however, these workers had held jobs that required greater skill. As a result, finding replacements was difficult. In Sam's case, his job was relatively easy to learn and thus, easily filled. Further, when the two skilled workers had decided not to quit, their jobs were still vacant. In these two incidents, the company had agreed to let the workers keep their jobs.

■ The labor contract stated that a worker lost seniority and ceased to be employed when he or she was discharged, quit, or exceeded a leave of absence.

a) What would you decided to do if you were Jan?
b) What might the consequences be if you were to decide Sam was right and you let him keep his job?
c) Assume you decide you cannot change your mind. Sam had quit and you cannot give him back his job. How would you explain you decision to Sam? What do you think the chances are of resolving this grievance?

2. Interview a union leader and a supervisor about labor relations. Among other things ask them about their feelings regarding the use of seniority in decisions affecting employees. If they have different views explain why those differences might exist. Do you think the goals of the two are compatible or incompatible? Why?

Notes

1. M. S. Trotta, *Handling Grievances: A Guide for Management and Labor* (Washington D.C.: Bureau of National Affairs, 1976).

2. *Ibid.*, pp. 44–45.

3. *Ibid.*, pp. 48–49.

4. Charles L. Hughes and Alfred T. DeMaria, *Managing to Stay Non-Union* (New York: Executive Enterprises Publications Co., Inc., 1979).

16

Working safely

Objectives

☐ Explain the supervisor's responsibility for safety in the work place,

☐ Identify potentially unsafe working conditions,

☐ Explain the importance of safety rules and procedures, and

☐ Identify topics that should be included in a safety training program.

The issue of safety

Twenty-year-old Tim Merkel of Detroit, Michigan, had a promising future. An A – student at the U.S. Naval Academy, he was working on an apartment construction project where his father was a carpentry foreman. On December 5, 1979, a two-and-one-half story brick wall suddenly collapsed on Tim, crushing the young man and all of his dreams.[1]

Joe Taylor, 53 years old, had discussed his upcoming retirement with his wife just a few nights earlier. Now his wife viewed his body stretched out on an emergency room table. A few hours earlier, Joe had been working on top of a large tank when a damaged section of it tilted. He fell 30 feet to the ground, eliminating any need to think about retirement.[2]

It is difficult to argue that worker safety and health is not a real problem today. Just in case you aren't convinced, here are a few facts:[3]

■ One out of every eight workers will suffer a job-related injury or illness in any work year.

- Every year some 2,000,000 workers become seriously disabled on the job and another 5,000,000 become somewhat disabled.
- Every year 14,000 to 15,000 workers lose their lives while working.
- Invisible contaminants found in the work place are believed to cause the deaths of some 100,000 American workers and disable another 390,000 workers every year. These estimates are admitted to be conservative.

Organizations have done much to improve the safety of the work place. A considerable amount of progress has been made. Much remains to be done, however. For example, we are just beginning to understand the extent of disease associated with invisible contaminants in the work environment. Pressures are mounting for organizations to take action in this area as they have done in the area of work-related accidents.

As a supervisor, you play a critical role in assuring a safer work place for your workers. You are expected to identify potential safety problems and implement safety improvement programs. In this chapter we will discuss pressures for safety improvement and approaches you can use to improve safety.

Safety and the law

Historically workers themselves were held responsible for any injuries suffered at work. Supervisors and employers were rarely held liable for workers' accidents under the law. Basically, it was assumed that:

- Employers were not liable if the accident resulted from workers' negligence (**doctrine of contributory negligence**);
- Workers who accepted a job also accepted the risks associated with the job (**doctrine of assumption of risk**);
- If a worker was injured by a fellow worker, the employer was not responsible (**fellow-servant rule**).

It is easy to see that this approach proved to be unsatisfactory. As a result, by 1920 all but three states had enacted workers' compensation laws.

Workers' compensation programs

Today, all states require employers to provide **workers' compensation plans** for their workers. While state laws differ, in general all plans provide workers who are injured on the job with payments for a specified time. The objective of workers' compensation is to offset the wages lost by injured workers while they are unable to work. The payment is typically a percentage of the worker's actual wages. In most cases, additional payments are made to cover medical expenses. In the event a worker is killed on the job, the survivor receives death benefits under most programs.

Organizations must spend money to provide workers' compensation benefits to workers. Just like a regular insurance policy, the premium organizations must pay in order to provide coverage is based largely on their past safety record. Organizations that have had many workers injured or killed at work pay higher premiums than those with better safety records. The cost of this experience-rating system has encouraged many organizations to implement safety improvement programs.

Occupational Safety and Health Act (OSHA)

Despite workers' compensation programs, the statistics show that U.S. employers made only limited headway in improving the safety of work places. Reacting to continued concern over workers' safety, Congress passed the **Occupational Safety and Health Act (OSHA)** in 1970. Whereas workers' compensation is designed to provide economic security to workers injured on the job, OSHA focuses on the crux of the problem—preventing industrial accidents from occurring.

OSHA requires that organizations take action to ensure safe working conditions for employees. Specifically, OSHA requires organizations to:

- Furnish a place of employment free of hazards which may cause illness, injury, or death to workers;
- Comply with the standards set by the Secretary of Labor;

- Permit inspectors to enter the work place without delay at reasonable times;
- Conduct periodic inspections for safety and health hazards if required;
- Post notices to keep workers informed of their rights and duties including applicable safety standards;
- Maintain records of all work-related injuries, illnesses, deaths, and exposure of workers to toxic materials and harmful physical agents;
- Provide physical exams for workers to determine if exposure to toxic substances or potentially harmful physical agents has exceeded permissible limits;
- Post copies of citations of violations at or near the site of the violations;
- Provide workers with protective equipment where required.[4]

Under the law, safety regulations are developed by the Department of Labor. All employers are required to know and comply with these standards. There are literally thousands of regulations covering everything from the specific to the general. The multitude of regulations resulted in so much uproar that in 1978, some 1,100 "outmoded" or overly specific regulations were discarded. These included specifications regarding the type of wood to be used in stepladders and the requirement for portable toilets to be placed on all construction building sites.

The Act is enforced through **safety inspections** conducted by OSHA officials. These inspections may be made on a "surprise" basis, or officials may visit the plant or office by invitation from the employer, union, or workers. When visiting a work site, OSHA officials check to see that safety regulations are not being violated. Organizations failing to comply with the law may face fines ranging from $1,000 to over $10,000.

While assuming supervisors will actually know all regulations is unreasonable, they are responsible for seeing that their workers follow the safety practices required by OSHA. Often supervisors work with OSHA inspectors during the inspection visit. And, of course, they must implement any changes the inspector recommends and the organization adopts.

The costs of poor safety

In addition to the legal requirements, there are other reasons for promoting safe working conditions. One is the cost of accidents. These costs are not as observable as workers' compensation premiums and OSHA fines. Often they are overlooked. These costs result from interrupted production, decreased morale, and a bad reputation in the local community.

When an accident occurs, fellow employees in the area stop working to see what has happened and to offer assistance. Injured workers are usually paid for the time spent in first aid. Further, many injuries require time to heal. As a result, injured workers may return to work on a restricted basis and their pay probably will not reflect the real value of their performance.

In the event an injured worker cannot return to work immediately, new workers or replacements must fill in. This requires training a new person to perform the job. In all likelihood, the temporary replacement will not perform at the same level as the more experienced but injured worker. As a result, there may be a loss in productivity.

When accidents occur, time must be devoted to investigating the accident and completing the paperwork required by OSHA. The people performing these duties are being paid.

There are also psychological costs. When accidents are more common than expected, workers begin to feel uneasy and uncomfortable while at work. Watching a friend lose a finger, break a leg, or worse yet, lose his or her life, results in reduced morale. It also paints a negative image of the organization in the community. Such events can seriously impede efforts to attract and retain good workers. Above all, a more important cost must be considered, that of a human life, a limb, or someone's sight.

How great are these costs? The National Safety Council estimates that on a national basis the costs of accidents exceed $14 billion a year. That figure averages out to $165 per worker.[5] In demonstrating the hidden costs of accidents, the *Journal of American Insurance* has estimated that to recoup losses suffered from a $500 accident, a baker must sell 119,000 loaves of bread, a restaurant must serve 3,788 lunches, a department store must sell 16,130 pairs of boys' socks, and a telephone company must handle 23,575 local pay phone calls.[6]

A recent survey of safety practices demonstrates that organizations are not taking these costs lightly:[7]

- Three-fourths of the companies surveyed had formal safety programs;
- 80% of the programs involved supervisory safety training;
- 75% of the programs involved worker safety training;
- On the average, $100 per worker per year was spent on safety programs.

The supervisor and safety

While top-level management is responsible for establishing safety policies and procedures in compliance with OSHA, it is the supervisor who ultimately is responsible for promoting safety at work. Supervisors are in constant contact with workers in the work place and as a result can directly observe and immediately correct safety hazards.

In larger organizations, supervisors often receive help from staff specialists in the personnel department, or in some cases, from a separate safety department. In many organizations safety committees have been formed. Ultimately however, supervisors are directly responsible for their workers and have an obligation to communicate and enforce all safety policies and procedures.

As a supervisor, you should be concerned with several areas. Specifically, you are responsible for:

- Ensuring safety is designed into each operation or procedure performed by workers;
- Telling workers about hazards on the job and how to avoid them;
- Seeking the assistance of safety specialists in determining safe practices, policies, and procedures and how to make operations and equipment safe;
- Assuring essential safety equipment and devices are provided for and used by all workers;

■ Taking prompt corrective action whenever unsafe conditions or behaviors are observed;

■ Assuring that all injuries are promptly treated and reported. When an accident occurs, it must be investigated and the cause determined so that corrective action can be taken to prevent future accidents.[8]

In light of these duties, it is clear that you have an important role in assuring safety at work. As one safety expert has suggested:

A prime requisite for any successful accident prevention program is to leave no doubt in the mind of any employee that his managers are concerned about accident prevention. . . . For the workers the supervisor represents management. He has to see that the intention and orders of management are carried out by exerting his personal authority and influence. If the supervisor does not take safety seriously, those under him will not either.[9]

Preventing accidents

To determine how accidents can be prevented, you must first determine what causes accidents. Three major causes of work-related accidents have been identified. They are chance occurrences, unsafe working conditions and mechanical failure, and unsafe behavior by workers.[10]

Chance occurrences

It is impossible for all accidents to be prevented. Some accidents occur purely by chance. A worker who is moving from one building to another and is struck by lightning has been involved in an accident while at work. There is little anyone could have done in this, or similar situations, to prevent the accident from occurring. Fortunately, the odds of **chance accidents** occurring are small. Less than 2% of all work-related accidents are due to chance.

Unsafe working conditions

A much more common cause of accidents is **unsafe working conditions.** Examples of typical unsafe working conditions include:[11]

- Improperly guarded equipment;
- Defective equipment;
- Hazardous arrangement of equipment;
- Poorly designed procedures for handling machines and equipment;
- Hazardous storage conditions;
- Inadequate lighting;
- Improper ventilation.

You must undertake a program of action to remedy any unsafe working conditions. Periodic safety inspections draw attention to potential trouble spots so that corrective action can be taken before an accident occurs.

The conditions listed here are the very problems OSHA regulations and standards are designed to eliminate. They are the first things to be checked for during an OSHA investigation. You can keep informed about the safety of working conditions in your unit by inspecting your operations periodically. Figure 16.1 provides a sample checklist you might use when inspecting your unit for potentially hazardous conditions.

All work places are susceptible to accidents. On the basis of past experience, however, we can identify certain working conditions more likely to cause accidents. Particular attention should be paid to these conditions when conducting your safety inspection.[12]

- Situations where heavy, awkward material is handled using trucks, cranes, and hoists account for one-third of all industrial accidents.
- Situations involving the use of machinery—metal and woodworking machines, machines with exposed gears, belts, chains, paper cutters, and even electric pencil sharpeners—can cause accidents.
- Walking or climbing at work, and using scaffolds, ladders, and axes are also likely to be the cause of accidents.

Department _____ Date _____

This list is intended only as a reminder. Look for other unsafe acts and conditions, then report them so that corrective action can be taken. Note particularly whether unsafe acts or conditions that have caused accidents have been corrected.

(√) Indicates Satisfactory

1. FIRE PROTECTION
   Extinguishing equipment ( )
   Hose, sprinkler heads, and valves ( )
   Exits, stairs, and signs ( )
   Storage of flammable material ( )

2. HOUSEKEEPING
   Aisles, stairs, and floors ( )
   Storage and filing of material ( )
   Wash and locker rooms ( )
   Lights and ventilation ( )
   Disposal of waste ( )
   Yards and parking lots ( )

3. TOOLS
   Hand tools ( )
   Power tools, wiring ( )
   Use and storage of tools ( )

4. PERSONAL PROTECTIVE EQUIPMENT
   Glasses, goggles, or face shields ( )
   Safety shoes ( )
   Gloves ( )
   Respirators or gas masks ( )
   Protective clothing ( )

5. MATERIAL HANDLING EQUIPMENT
   Power trucks, hand trucks ( )
   Elevators ( )
   Cranes and hoists ( )
   Conveyors ( )
   Cables, ropes, chains, slings ( )

6. BULLETIN BOARDS
   Neat and attractive ( )
   Display changed regularly ( )
   Well illuminated ( )

7. MACHINERY
   Point of operation ( )
   Belts, pulleys, gears, shafts, etc. ( )
   Oiling, cleaning, and adjusting ( )
   Maintenance and oil leakage ( )

8. PRESSURE EQUIPMENT
   Steam equipment ( )
   Air receivers and compressors ( )
   Gas cylinders and hose ( )

9. UNSAFE PRACTICES
   Excessive speed of vehicles ( )
   Improper lifting ( )
   Smoking violations ( )
   Horseplay ( )
   Running in aisles or on stairs ( )
   Improper use of airhoses ( )
   Removing machine or other machinery ( )
   Removing machine or other guards ( )
   Work on unguarded moving machinery ( )

10. FIRST AID
   First-aid kits and rooms ( )
   Stretchers and fire blankets ( )
   Emergency showers ( )
   All injuries reported ( )

11. MISCELLANEOUS
   Acids and caustics ( )
   How processes, chemicals and solvents ( )
   Dusts, vapors, or fumes ( )
   Ladders and scaffolds ( )

Figure 16.1 Safety inspection check sheet.

Source: M. G. Miner, *Safety Policies and the Impact of OSHA* (Personnel Policies Forum Survey No. 117) (Washington, D.C.: Bureau of National Affairs, Inc., 1977), p. 45.

■ Situations requiring electricity other than that used for usual lighting have high accident potential.

■ Blocked aisles, unsafe passageways, and blocked stairways may cause accidents.

■ Lack of access to fire alarms and fire extinguishers is dangerous.

In many cases, you can make the necessary corrections. However, if the correction requires a substantial rearrangement of physical facilities and/or costs, you may have to draw higher management's attention to the problem.

Unsafe work behavior

Without a doubt, unsafe actions by workers are the single most common cause of work-related accidents. On the average, for every accident caused by unsafe working conditions, four accidents are caused by unsafe actions. You can regularly inspect the work place and see that safe conditions prevail, yet still find accidents occurring in your unit. If your workers do not share your safety-consciousness and if they do not know and use safe practices, even the safest work sites will not remain so.

Unsafe work behaviors are commonplace in all organizations. Either intentionally or unintentionally, you may see workers:

■ Acting without authority;

■ Failing to secure equipment before using it;

■ Failing to warn fellow workers of possible danger;

■ Failing to use safety or protective equipment provided by the organization;

■ Throwing materials;

■ Operating equipment or working at unsafe speeds;

■ Removing, adjusting, or disconnecting safety devices;

■ Using unsafe equipment or using equipment unsafely;

■ Using improper procedures in loading, placing, mixing, or combining materials;

■ Lifting things improperly;

■ Working on or moving dangerous equipment;

■ Distracting, teasing, abusing, scaring, quarreling, or otherwise engaging in horseplay while on the job.[13]

Admittedly, most unsafe behaviors are not intentional. Most workers do not want to cause another worker or themselves to become injured or worse yet, lose their lives. However, intent is not the issue. Supervisors are obligated to ensure that their workers behave in a way that prevents accidents.

To eliminate unsafe behavior you should:

- Detect accident-prone workers and take corrective action;
- Enforce safety rules and procedures; and
- Adequately train workers to behave in a safe manner.

Accident-prone workers

We have all known "Calamity Janes and Jims." Some people just seem to have a knack for causing accidents no matter what they do.

For years, psychologists have tried to describe the personality of people likely to cause work accidents. If you can identify the "Calamity Jane and Jim" at work, you can place them in jobs where they could do the least damage.

Unfortunately, no such personality type exists. However, certain personal characteristics do tend to be associated with accident-proneness in certain situations. Surprisingly, younger workers (under age 30) tend to be more accident-prone than older workers. In fact, the frequency of accidents is lowest for workers in their late 50s and 60s. Workers who are impulsive and adventurous also tend to be more accident-prone.

Workers who have stress, alcohol, or drug problems are also accident-prone and the safety-conscious supervisor cannot ignore them. As discussed in Chapter 8, these employees cause problems wherever they work. They can present severe safety risks as well. For example, job-related accidents are two to four times higher for alcoholic workers. Their rate of off-the-job accidents is even higher.

Accident-prone workers thus can be many different types: younger, impulsive workers or alcoholics or drug abusers or workers undergoing temporary psychological stress. To further complicate the matter, some workers may be accident prone on some days and not on others. And as if the situation were not complicated enough, you cannot deal with all accident-prone workers in the same way and expect your strategy to work.

You can, however, attempt to anticipate potential unsafe behavior before it occurs. Of critical importance is detecting workers who are not mentally or physically capable of performing their jobs safely, keeping them away from potentially dangerous assignments, and attempting to help them get rehabilitated. The counseling guidelines discussed in Chapter 8 also apply to helping accident-prone workers.

Enforcing safety rules and procedures

Many work accidents are caused by sheer stupidity. Workers (and supervisors) willingly ignore established and known **safety rules and procedures** while at work. It is not uncommon for workers to bypass safety procedures because they feel they "would never be hurt on the job." Once a safety rule or procedure is successfully ignored, workers tend to regard it as silly and useless and will continue to push their luck. An example of general plant safety rules is shown in Fig. 16.2.

This general disregard for the consequences of unsafe work behavior on the part of workers is a continually perplexing problem for supervisors. Workers resent the discomfort of wearing protective shields (such as eyeglasses, hard hats, or closed-toe shoes). They resent being required to take the time to do something the safe way. As a result, workers often ignore safety rules and procedures.

1. Report all injuries to your supervisor immediately.
2. Running on plant property, except in case of an emergency, is prohibited.
3. Removal of "Danger-Do-Not-Operate" tags or locks on any machinery by unauthorized personnel is prohibited.
4. Never attempt to catch falling objects.

(continued)

Figure 16.2   Example of general plant safety rules.
Source: Adapted from M. G. Miner, *Safety Policies and the Impact of OSHA* (Personnel Policies Forum Survey No. 117) (Washington, D.C.: Bureau of National Affairs, Inc., 1977), p. 40.

Figure 16.2 (continued)

5. Only authorized equipment may be used in specific operations. Never attempt to use defective machinery.

6. Use a ladder when required. Do not climb on machinery.

7. Smoking is permitted in designated areas only.

8. Tampering with or unauthorized use of any machinery is prohibited.

9. All emergency equipment, such as fire extinguishers, fire alarms, and exit doors, must be kept clear of obstacles.

10. The wearing of any type of jewelry, such as watches, rings, bracelets, necklaces, or long ties while working around or operating moving machinery is prohibited.

11. Know the location of fire and safety exits.

12. Safety glasses will be worn in all specified areas. All safety glasses areas are marked by green tape and warning signs.

13. A safe shoe will be worn at all times. Sandals or canvas-type shoes are not acceptable.

14. A clean work place is a safe place. Keep your area clean by adopting a "pick-up as you go" method of housekeeping. Remember that safety rules are for your own protection. Your adherence to them is part of your responsibility.

15. No one will be permitted on the plant premises who has in his or her possession firearms, ammunition, or articles of a similar nature unless he or she has a permit signed by the plant manager or assistant.

16. It is the duty of each employee, when going on or off duty, to carefully examine buildings, apparatus, and equipment in their charge to see that everything is in good order. Any needed repairs and other attention should be reported promptly to the shift supervisor.

17. Each employee is expected to be responsible for his or her own safety and at the same time to exercise care in avoiding injury to fellow workers and others.

18. Horseplay and practical jokes are forbidden.

19. If machinery must be cleaned or requires adjusting while in motion, special permission must be obtained from your supervisor.

20. Compressed air is not to be used for the cleaning of clothing which is being worn.

21. Be sure that all tools are maintained in a good state of repair.

22. Forklift trucks are built to accomodate only one person. No one other than the driver shall ride on the fork truck at any time.

Supervisors also fall prey to the assumption that safety rules and procedures are not really necessary. This feeling is particularly evident in nonmanufacturing settings. Unfortunately, this is a false assumption. Table 16.1 reveals the incidence of occupational injuries and illnesses in U.S. industry. The incident rates given in Table 16.1 are the number of injuries and illnesses per 100 full-time workers.

You are responsible for ensuring that safety rules and procedures are followed by all workers in all situations. You should also remember to lead by example. It is difficult to enforce a rule when you violate rules. When violations occur, prompt and consistent corrective action must be taken to assure similar infractions do not reoccur. In fact, OSHA requires all employees comply with the safety standards, regulations, and orders that apply to their actions and job conduct. If OSHA inspectors find workers failing to meet these obligations, they can fine the organization for violating the act. For serious or repeated violations, the fines are quite large.

Table 16.1

Occupational injuries and illnesses incidence rates, U.S. private industry, 1974

Industry	*Total Cases per 100 Full-Time Workers*
Agriculture, Forestry and Fisheries	9.9
Mining	10.2
Construction	18.3
Manufacturing	14.6
Transportation and Utilities	10.5
Wholesale and Retail Trade	8.4
Finance, Insurance and Real Estate	2.4
Services	5.8
Total	10.4

Source: Bureau of Labor Statistics, U.S. Department of Labor.

Safety training

To ensure safe working conditions prevail, training is critical. **Safety training** concentrates on:

- Making supervisors safety-conscious;
- Making workers safety-conscious;
- Specific job-safety training.

Safety training for supervisors is necessary to achieve efficient operations. Research shows that supervisors who manage their units with an overriding concern for safety also achieve higher efficiency and productivity.[14] As we have discussed earlier, the key to safe working conditions is eliminating the causes of accidents. As a result, most supervisory safety training teaches supervisors how to prevent accidents. The topics often included in such programs are shown in Fig. 16.3.

Many organizations offer safety services for companies that do not have formal in-house supervisory safety training programs. Most insurance carriers, state departments of labor, and other organizations such as the National Safety Council provide training services.

When investigating work-related accidents, it is amazing how often workers reveal they didn't know a hazard existed, were not given special instructions, or were not aware of safety rules. The frequency of this ignorance of safety rules and procedures illustrates the critical need to provide safety training for workers.

General safety training is often provided by the safety or personnel department. However, with or without this service, supervisors are the only ones who can give workers specific on-the-job safety training. Several opportunities exist for supervisors to indoctrinate their workers in safe work behavior. Situations requiring safety training include:

- A new worker joining the unit;
- Current workers' being assigned to new jobs;
- New processes implemented or established procedures modified;
- Workers' returning to work after a layoff.[15]

To ensure safety training is effective (that workers do become safety-conscious), you need both oral communication and written

1. Safety and the Supervisor
   - OSHA and governmental regulation
   - The costs of accidents
   - Supervisors' responsibility
   - Employees' responsibility

2. Accident Problems
   - Recognizing job hazards
   - Unsafe conditions
   - Unsafe acts
   - Accident investigations
   - Accident reporting procedure

3. Safety Consciousness
   - Safety contests
   - Safety posters
   - Off-the-job safety
   - First aid

4. Housekeeping
   - Inspection procedures
   - Aisles and floors
   - Storage facilities
   - Machine and equipment placement
   - Office safety

5. Industrial Hygiene
   - Chemicals and solvents
   - Dust, fumes, gases

6. Personal Protection Equipment
   - Eyes
   - Face
   - Ears
   - Respiratory
   - Safe work clothes

7. Material Handling and Storage
   - Lifting and carrying
   - Equipment for handling materials
   - Material storage methods

8. Guards
   - Guard design and mechanisms
   - Lookout procedures

9. Operating machine safety instructions

Figure 16.3   Sample contents of safety training programs.
Source: Adapted from M. G. Miner, *Safety Policies and the Impact of OSHA* (Personnel Policies Forum Survey No. 117) (Washington, D.C.: Bureau of National Affairs, Inc., 1977), pp. 31–33.

materials. In all cases, you should explain the job safety rules and procedures to workers, inform them of potential hazards, and explain why the safety precautions are necessary. This communication should be reinforced by written instructions. When possible, safety rules and procedures should be posted at or near the work site.

Often, the only safety training workers receive is a list of safety rules and procedures as part of the employee handbook. Past experience has demonstrated that this is hardly enough; it does not make workers safety-conscious. You must continuously seek to establish an environment which encourages safety-consciousness. As a result, much of your safety training may be informal rather than formal. Even though new workers are given specific on-the-job safety training upon entering the unit or assuming new assignments, your obligation does not end there. You need to remind workers continually of safety considerations and observe to ensure they are working safely. Safety training should be a part of the day-to-day interaction with your workers.

Summary

☐ Supervisors play a critical role in ensuring a safe work place exists. They are in a position to observe workers on the job and are expected to identify potential safety problems and implement safety improvement programs. They are responsible for promoting safety at work.

☐ Safety on the job is the subject of legal regulation. Worker's compensation laws establish programs which provide workers injured on the job with payments for a specified period of time. The Occupational Safety and Health Act requires organizations to make sure working conditions are safe. Its regulations and standards are enforced through official inspections. Organizations violating the law may be fined.

☐ Unsafe work practices are costly. They result in decreased morale, poor organizational reputation, and interrupted production. Intangible costs are also involved. How can you place a value on a human life or limb?

☐ Work-related accidents result from three major causes: (1) chance occurrences, (2) unsafe working conditions, and (3) unsafe behavior by workers. Unsafe behavior is the most common cause of accidents.

☐ Supervisors should inspect the work place periodically for potentially unsafe working conditions. If unsafe conditions exist, they should see that corrective action is taken before an accident occurs or alert upper management to the problem.

☐ Unsafe behavior may not be intentional but it cannot be tolerated. To eliminate unsafe behavior, supervisors should (1) detect accident-prone workers and take corrective action, (2) enforce safety rules and procedures, and (3) adequately train workers to behave in a safe manner.

☐ Safety rules and procedures must be communicated to workers and enforced in all situations. Supervisors must observe the same rules workers are expected to observe.

☐ Safety training should include making supervisors and workers safety-conscious as well as specific job safety training. Supervisors should make sure workers receive job safety training when: (1) new workers join the unit, (2) current workers assume new jobs, (3) new work processes are implemented or current processes are modified, and (4) workers return to work after layoff.

☐ The supervisor's responsibility for workers' safety is a continuing one. Workers must be reminded daily to perform their jobs safely. Supervisors must be alert to potential safety hazards at work.

Questions for review and discussion

1. What is workers' compensation?

2. What specific requirements are placed on organizations by the Occupational Safety and Health Act of 1970?

3. What are the three major causes of work-related accidents? Which is the most common cause?

4. What are five areas you should check in any safety inspection?

5. How can you reduce unsafe working conditions?

✗ 6. How can you reduce workers' unsafe behavior?

7. What role does safety training play in promoting a safe work environment?

8. How would you react to a worker who says, "All these safety rules set by the organization just prevent me from doing my job"?

9. Some people argue that OSHA regulations and standards add substantial costs and lower the productivity of workers. Discuss both sides of this issue.

Key terms

Accident-prone workers

Chance accidents

Doctrine of assumption of risk

Doctrine of contributory negligence

Fellow-servant rule

Occupational Safety and Health Act

Safety inspections

Safety rules and procedures

Safety training

Unsafe working conditions

Unsafe worker behaviors

Workers' compensation plans

Cases for discussion and practical exercises

1. L & M Metal Products was behind on sawed bar deliveries. This was a serious problem and Joe Wyatt, plant manager, was determined to find out what the trouble was. He went directly to Phil Stewart, production supervisor, for an explanation.

"This has got to stop, Phil. We have the capacity to get these bars and more out. Why can't we get them out the door?" Joe fumed at Phil.

"Because our saw operator is out," Phil responded. "He cut his hand last Thursday and severed some tendons. He won't be back for a while. I've brought in a replacement. But you know as well as I do that it takes at least three weeks to train a good saw operator. Until this new one gets broken in, things are just going to run a little slower."

"That one accident is sure costing us a pretty penny. There's just not enough business out there for us to be fooling around like this. How did it happen anyway?" Joe asked.

Phil quickly replied, "I filed a report. It's somewhere in your office. He's operated that saw for five years now, so it's his baby. I guess he got a little careless or cocky. At any rate, he forgot to put the guard in place."

"What do you mean, he forgot? You know the rules around here. What are you doing, sleeping in your office all day?" Joe exclaimed.

Phil responded, "Hey, don't get on my case. He is an experienced operator. All my workers know the rules. Why that's the first thing they learn when they're hired. But what can I do? I have lots of other things to keep me occupied during the day. I can't spend my time watching over their shoulders. We would never get anything done around here that way."

"Well, it's not going to matter if we have many more situations like this one," Joe declared. "You're right, you can't be everywhere all the time. But somehow, you've got to get control of the situation. You know this isn't the first accident your crew has had. For some reason, your crew seems to be more accident-prone than any of the others."

"Something has to be done and you'd better do it soon," Joe continued. "We can't keep investing three weeks in training a new operator just because someone takes a gamble and refuses to put the saw guard in place. And we can't afford these delivery delays. You should realize, we pay good money to make our equipment safe. And we don't create safety rules just for the sake of filling up an employees' manual."

a) Is Phil right? Does he have to watch over his crew to ensure they work safely?

b) If you were Phil, what would you do in an attempt to decrease accidents in your area?

2. Conduct a safety inspection of a work place with which you are familiar. You may use the checklist (Figure 16.1) given in this chapter, or make up your own checklist. Note what actions should be taken to correct any unsafe conditions. If you do not have access to a work place, make a safety inspection of your home or of an area at your school.

3. Outline a safety training program, consisting of four 15 minute sessions, for workers from the work place (or home or school) you studied in exercise 2 above.

Notes

1. Stephen Franklin, "Workmen's Compensation Here: Small Fines, Low Benefits," *Detroit Free Press*, August 25, 1980, pp. 3,5A.

2. Stephen Franklin, "Earning a Living Sometimes Means Sudden Death," *Detroit Free Press*, August 24, 1980, p. 3A.

3. "Safe," *Industry Week*, April 26, 1971; "Struggling for Safety," *Time*, May 22, 1972; "Is Your Job Dangerous to your Health?" *U.S. News and World Report*, February 5, 1979, p. 3.

4. *ABCs of the Job Safety and Health Act* (Washington, D.C.: Bureau of National Affairs, Inc.), 1971, p. 15.

5. James F. Van Namee, "Occupational Safety and Health," in Dale Yoder and Herbert G. Henemen, Jr. (eds.), *ASPA Handbook of Personnel and Industrial Relations* (Washington, D.C.: Bureau of National Affairs, Inc., 1979), pp. 1–45.

6. Jack Halloran, *Supervision: The Art of Management* (Englewood Cliffs, N.J.; Prentice-Hall, Inc., 1981), pp. 328–383.

7. Mary Green Miner, *Safety Policies and the Impact of OSHA*, Personnel Policy Forum Survey No. 117, (Washington D.C.: Bureau of National Affairs, Inc., May 1977).

8. James F. Van Namee, *op. cit.* pp. 1-27-1-59.

9. Willie Hammer, *Occupational Safety Management and Engineering*, (Englewood Cliffs, N.J.: Prentice-Hall, Inc. 1976).

10. Gary Dessler, *Personnel Management: Modern Concepts and Techniques.* (Reston, Va.: Reston Publishing Co., 1978), pp. 423–431.

11. "A Safety Committee Man's Guide," Aetna Life and Casualty Insurance Company, Catalog 872684.

12. *Ibid.*

13. *Ibid.*

14. L. M. Long, "OSHA Brings Out the Super in Supervision," *Supervision*, April 1975, pp. 31–32.

15. J. Gardner, "Employee Safety," in J. J. Famularo (ed.), *Handbook of Modern Personnel Administration* (New York: McGraw Hill, 1972), Chapter 48.

Cases for section V

The education of Greg Horning: May 24

The gripes from the crew about the night shift had been increasing. Greg's crew often would come in in the morning and find a lot of unfinished work left for them to do and the shop in a mess. Another gripe came frequently from the workers about inspections. The night shift had no one in particular to do their inspecting, as the operators did it for themselves. According to Helen and Jeannette, they couldn't care less. They let a lot of shoddy pieces go through and the workers had to reinspect the night shift's work and flash a lot of their output before they could let it pass.

As a result, they wasted a lot of time redoing the night shift's work, and this really slowed the whole department's production. Greg checked the complaints and they were legitimate; if anything the mess was worse than they had claimed.

Greg had tried talking to the night supervisor about the problem, already, but it hadn't had any effect. He was in charge of the whole plant for the night shift, and he didn't have the time to keep a close watch on any one department. So he had no choice but to leave them pretty much on their own, hope for the best, and leave the problems to the day shift supervisor.

Greg was not sure what to do. He could bring the problem to Phillips' attention, but he knew better than that now. Phillips would chew out the night people, maybe fire some of them and give a warning to the others. It might make them shape up, but the bad feelings it would generate wouldn't be worth it. In spite of the fact that the night shift was causing his crew trouble, they'd all join together against him if he went upstairs. It would get back to his people through the union and they'd think he'd been a fink, running to the big boss instead of handling the situation himself.

The union! That was it. This was a problem that the union should be brought into. He'd better have a talk with Phil Martello.

Martello was not exactly enthusiastic when Greg called him in to talk about it.

"I don't like the sound of it, Greg. You're putting me in the middle of a very sticky situation."

"I know it's sticky, Phil, but you've complained yourself about the mess they make. They're the worst crew in the plant and we have to take the rap. Something's got to be done about it."

"Listen, Phil," Greg said carefully, trying to be persuasive. He knew how Phil must feel. He knew what it was like to be boxed in. "Think about it. What could I do? I could get some of them fired and it would stick. The union wouldn't like that much, would they? Or I could get Phillips to hand out a bunch of layoffs. Your people wouldn't like that much either. There's got to be a better way. That's why I'm talking to you."

Phil smiled reluctantly. "You sure have learned a few things in five months!"

Greg laughed.

"But, honestly, Greg," Phil went on, shifting in his chair, "I don't know what those people do at night. Maybe they have it good—maybe too good—but I don't know what I can do about it."

"But you do know what this place looks like in the morning. And you do know how you gripe all the time about your machine being all fouled up with dirt."

"Yeah."

"And you know the people on the night shift," Greg persisted. "Now you can talk to them, see, where I can't. You can tell them how you feel, that you're not going to fight for them because you know they've been goofing off. And you can tell them what I'll do if they don't shape up. From you it's a friendly tip. A word to the wise, that kind of thing. You know."

"Yeah," Phil said, a little more positively. "I guess I could try that. I know some of the people in the union. We have a meeting next Thursday night. I guess I should tell them they've been getting away with murder."

"You sure should," Greg said, closing in. "After all, it's our own people they're hurting. Our crew. It's not as though it was something that doesn't affect us. It does. It hurts our whole operation. And you can talk to them. You're a union steward. They'll listen to you."

"Well, all right, Greg," Phil said. But he was still doubtful. "I'll give it a try. Maybe they'll listen to me."

"Okay, Phil," Greg said. "I won't move on this until I hear from you. Let me know what happens."

"Yeah. I'll let you know," Phil said, nodding his head. "Yeah. I guess they'll listen to me. Anyway, it's worth a try."

Questions

1. Is Greg being realistic in hoping that the night shift will listen to the steward, Martello? (Are members expected to take instructions from their elected officials?)

2. At what point in dealing with the night shift could the steward best be brought into the picture?

3. What should Greg do if the steward were to tell him he wouldn't cooperate?

4. How would you cope with Martello if he agreed to help only if Greg would promise to get the day crew a 15-minute wash-up period in the afternoon?

Source: Adapted from William F. Dowling, Jr. and Leonard R. Sayles, *How Managers Motivate: The Imperative of Supervision* (New York: McGraw-Hill Book Company, 1971). Copyright 1971. Reprinted by permission of the publisher.

Beamon Plating Company

The Beamon Plating Company specialized in cleaning and plating all types of small metal objects. Its service was good, its prices were reasonable, and its work was guaranteed. As a result, it enjoyed a healthy business, mostly from industrial concerns located within a 500-mile radius. Some of its work consisted of silver-plating and gold-plating objects of art as well as other silver services.

Several hazards exist in any plating shop, and die precautions must be taken. Fumes from the plating tanks, for example, are very dangerous and can cause sickness, and even death, from prolonged exposure. To preclude such a mishap, the management of Beamon

Plating installed one of the most efficient air exhaust systems obtainable. In fact, air purity tests showed that the air in the plating room contained less toxic gases than air elsewhere in the plant. In addition, three emergency showerheads were installed beside the plating tanks. If an employee were to spill acid on himself, he or she could quickly step into the closet shower and pull the chain. This automatically opened a valve sending out a full-force shower, thus dissipating the effects of the acid. The company also furnished all its plating room employees with special uniforms, rubber boots, rubber aprons, and rubber gloves. These protected the employees from the plating fluids and acids.

Chemicals used in the plating tanks were purchased in 50-gallon drums, and acids came in large glass containers called carboys. Both the acids and the chemicals in drums were stored under a shed, which was 150 feet from the main building. Other less bulky items such as cadmium balls or soda ash were stored in a small storeroom in the plant. When material from either of these storerooms was needed, any one of the employees who wasn't busy at the time was sent to get the material. If it was not too heavy, the employee usually carried it by hand. If it was heavy or bulky, the employee could choose one of the several handtrucks that were always available. Occasionally, the material fell off and spilled on the floor. In several instances, employees dropped material on their feet, causing a lost-time accident. Some of the workers complained of straining their backs from lifting, but this could not be positively linked to lifting the material for the plating shop.

Despite all the precautions and the provision of protective equipment, the company had some trouble in the plating room. Several of the employees almost refused to wear the rubber boots and aprons provided by the company. In fact, they removed them quite frequently, claiming they were bulky, hot, and uncomfortable. Management realized that this was a dangerous practice, but if the employees would not wear the safety equipment, management admitted it did not know what to do about the situation.

Several accidents of a minor nature occurred recently. For example, one of the women who wired parts to racks so they could be individually plated stuck one of the sharp parts in her finger. This would not have happened if she had been wearing the gloves furnished by the company.

Although this may seem a minor item, the Beamon Plating Company does not want its employees to forget that serious injuries can occur. It also wants them to realize that the company is trying to provide maximum protection for its workers during their workday.

Questions

1. What do you think of the safety program of the Beamon Plating Company?
2. What changes, if any, would you recommend? Explain why.

Source: Adapted from Claude S. George, *Supervision in Action: The Art of Managing Others*, 1979, pp. 339–340. Reprinted by permission of Reston Publishing Co., a Prentice-Hall Co., 11480 Sunset Hills Road, Reston, Va. 22090.

Andy Stenkowski

"For a company the size of Ajax, you would think they would have some standards already," complained Andy Stenkowski after a particularly trying day. Today was the frustrating culmination of about two months of managerial ups and downs for Andy.

He had been in the supervisor's job for about a month when top management called a meeting of all the supervisors. "We're not getting the product out fast enough. Some of our smaller grocers are starting to complain that we're letting them down. Now each of you people has some slower workers in your sections; let's see if we can get them speeded up."

"About how much should each person be picking an hour?" asked Andy. "There's nothing in the union contract that specifies standards for each job."

"No, that means that the authority is left to management. We can set those standards if we want to," replied the vice-president. "We've thought about it, and maybe we'll have something in the next year or so. Meanwhile, though, we've got some real loafers out there, and you people had better shape them up."

Andy's section generally met their day's orders, but often just barely. There was very little slack, however, and when an unusually large order or a new account came in, the section would leave some orders for the next day or the next shift, depending on the next shift's work load. But Andy knew that the productivity of his people varied. Whereas his best person could pick over 180 pieces an hour, his poorest barely did 90. Andy suspected that the average was about 140.

Andy decided to chart the production of his workers for about a month. Then he would establish an average "pick" rate, which he would use as a standard against which to push some of the less productive pickers. He also wanted to check any industry publications to see what other companies the size and type of Ajax were doing.

A month later, Andy called his crew together and announced that the average pick rate in the unit was 142 pieces an hour, compared with an industry average of 144. He said that he wanted those pickers at or above the average to stay with their production, but that he was going to work on those in the 90 to 125 range to get them up to average.

"Hey, Andy, when did you turn into a company slave driver?" called out one worker.

"I hope you people realize that the top brass is on my back to increase production," replied Andy. "Now, let's get back to work."

Only four people were picking fewer than 130 pieces an hour, but one was Charlie Vitrello, whose output rarely exceeded 100 pieces an hour. The three others gradually inched up to 130 and over, but Charlie stayed under 100. Andy spoke to Charlie and asked him why he wasn't cooperating.

"Hell, Andy, you've got no authority to set standards. Look, there's nothing in the contract, management has set no standards, so I can set my own pace. Now, just stay off my back, will you?"

"C'mon Charlie, we're old friends, and I know you can do a better job. I'll give you another month. Let's see if we can come near the average."

"Or what, Andy?" asked Charlie.

"Let's not get to that, Charlie," replied Andy as he walked off.

Another month went by and Charlie's output stayed under 100. Andy finally went to Charlie and said, "Look, Charlie, I've tried to be good to you. Everyone but you is trying to meet the standards.

I'm afraid I'm going to have to send you home for a week without pay."

"What? What for?" yelled an irate Charlie.

"Disregard of orders and unwillingness to meet a management standard," replied Andy.

Charlie marched off and an hour later, accompanied by Louise Votrovich, the shop steward, approached Andy. "Andy, what is the nonsense about standards?" asked Louise. "You know that no standards are specified in the contract."

"Then it's up to management to set them," replied Andy.

"And management hasn't set any in this plant," said Louise.

"I'm the supervisor and I set them for this section," said Andy. "Charlie refuses to cut it here."

"C'mon Andy. Don't let the power go to your head. Who gave you the authority to set standards?"

"Sorry, Louise, but Charlie stays out. I'm not budging on this one. Top management gets on my tail, and I've got to get output out of this group."

"Okay, Andy. We're going to grieve. I think we've got a winner here," announced Louise.

"Be my guest," replied Andy.

Andy reported the incident to the vice-president of operations and got very little response. "Okay, Andy, we'll see you at the first-level hearing. I'll be there and so will the personnel manager. Let me sleep on our case for a while."

At the hearing, the company and the union were working on four grievances, this one being the first. Andy recounted how he set the standards and that the rest of his crew was trying to meet them.

Charlie replied that Andy was overstepping his power. Louise Votrovich and the local president reasserted that there were no standards in the contract and that management had set a precedent by not enforcing company-wide standards. "Now, how can they justify one supervisor setting standards unilaterally? Besides," argued the president, "Charlie didn't even get a proper warning."

The vice-president for operations replied that for the record, he was not conceding management's right to set standards, but they would not press this case. Charlie would be reinstated with back pay.

Andy sat there stunned for a moment and then got up and left the hearing room. Charlie could barely conceal the grin on his face.

Later in the day, the vice-president of operations called Andy in and said, "Andy, I think you're on the right track, but this case wasn't as important for us to win as two of the others. We're going to set company-wide standards, and I'm glad you started the ball rolling. At least the union knows we're moving in that direction. I want you to keep trying to get your production up. For the time being, you'll just have to find another way."

When Andy got home, the first words out his mouth were, "Darn it, why did I ever take that supervisor's job?"

Questions

1. Why did Charlie Vitrello react negatively to Andy's attempt to set standards?

2. What managerial actions made it difficult for Andy to get Charlie (or any other reluctant employee) to respond to the new standards?

3. What now remains of Andy's capacity to lead, motivate, and in particular, control?

Source: Adapted from Arthur Elkins, *Management: Structure, Functions, and Practices,* © 1980, Addison-Wesley Publishing Company, Inc., Chapter 18, pages 419–421. Reprinted with permission.

Glossary

Accident-prone workers. Certain workers likely to cause work accidents. Such workers include those who are impulsive and adventurous, those under stress, and those with alcohol or drug problems. These individuals often have specific characteristics proven to fit the category of youth (under 30).

Action requests. Category of paperwork that includes all requests to take action.

Affirmative action plan. Establishment of goals and timetables for hiring women and minority workers, with hiring decisions based solely on applicant's ability to perform on the job; positive action to seek out, hire, and promote qualified members of groups previously discriminated against.

Age Discrimination in Employment Act. Law enacted in 1967 that prohibits discrimination on the basis of age. The act specifically covers individuals between the ages of 40 and 70. Under its jurisdiction are private employers of 20 or more persons, public employees, employment agencies, and unions.

Aggression. Behavior characterized by some kind of attack that can be a reaction to frustration. Direct aggression involves action taken against the actual source of frustration. Displaced aggression is directed at some person or object other than the actual source of frustration.

Alcoholism. Disease suffered by workers that often results in job performance problems.

Application blanks. A source for obtaining information about an applicant's education, work experience, skills, abilities, and personal background.

Arbitrator. A neutral person brought in from the outside to resolve disputes between labor and management over contract interpretation.

Authority. The right to decide and take action while using organizational resources.

Authorization cards. Cards signed by workers stating support of their union as their representative in collective bargaining.

Bar charts. Also called Gantt charts, these are techniques for planning and controlling work activities. On a bar chart, activities are listed on the vertical side and a time scale along the bottom. The length of the bars contained on the chart reflects the estimated time each activity requires. These charts are useful for planning and controlling repetitive projects or projects involving relatively few activities.

Behavior modification. A motivational strategy based on the assumption that behavior is a function of its consequences. Behavior modification assumes that behavior followed by positive (rewarding) consequences tends to be repeated and that behavior followed by negative consequences tends not to be repeated.

Brainstorming. A method of problem solving that involves having an individual or group think of as many alternatives as possible without pausing to evaluate them.

Break-even analysis. A planning and control technique for studying relationships between levels of output, revenues, costs, and profit or loss. Break-even analysis may be performed by using either a break-even chart or a formula.

Budgets. The primary financial planning and control technique in most organizations.

Central tendency. Evaluation of all workers as average performers.

Centralized organizations. Organizations where the authority to make decisions is located within top management.

Chance accidents. Accidents beyond control and impossible to prevent, such as lightning striking (natural disaster).

Civil Rights Act. Law prohibiting discrimination in all terms and conditions of employment on the basis of race, color, national origin, religion, and sex. Applies to private employers with more than 15 employees, unions, employment agencies, state and local governments, and educational institutions. Originally passed in 1964; Title VII amended by Equal Employment Opportunity Act of 1972.

Coaching. A method of providing workers with feedback on their performance and instruction to improve performance.

Coercive power. Power based on workers' fear that if they do not conform to what their supervisor expects, they will be punished in some way.

Collective bargaining. A process involving both the union and management in negotiating, interpreting, applying, and enforcing labor contracts.

Communication process. The passing of information and meaning from one person to another. This process involves at least two people (a sender and a receiver) and includes six stages: The sender has a thought, which is developed into a message, which is in turn transmitted to the receiver, who receives the message, attaches meaning to the message, and gives feedback to the sender.

Comparison evaluations. Involves comparing each worker to all other workers in the group.

Connection power. Power based on the connections the supervisor has with others, which enables the supervisor to obtain rewards for workers.

Consideration. Leader behavior identified by the Ohio State Studies, which involves a showing of mutual trust, respect, and friendship between leaders and followers.

Consultative decision making. Approach to decision making whereby the supervisor shares the problem with workers, obtains their ideas and suggestions on how to resolve the problem, and then makes the decision and communicates it to the workers.

Consulting style. Leadership style that involves obtaining input from workers and considering their ideas. The leader still makes decisions and provides clear instructions. However, the leader explains the reasons behind decisions and attempts to persuade workers to agree with the instructions given.

Consumer protection. Legislation and regulation intended to protect consumers' rights to safety, to be heard, to choose, and to be informed.

Contrast effects.   Worker is evaluated in relation to other workers rather than in terms of the actual performance requirements.

Control process.   Process wherein the performance objectives become standards against which actual performance is checked, and corrective action is taken if necessary.

Controlling.   Management activity that involves collecting of information on accomplishments, comparing these to planned accomplishments, and taking corrective action when necessary.

Counseling.   Process that provides troubled workers with ways to solve the problems affecting their job performance before more drastic action is taken. Counseling involves: (1) identifying problems troubling the worker; (2) taking action to resolve the problems; and (3) following up to see that the problem is solved.

Counseling interviews.   Interviews addressing workers' personal problems with the objective of resolving problems before job performance is seriously affected.

Critical path.   The series of activities in a network that takes the greatest amount of time from the beginning event to ending event. The time required by the critical path is the estimated completion time for the project.

Daily work plan.   List of tasks taken from a master list to be accomplished on a particular day, taking into consideration time for unanticipated demands. Also called a "to do" list.

Decentralized organization.   Organization where the authority to make decisions is delegated to lower levels of management.

Decision-making process.   Process that involves (1) identifying the problem and determining the cause; (2) developing alternative solutions to the problem and selecting the best alternative; and (3) putting the decision into action and following it up.

Delegating style.   Leadership style in which workers are given the authority to make decisions or determine courses of action within certain limits. The leader is not directly involved but retains responsibility for the activities of his or her workers.

Delegation.   Giving workers additional authority and tasks.

Delegative decision making. Approach to decision making in which the supervisor delegates the authority to make the decision to one or more workers but retains the responsibility for resolving the problem.

Demotion. A step sometimes included in progressive disciplinary procedures that involves placing the worker in a lower paying, lower status job.

Department. Groups of jobs related on the basis of function, product, location, or some combination of these factors.

Directing. Management activity that involves the guiding and influencing of people to perform work, communicating with them, creating positive motivation, and handling people problems.

Directing style. Leadership style in which the leader closely structures the activities of workers and exercises close supervision.

Directive decision making. Approach to decision making in which the supervisor collects information, analyzes the problem, makes the decision, and then communicates the decision to those who must implement it.

Discharge. The last, most drastic step in progressive discipline, which is used only for serious violations or for a prolonged series of violations that have not been resolved through prior disciplinary action.

Disciplinary interviews. Interviews during which information regarding unacceptable job performance or behavior is exchanged and action is taken to correct the problem.

Disciplinary layoff. A step in progressive discipline, which involves the suspension of a worker for a period of time without pay.

Discipline. Action taken to ensure that established rules and standards are observed and that workers behave in an acceptable manner.

Distributed practice. Shorter and more frequent practice sessions. Better for slower learners as well as for learning complex and difficult tasks.

Doctrine of Assumption of Risk. Workers who accept a job also accept the risk associated with the job.

Doctrine of Contributory Negligence. Employers are not liable if an accident results from workers' negligence.

Downward communication. Information flowing from higher-level managers to supervisors and workers through formal channels. Examples include job instructions, policy statements, procedures, and memos.

Drug addiction.   A personal problem that often results in job performance problems.

Dual-career marriages.   Marriages in which both husband and wife work and view their work as a central and important part of their lives.

Economic order quantity.   Technique for determining how much inventory to order that minimizes ordering and carrying costs. The economic order quantity (Q) can be determined by the following formula: $Q + 2(DXC)/(VXP)$, where D is the yearly demand, C is the ordering cost, V is the value per unit, and P equals the carrying costs for the inventory.

Emotional stress.   A personal problem that often results in job performance problems.

Employee assistance program.   Programs sponsored by organizations that provide specialized services for workers to resolve personal problems that hinder job performance.

Environmental protection.   Legislation and regulations concerned with protecting the quality of the environment.

Equal employment opportunity.   Prohibition of discrimination in all terms and conditions of employment on the basis of race, color, national origin, religion, and sex.

Equal Employment Opportunity Commission (EEOC).   A federal agency reporting to the President, which is responsible for enforcing Title VII and several other antidiscrimination laws. Investigates charges to determine if there is reasonable cause to believe that discrimination has occurred.

Esteem needs.   Need category identified by Maslow that includes needs related to respect and prestige both from oneself and from others.

Expectancy theory of motivation.   A theory of motivation suggesting that people's actions are based on their expectations as well as on their needs. It points out that individuals will not take action unless there is a positive expectation of receiving a reward that will satisfy a need.

Expert power.   Power arising from the respect workers have for the supervisor's knowledge, skills, and abilities.

Extinction.   The withholding of rewards when undesirable behavior occurs so that the behavior will eventually disappear.

Feedback. The final step in the communication process, which involves determining whether the receiver understood the message sent.

Fellow-servant rule. If a worker is injured by a fellow worker, the employer is not responsible.

Final employment interview. A procedure designed to provide an opportunity for the supervisor to meet and evaluate the remaining candidates and to provide candidates with a chance to meet their prospective supervisor and ask questions.

First impressions. Impressions based on initial exposure to an individual, which are generally lasting and which can lead to an inaccurate evaluation of the individual's abilities.

Fixed costs. Costs that are constant regardless of the level of output.

Formal communication. Communication flowing through formally established channels in the organization that involves work-related matters. Formal communication involves downward, upward, and lateral communication.

Formal control system. A control system having explicitly stated standards by which performance is systematically observed and measured. Written and documented reports of measurements and comparisons are compiled.

Formal performance review. Meeting with workers specifically to evaluate their performance, with outcomes generally affecting their employment status.

Frustration. Frustration results when need satisfaction is blocked, i.e., when a person acts to satisfy a need and is unable to reach the goal.

Functional department. Groups of jobs requiring similar skills or related activities.

General gripes. A non-contract-related problem. A general dissatisfaction that is voiced by a worker.

Goal. Something that will satisfy an unsatisfied need.

Government regulation. Directives issued under laws, orders, or regulations limiting business activity or specifying action.

Grapevine. Informal communication that carries both work-related and people-related information.

Grievance interviews.   Interviews in which information regarding a worker's complaint is exchanged and action is taken to resolve the complaint.

Grievance procedures.   A formal appeals process established in the contract to resolve union-management disputes over contract interpretation and administration.

Grievances.   Formal challenges made by the union regarding the way the contract has been interpreted and applied.

Group cohesiveness.   The extent to which group members desire to remain members of the group. How "closely knit" the group is or how tightly group members "stick together."

Group decision making.   Includes decision making by a group of people through informal or formal participation.

Group norm.   An informal rule, stated or unstated, regarding how members of a group should or should not behave. Norms may be positive and facilitate organizational goal attainment. Or they may be negative and hinder organizational goal attainment.

Group think.   Problem encountered in group decision making that results from a closely knit, cohesive group whose members are overly concerned with maintaining friendly relations and avoiding conflict and less concerned with making good decisions.

Halo effect.   A common error made by supervisors that occurs when one particular action or aspect of work performance influences the supervisor's overall opinion of the worker.

Herzberg's Two-Factor Theory of Motivation.   A theory of work motivation that involves maintenance factors and motivator factors. The theory suggests that the presence of maintenance factors may prevent dissatisfaction but will not produce higher levels of motivation. Only motivator factors can produce higher levels of motivation and satisfaction.

Higher-level review.   A method used to reduce errors in performance review by requiring supervisors to justify evaluations to superiors or members of the personnel department.

Hiring interviews.   Interviews designed to gather information about job applicants as well as to give information to applicants so that good hiring decisions can be made.

Human factors. Factors influencing leadership effectiveness that reflect the state of the human resources in an organization. They indicate how well people are working together and how well satisfied they are with their work (i.e., morale, amount and type of communication, level of motivation, commitment to objectives, and level of interpersonal and intergroup conflict).

Informal communication. Communication in organizations that flows through informal channels and involves work-related and people-related information. The grapevine is informal communication.

Informal control system. A control system in which performance standards are assumed or established in a nonsystematic manner. Oral, informal reports are used.

Informal leader. A leader who emerges from within the group's membership and to whom group members look for guidance.

Informal organization. The network of personal and social relationships that develops as people associate with one another in the organization. It is not established by the formal organization structure. Emphasis is on people and their relationships.

Informal performance reviews. Reviews based on the day-to-day conversations supervisors have with their workers.

Information power. Power that stems from the degree to which supervisors have information, or access to information, that is valuable to workers.

Initiating structure. Leader behavior identified by the Ohio State Studies that refers to the structuring of jobs performed by followers and the establishing of well-defined patterns of organization and communication.

Interviews. Formal conversations planned to meet specific purposes. Supervisors typically conduct hiring interviews, performance review interviews, counseling interviews, disciplinary interviews, and grievance interviews.

Job definition. A framework for training new workers that defines each task required to perform the job, describes how each task is performed, and defines the level of competence workers must achieve on each task.

Job description. A written statement of the tasks, duties, and responsibilities required by the job. A job description directs recruitment efforts and guides decisions made during the selection process.

Job enrichment. A motivation strategy based on Herzberg's conclusion that work motivation can be increased by building motivator factors into jobs. Job enrichment involves adding more responsibility and more opportunities for achievement, recognition, growth, and development to jobs.

Job Instruction Training. JIT is the most commonly used training approach for developing job skills. Four steps are included: (1) prepare the worker for training; (2) present the job; (3) have the worker practice; and (4) follow up.

Job specification. Description of the skills, knowledge, and other personal characteristics required to perform the job satisfactorily.

Kepner-Tregoe process. An approach to resolving problems that can help collect and organize information incorporating answers to four questions: (1) What is the deviation? (2) Where is the deviation located? (3) When did the deviation appear? and (4) What is the extent of the deviation?

Labor contract. A binding agreement between labor and management establishing the terms and conditions of work for the group of workers represented by the union.

Landrum-Griffin Act. A law governing the internal affairs and regulating the leadership elections and financial reporting procedures of unions; it guarantees union members freedom of speech, voting rights, control over union dues increases, the right to sue the union, and the right to have copies of the labor contract.

Lateral communication. Formal communication that flows horizontally in an organization, thereby helping to coordinate the activities of different departments.

Leadership. The process of influencing the activities of indivduals or groups toward goal accomplishment.

Legitimate power. Power based on the supervisor's position in the organization and the formal authority associated with that position.

Line authority. Authority involving the right to direct the work of subordinates within the chain of command.

Listening.   The process of hearing, understanding, and remembering what someone is communicating.

Location department.   Jobs grouped on the basis of where the work is performed or where the market areas to be served are located.

Maintenance factors.   Factors relating to the conditions and environment in which work is done. When these factors are not present, dissatisfaction results. Their presence helps avoid dissatisfaction. As identified by Herzberg, maintenance factors include fairly administered company policies, supervisors who know the work, good relationships with supervisors, good relationships with co-workers, a fair salary, job security, and good working conditions.

Management by Objectives (MBO).   A planning and control technique that formalizes the informal planning and control process that occurs in the organization. It involves an objective-setting discussion between manager and subordinate, which results in joint decisions regarding (1) objectives to be accomplished; (2) time required to accomplish each objective; and (3) how progress will be judged. A follow-up discussion is held to review accomplishments and establish new objectives.

Managerial Grid.   Developed by Robert Blake and Jane Mouton, this view of leader behavior identifies five leadership styles based on various combinations of concern for production and concern for people.

Maslow's need hierarchy.   A classification of human needs into five categories that form a hierarchy. The categories include physiological, security, social, esteem, and self-fulfillment needs. According to Maslow, people attempt to satisfy dominant, lowest-level needs first. Once a need is satisfied, it no longer serves as a motivator.

Massed practice.   Practice sessions scheduled for long, uninterrupted periods. This process works best with quick learners and for short, simple tasks.

Master list.   List of routine and nonroutine duties and tasks facing you in the foreseeable future.

Modeling.   One of the basic approaches to learning, which suggests that skills are more easily learned through demonstration or giving workers a model to copy—observing another worker perform a job correctly, showing a movie or videotape.

Motivation to learn.   Learning principle that suggests learning is more likely to occur if workers are made aware of benefits to be gained, want to perform more effectively, and are stimulated and interested by the training.

Motivation process.   The process begins with an unsatisfied need. Individuals identify a goal that will satisfy the need and then take action to reach the goal and thereby satisfy the need.

Motivator factors.   Factors that relate directly to the content of the job itself, which, if present, can create higher levels of motivation and satisfaction. When not present, no strong dissatisfaction results. As identified by Herzberg, motivator factors include the opportunity to accomplish something significant, recognition for significant accomplishments, chance for advancement, the opportunity to grow and develop on the job, and the chance for increased responsibility.

"Must" objectives.   Outcomes that the alternative action has to achieve. They are constraints on actions that have to be met. If an alternative does not meet a "must" objective, it is eliminated.

"Must" tasks.   Tasks that are demanded by your boss, organization, or customers. Tasks that must be done on time to avoid threatening your job or career.

National Labor Relations Board.   A federal agency responsible for enforcing labor laws and conducting elections to determine whether a union will represent a group of workers.

Negative reinforcement.   The removal of unpleasant consequences so as to increase the likelihood that a certain behavior will be repeated.

Negotiations.   The process wherein management sits down at the bargaining table with the union to jointly establish procedures for making certain decisions, thereby resulting in a contract.

Network techniques.   Techniques for planning and controlling work activities that show the activities and events required to complete a project, time required for each activity, and the relationships among the activities.

Nonverbal communication.   The communication of feelings and emotions through facial expressions, posture, gestures, and other types of body language.

Objectives. The goals, aims, or purposes that executives, managers, and supervisors want the organization, or organizational unit, to achieve over a period of time. They are the targets toward which the organization or unit is moving.

Occupational Safety and Health Act. Legislation created to improve safety of workplace.

Ohio State Studies. View of leader behavior that identifies four leadership styles based on various combinations of initiating structure and consideration behaviors.

On-the-job training. Training that occurs at the regular job station with the normal tools and equipment.

Operating information. Category of paperwork including all information received that is necessary for keeping abreast of your operation.

Operating plans. Programs, policies, procedures, and rules developed within the framework of the strategic plan.

Oral warning. Step in progressive discipline involving a formal discussion of the infraction with the worker, during which expected behavior and the consequences of continued misbehavior are communicated to the worker.

Organization. Entity possessing the following characteristics: goals; people working together to accomplish something they could not do individually; division of labor; formally established structure; and hierarchy of authority.

Organization campaign. An effort by the union to gain worker support while management campaigns against it.

Organization charts. Graphic description of organization's structure, which identifies departments and jobs and shows the flow of authority within the organization.

Organizational politics. Political maneuvering within organizations to increase your visibility and to publicize your activities to your boss, peers, and subordinates.

Organizing. Management activity involving the assignment of jobs to individuals, the grouping of jobs to coordinate effort, and the delegation of authority and responsibility.

Orientation. A program whereby new workers are introduced to the job, their co-workers, and the organization.

Output factors. Factors influencing leadership effectiveness that indicate how well the organization is accomplishing its objectives (i.e., productivity, quality, profit, and cost-effectiveness measures).

Part learning. Learning in which the job is broken down into parts and workers are taught one task at a time. Better method for long, complex jobs or for those that involve loosely related activities that are meaningful by themselves. Also the better method when teaching slower learners.

Participating style. Leadership style in which the leader shares decisions with workers, discusses problems, and attempts with the workers to decide on courses of action acceptable to everyone. The leader's role is to minimize differences and to get a commitment from workers before taking action.

Participative decision making. A kind of decision making in which the supervisor shares the problem with workers. Together they analyze the problem, generate alternatives, and make the decision.

Performance aids. Simple, graphic descriptions of how to perform a task.

Performance review. An approach to determining training needs, generally used when upgrading workers' skills.

Performance review interviews. Interviews designed to assess workers' activities and let them know where they stand, to determine training needs, and to motivate workers to higher levels of performance.

Performance review process. A formal and systematic evaluation of workers' performance conducted on a yearly basis along with day-to-day conversations regarding performance, goals, and plans for improvement. A system established to communicate to workers how they are doing and any desired performance changes.

Physical exam. A requirement for some jobs when certain health standards must be met.

Physiological needs. Need category identified by Maslow that must be at least partially satisfied for continued survival (i.e., food, water, air, shelter).

Planning. Management activity that involves determining goals, deciding how goals can be accomplished, setting courses of action, and establishing policies and procedures.

Planning process. The setting of performance objectives and the determination of how these objectives will be achieved.

Plans. Procedures by which set objectives will be accomplished.

Policies. A specification of the range of acceptable behavior. Policies are general statements that guide decision making, define the boundaries within which decisions can be made, and direct decisions toward the accomplishment of objectives.

Positive reinforcement. Providing rewards to individuals as a result of behaving in a certain way so as to increase the likelihood that the deserved behavior will be repeated.

Power. The supervisor's influence potential stemming from a variety of sources. Sources of power include coercive, connection, expert, information, legitimate, referent, and reward power.

Preliminary interview. A short and to-the-point interview whose objective is to eliminate those applicants who are obviously not qualified. Sometimes conducted in conjunction with the completion of the application blank.

Primary needs. Lower-level needs, including physiological and security needs.

Probationary period. A period of time during which it is determined whether the worker can perform the job and qualify for permanent status.

Problem-solving approach. A method that enables the worker to become involved in discussing performance, resolving problems, and setting goals.

Procedures. Courses of action arranged in a sequence and designed to meet specific work objectives; a listing of specific steps to be performed in a sequence to accomplish a specific task.

Product departments. Jobs grouped together on the basis of the product produced or the service provided.

Productivity. The relationship between the amount of resources used and the level of output achieved. A major problem facing the United States.

Programs. Plans for action designed to accomplish a single objective (single-use plans).

Progressive disciplinary action. An effort made to improve the worker whenever possible.

Progressive discipline. A problem-solving approach to disciplining workers, which calls for instituting penalties appropriate to the violations. The steps typically followed in progressive discipline include (1) informal talk, (2) oral warning, (3) written warning, (4) disciplinary layoff, (5) demotion, and (6) discharge.

Punishment. Reinforcement to reduce undesirable behavior whereby an unpleasant consequence follows undesirable behavior so as to increase the likelihood that the behavior will not be repeated.

Quality circles. Autonomous units established within work groups that are voluntary study groups focusing on job-related problems. Emphasis is on improving productivity and the morale and motivation of the work force.

Quality of Work Life (QWL) programs. Programs involving QWL committees, which are cooperative problem-solving groups determining their own goals, analyzing problems, and developing action plans to improve the work place. The objectives are to improve quality of work life and organizational effectiveness by focusing on providing employees with more responsibility and decision-making authority.

Rating scales. A method of evaluating workers' performance, designed to indicate the worker's relative strengths and weaknesses in specific aspects of performance.

"Real" grievances. Contract violations

Recent behavior bias. An error often committed by supervisors that occurs when their opinion of a worker is influenced by the worker's most recent behavior rather than behavior over a period of time.

Reference checks. Information regarding an applicant's past behavior obtained from personal and business references. Also provides a check on the accuracy of information given by the applicant.

Referent power. Power based on the charisma and personal traits of a supervisor, which influences the extent to which workers like and want to be liked by the supervisor.

Relationship behavior. Dimension of leader behavior identified by Hersey and Blanchard that involves actions taken by leaders to recognize people for good work, to open channels of communication, to provide emotional support, and to involve workers in job decisions.

Reorder point. The inventory level at which an order for inventory must be placed. The reorder point (R) can be determined by using the following formula: $R = U + L + SS$, where U refers to the usage rate, L is the lead time, and SS indicates the safety stock level.

Representation election. A secret ballot election conducted by the NLRB after the union has obtained signed authorization cards from at least 30 percent of the workers.

Review discussion. A planned meeting to help supervisors better understand their workers, plan for improved performance, and relate rewards to performance.

Reward power. Power based on the workers' feelings that the supervisor is able to provide rewards—both tangible and intangible—that are meaningful to them.

Robot assembly. Computer-aided manufacturing intended to increase productivity, enhance the quality of working life, and increase product quality.

Rules. Official statements specifying what may or may not be done.

Safety inspections. Visits to work sites made by OSHA officials to see that safety regulations are not being violated.

Safety rules and procedures. Promotion of safety at work through awareness and implementation of safety standards, regulations, and orders that apply to workers' actions and job conduct.

Safety training. An ongoing procedure to make supervisors and workers safety-conscious; includes specific job training when new workers join the unit, current workers assume new jobs, new work processes are implemented or current processes are modified, and workers return to work after layoff.

Secondary needs. Higher level needs including social, esteem, and self-fulfillment needs.

Security needs. Need category identified by Maslow; includes need to feel free from threat and harm.

Selection. A series of activities involved in the determination of who will be hired for a specific job.

Self-fulfillment needs. Need category identified by Maslow that includes needs for realizing one's potential; also called self-realization or self-actualization needs.

Seniority. The length of time a worker has been employed.

"Should" tasks.   Tasks no one is forcing you to complete, but, if done, will provide real benefits.

Similar-to-me effect.   Situation that exists when supervisors evaluate those workers who are similar to them in attitudes or background more favorably than those who are not.

Social needs.   Need category identified by Maslow that includes needs to associate with people and to be accepted by them; also called love needs or need for affiliation.

Span of control.   The number of workers a supervisor must work with.

Spillover effect.   Situation that results when a supervisor gives a good performance evaluation (even when actual performance is not satisfactory) based on a previous performance review.

Staff authority.   Authority involving the provision of advice or service to the line.

Staffing.   Management activity that involves selecting people to fill jobs, placing them on jobs and orienting them, training them, and evaluating their performance.

Staffing process.   The hiring and training of workers and the reviewing of their job performance in order to achieve positive results.

Standards.   Targets representing desired or expected performance for a given activity. Standards are statements of objectives for the activity being controlled.

Stereotyping.   The forming of an opinion about an individual on the basis of readily identifiable characteristics such as race, sex, or age.

Stereotypes.   Preconceptions that introduce bias into the evaluation during performance reviews.

Strategic plans.   A course charted for the organization over the next three, five, or ten years, which identifies products, services, and/or activities that will be emphasized as well as those that will be de-emphasized.

Strictness/leniency.   Contradictions in review due to the differing expectations supervisors have of workers' performance.

Structured interview.   A set of predetermined questions is asked in an open-ended, general manner allowing applicant to talk freely about specific topics.

Supervision. Working with and through hourly-level workers to accomplish established work-unit goals.

Supervisor. First-line managers in organizations who have people working for them and get work accomplished through other people.

Supervisor-centered styles. Leadership styles that require greater involvement by supervisors than workers. Directing and consulting leadership styles are supervisor-centered.

Taft-Hartley Act. An amendment to the Wagner Act restricting union activities much as Wagner Act had done for employers.

Task analysis. The analysis of a job, a description of the tasks involved in its performance, and a definition of minimally acceptable levels of performance.

Task behavior. Dimension of leader behavior identified by Hersey and Blanchard that involves actions to organize and define the jobs and activities of workers.

Technical skill. Supervisors' knowledge of the technical aspects of the jobs performed by their workers.

Tell and listen approach. A method of discussing performance by telling workers their strengths and weaknesses, then giving them an opportunity to express opinions.

Tell and sell approach. A method of discussing workers' performance, with supervisor relaying evaluations and persuading them to improve.

Testing. Procedures designed to measure characteristics that cannot be accurately assessed through application blanks or interviews.

Theory X. A set of assumptions about people that represents a negative view of workers. According to McGregor, these assumptions include the following beliefs about workers: they are lazy and will avoid work if they can; they are not ambitious, they do not want responsibility and prefer to be directed; they must be closely controlled; they are unwilling and unable to help solve organizational problems.

Theory Y. A set of assumptions about people that represents a positive view of workers. According to McGregor, these assumptions include the beliefs that work is as natural as rest or play; that workers will accept responsibility and even seek it under proper conditions; that they will exercise self-control when working toward objectives to which they are committed; and that they are generally willing and able to help solve organizational problems.

Total costs.   The sum of fixed and variable costs.

Total revenue.   The product of unit sales price and the level of output.

Training.   The development of workers' skills through various teaching methods.

Unfair labor practices.   Violations of labor laws.

Union.   An organization chosen by workers to represent them in dealings with their employers; union representatives bargain with management to establish terms of employment, wages, hours, and conditions of work.

Union steward.   Locally elected or appointed leaders who see that contracts are enforced.

Unsafe workers' behaviors.   Unsafe actions due to workers' lack of safety consciousness and ignorance of or refusal to use safety practices.

Unsafe working conditions.   Potential trouble spots or hazards such as improperly guarded equipment, defective equipment, hazardous arrangement of equipment, poorly designed procedures for handling machines and equipment, hazardous storage conditions, inadequate lighting, and improper ventilation.

Upward communication.   Formal communication that flows from workers to supervisors and to higher-level managers.

Variable costs.   Costs directly related to the level of output.

Vestibule training.   Occurs away from the actual work station (off-the-job) and involves recreating the workplace in a training room or facility.

Vocational Rehabilitation Act.   Legislation that prohibits discrimination against individuals on the basis of their physical and mental handicaps and requires that employers develop specific programs aimed at increasing employment opportunities for the physically and mentally handicapped. All organizations doing more than $2500 worth of business with the federal government are covered.

Wagner Act.   Legislation that gives all nonmanagerial workers employed in the private sector three basic rights: the right to join unions; the right to bargain collectively with employer over hours, wages, and working conditions; and the right to strike.

"Want" objectives.   Desirable, but not necessary outcomes from a decision. For example, to correct a problem (1) at the lowest possible cost; (2) in the shortest possible time; and (3) with a minimum of customer inconvenience.

Whole learning.   Teaching a job in its entirety. A general and simple method best for quick learners and when jobs are short and involve highly related activities that join together in a meaningful sequence.

Worker-centered styles.   Leadership styles that require greater or equal involvement of workers relative to supervisors. Participating and delegating leadership styles are worker-centered.

Workers' compensation plans.   State-required programs for workers injured on the job, with payments made for a specified time to offset wages lost while unable to work.

Written warning.   A step in progressive discipline that involves issuing a written statement regarding the problem, the consequences of continued misbehavior, an indication of the worker's commitment to changed behavior, and the follow-up action to be taken. The written warning is placed in the employee's file.

Indexes

Subject index

Name index